Tuesday 'n' Me

DAVID FOREMAN was born in 1947 and comes from the Suffolk coast of East Anglia. He has been sailing yachts, dinghies and experimental model boats since his earliest childhood.

He worked as a family doctor for 33 years but always held on to his ambition to live in the open ocean for a while, and to utilise his interests in meteorology, geology, navigation and ham radio. He was particularly keen to see some of the wildlife in parts of the Atlantic where very few people have been, and he made a film showing what he found.

He wanted to meet some of those most resilient seaman, the long distance single-handed sailors whose sole homes are their own ships, and the only effective way to do this was to become one of them for a while. He feels a great sense of pride that this community of thinly spread specialists, some of the quietest but most resourceful humans one could hope to meet anywhere, welcomed him warmly and gave him some insight into why they have chosen their lifestyle. This book is dedicated in part to them.

David has returned home to Suffolk now, where he lives with his family.

Tuesday 'n' Me

David Foreman

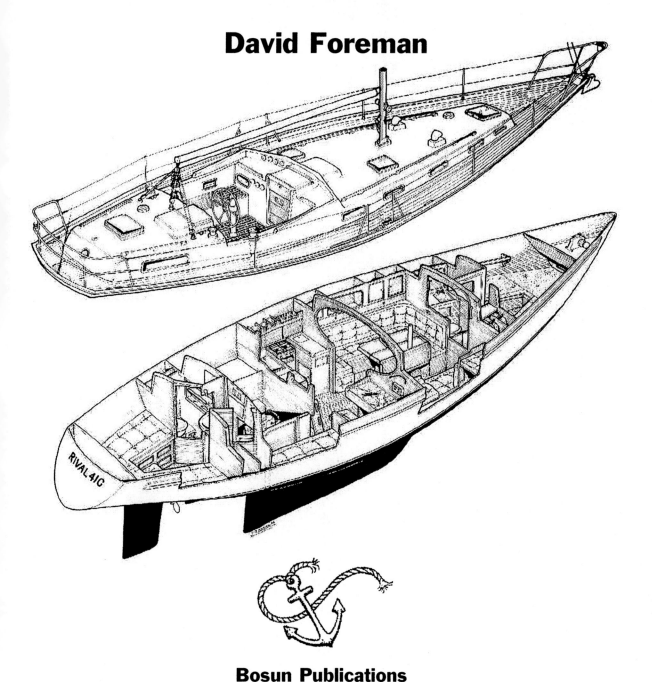

RIVAL 41C

Bosun Publications

Published by Bosun-Publications
The Ferry Point
Ferry Lane
Shepperton on Thames
TW17 9LQ
Tel: 01932 242436
Email: info@bosun-press.demon.co.uk

ISBN: 0-9546932-8-0
ISBN: 978-0-9546932-8-2

Tuesday 'n' Me

A CIP catalogue record for this book is available from
the British Library.

British Library Cataloguing in Publication Data
A CIP catalogue record of this book is available from the British
Library.

Typeset in 11pt Minion
Printed in England by
Lightning Source UK Ltd

Book design and production by
FW Barter ARCA
Bosun Publications

CONTENTS

Dedication

This Book is dedicated to my family, (and I include those very special few friends who have become a part of my family), without whose tremendous support and encouragement it would have been very difficult for me to fulfil my dream. The book would not exist without their messages to the ship.

Grateful Acknowledgements:

My son, Ben Foreman, without whose expertise and patient tuition the DVD would never have been created, nor would I personally have begun to master the art of Emails.

Mike and Alan, and the lads at Robertson's Boatyard in Woodbridge, who let me work on the ship at all hours of the day and night while she was in their shed for 15 months during her rebuild. The place has a warm friendly atmosphere, and they gently kept an eye on me to make sure that I worked only to the highest standards. It is entirely due to their skills that the hull was rebuilt so strongly.

My publisher Fred Barter and Geoff Doggett for their remarkably patient and kind advice, ideas and guidance while assembling this book.

Why "Tuesday'n'me"?

In 1883, in the south-east of England, a Thames barge was launched and named "Tuesday of Rochester". Her history deserves a separate story of its own, but after over 50 years of hard work her tired hull was pulled up on the saltings at Orford in Suffolk, where even today her name can still be seen carved on the remains of her transom. When I was a boy I used to row my dinghy through her bones when the tide was high enough, and I used to imagine how she must have been when under sail at sea.

I found some of her oak deck timbers were floating freely inside her hull in 1998, and so they were incorporated into the rebuild of my own boat over the next 4 years. As a result, it seemed natural to me to name my ship "Tuesday of Ore" (the River Ore runs through our home-port of Orford). It has been a pleasure to me to know that parts of the original "Tuesday" are still sailing the seas today, 120 years after they were first carved.

Since then, "Tuesday of Ore" has sailed beyond the Arctic circle in 2002, and (with only one person on board) across the Equator and south of the Tropic of Capricorn in the Southern Atlantic during 2003 and 2004. During these voyages the partnership between the ship and myself had been forged and strengthened, to the point where we seemed almost to have merged into a single entity at times, during our travels. There were times when we were both in very difficult and frightening circumstances when neither could have survived without the other.

As a result, most messages sent from the ship were signed "Tuesday'n'me", and my thanks go to Graham Haynes who first suggested it became the title for this book.

TUESDAY'N'ME

The story of a singlehanded voyage of discovery.

A selection from messages sent and received during a solo sailing trip from Orford, Suffolk, into the South Atlantic and back, in 2003/2004.

RISKS:

The greatest hazard in life is to risk nothing......
To laugh is to risk appearing a fool..
To weep is to risk appearing sentimental..
To reach out for another is to risk involvement.
To expose feelings is to risk exposing your true self..
To place your ideas, your dreams, before a crowd is to risk their loss..
To love is to risk not being loved in return..
To live is to risk dying..
To hope is to risk disappointment..
To try is to risk failure..
But risks must be taken,
because the greatest risk is to risk nothing.
The person who risks nothing has nothing, knows nothing,
and IS nothing.
They may avoid suffering and sorrow,
but they cannot learn, feel,change, grow, nor love nor live.
Chained by their certitudes they are slaves;
they have forfeited their freedom.

Only a person who risks is FREE.

PLEASE NOTE:

The chapters of the book correlate with the "chapters" in the DVD title screen. Together with the date visible in the bottom left corner of the picture when running the film, this will help to cross reference the film and the Emails. All times are UTC unless otherwise stated.

Some comments before running the film.

There was vicious editing and cutting of the 22+ hours of video, so the film consists of very short clips ... blink and you'll miss it.

All the sounds you hear were made at the time .. there is NO editing of the sound, nor added commentary, so my apologies for all the wind noise, the squeaks from the rubber camera case and the unsteadiness of the camera. Note that the noise from the wind generator indicates the windstrength, and you will hear one of the home-brew electric selfsteering gears which is used when near land.

The Eddystone lighthouse appears both at the beginning and towards the end of the film.

Note the Aries self-steering gear, at times steering by a compass, not by wind direction.

You will see a dog bowl on the table at mealtimes .. stainless steel, with a wide rubber-covered base which makes it very stable for humans. Note the tray on the cooker which allows a mug of tea to sit safely without spilling, and the gimballed seat made from an old bosun's chair.

Biscay was calm .... Finisterre was not.

In the Canaries I did work on other yachts' masts, to earn a cold beer.

Look out for the animals ..

- Gannets 234 miles from the nearest rocks/land .. (I had not seen this recorded before).
- the Fifty Quid bird (also called Bem-ti-vi (meaning "I SAW you!") and Kiscadee (meaning "What did they say?") ..
- the Alien (turns out it's a type of Buoy Barnacle, called Dosima Fascicularis).
- Portuguese-Men-of-War .. (Notice the carpet of baby ones, by the million, continuously for 3 days between the Azores and Plymouth, while the dolphins play .. but how are the dolphins apparently immune to them? .. It's dangerous on deck, and would be fatal if you fall in the water ..
- Dorado/"Dolphin fish"/Mahi-Mahi .. (excellent food) .. in the whole trip only TWO fish (both were Puffa Fish) were returned to the sea, all the others were eaten, including the flying fish ..
- Many Whales were seen, but to keep the film a reasonable length I had to edit out all but two of them. Note the extra "Super-numerary Arcs" on the inside edge of the rainbow, (the violet edge) ... they depend on the size of the raindrops .. they prove the "wave" characteristics of light.

Note radio conversations (other maritime/mobile radiohams) and the type of weather forecast being read to a fellow radioham at sea (1000 miles south of me) by Gerard, the retired gentleman near Brussels ..

6 out of 10 islands visited were actively volcanic still, but because of time restraints they've had to be edited from this film. Brava Island, one of the Cap Verdes, was seen again briefly on the way home northwards (I hadn't expected to be able to get so far eastwards, a great help).

You will note there is much more windward sailing than anticipated.

The Fireworks in Plymouth .. no, not actually a celebration of Tuesday's return .. in fact part of the British National Fireworks Championship.

HOPE YOU ENJOY IT!

Chapter 1

Leaving England

(June 2003)

Dear Nick and Denise,

It's probable that you don't remember the occasion, but in January 1998, I came to see you in Mallorca to buy a tired Rival 41 (centre-cockpit), at that time known as "SEBARAU". Both you and Denise were extremely helpful to me, allowing me to do my own survey of the vessel over 2 days, and then being most supportive trying to organise her return to the UK through Biscay in mid winter, (even getting in touch with a Man-With-A-Van to deliver the aluminium dinghy by road to my work address, which gained me considerable street-cred with my customers when it arrived during office hours!)

This is just my way of saying Thank You, as the 5 Year Refurbishment is now completed, and the ship is setting off on a 15 month solo South Atlantic circuit in the next few days.

I retired last year, and promptly took her off on a shakedown cruise, partly singlehanded, up the western Norwegian coast, into the stunning scenery of mountains, glaciers and snowfields north of the Arctic circle. Everything seemed to work OK, so here we are again, ready for the main trip.

Just for interest, the refettling of the boat involved removing nearly 1cm thickness of pox-ridden fibreglass (which was expected), then replacing the glass but in solid epoxy. There followed a complete re-rig to my own design (a taller, cutter rig with a boomed staysail, which Selden agreed to build for me, and even put their name on it!), and a new 5-pot Nanni engine etc, etc, etc,. So she's now a 1 year old boat with a revamped 28 year old interior, probably the toughest Rival 41 around, for about a quarter of the price of a modern equivalent.

So I'm most grateful to you for the good start to this project you gave me, 5 years ago.

Many Thanks, and Best Wishes!

David and "Tuesday".

(RECEIVED) Tue 01/07/2003 13:22

Hi David

What a blast from the past!!!

Guess what, Denise and I are working together at Sunbird in Puerto Portals now! Still hopefully looking after clients like we looked after you. Do you remember you said to me that "if you can get her aluminium oversized Optimist dinghy back to my home for under £300, then send it." I managed to get the job done for £285, so for the sake of that £15 I could have kept the dinghy!!!!

Still, a deal is a deal.

Really great to hear that the boat has done everything that you expected of it, and had you told me you were going to Norway, I would have scrounged a lift with you. One of the places I have also wanted to go to.

Like you say, a lot of boat for quarter of the price of new, even with all the work you have done to it. One thing is for sure, the boat will take you anywhere you want to go.

I can't believe it's been 5 years since the deal was done and it is really good to hear that you are fulfilling your retirement dream. You now have our new e-mail address at Sunbird, it would be lovely to hear from you during your travels.

Both Denise and I wish you bon voyage on your coming trip as we are sure you are going to have a ball. Please keep in touch.

Kindest regards

Nick and Denise

P.S Is there a doctor on board?

(RECEIVED) Thu 03/07/2003 18:30

Things won are done; joy's soul lies in the doing. Good luck, our thoughts are with you.

Regards Joyce & Joe

(RECEIVED)Tue 24/06/2003 20:46

Subject: Words can't say enough

Just remember, it's not an adventure if you are always at home. It only becomes an adventure when you leave your home behind! Also, an adventure is when things don't go quite as you planned.

Thinking of you. Have an excellent time.

Lots of Love

MOL

(RECEIVED) Fri 13/06/2003 11:53

cheers daddy. Hope plans go well, you may have even left by the time you get this. wishing you favourable winds, and all that sh*t. Am free for 2 weeks Mon 7th July until Sat 19th, so would love to meet up wherever you may be, but not if it interferes with other plans etc.

Lots of love

TOT x.......

(REPLY) Tot,

I'm sorry I can't give you any definite dates of future arrivals and departures yet, not only because I'm vague and disorganised but simply that I'm allowing myself to be driven entirely by the weather and the seasons....It's a totally different outlook to my usual attitude of trying to run a scheduled shipping line, and doesn't come naturally at first, but I'm learning!......

All the Best,

Dad.

(RECEIVED) Sat 05/07/2003 01:53

Safe Passage!

Lots of love,

Woddy

Tue 24/06/2003 19:53

Dear Everybodies,

Well, we're on the way!..the journey across the Thames estuary, through the busy Staits of Dover, and along the South Coast was calm and sunny, but I found it very tiring as I was so short of sleep from all the preparations before we'd started. But with two of us on board just to see us safely through the Straits it all went well, and James was brilliantly supportive as he listened to my fears .... I remembered being in Newtown Creek (Isle of Wight) 38 years ago, so we decided to ride out some aggressive adverse winds at anchor there .... a really delightful place, even though the National Trust charge a fee for slinging your own hook.

Spent my birthday there ...... the two Happy Birthday balloons I'd salvaged from the sea in the Dover Straits jumped ship the day before (a gust of wind blew them out of the forecabin), but my sincere thanks for all the cards and presents which I thoroughly enjoyed ...

James had other commitments so we paddled him ashore through the mud of low-water on 19/6/03 ....

So from now on I'm on my own ....

By 20/6/03 there was a window in the weather, so I jumped at it.. a hard punch out of the Solent against the last few hours of the blow, in lumpy seas, to be nicely set up to carry the tide to beyond Portland Bill, but it was so busy with ships, fishing boats and yachts that I found it very difficult to get any rest.. spent most of the night catnapping in the cockpit with the kitchen-timers set to 7-8 minutes.. so after an excellent sail from Start Point, I was glad to put in to Plymouth before thundery showers and fog set in..

Plymouth is a lovely place, and also I've discovered an inexhaustible power supply (croc-clips and an overhead power-line?), which means unlimited computer time ..The marina here is very friendly but horrendously expensive ..Security is the best I have seen anywhere..

I think I might have worried a shopowner today when I bought the speargun; I suspect my mistake was asking him to show me how it worked, but he was very nice about it, later.......

I spent one hour fixing a fairlead and cleat on the ship today, then four and a half hours retrieving my spanner which fell down between the ceiling and the inner lining...

Please don't laugh, but I think I've pushed the boundaries of what is normally accepted as "cooking" to new heights..God only knows what it looked like (it was dark at the time) but it tasted really quite..um..well..I think "interesting" sums it up best..I suspect it would allow me to starve more slowly, anyway....So far I've only used fresh stuff, and not touched the Ship's stores at all..but I have a ghastly feeling that all these greens and roughage and stuff might be good for me...total culture shock...

The plan at present is to take a breather for about 10 days, then hopefully Hedley might be free to help just for the Biscay crossing..but it depends totally on getting a fair wind to make progress west first....

I've been to see Pantaenius personally here in Plymouth, and they've been most friendly and encouraging, and I've been able to gather additional info ref Canaries and Cape Verde Islands from other yachtsmen here....All in all it's beginning to take shape at last!

This is going to be the longest E-mail of the voyage I suspect, so apologies if any future ones are a bit brief....

Thanks for all your support,
Take good care of yourselves!
Byee!
TUESDAY

(RECEIVED) Wed 25/06/2003 12:10
Subject: Amazing!...
......to get your email. Never expected that!!
Think I'll print off your email and start a folder, so you'd better send lots more. Try connecting your leads to the lightening flashes when you leave harbour, to ensure you continue to get a good (and FREE) power supply for email sending. But I understand the voltage may be a bit high.
Woddy.

(RECEIVED) Wed 25/06/2003 13:30

   David,

   Bless you for the wonderful letter. Needless to say Daddy is longing to see the photos! We gather from the TV that you are probably having heat, rain sun, and thunder .. hope it isn`t too muggy.

   It is aleady very lonely without you but we are both glad that the voyage is already underway, although for the moment stationary in Plymouth. We will be keeping all your EMs so when you are our age you will be able to re-live all the events. Heaps and heaps of love,

   Mother.

(RECEIVED) Wed 25/06/2003 18:40

   Hi Doc,

   On my way I will bring the new pump down to Plymouth tomorrow. But I guess you may not open this before I get to you so I will phone. (So I suppose this message is a bit of a waste of time really).

   James

Wed 25/06/2003 22:14

   Please,

How do I stop the bacon sticking to the inside of my kettle?...Should I grease it first or something?..(although it felt pretty slippy already, when I picked it up to poke it in the spout....)

   Any advice?..

   TUESDAY

(RECEIVED)Thu 26/06/2003 12:30

   Put it on the bread first. The bread might stick, but at least the bacon won't. Only downside is it might take a little longer to cook. Otherwise problem solved.

   MOL

(RECEIVED) Wed 25/06/2003 23:31

   Don't worry about it.

Once it has gone crispy inside the kettle, it will not be possible to remove it via the spout anyway.

I understand salty-bacon flavoured tea is an acquired taste. Personally, I prefer coffee.

   Woddy

(RECEIVED) Thu 26/06/2003 16:37

   After a great deal of intensive brain power I remembered my culinary skills. First of all you must get one pound of Australian SALT FREE butter and (first remembering to remove most of the wrapping very gently lower it into the kettle either via the spout or more easily through the lid orifice. Immerse the kettle in the same water you are either bathing or showering in. Make sure the water is hot enough to melt the butter. Then put in the bacon and give kettle a good shake. Leave the kettle and the butter at the top of the mast so that the hot sun will gently fry the contents. When evening comes lower the kettle and remove and consume the bacon. You are now left with a kettle full of butter (SALT FREE) ready to put on your toast with marmalade for breakfast. The bacon has NOT stuck to the kettle which remains ready greased for the next meal. Heaps of love from **Mother**

(RECEIVED) Thu 26/06/2003 00:44

   No. You obviously have a faulty kettle ... probably wrongly assembled in some foreign village.

   Carry out the following modification:-

1) *From roughly the centre of the handle, saw out a section exactly the same length as the spout and put it aside for use later.*
2) *Saw off the spout.*
3) *Solder the spout into the gap in the handle and the handle bit onto the original spout location.*

In use, you put the bacon into the houndle ... never into the spite.   I have been using this method for 40 years and there haven't been any complaints yet.

By the way, don't use an aluminium kettle. It must be a "tin" one, so you can solder it. If you bring a tin one aboard you will of course, as I am sure you are aware, have to box your compass again.

Take care ......   BA

Sat 28/06/2003 22:03

Thanks for all your expert advice and guidance! A really fascinating series of responses to my problem with the kettle, (which has quite a few tooth-marks on it now). It would have been much easier if the lid hadn't got jammed into place when I got a little too enthusiastic with the Molegrips and scewdriver...There wasn't room to line it with bread or butter I'm afraid because by that time it was already full of cremated bacon, but I will try these things with a new kettle next time.....I haven't got a spout-cutting-tool on board, so eventually I hammered off the base of the kettle with the sharp bit of a winch-handle, (perhaps a bit too noisily because a very nice gentleman came along to help, as he thought I was despatching cockroaches) ....
I hoped I could carve out the bacon residue,(now cold and opaque, but the bloodstains were fresh), but I think this is where I went wrong again........

I've got an idea for efficient "fast cooking"!.. to save gas .... the main principle is to use the pressure-cooker, but to produce the heat INSIDE it, instead of outside ..... you see, I've got several out-of-date emergency flares, and as I hate wasting anything I'd love to put them to good use.....(I mentioned it to my neighbour, but he's now left the marina in a hurry, muttering something about a "clucking bell" I believe)....If it works, it could make me famous, one way or another...

Anyway, I must get back to constructing tonight's offering of cabbage-cheese (haven't got any cauliflower)....it doesn't exactly make your mouth water, but it certainly makes your eyes run, so I must be getting it nearly right....

Take care, and Love to all,
TUESDAY

(RECEIVED) Sun 29/06/2003 18:43

Glad you received my expert advice on kettle cooking bacon. I forgot to tell you after removing bacon you should then add some mashed potato and two eggs to the buttery kettle contents. Then go for a sail in really rough weather. On your return scoop out the kettle contents onto a platter and you will now have a good nourishing meal of "EASY POTATO"!.

God bless you. The very best of luck and peace of mind to you throughout the voyage. We love you very, very much.

Heaps of love from Mother.

Fri 04/07/2003 23:07

Just a quickie, to say that Hedley can't come after all.... but I will press on alone, as I must use the last few hours of this unusual weatherwindow, so that I can try to get clear of the Channel Approaches before the prevailing (adverse) wind sets in again (I wish I'd set sail 3 days ago really.....) It looks like it's going to be a slow passage, so please expect no news for at least two weeks. If anything goes wrong you will know about it almost as soon as I will! No news is good news, but I will try to use the Sat-phone every few days...briefly!

The Ship and crew are in good shape, and keen to get started, now that the decision has been made. Planning to set sail early on Saturday 5/7/03, hoping to get clear of the coastal traffic as reasonably quickly as possible.

> Take good care of yourselves too!
> Warmest Love to all,
> **TUESDAY.**

(RECEIVED) Sat 05/07/2003 01:18
> *Subject: Leaving Plymouth today!*
> *David ... Thanks for that. Have a safe and happy voyage. We have, of course, complete and utter confidence in you and your ship. Bong Thingy.*
> **Much love,   Mother and Daddy**

(RECEIVED) Sat 05/07/2003 01:53
> Safe Passage! Lots of love,
> **Woddy**

Sat 19/07/2003 01:10
> **Dear Everybodies,**
Arrived in VILAMOURA, Portugal, Wednesday 16/7/03, after an 11+1/2 day, solo, non-stop 1340 mile, slow passage outside Biscay, keeping about 150-200 miles off the headlands...just for practice!.........
And the things you see!..(when was the last time you saw a 35' ketch being towed at 14+ knots behind a large ship?...you should see its wash!......(got it on film))...
Absolutely fascinating, the Highs (and Lows) of life....

For example, a Low was during the days before setting off on this trip, going through the "horrors" when I wasn't sure if I would be able to manage......Another was when it was too rough to be able to rest and cook, being thrown around a lot, as well as feeling cold and a bit "tom & dick"..("Beam me up, Scotty" didn't produce any result, so I satellite-phoned home which really cheered me up no end......that, and a cup of tea...)

A High was when completely becalmed at night (fishing line vertical, and only making 10 miles in 12 hours), the ship was surrounded by scores of Common Dolphins (5-8 feet long), feeding in formation on sprats shoaling under the ship, for over one and a half hours, all within touching distance. Dolphins' eyes don't seem to reflect back much light from a torch, but boy, sprats eyes do! Thousands of bright orange fire-flies, it seemed, rushing everywhere, with the dolphins following them even into the air to catch them ..... And the commotion and noise!.... Eventually I told them to shut-up and let me get some rest, but to no result...

Then next day seeing large schools of Dusky Dolphins(6-8 feet),(each school being made up of at least 50 animals, many of the jumping and splashing rather than just breathing), charging close under and round the ship as they headed north-east to the upwelling currents of the continental-shelf for food. During this I heard a different sound, turned round, and was gobsmacked to see three Minke Whales (20-30 feet) about 150 yards away cruising slowly by...

But the cream of this "High" was 2 days later when three pods of Fin Whales came up, doing about 6-7 knots 400 yards away, heading west. The first lot were 4 in number, the second lot maybe 6 (one had a smaller bushier spout than the others, perhaps a calf?) and only 2 spouts seen of the last. But boy are they BIG!(and I mean SERIOUSLY...).The book says 50-70 feet, but all I can tell you is that they're a LOT bigger than Tuesday and me, and I'm not at all keen on getting any closer to them .. And the spout seems so remarkably high too .. I thought it was distant smoke at first.... got it all on film........These animals are also very noisy when they breath...when it's calm you can hear them from a long way off.......small dolphins go "fpa!", Minke go "fff-ah", but Fins go "FFFFFfffff..."............... I really can shout "THAR SHE BLOWS, CAP'N!" now.. certainly didn't hope to see these things so early in the voyage ...

But the whole point of this saga is that if the sea had been lumpy, or if we had been doing the conventional thing and motoring through the calm, I would have missed it all! I wanted to feel a little of what the ancient sailors felt centuries ago, and they clearly HEARD a lot more than we do today, and they had a lot more TIME too.......(Ah, the joys of Retirement....)

Because it was flat calm as we drifted slowly over the edge of the continental shelf, I was able to note those upwellings of water which in bad weather cause the seas to break and behave badly, and I was able to demonstrate this later in Force 6 going over the Galicia Bank (which is still deep at 1600 feet!) when it all got a bit violent...... incidentally, the deepest bit was a gnats-whisker under 17,000 feet..a bit different from the Thames Estuary!.....need a longer piece of string for my echo-sounder....

Just for completeness;   I had delayed too long in Plymouth, learning how to cook, bicycle, wash, worry, shop for provisions, improving the ship(= more "toys") etc, and I missed the weather-window for a fast voyage. So Biscay was calm for several days.... catching mackerel for lunch and supper,..... then strong winds from the North (helpful but kicking up a most unpleasant sea, with awesome waves the same size as our house in Saxmundham), then very heavy rain for a whole day and a half, followed by some really gorgeous weather in the Portuguese Tradewinds 200 miles off the Spanish and Portuguese coasts...For 20 hours at one point I touched neither helm nor sheet, as the Aries-self-steering gear kept her on a dead run at hull speed, following the wind shifts, goosewinged with the genoa on a pole, the staysail pinned in flat to reduce any tendency to roll... Clear skies day and night...long rolling Atlantic swell (one smooth 8 ft crest every 11-12 seconds.)..I've NEVER sailed in such perfect conditions for so long.... Magic!

Sextant sights were mostly within 1 mile, using a small, wartime, Coastal Command sextant very kindly lent to me by Paul Spens (the one he used in his own Atlantic crossing in the 1950s). Much easier to use than my full-size one...........

It was interesting to see land the first time for 11 days...I felt almost resentful at its intruding into my own little world.....Didn't expect THAT emotion at all.....

And then I blew it all by getting an invisible lobster-pot-line round the prop in the last 3 miles (had to cut my way out of it), made a pig's-ear of tying up in Vilamoura in the fresh and gusting wind, so circled round carefully and b*llsed it up a second time as well, (thanks mainly to the excessive enthusiasm of the non-english-speaking marina staff who grab any rope on the ship's rail and pull like hell) ...

Vilamoura takes a bit of getting used to..culture shock with the Monaco Set, etc...but it has a good super-market, and the best loo-seats I've ever seen..press a button and the polythene covering trundles round by itself..Well, it said "press", so, poor fool, I did... the first time it nearly made me do a brisk "about-turn" while in full strain..now I know how the Old Man of Kent felt........We don't get that sort of technology in Sax...(take yer own shovel and yesterday's copy of the East Anglian, more like).........

Spending 3-4 weeks on the Algarve coast, planning to move every few days....after that, hopefully further progress south and west..........

There's so much more..literally could write a book.... but you've suffered enough, so Stay Well, and once again, Thanks for all your support, each and every one of you.
          "TUESDAY".

(RECEIVED) Sat 19/07/2003 06:41

David, Your wonderful EM had been printed for me and was waiting on my table when I got up an hour or so ago. Bless you! It is now safely enclosed in a folder we have for your letters. It is a great relief to know you are more or less motionless. Fin came over a few days ago and is obviously longing to going out to you.

*Your EM reads like a first rate book. Gran would have been delighted for she was keen on descriptive letters. When I used to complain there was nothing to say in a "thank you" letter I would be told "write as if you were talking to her" which is exactly how your EM sounds. I can hear you speaking as if you were in this room. Take care! Heaps of love, **Mother**.*

Sat 19/07/2003 01:11
    Subject: (The real story).

      B. hard work much of the time, but the rules are completely fair and unchanging. There were times of severe tiredness verging on exhaustion, when you can't think, if you're not careful, but even at the worst it was much preferable to being back at work. When the weather is kind it's Magic...when it's not it can get to you a bit, after surviving the first 18 hours by running down your own batteries. Then you need extra rest to cope with the violent motion, but with sail changes etc. you can't always get a break ...

    Another problem I've found is that when we're running away from the wind, although the wind generator continues to produce electricity, it's often not enough ...I'd already considered the problem, but I miscalculated ... so I've ordered a towed-generator (a propeller on a string spinning in the wake) from England to supplement it .. I'll wait here for it to arrive .. soon, I hope ....

    The probability of other shipping is a main worry, but it's a lot easier the further you get from land, although big waves make it difficult to rely on Radar watch, because the echoes from waves and rain confuse it.

    Only about one ship within 8 miles each day, on average, but twice I had near misses from ships...one of them, at night, probably a large fishing boat, certainly had no-one awake on the bridge, and for sure there would have been a collision if I hadn't spotted him (before the radar did, even) and stopped 600 yards short of impact. It left me feeling angry that if I could keep a lookout then why the h*ll can't these so called professionals, and I called him by radio to quietly wish him "Thank you, sir, and a Good Watch for you too, sir". Needless to say there was no reply, but as we were over 200 miles away from land, he would have known something was VERY near to him (if he woke at all)....

    The other ship I spotted in poor weather at 4 miles, and called him up to ask if he would like me to move a bit to the west to give him more room, knowing that almost certainly he couldn't have seen me yet, because of the waves. "Er..no , thank you" came the calm and capable reply, and it was obvious that he knew I was merely letting him know I was there. He altered course slightly nice and early, and never came closer than 3/4 mile.... That cooperation made up for the first ship's incompetence, and restored my faith a bit .... Last year's trip home from Bergen was certainly necessary as a dress rehearsal for this!

    But overall, the good bits easily outweigh the nasty bits, and in the last 2 days of the trip I was making a profit on sleep.   But I am definitely NOT looking for hard weather and heroic and fast passages, just a gentle breeze, and lots of time to soak up this kaliedoscope of new images and information.

    There's just so much to tell you about that I think it better to dwell on one subject, and talk about the other stuff another day.

    Going to move 15 miles East of here in about 4 days time, to a sort of Orford river bird sanctuary, if I can get in over the bar, and hopefully that's where Fin and I can have a holiday on our own....longing to see her again..though we're going to get wet going too and fro by dinghy (there's nowhere deep enough to tie up..have to anchor off),

      That's enough for now...Stay well!
        David & TUESDAY.

Sun 20/07/2003 00:33
   Dear all,
      Now that I've been well advised as to how to stop the bacon sticking to the inside of my kettle, (incidentally, if you wait long enough in this Algarve heat, it changes colour and crawls out by itself), I've been exploring the edges of culinary expertise a bit more.....I agree though that the Cabbage Cheese was not completely successful, not as a means of nourishment anyway, but it has possibilities in the world of pharmacology, for both your innards and your eyes......I expect you're already taking bets whether I damage myself by bacterial means, or by chemical poison (Pot Noodle pots go runny in the oven)......

Yesterday I bought some rather tasty-looking meat with veggies bits on it, but when I started to assault it, it began to fall into little chunky cubes.....very convenient I thought, until I bit into the middle and came across rather chewy WOOD, (please bear in mind that I was eating this in the dark as usual)......at least now I know the Portuguese for Kebab....at least, I did, 'cos I've gone and forgotten it again....Apart from the bits of tree, it was simply delicious!........

Some of you already know that fish is delivered direct to you here....by SEAGULL!........Shortly after I arrived here there was a "Snick!" sound and a "squawk", and from the staggery flight of a large seagull and from the two freshly cut halves of a sizeable fish dropping in the water close by, it became clear that the poor bird, basking in the warm glow of having landed a big'n, suddenly realised, with the extra payload, it wasn't going to clear the rigging..... dropping the fish unerringly into the wind-generator, (which has needle-sharp carbon fibre blades going at just sub-orbital speed) ....surprisingly no damage to the heavily bloodstained whirlything at all, but now I know the damage it can do I'll treat it with a bit more respect in future!.......

Lots of catchable fish here... but I'm not going to bother, because I've seen how they eat weed from the antifouling-painted bottoms of the boats......they're probably laden with heavy metals etc.... only good enough for the local restaurants ....(you should see the prices!..must be all that high serum platinum...)

The fruit here is better even than Tesco's...nectarines and bananas taste much fresher, but I'm having problems finding TINNED fruit for the longer bits of this voyage...I've got quite a bit already, but I learnt in Biscay that I need more... I've still only used fresh stuff, apart from a couple of tins when it was rough.....Oh, and I've only had one Pot Noodle in the whole trip so far.....(NOT the oven one!)

Saw a boat with the guardrails laden with drying clothes today....looked out of place with the Monaco set here......sure enough it turned out to be a British yacht.... I went to say hello, explaining that they were the first people I could relate to since I arrived here (which they took as a compliment, since they are also of the opinion that this is NOT the place for "Rag-and-Stick" men).....turned out to be a charming couple, waiting to pick up family from the airport) ..... Later in the day, a gentle tapping on the deck turned out to be a really nice Welsh couple sailing their way to Greece, wanting to know if there are any bookshops with English books in them.....I said Sorry, Don't Know, but I explained that I had 3 novels I read in Plymouth and could we do a trade later? ....They found a bookshop, but too expensive......So in the evening they came back to swap books over a cup of tea and a chat.......this is precisely the sort of community I was hoping to meet, but rather lost faith that it existed. They've given me lots of useful advice about this coast and marinas ....(they also dislike the Monaco Jet set, just accepting it for its stores/fuel/repairs etc)..........................so it's not just me being paranoid..there are several of us!...

Oh, another little thought....Daddy, do you remember once commenting on just how powerful music can be, at the right moment?... well, that certainly came home to me late the other night on hearing (on CD) a piece I often play on the organ at home....... tears running down my face for no other reason but the music.......... it wasn't Sadness, nor Homesickness, nor Happiness, nor anything,..... just the triggering of a sensitive part of some deep recess of the brain somewhere.....or a distant memory..........not in the least unpleasant.......in fact slightly comforting somehow ....

17

Interesting ....Wonder what the mechanism is...... and why it helps ....

It's late...time to stop.................If these Emails are too long or too often, do please let me know.

All the Very Best,

Love,

TUESDAY.

(RECEIVED)Sun 20/07/2003 01:31

Lovely stuff. Please do not hesitate, even for one second ... just keep sending more and more episodes of "The Voyage of Tuesday". We love 'em and can't get enough of 'em.

About the music:- I spent 90 minutes listening to an old very favourite cassette last night on my new super-headphones... while observing myself. No tears, but twice I grimaced and banged my fist down on the table (from sheer exhilaration you understand). And once I held up my finger and glanced up and to the right, to bring in the next soloist exactly on cue, which he was.

Love, and take care.   BA

Tue 22/07/2003 00:48

Another excellent day!....

I've had long chats and pots of tea with the couple waiting to pick up family from the airport ....turns out he's ex merchant navy (2nd mate's ticket, same as Fin's dad), and he's been using his 25 year old Moody as a base for Ocean Yachtmaster exams, though he's not actually an instructor himself...result is that he had a look at both the ship's log and my celestial navigation log to see if what I have been doing is adequate etc... Answer "yes", but he suggested I ought to put my sights on a graph each time (I normally take half a dozen or so and then average them) so that it would be easier, quicker, and show up any "rogue" readings better. I used to, but changed to try and reduce the amount of paper needed....but I'll try to find a child's exercise-book with squares already drawn in it, and do what he says.....

Swapping stories of travels, sitting on deck in the sun is really fun....this is one of the things I came for ....

The other success today, apart from finding my way round the supermarkets better, is that I have spent quite some time setting up the Ham Radio a bit better than its previous "lash-up" (literally), and although it's not finished, it's a lot better...apart from getting through to Trudi's net in Bermuda (a long established Ham network for Atlantic crossings, where they will give you any forecast you request for the waters round you, and you can talk to other yachts in your area), and in the last 3 days having spoken to hams in N. America, Poland, Germany, Belgium, Malta, Wales, Scotland, and somewhere totally unpronounceable in Indonesia (couldn't even find it on the map!), this evening I spoke direct to John in Farnham/Benhall, having established contact initially by Morse............always nice to talk to "home"....

And there lies a story in itself......... in a fit of panic I discovered I'd left my special Morse Key at home.......(the beauty of Morse is that it will get through when no other radio mode will succeed..... and it's FUN too)......... anyway I thought, well, I've got to be self-sufficient, so I made one out of copper wire and bits..............but the daft thing is that when I got the instruction book for the radio out, to check the wiring of the plug for the key, I discovered that these modern sets have everything built in, including a semi-automatic keyer......so I've altered so that it can work by using the "up/down" buttons on the microphone ("up" for dots, and "down" for dashes)...it works far better than I could have hoped!..............

Still got to find a safe and permanent place for the antenna, though...It's still only a fair-weather set-up......

(Jonesy, I'm usually on the air around 14.150 or 21.150 MHz)....

Planning to leave here very early on Wednesday,23rd July, to try to wriggle my way over the bar into the Faro rivers, about 15 miles east of here, but only if the strong wind here eases a bit,.......and only if the Towed Generator ordered from the UK has arrived (hopefully tomorrow, Tuesday)...

By the way, it's interesting how materials behave differently in this climate....plastic becomes well, "plastic", I suppose, and sticky tape can be made to accept the most awful compound curves.........but then it makes up for it by losing its "stick".......at least, it doesn't exactly lose it, but transmographies it into "Sticky-creep".....

Oh, I've just realised I've scoffed a whole box of deliciously sweet local tomatoes.......?anyone know what effects they have, and how long before it all happens?.......... No new culinary adventures of note in the past 2 days....gone back to 1001 dubious things you can do to an egg (!)...........the boat is restocked now, actually better than when we set off.....

Time to stop, before those tomatoes work, (or whatever) ....

Probably no Emails for a few days, 'cos I shan't have a decent mains supply....will have to run off Ship's supply.... but I will keep smothering you with this drivel if and when I can..........

Bye for now!

Tuesday & me.

Tue 22/07/2003 20:13

The Towed Generator didn't arrive in spite of all the sworn-on-the-Bible promises, so have to delay 24hrs. or more, as I need High Water to be safer for this next river-entrance, and they don't like you mucking about in the dark on this coast (?smugglers?).........Another day costs another arm and a leg in Marina fees too.......

Took only 3 minutes to fill up with water today (first time since Plymouth three weeks ago)......from "empty" usually takes about 40+ minutes, so I'm confident I can make the water last on a long trip.......The ship carries over half a ton of the stuff, (and only dirty people need baths)..........

My eyes feel gritty all the time, though no sign of redness......it's either ultraviolet, my cooking, or bad habits in my youth I expect.....but I'll try sunglasses first.....

No other news here really........gradually beginning to get my jaw off the ground at seeing all these VERY beautiful young ladies with virtually nothing on parading around, or draped over the decks of Gynormous speedboats (70ft+), or serving drinks in the bars and cafe's which surround the marina/town...............Please hurry out here Fin, and save me!.................

So far I've only eaten Ship's food, but I very nearly weakened and bought an ice-cream today.......Didn't though, 'cos I thought it might put me off what I've been living on.......You can get used to catfood as long as you never get to taste anything better...........

I feel a bit ashamed, (only a bit though), because I thoroughly enjoyed watching several of these enormous gasguzzling-stinkpot-boats trying to berth in quite awkward strong gusty winds,........especially when they run out of sufficient bowthruster power..(that's fun!)........Some use their RIBs (=ship's tender) as a bow-pusher, but communication seems a little vague at times.......... Most of them seem to have professional crews and skipper.......... but it amuses me the order of priorities sometimes.......Mind you, you don't want to get anywhere near them, because when they try to fend off from another boat they use the longest, pointiest, sharpest boathooks, powered by several young studs out to show off to the girls how tough they are.......no wonder these Bonkatorial vessels have so many portholes!...

Sorry if the flow of Emails dries up a bit when I escape from here "into the sticks", but I'll do my best.............................

More in a day or two I hope......

Take good care of yourselves, Love, **Tuesday.**

(RECEIVED) Wed 23/07/2003 02:26
Subject: Missing the boat.
    Now I understand what missing the boat means. This, presumably, would have missed the boat were it not for captain being delayed 24hrs with generating something. LOVE getting emails. Book growing, but printing ink fast running out.
    Flying to Helsinki end of August (judging again) and Dublin next June (same reason). Now need a housekeeper, spiders can't remember which web is who's.
    Jonesy tried radio tonight, after speaking to John. Not a dickie.
        LOTS of love, **Woddy.**
P.S. Strongly suspect a connection between gritty eyes and dolly birds. Cure is blindfold.

Wed 23/07/2003 21:10
    Thanks for all the Emails...they're really fun to open......and poor Woddy having to tear around Europe so much......it's the price you pay for being famous, my dear, I'm afraid..................And I like the idea of Mother's cooking fish on the asphalt...............but I see the weather's breaking for you a bit now, from my weather maps.......(can't get any change out of local forecasts here.......they're stuck on Cloudless, NorthWest Strong, at present, which would make getting out of this berth a bit tricky)............perhaps it's all to the best that the bits STILL haven't arrived, but I sold another arm-and-a-leg today, for another 48hrs here...... any more delays and I will have run out of arms and legs .... may have to sell my body........

    Pity, though,............cos I feel like I'm all dressed up but with nowhere to go, being fuelled-up, watered-up, freshfooded-up, etc.....just waiting for these ****** bits.......If the worst comes to the worst, I'll leave here, in a weather-gap, and come back to collect them in a fortnight or so.....

    It's really nice to speak to home by radio.......much more "real" than by modern-magic-means somehow, but the airwaves are as unreliable as the weather, though..........nothing heard at all this morning, and only very weakly around 11pm last night.....will try again in half an hour, but a little while ago it was "solid" with machinery noises.........

    Sore eyes are associated with sore elbows, I've discovered........no, not what you think....I suspect it's a combination of U/V light, and too much computer-time (staring at the screen thinking "wottheh*lldoIdonext?", and elbows on the table)........Marvellous ain't it, all those years of work and it's only now I have to suffer from Repetitive-Strain-Injury!..........

    Here are some sensations of Vilamoura:-

    Windy/Hot sun/cloudless/but the air is dry so clothes dry very quickly/dry dust/exotic spicy herbally smells of plants and trees/and the smell of dried sewage/playful screams of tourist-girls getting wet/kids and their ice creams/beat-music from the bars & cafes/noise of powerful multicylinder big gasguzzlerstinkpotboats' engines/aeroplanes low overhead towing advertising banners/posing Ferrari's and Maserati's 'n Mercs 'n BMW's 'n stuff/little electric motor powered scooters/the armed cops on bicycles complete with tadpole crash-hats/speech which is sometimes English (all types of accent) German, French, Spanish, and the almost Russian-sounding Portuguese/never heard any aggression/rare dogs and NO cats/......and all these dollybirds parading.....................Ain't life HELL!

    Byee! **Tuesday.**

(RECEIVED)Wed 23/07/2003 21:32
    Subject: Spelling Error
    Glad to know you got my email.
*Have just read your latest. Re your waiting for the bits (described by you as ****** bits). Please note this word*

*has a "g" on the end of it..... you're missing the additional * in your email.*
*From **Know-all**.*

(RECEIVED)Wed 23/07/2003 09:59
   Subject: Docs world tour
      Hi David,
            Thanks for all the e-mails.
It seems you have experienced more sea life in your trip so far than I experienced on the whole of my transatlantic trip in '92 .. such are the fortunes of life.
   Keep on enjoying your experiences and we look forward to receiving the next chapter.
*Good luck **Ruth and Chris***

(RECEIVED) Thu 24/07/2003 02:45
   David ... Gee, thanks for Emails.   On my computer road map, on the coastline near Vilamoura, I can see a little inlet looking rather like a spheroidal diverticulum.   Is that where you are?
   It's not the dollybirds you want to watch out for, it's those mucking dogs.   Believe me, I've had a lifetime of it.
   Yes, we are all well.   Send more whenever you can.
      *Love,   **BA***

Sat 26/07/2003 19:10
   Dear Everybodies,
         This is MUCH better!.........
Imagine Poole Harbour with a tenth of the number of the boats, sand instead of mud, blazing sun-sun-sun, force 3-5, not much run of tide so we're wind-rode all the time and head into any waves, in about 18' of water, lots of space so the noise of the wind generator doesn't upset anyone, and a wonderful view of towns over a mile away, with the mountains (well, big hills anyway) behind them....and it's really WARM!(minimal clothing).........
There are other anchored yachts, mainly British and Dutch, well scattered, (until a Portuguese boat from Lisbon came in and spoilt it all and slung his hook about 75yards away.....but he's gone away again now)...............Every so often a passing fishing boat, or a gasguzzlin'stinkpot, kicks up a nasty wash....... and occasionally there's a sonic boom from the fastest jetskis I've ever seen, but I believe their drivers are quite high on the list for Darwin Awards (those who do dangerous things, die young, and thus fail to breed, removing themselves from the Human-Gene-Pool), so I don't think they'll be troublesome for long......
And the aeroplanes landing at Faro international Airport all seem to straighten themselves up overhead here, lowering their wheels as they do their final turn to line up with the runway, so there's lots to look at........
And, as a special bonus, I'm surrounded by relatively smooth water in all directions, so the Ham Radio aerials should work much better......we'll see, this evening.......
Moved here early this morning......couldn't move any other time as it was a bit tricky to get out of the berth in Vila-(I'll-take-your-money-for-you-sir)-Moura in the winds we've had there (so I got out of there at dawn when the wind was at its least)......that, and I needed the tides right for here..........
Had a lovely quiet sail the 15 miles along the coast to here, but wretched lobster-pot-buoys made life difficult......... every 120 yards the whole way, virtually none of them marked with more than a weed-covered empty plastic detergent container, totally invisible except on calm days like early this morning........But I could see the mountains of AFRICA in the far distance though!.......

The entrance is very like Shingle Street, with its swirling crosstides and powerful eddies, and a mixture of 100' deep channel(in the entrance at least) and cliff-edged shoals demands a little respect I would think, when it's windy ....

At present anchored in the area which leads up to OLHAO ("ole-le-ong", apparently), just to the east of FARO, which I can see about 4 miles away........Tomorrow planning to start exploring places to meet Fin next week.......

By the way, the bits from England never arrived, but the gentleman who organised it all as a Special Delivery says it reflects badly on him and his firm (he's the boss in Plymouth), so he's started a war with the shippers to make things happen and to return the extra charge for the rapid delivery to me, (which I told him was well beyond the call of duty but most welcome to hear).......Apparently the packages left the firm on the 18th., the same day I'd ordered them ....so the plan is to keep in touch with Vila-thingy and to poke my head back into the lion's den in 2-3 weeks' time before setting off towards Madeira (weather permitting).....I'd also be able to top-up fuel and water tanks, but the chances of an overnight berth there in August are minimal, I gather...........

One other thing....the insurance company have agreed, as a one-off special, to cover me, fully, as far as Brazil, singlehanded, as they know me personally now..........I have to thank James for that one, as he sort of told me to "go and tell them you're God's Gift to Sailing and Humanity because your Mother says so, and they can't argue with facts like that", and it's worked!..........(actually they've been very generous to me, but I'm under strict instructions not to tell any other singlehander I meet)..........during and after Brazil should be 3rd party only..........

Must stop... British Maritime Mobile Radio Net on 14.303MHz in 5 mins, so...

........Stay Well!

Love,

Tuesday.

(RECEIVED) Mon 28/07/2003 15:26

Daddy

Great to hear things are going well. Your recounting of events are great to read. Makes me really long to be back sailing.

Missing you greatly.

Hope weather & things continue to be favourable. Enjoy Mummy's visit & am sure I will hear all about it.

Have 2 weeks holiday towards the end of August, so will contact soon &, again, depends where the weather takes you, maybe can meet up.

Keep safe as you're my only DAD and I like it that way,

loads of love

TOT xxx........

Sat 09/08/2003 23:03

Dear Everybodies,

There are two types of sailing.....mucking about in boats, and boating about in muck..........Olhao Harbour is one of the latter, but its such a gorgeous place it's completely forgivable........You have to be careful to wash anything which gets harbour water on it, eg. hands etc, but Tuesday's only been in there for shopping etc., and meeting Fin, Jan and Andy..........Drinking water for the ship has to be collected by dinghy, in your own container, from the nice clean town tap on the waterfront....... and because the berths here are not finished (so they're FREE), they're not connected to the land, so the Green Bladder (rubber boat) has been put to good use............

There's a Karaoke cafe here.......I've never heard such AWFUL singing.... I asked what the penalty was for despatching a perpetrator, and was told by local official that probably no crime would be committed .... might even get a medal ...... in actual fact it's so bad that it's really quite fun sometimes, and although it starts at 8pm and dies at 4am, you become immune.......even my playing of my new harmonica is no worse than them, but maybe Fin disagrees..........

But most of the time is spent out in one of two anchorages about 2 miles away, near extensive sandy beaches, and the spotless Atlantic waters over the other side of the island of Culatra, (lovely for secluded swimming)........The wind is peculiar, in that it follows the sun each day....east in the morning, south after lunch, west at sunset, and the northerly "land breeze" at night.....so we're always head to wind and head to sun.........doesn't half wind up the anchor chain though..........

Have met some wonderful characters, including Clive-the-Junk-Man, who has nearly completed his 13 year circumnavigation in the 28 ton steel junk he built himself in Canada.......everything about the boat and its fittings is begged, borrowed or bargained for, and to pay for his food etc. he either has to sell a part of his ship, or try to persuade backpackers to pay money to sail with him....(some wit locally has suggested that he EATS the backpackers, but there are no bones around to substantiate the story).....recently he's been taking widows out to sea to scatter wreathes and flowers in memoriam......at least, that's his explanation, anyway............He's writing a book of his adventures.......

.............This is the person who was SO grateful when I donated a new ensign from Tuesday's stores to his ship (she's British registered somehow, because it was the easiest way into the EEC) because his old flag was such a disgrace that no backpacker would look twice at the boat............ he insisted that I accept a book that he'd just finished reading, which he reckoned was a really good story........surprisingly it turned out to be *"Great Expectations"*, (Charles Dickens), which I wanted on board anyway..........

Fin and I had a smashing holiday, in the hot sun each day, a real Holiday.......... swimming, and a little exploring on board "Tuesday" up the Faro river till it was too shallow to go further, with Jan and Andy................. and we had a wonderful day with them in their car when they very kindly drove us to Vila (-Most-Expensive-Rat-Hole-On-The-Algarve)-Moura to collect my water driven electricity generator (yes, it finally arrived!)........then we spent the rest of the day, till late, in and around their Chateau-on-its-own-Mountain (well, OK then, their lovely holiday bungalow on its own hill), and had a delightful meal in the village nearby in a real rustic environment........What a wonderful place this is!....I can see why many people come here and forget to leave............

But yesterday the boat was horribly empty without Fin....a most unpleasant feeling.............but I suppose she has to work, otherwise she can't afford me...............

Hot water (heated by the sun in a black bladder).........Electricity from the sun and the wind.........Oh, and I've found how to keep cool outside on deck...simply wash your clothes in the hot water, don't bother to dry them, just put them straight back on again..........mind you, I overdid it yesterday and actually felt cold for a while.....started looking around the horizon for a weather change till I realized.............Temperatures outside in the shade have been over 40 centigrade, but never more than 36c (=98 Fahrenheit) in the cabin............Butter and cheese melt, and seawater on deck becomes solid layers of salt very quickly.........Plastics become "plastic", paint peels,varnish crazes.....there's going to be lots to do!..............But very little build up of weed as yet,surprisingly........

I've tried every time I've been ashore to find a shop which sells ammeters and fuse holders for the new watergeneratorthingy........no luck.......so today I had a deeper rummage in the ship's stores, and would you believe it, I found exactly what I needed (with a bit of borrowing-from-Peter-to-pay-Paul)........all broken, but repaired with little difficulty..........Will test it tomorrow with temporary wiring.......

Spent the rest of the day getting the ship back into "going-to-sea-mode"......things like reversing the forehatch again, which I had turned round in Vilamoura so that it directed air into the cabins.......

Planning to try to sail westwards a bit tomorrow, to fill up with fuel, water, and fresh stuff in Portimao, about 40 miles from here............then I want to have a go at a tiny river and its tight entrance 4 miles beyond that, for a day or so, ready to attack the next leg out into the Atlantic again, towards Porto Santo, the second main island of the Madeira group............but more details in 2-3 days I hope.........

Getting dark, and much to do on deck before tomorrow's early start ....so Stay Well, and enjoy the unusual weather I hear you have in the UK!.....(and thanks for all the Emails....I really enjoy them!...thanks too for keeping to plain text only as it's programmed to reject anything more than that)........

Love to All,
"Tuesday".

(RECEIVED) Mon 11/08/2003 01:32
Subject: Monday .... I think.

Dear Tuesday,
Lovely stuff! We are following you on our maps. We are, of course, absolutely thrilled that you are enjoying it all so much.
Fin phoned (Monday) to say that she is home and in good nick.
We are well, and send our love, and wish you bong continuing. *(It's Tuesday now).*
BA

Sun 10/08/2003 22:50
Dear Everybodies,

Crept out of Olhao, near Faro, just after dawn Sunday 10/8/03.........Lumpy sea outside at first, then it all settled down to a light breeze, but with an aggressively hot sun..............

Saw my first wild Turtle today...well it wasn't really "wild", just a bit upset.... because quite clearly I startled it when it was sunbathing on the surface.............It dived before I could film it unfortunately.........about 2'6" long, and 2' across.....about 6' from the side of the boat......

I managed to get the towed generator up and running, though not much output yet as the wind was light......more tests needed.....but looks promising.......

And then it happened........"fpa!" all round the ship again, only this time they weren't feeding, just playing.............between 20-30 Common Dolphins, playing, rolling over and over, cuddling each other, jumping, and tail-slapping the water, zigzagging either side of the bow, etc..............But the wind died after 20 minutes or so..... "Tuesday" stopped, and they got bored..........but when I started the engine 10 minutes later, as time and tide were pressing a bit, they all came back to have a look again............quite fascinating!........ a couple of babies amongst them sticking tight close to their mums ...... and a dominant leader big chief, with a damaged fin....... I feel really privileged to see these things we read about..............Magic!

PORTIMAO is where we are now.........it's another Vilamoura ("Tuesday" is a baby yacht here), but a lot more "rag and stick" friendly......but not a place to stay in........This time I discouraged assistance when mooring up and warping the ship along the fuel pontoon, and everything worked beautifully for a change......a bit embarrassing really, as the marina reception organised for two of their staff to come and help, but when they laid a hand on the warps it all started to go pear-shaped........took great tact to show them I'd got it all carefully balanced, by quietly taking over again........("Oh, I see now" said one in English, "keep the boat head into the wind").....................typically Foreman/Pettigrew isn't it!.............

The Customs officer was a bit suspicious of my appearance, until he overheard my answers to the reception girl ("and where are your next ports of call, sir?").........and within minutes the word had got round, and a couple of Spanish yachtsmen came up and wanted to know all about the trip........then a Belgian from Antwerp ("nice boat, Beauty of Ore").......I feel a fraud 'cos I haven't actually been anywhere yet!............A lady behind the counter in a marina-shop here asked where I was headed, and then told me in good english that she thought the east coast of Brazil was absolutely lovely ("you will be much liking it")........

Planning to take the Courtesy Coach into town tomorrow morning to do final shoppings, then to anchor by the harbour mole for a night, before trying for this narrow river at Alvor, 4 miles west........then to head towards Madeira in 3-4 days time, weather permitting, but I'll keep you informed..........

So..........Bye for now!

Love,

"Tuesday".

Wed 13/08/2003 19:51

Spent a night anchored under the harbour breakwater in Portimao (free!), then quietly sailed out Tuesday morning........

Dawdled along the coast to this delightful small lagoon at ALVOR, just west of Portimao.......They say do not attempt it in onshore winds, but luckily the wind was light until just after I arrived here..........Really very pretty, warm sandbanks everywhere, sandy cliffs, with the mountains as a backdrop .... but many speed boats etc., and very little water at low tide (like now)........had to move to ferret around to find a hole deep enough to float in, and even so only 6" under the keel.............(I've discovered, very gently, the sand is HARD!).....

Eight swimmers washed out towards the sea on the tide in the afternoon......four of them collected by Tuesday (not by me...the dinghy's all packed away), three on the gunwale and one on the anchor chain...... collected by various rubber boats soon afterwards and returned to their rightful owners........ all looked some-what shaken by the episode....there's quite a tidal run here ......swimming isn't fast enough......

Then the wind changed........visibility collapsed to 400 yards in the smoke haze from the forest fires a few miles inland......saw them earlier from out at sea.......quite scary, with the air full of soot, smuts, cinders, which get EVERYWHERE, and smoke which stings your eyes after an hour or two......the smell of burnt timber...... I was jolly glad to be afloat......must be nasty inland, 'cos you wouldn't be able to see the fire coming at you..........Helicopters have been ferrying to and fro all day, collecting water from higher up the river to bomb the fires from large buckets slung underneath them......and a large twin engined flying boat appears occasionally, looking busy.................It's the first time I've gained an inkling of just how powerful these fires are...............the air didn't clear until today's seabreeze filled in around 3pm.....but the smuts keep falling even so.......everyone's sluicing their decks to shift the cinders......expecting more this evening......

Just got your Emails, for which many grateful thanks......always a pleasure!........In answer to the questions:-

Water powered generator should produce .06volts per rev/minute, and 0Amps into 12v @ 3knots, 4Amps @ 5knots, 8Amps @ 6knots, and 11Amps @ 8knots...........Hoping to average about 5Amps, but the drag does slow the ship a bit....

No, sorry, Mother, I couldn't hear the rain on your roof....... but we could do with some here........

Paul rang me on the mobilephone, (a pleasant surprise!), about the Ocean Cruising Club, as you gathered, but I think the best thing to do is nothing until I get back, because I won't have a reliable address anywhere I suspect.........I've briefly looked on their website, and seen the application form, but let's leave it till it's easier to do........And besides, my route to Portugal was not the most direct, and may not qualify..........

Planning to leave here tomorrow, Thursday 14/8/03, early afternoon, but going through the pre-voyage-horrors as usual at present (not nice)...............forecast looks OK, and I'm now accepted onto the Italian Maritime Mobile Ham Radio Net on 14.297Mhz at 1900hrs UTC each day......they will give me, personally, predicted forecasts for every 6 hours en route, from various official sources on the worldwideweb .....very kind and helpful gentleman called Alfredo runs it from near Rome......... and in Porto Santo (island near Madeira) it looks like there should be an anchorage to start with, which I would prefer instead of manoeuvring into a pontoon berth on first arrival...............distance is less than 500 miles, expecting a close fetch to balance the southgoing currents, but a few shipping lanes to cross first...........Hope to be there within 7 days, but no news is good news......

     So..... Take good care of ourselves.....and I'll try to keep in touch as before......

       Lots of Love,

        Tuesday & Me.

PS.(4pm) Since I started typing this, the forest fires have appeared on the horizon and I can assure you it is a very frightening sight....... whole hills and mountains (approx. 30degrees of view) ablaze.....and it moved so FAST as it breasted the skyline and raced down the hillside towards us......the sky is a deep red/orange colour........the flames are a brighter, fluorescent, orange.... twisting, leaping, moving over the landscape........."alive"...........all the holiday makers have gone very quiet, realising we're seeing peoples' HOMES burning ...everyone is watching....(apart from one brain-dead youth on a jetski).........the smoke cover so thick that it's so dark that ashore the streetlights have come on, and cars are using their headlights..........worrying till you realize it's over 5 miles away....... you can actually HEAR the fire, like distant summer thunder, but continuous............quite an experience....... hope the wind changes again soon....

    (7pm) Wind eased......now only smoke, no flames visible......

(RECEIVED) Thu 14/08/2003 01:17

   David,

     Thanks. Fire sounds very scary. Are we to take it that you will not be able to e-mail us once you have got to sea? And will mobile fones work on Madeira and Porto Santo? In which case can I presume that you will be able to send/receive e-mails when you get there?

     I know that my seagoing escapades are absolutely nothing compared with yours, but think of me when you cross those shipping lanes ... it was 56 years ago!! (Good God, where did it all go? Raising kids I s'pose!).

     All well here.

     I know that you will, but take care won't you.

       BA

(RECEIVED) Thu 18/09/2003 14:56

   Dear David,

     Thank you very much for your e,mails, keep them coming, they are now required reading by us.

     Re- the Forest fires you experienced whilst anchored off Portugal, I am rather surprised that you allowed the authorities to get away with dirtying Tuesday's deck with smuts; I seem to recall you were unhappy once when someone wearing old wellies (not the yachting variety) marked the deck of one of your other boats!.

     Once again, take very good care of you and yours, enjoy your adventure and it's challenges.

     *Regards, **Bob & Brenda.***

Chapter 2

Leaving mainland Europe

Thu 21/08/2003 23:18
    Dear Everybodies,
        More Highs and Lows.......

The forest fires in Portugal were really quite worrying .... and the cinders could easily damage sailcovers etc.,(they still reek of woodsmoke), but no significant harm done........spent ages washing the decks ....

I needn't have bothered........Left Alvor on 14.8.03, but everything went wrong from the start (just as though the ship didn't want to play that day).........and the final blow was charging headlong into 35-40 knot winds (certainly NOT forecast) in the "acceleration zone" off Cape St.Vincent........gave myself one hour so see if I would stick it, but gave in after another 5 minutes and turned back.......found (from the book) a small bay tucked under the Cape itself, and, feeling rather "hammered", tentatively clawed the way in against the wind (first time I've used ALL the reefs in anger), to anchor in about 20 feet on good sand........still heavy gusts to 45 knots, so a wretched night spent at anchor-watch with ruined confidence and little sleep, thinking of every individual link and shackle in that anchor chain........(Joe, your Anchor "CHUM" you gave me was really useful, thank you)....... I thought I was stuck there for ever, but noted it calmed down a bit at dawn, so after 36 hours, took a big breath and had another go on 16.8.03............

No problem, scampering away from that terrible Cape at an averaged 7.5knots ....desperate to get clear of the land effects.......and you could see it very clearly in the cloud patterns..........excellent progress towards Madeira, once across the shipping lanes.........

But the second day out, still literally battered and bruised, I got miserable again (usual on the second day I think?)..........couldn't tell the difference between Fear and Hunger and Seasickness (same symptoms), and I certainly didn't feel inclined to cook...... although the sailing was excellent in 25+ knots of wind, I was tired and fed up with the motion in a decidedly awkward sea, and hadn't yet settled into a daily rhythm...... couldn't go outside to play as it was still wet on deck............Gave myself a blunt talk, had a cup of tea, and felt a bit better.......

Had to stop for one ship at night (hadn't seen me), but otherwise only one ship every 24 hours.........

No wildlife at all....no birds (until within 40 miles of land), and no dollyfins (except for 3 minutes at sunset one evening)............but perhaps it's because I'm learning to play the Chromatic Harmonica and the dolphins do have SOME musical taste............

Ampere Seamount was interesting........The seabed rises from 15,900ft deep to 8,000ft, then abruptly up to only 150ft deep briefly, before diving again........(though I personally didn't notice any change at all.......but then I was 1.5 miles to leeward of it ......and it was dark, after all)...

Very dark at night, especially when it's cloudy.........none of the northern glow we get in higher latitudes.......stars are bright, but the sky is blacker than I expected......Mars is at its closest around now.....impressive....

Ham Radio has been very helpful indeed, both physically and morally.......trying a new antenna tonight, made of old wiring and a telescopic 12 ft. fishing rod.....it worked OK earlier today........

Settling down nicely into the life, when suddenly all change again at sunset on 19.8.03 .... LAND HO! at 40 miles.....approx 450 miles in three and a half days......To avoid entering the place at night (unlit buoys and boats), hove-to at 30 miles out, at 0.5knots, for 12 hours)....... overslept, twice, getting a grand total of 4 hours sleep in all that night, knowing I was headed AWAY from land, in a more comfortable motion.........

Got her going again at 0500 (the sun here is an hour BEHIND yours)......and fetched up in this enchanting spot in the large sheltered bay that is PORTO SANTO Island (size about 6x2miles), Madeira...........clear pale blue water, clean sand, palm trees, volcanic ash hills, hot sun, temperate breeze (strong at times), and the occasional brief and warm rainshower ....and CHARMING people...............Harbourmaster came haring out to sea to meet me in his little speedboat, and said in English, with a big smile, no need to clear the formalities today, have some sleep and food, and come and see Immigration, Customs, Police and himself tomorrow, (once I'd explained I was going to anchor off, and there was only me on board).........lovely welcome!....

So I inflated the Green Bladder today, paddled ashore with the ship's papers etc, cleared with all Authorities very peacefully............ met several other yachts I've already seen in Portugal........ ("aren't you the skipper of "Tuesday"?", said someone in the shop today......... turns out he's from a Maltese yacht who also got cindered near me in Alvor)................I suppose it's inevitable since we're all going down-wind in the Trades.....bit like last year in western Norway, where everyone's taking the same route........nice!.........they have told me there's a new marina in Madeira, not in the books yet, which has empty places (Funchal is always full) so, when Tot arrives tomorrow for a week, we'll get more details from a French yacht I met in Portimao..........

Blimey, this was a long waffle.... sorry about that!......................Take good care of yourselves................more soon......

    Love,
    Tuesday.

(RECEIVED) Sun 24/08/2003 14:02
 Hello David
 Love your story so far, after each read I have to shower to remove the salt and smuts!
 The fact that you have found the anchor 'chum' useful is good news, it spent its previous life idle in the chain locker of Ferrikee and before that, my father who bought it, had it on board his Twister "Softly", where I know it was used, but these ships were both 'tiddlers' compared to Tuesday, 31 & 28 ft respectively.
 Regards Joe

21/08/2003 23:18
Greetings and Salutations to Manuel(sorry if bad spelling!) and Alfredo, from David on yacht "Tuesday", Porto Santo,Madeira. This is in answer to your radio request for more details....

My information about NATAL (05:45N/35:11W) is dated Autumn 2002. It suggests :-

Leave the two GREEN buoys on your PORT side when in the Rio Potengi.   The channel appears close to the NORTHWEST bank for the first 1.5 Km.   The Iate Club de Natal is approx 2 Km inside the river, on the EAST bank, just before a ferry jetty.   My information suggests you tie to a mooring buoy near the pontoon, or anchor by the moorings.   The current and wind are reported as being strong.   There is river traffic so anchor light is necessary. Not many facilities for repairs, but I believe there are showers and restaurant, and the club is friendly.. There is NO mention of pontoons to actually moor to, and my impression is that it is a "club" and not a "marina".

I am sorry, Manuel, but that's the best I can do from here.

I wish you good luck, fair winds and safe landfalls.

I hope to be following a similar route this November, cruising the Brazilian east coast from December to April 2003/4, so any advice you can pass on would be useful!

   73! PS.Alfredo,(and Gerard) thanks for all your support....I promise to try to rig up a better antenna system on "Tuesday", to make life easier for everyone! May your shadows never grow less, Sirs!

(RECEIVED)Sat 23/08/2003 01:06

thanks dear om 4 that valid information......
i have only the british big ship pilot on board and so no mention of that club or marina. well, so it's not a marina, suites me even better, i'm not the marina type at all.....
thanks again, 73
manuel

Sun 31/08/2003 22:01
Dear Everybodies,
I think it was the French who caused it..........Water in Porto Santo is only available to yachts which are in the harbour itself (which means you have to pay for it).........us hardy types ("moneypinching" more like) anchored outside aren't allowed it officially..........we suspect a French yacht, inside, was filling everyone else's water containers............anyway it appears they were asked to leave........next thing is the whole French contingent came outside to anchor in the bay, so instead of only four boats, we were suddenly fourteen!.........the marina was very empty afterwards too........

There are some wonderful people here.........I won't name them all, but the variety, and the low cunning of them is fascinating..........The "mad" Finnish solo-sailor on a steel yacht called "Snoopy", who never goes ashore, and sings VERY loudly some rambling reindeer-calming-sagas in Finnish at strange times, turned up alongside one day in his rubber boat, immaculately dressed, spotlessly clean, completely sane and utterly CHARMING.........his name is Matti and he spent quite some time chatting on board "Tuesday", confessing some of the mistakes he's made during his trip from Finland this year........nice chap........he's also aiming for Brazil, but he'll get there long before me......... we'll keep in touch ....

He told me nobody bothered about putting up a black ball shape, or lowering their ensigns at night, or anchorlights, till "Tuesday" turned up with all her traditions.............now they're all doing it in Porto Santo...........(how embarrassing!).........

Tot came out by air, via Lisbon and Funchal, and we had a smashing holiday ....we climbed up the solidified remnants of an eroded volcano-"chimney" with our new-found American friends from "Free Spirit" and "Forever",..........we went UNDER a cliff/mountain in a newly carved tunnel,.........we found fields absolutely packed with white snails (every single one of them dead) on every single grass-stem, looking like cotton bolls till you look closer....(never did find out why,what,how etc)...............

We covered a lot of miles on foot that week........it takes 25 mins to walk to the shops, and that's after you've rowed ashore by dinghy,.....then you've got to carry all the stores back again........and it's HOT.........

But swimming off the boat in such clear water was a real revelation..... ....Tot spent ages snorkelling, looking for a stainless steel nut I'd dropped overboard.........(I suspect it buried itself in the sand).....

We discovered that what I had taken to be Peruvian Beef, called "Peru Bife", (and it was delicious!) actually means "Turkey Steak"..... ....pity...seems better my way........

I have often wondered why graffiti exists..............now I know...........The painting of a motif and ship's name on the harbour wall, by visiting vessels, is positively encouraged here (the port-policeman said "it's not actually compulsory, but....") ..... so Tot and I did our best, just beside the red lighthouse at the entrance..........it went horribly wrong at first, but thank heavens for Polyclens and kitchen rolls!...........Anyway, we left our mark in Danboline Bilge paint, even though we had to go and find a rubbish bin, to stand on, to do it.........should be there quite some time I would think..........

All was calm and idyllic, but then Tot had to return to Oxford (very sad, that was) .... and David-the-local-Porto-Santo-marine-mechanic was most upset about it too, wailing "where's Tot?" from the harbour wall as I rowed back..... (You made a hit there, girl!)........and then it all went pearshaped..........The wind swung into the bay and turned it into a very uncomfortable place to be anchored...........only one boat gave in, paid the marina dues, and went into the harbour..............the rest of us sympathised with each other, by sign-language or by dinghy,..........and decided to go to Madeira as soon as the wind was favourable.......

So that's why "Tuesday" is here, since 1745 this afternoon, in CANICAL near the eastern end of MADEIRA, behind a brand new breakwater, tied to a brand new pontoon,..........so new that the whole place is still feeling it's way at present................long chat this evening with the local Customs/Policeman, helping him fill in his forms which are quite clearly a novelty for him...........but again, everyone's so pleasant here, even though it's moderately expensive (still only about one third of what an English place would be!)...............

Had a very pleasant daysail to get here, with balmy headwinds in unlimited visibility and sunshine ....TOO hot in the sun, so I kept filling a bucket with seawater and dunking my feet and ankles in it (it works!).............met a strong and unexpected adverse current near the eastern cape of Madeira........must be because the wind at present is opposite to what it should be too?.................

"FREE SPIRIT" and "FOREVER" should arrive here tomorrow all being well............I'm planning to stay a week, but I don't know yet if they will..................But I bet this is the only marina in Madeira with spare places..............so new it's not in the books yet........tucked under a cliff of fossilised volcano-ash.......really quite pretty!.........

But being virtually underground means Ham radio may not work very well, in spite of my new antenna made of domestic wiring pushed up the inside of a 5 metre fishing rod.......I'll keep trying though...............

So much more...........but that's more than enough for now..........

Take Care!
"TUESDAY".

(RECEIVED)Sun 31/08/2003 22:16
dear om,

once again thanks 4 the advise about natal and my eta is 02.09.2003 around midday 2 evening. so it would have taken us 18 days from banjul, (Gambia) 2 cross, noytb so bad when u consider it's only a 10m boat, heavily loaded with presents 4 the family. well we had thew first 4 days 2 make south against the sw monsun what was quite hard going. well, any information i gather will passed by 2 u 4 sure, and by the way: i have exellent results with a 8m fishing rod just tied 2 the stern sea fence and connected 2 a sg smarttuner. only thing 2 considerf must be a fishing rod not made from carbon cause that is a conductor. the rod set me back 20 euros and is asm good as a commercial antenna 4 over 400 euros, so give it a try and surely is better than the backstay.

73 fair winds always
manuel

Mon 01/09/2003 23:36
Dear Manuel,

Many thanks for info.....and for all your reports to Alfredo & Trudi etc.. which I have been monitoring as a "dry-run" for my own trip.....

Like you, I have found the best antenna for my purpose is a glassfibre fishing rod I bought in Porto Santo for only 8 euros, but it's only 5 metres long......I use the supports to the radar pole as the counterpoise, so the base is already up at 4 metres above the sea........... it's working now from 7 MHz up to 52 MHz, so I dare not alter it!....(Pity I have only 8-10 watts tho')..........

Stay Safe!....73!
David

Mon 01/09/2003 22:50

Dear Everybodies,

Personally, I quite like small mammals/rodents ....but I understand there is at least one highly intelligent RAT in this harbour, which is an expert at boarding boats.........not met him yet (harmonica may have put him off), but can't leave any food anywhere, just in case..............please don't laugh, but I do have a rat-trap on board..a battery powered ELECTRIC one, believe it or not.... but I've not had the opportunity (or courage) to fire it for real yet.........

The chap who invented the spoon was a clever fellow............ it's a superb tool for transferring butter (which is permanently liquid now) from container to bread............don't know how I missed the obvious use for it before, really........(actually it's not butter, but some sort of vegetable goo which I've come to quite like now...............I've a nasty feeling it's probably good for me or something, though)..........

I was wrong about this place being just a fossilised ash cliff/mountain..... ....in daylight today it became obvious that we're right in the middle of an old volcano which has been eroded by the sea...........just like it had been sectioned vertically with a knife.........so there is a vertical "chimney" blocked by solidified magma/basalt, and on either side of it are the layers upon layers of ash-rock, in the classical volcano shape, all of it sitting on the original bedrock.......Fascinating!.................just like a diagram in a geography book............

I gather there has never been an eruption here in living memory.... ....Fair enough, I thought........till it dawned on me that this place was only discovered about 600 years ago...........(Puts a different slant on it, doesn't it!)......

The video-camera is misbehaving.........very sad......but advice from home (for which my most grateful thanks) may well hold the answer........ I really do need to record all of this trip, so I can relive it later.........

The two American boats arrived today from Porto Santo, and being able to radio to them the latest pilotage information when they were still an hour away was fun..........Also met up with two British yachts (one from Shotley which I've seen in the Orwell before).........nice people on board (as usual, a married couple on each)..........a great deal of information pooled between us all................but the Brits are not going our way after the Canaries............

Planning to stay one week here, (not far from the airport, incidentally) probably hiring a car for us all to go up into the mountains one day I hope.................might even see some proper RAIN!........... Spent today washing clothes, cleaning, improving the ship, setting up someone's radio etc.........First exploratory expedition on foot tomorrow morning, towards town of Canical itself, two miles away.........

(Not much about Boating this time, is there..............)

Love to all, **"Tuesday"**.

(RECEIVED)Tue 02/09/2003 13:17

Hello David,

I wanted to visit you again, but this morning you were gone. The anchor place in Funchal has been a bit noisy. What is your sailing plan? Have you a mobile phone? I will leave towards Canary Islands tomorrow or day after. Originally I wanted to sail straight to Las Palmas, but now I am thinking of checking some of the other island on the way. I am then planning to sail to Cape Verde, Brazil, Trinidad, Grenada, Netherlands Antilles. Venezuela and Panama. I fly to Finland for couple weeks in the middle of January. If needed I take the boat up in Trinidad or Netherlands Antilles.

With best regards

***Matti** S/Y Snoopy*

PS. I keep the mobile usually open when there in a net. Satellite phone I open only when I use it, but then I can also read last messages.

Thu 04/09/2003 02:18

Hello Matti,

What a pleasant surprise! Nice to hear from you! I hope all is well with you....

I didn't leave Porto Santo until Sunday Aug. 31st.....but came to a new marina at CANICAL in the East part of Madeira......planning to anchor at Funchal for maybe one night next week, then (if wind is fair) to Lanzarote. Probably 2-4 weeks around the Canaries, then on to Cape Verdes (probably Sal at first).........hope to be in Recife/Salvador about Christmas,..... then s-l-o-w-l-y towards 35 degrees south................then (around Easter-time) eastwards round to St.Helena Island,..... north to Ascension Island......maybe Cape Verdes again.......to Azores early next summer.

Then to stop for 2 months holiday with my wife on board, before returning to England in mid summer 2004.

But plans are not timetables, so who knows what will happen!   But maybe we will cross paths again............that would be nice....

(Yes, I use mobile-phone and satellite-phone exactly the same way as you do......but probably less Email than you....usually only use Email in port, and very little even then, I'm afraid....(very slow at typing!)........

I'm often on Ham Radio around 14.150 MHz at 2000hrs utc, or on the English net, Alfredo's net, or with Trudi's net when actually at sea.

Stay Safe, good friend,

Fair winds and Safe landfalls!

"Tuesday" and David.

(RECEIVED)Tue 02/09/2003 20:35

This is to prepare you for your return next year and it comes with love from Michael who found it - so he

"Being a very occasional sailor (two weeks of fair-ish weather a year) it normally takes me several days to readjust to the physical constraints of a thin, 30 foot home with no standing room. So, this year I thought I should get into training and I developed a regime which I now offer to like-minded water caravaners, much as I did my ski training tips earlier in the year:

Sleep on a shelf in a broom cupboard. Replace the cupboard door with a curtain.

Then: six hours after you go to sleep, have your shipmate whip open the curtain and shine a torch in your eyes,

OR set your alarm clock to go off at random times during the night:

when it does, jump off the shelf and get dressed as fast as you can, run into the garden and shower under the garden hose,

OR wake up at midnight and have a peanut butter sandwich on stale bread,

OR, any combination of the above.

Renovate your bathroom. Build a wall across the middle of the bath and move the shower head down to chest level. When you take a shower, make sure the water mysteriously shuts off just as you've got the shampoo/shower gel into a good lather.

Dispense with your dustbin. Place all non edible household waste in small plastic bags, and store them in other half of the bath. Throw edible waste out of the window.

Every time there's a thunderstorm, go outside and sit in a wobbly rocking chair and rock as hard as you can until you feel nauseous.

Bring indoors some form of petrol engine (a lawn mower will do fine), start it and leave it running while trying to listen to your favourite CD or hold a conversation.

Once a month select a major household appliance, take it apart and put it back together.

Have a fluorescent lamp installed on the bottom of your coffee table and lie under it to read books.

Raise the doorsteps and lower the top sills on your front and back doors so that you either trip over the threshold or hit your head on the sill every time you pass through one of them.

I certainly found that these few exercises more-or-less did the trick this year although next year I think I'll add one more. Instead of using a ladder to get onto my roof, I'll sling a line around the chimney and tie around my waist: then I'll pull myself up hand over hand. I'll fix the flashing around the chimney with tape while hanging from the line. And I'll make sure I do this during a thunderstorm at 3 a.m.

And the other thing you have to do once a year is to reacquaint yourself with the technical jargon. So while it is helpful to know how to say "please" and "thank you" in Turkish, it's much more important to understand the following:

Beam Sea - A situation in which waves strike a boat from the side, causing it to roll unpleasantly. This is one of the four directions from which wave action tends to produce extreme physical discomfort. The other three are 'bow sea' (waves striking from the front), 'following sea' (waves striking from the rear), and 'quarter sea' (waves striking from any other direction).

Boom – So called because of the sound that's made when it hits crew on the head on its way across the boat. For slow crew, it's called 'boom, boom'.

Bulkhead - Discomfort suffered by sailors who drink too much.

Calm - Sea condition characterized by the simultaneous disappearance of the wind and the last cold drink.

Companionway - A hole to fall into.

Course - The direction in which a skipper wishes to steer his boat and from which the wind is blowing. Also, the language that results by not being able to.

Crew - Heavy, stationary objects used on board ship to hold down charts and deck cushions, and to dampen sudden movements of the boom (q.v.).

Current - Tidal flow that carries a boat away from its desire destination, or towards a hazard.

Fluke - The portion of an anchor that digs securely into the bottom, holding the boat in place; also, any occasion when this occurs on the first try.

Gybe - A common way to get unruly guests off your boat.

Halyard - Something that only breaks or jams when you're winning.

Hatch - Another name for a hole to fall into.

Helmsman - The nut attached to the rudder through a steering mechanism.

Keel - A very heavy depth sounder.

Leech - A crew member who never seems to have any money when its time to pay for drinks or meals.

Luff - The front part of a sail that everyone but the helmsman seems to pay attention to.

Sheet - A line made to rip gloves or hands part; it also has the ability to tangle or snag on just about anything.

Torch - Tubular metal container used on board ship for storing dead batteries prior to their disposal.

Zephyr - Warm, pleasant breeze, named after the mythical Greek god of wishful thinking, false hopes, and unreliable forecasts.

Thu 04/09/2003 02:18

LOVED it, thank you! Favourite is "Helmsman:-a nut, etc.."

Many thanks to you both......

Tuesday'n'me.

Thu 04/09/2003 00:53

Dear Everybodies,

Puzzled one of the American boats the other day..........they can't understand how many more spares there are on board "Tuesday".................but it was their own fault really.........

You see, I was wondering how to stop one of the fenders (protecting the ship's side from chafing on the dockside) from going "sticky" in the hot sun (the plastic material is old).........Ron on "Forever" suggested fender-socks........I thought, yes I've got some old bits of towel I could use........but better than towel, he suggested, "try old tee-shirts" ....

BINGO!..(all the little light-bulbs lit up in my brain).........

Let me explain.......

Over the last 30+ years, I've sponged ANY free, out-of-date samples from the medical reps at work, even though I couldn't think of an immediate use for them..............one of these gifts, out of the bottom of the boot of a rep's car, was a dusty plastic bag full of about a dozen tee-shirts which fit no known human shape........thought to be totally useless................so, after considerable rummaging in the ship's stores, I found them..........PERFECT fit on a fender!.....(apart from the arms, which wave around in the breeze a bit..........Alan on "Free Spirit" said "Who's your new little friend?")..........

Certainly it caused a stir amongst the German and French crews here, who stopped, gawped, discussed it in their own language, then moved on, scratching their heads, totally mystified!.............Later, the French admitted that the Germans said "That's strange..That should not be".............

.......Because it would appear that poor old "Tuesday" must now be the only yacht around apparently heavily sponsored by "NATIONAL MIGRAINE AWARENESS WEEK 1989".....................................on every fender!.............

Love to all,
"Tuesday".

Dear david,

so i'm now 1 week in br and what can i say about. in natal just anchor in front of the yachtclub, i'm with a shoreline tied 2 a palmtree and sternanchors, one river up 2 hold against the tide, so i'm nearer 2 shore and just pull the dingy along the bowline.

paperwork was fullminant, never seen such amount of papers and the ofices are quite a stretch away. an american couple needed 4 days, i did it in 2, might be cause i speak the language. english is not quite common spoken, so b prepared. the secretary of the yachtclub is helfpul, sending your arrivel papers by fax 2 the authorites so they are awaiting u. by the way: u need yellow fever vaccine, i u don't have u get it free and on the spot. yachtclub costs 3 dollar a day 4 my 35' boat, facilities are good. living is dead cheap compared with europe, also somewhat cheaper than westafrica. a meal in the little places is 1 euro with a nice juce included, portion are served quite big, so if ppl are no big eaters one plate serves 2.

well, my trip was not a typical one. becasue no northern tradewind where blowing i had 2 go south seeking the southerly ones and that meant 4 days beating in the southwest monsun 2 make enough south, but than it developed quite fine.

shops and intenet not being nearby a taxitrip or bicicle ride is needed, or with a 1km stroll u raech a fishercomunity with basic shopping and fish of course. but in the town i saw/found everything i was looking 4. just a couriosity: u need a br taxnumber if wanting 2 make interurban or international calls with ur cellphone if u get u a br card, receiving no problem.

guess 5m is a bit short as an antenna, at least when i tried such lenght swr was worst always than now with my 8m stick, but don't worry about qrp,l i often go down 2 10 w and works just fine. is the band open no problems, if it's closed Kw's will not help. also with my emergency rig, this little yahesu 917 and 5W i almost get always throuh.

so, this 4 2day,

have fun and safe sailing always

73, manuel

Sun 07/09/2003 14:46

Dear Everybodies,

Canical is a hot and hilly, 40 minute, walk from here.........hard work on the way back, laden with stores etc..............nice little town with a very thought-provoking whaling museum, (upsetting movies, taken locally 40 years ago, of killing Sperm whales by hand)........ and also a unintentionally fossilised supermarket, the shelves immaculately packed with barely-in-date produce, quite obviously a place where no one shops..(?why not?..couldn't find out)...........

Funchal by bus was interesting, (driving UNDER the active airport runway).......Managed to buy the only video-camera for sale on the island (cheaper and better than my existing one which hasn't responded to resuscitation measures).............can't track down spare batteries yet........and the instructions are in Portuguese,Italian,Spanish and Greek only.......(but by comparing words in different languages, it's possible to sort of bumble my way through them).....

Four of us hired a taximan, who gave us a good tour.....up to over 5,000ft, above cloud, then he left us at the start of a 12km hike over rocks and streams (VERY pretty scenery, in deep ravines and gorges, through tunnels and caves too....... the others all slipped/fell over at different times....I banged the top of my head on a rock instead).........4+ hours later, with perfect timing, the taximan met us (bloodstained, bruised and battered) at the bottom of the trail, 2000ft lower, and took us back to our harbour........A really good day out!......

We've had some falling water! (RAIN)......... warm, dries rapidly, ...and so refreshing!...............Strong winds keeping us here for the moment, and a Low over the Canaries, ...probably all will leave about the same time next week........(all the various crews get on so WELL together!)......... ....Many of the boats I met in Portugal are anchored off Funchal, rolling around quite a bit in the swell......but it's cheaper there..........

MASSIVE Rave Party here the past 2 nights....trying to get this marina on the map, I think........all the boats given free tickets, to bribe us to tolerate it.........VERY professional sound systems and laser lighting etc, using the mountains as a projection screen.....but the brain-dead-pounding-beat is so BORING......superb quality, but at a volume I found literally incredible until I experienced it.......wondered if it would upset the volcano...............puts British Shows to shame, though......9pm to 8am, continuous beat........but I slept well eventually, though no-one else did, I gather...........everyone's wandering around saying "what?" and "pardon?" and "say again?" today, in their respective languages.........Many young people reported to be walking/zigzagging all over the road back to town this morning.............

Met a game I've not seen before, last night........ Dominoes....but WHITE ones, with up to 15 dots on them......different rules....MUCH more interesting.........The Americans thrashed me at it...........Must try to find a set for "Tuesday"................

Made a rash promise the other day......threatened to cook/prepare part of supper for "Free Spirit".......PANIC! (can't even make "shaving" water.........this could ruin many years of carefully cultured relations between the two countries).............so gave them "Blazing-Dog-Poo-in-Gravy" (*) , as demonstrated by The Woodcutter in Butley Creek, but this time, although the fire extinguisher WAS necessary, didn't actually set fire to the cockpit seats............(and Allen and Marsha are still alive and well!)........

35

Spent all yesterday returning the ship to its original kit of parts...........then rebuilding it again....................all to re-route the towed-generator-power-cable through bulkheads below decks safely.........finished in the dark (as usual!)..........

I thoroughly enjoy your Emails, though I only look about once or twice a week...........I'm sorry I can't reply to everything........but all noted, thank you............(Bob, those screw-on porcelain wire connectors you gave me are excellent for certain jobs, because of minimal dissimilar metal joints in the wire...better corrosion resistance....many thanks!)..........

Sorry no "Boaty" stories these last Emails........ haven't been Boating for past week........

(More later)

Stay Well!

Love to all,

Tuesday'n'me.

PS. (*) (for those who don't know Oford)....."Dog-Poo-etc"...because it looks like it, if the bananas are cut longitudinally........otherwise known as Caramellised-Bananas-in-Cointreau....set fire to it...then put out the blaze with the fire extinguisher (Whipped Cream in an aerosol, that is)..........Most people keep coming back for more "Gravy", for some reason...............

Mon 08/09/2003 21:19

Dear Everybodies,

Today, a heavily laden pickup truck, with several navvies in the back, finding a steep hill a bit much for it, lightened the load by literally chucking a dog out of the back, onto the road..........I thought, I don't believe this........dog rolling over and over, without a sound......makes you feel sick watching......................dog suddenly picks itself up, and with a perfectly happy expression on its face, sets off to catch up and run   alongside the vehicle ....obviously quite used to it..........(left me with somewhat mixed emotions, though)...............

The Intelligent Rat turned up again, this time on the Danish boat............but they only found it on board when they anchored off Funchal!...............Ray denies it, but we wondered if he quietly encouraged it to board their boat, just before they sailed..............

Old saucepan-base rusting (non-stick coming off).........Last week, saw a nice new one (which fits the other saucepanny-bits) in a shop.......took 2mins to find it, but the lady wouldn't sell it to me at first..........insisted I wait.........and wait..........and wait..........25mins later, young girl employed in the shop appears, hot and bothered, from down the road......with the LID for it......................NOW the bosslady WILL sell it to me!....................I hadn't the heart to tell her by sign language I don't need the lid anyway ....(?anyone want a spare, brand-new one?....going cheap?)............

Went into the same shop today, for fresh vegetables, fruit, etc.........her nephew (speaks English) was there..........asking who?where?what? etc while demonstrating his linguistic skills (spends time in Kent, I gather) ....I asked him to thank the boss for all the effort she went to.....she looked really pleased about that........................(leaves me feeling really cheap and two-faced......by now I'm wishing I'd never bought the bl**dy thing)....................... Quite a little crowd of customers etc. gathered by now, overhearing the conversation relayed to the bosslady by the nephew, particularly about sailing solo to Brazil...........hastily changed the subject.................but no, the boss started rummaging again for about one minute...... then absolutely insisted that I accept a tiny little rubber doll on a keyring, "as a gift from Madeira", as the nephew explained......so I let her keep the 10cents change......everyone smiling, patting me on the back, shaking my hand, etc ....(I felt a complete fraud!) ....Lovely people here......makes you feel warm......

Hope to leave Madeira early tomorrow (Tuesday 9th Sept).......two boats left today, but probably quieter winds tomorrow........all planning to meet up in a bay on an island near Lanzarote..........maybe in 2-4 day's time (about 300 miles from here).....................

No news is good news, but I'll get in touch when I can......

Stay Well!,

Love to all,

Tuesday'n'me.

(RECEIVED) Mon 01/09/2003 09:47

Hi David

Its really good to get your diary-type missives; they get printed out & put up in the staff room for everyone to share.

Keep well, smiling, & writing emails

Jan

Tue 09/09/2003 22:19

Hi Barry (on St.Helena Island)

I gather my brother Gerald (G0UFI) has very kindly been in contact with you about my present trip......

My name is David....ship's name is "TUESDAY" (why, is a long story ...another time maybe!).....Single masted sailing yacht....Boomed-staysail-cutter-rig.....British built in 1975.....43ft overall....approx 14 tons displacement...only me on board...

Left East coast of England in June 2003...At present in Madeira, via Portugual.....planning to sail to the Canaries in next two days.....then Cap Verde Islands...then to east coast of Brazil by Christmas 2003.......then s-l-o-w-l-y down Brazil coast to near Uruguay........Leave Brazil around Easter-time 2004.......to ride the south and east sides of the South-Atlantic-High round past Tristan de Cunha, St.Helena, and Ascension Island......then to the Azores by early summer 2004............Then back to England during summer 2004..................(hopefully!).........

Why?.........I like sailing, physical geography, zoology and meteorology.... and have always wanted to do this trip......I retired last summer (2002) after 35years in Medicine in England.....immediately sailed "Tuesday" up the western coast of Norway into the Arctic, as a shake-down-cruise, to catch the midnight sun (successfully, standing under a glacier in bright sunlight, at midnight, hacking off ice samples with a screwdriver!).......

But the special thing for me about St. Helena has always been due to our deep friendship with the Spens family, of whom Teresa was very instrumental in setting up your Social Services/Red Cross on your beautiful Island ....so to be able to sail there has always had a sort of very personal interest for me....

So, nothing to do at present.......but when I get further south at the end of the year, maybe I could try to contact you again?....just for interest?....

Oh, nearly forgot.....radio here is an Icom, only 8-10 watts output (I'm severely limited on power (from wind and sun!)).....into a 5 metre wire rammed up inside a 5 metre fishing-rod, the counterpoise being the insulated metal supports for the 4 metre radar mast it's mounted on.....seems to work well on all ham bands between 7MHz to 52MHz (a relatively new band in the England) with only a small amount of antenna-tuning for each band..........my experiments with mast-stays, suspended end-fed-coax-dipoles, and loaded whips were not as successful as this very primitive set-up, so I daren't alter it!.......

Sorry....long Email.....no need to reply, no action required, and my access to Email is limited anyway................at present I'm calling in on the Italian net (14.297 @ 1900z), British net (14.303 @ 0800z and 1800z) and Trudi's net (21.400 @ 1300z) when actually at sea...............but will start to listen on 14.136MHz @

1130z when further south..........
> Thanks for "listening".......
>> 73!
>>> **Tuesday'n'me.**

Tue 09/09/2003 22:19

Winds still strong.....the two boats from here to Lanzarote (should get there tomorrow) report by radio that the seas are big, short, wet, and thoroughly uncomfortable......they're clearly getting hammered.....they sound tired...........

So the rest of us (3 or 4 boats) are staying put for 24-48 hours........?maybe leave on Thursday 11th Sept?
> **Tuesday'n'me.**

(RECEIVED) Thu 28/08/2003 22:17

Daweed,
LUVVLY to hear you on radio!
Take great care, I don't want to lose you.
> *Lots of love,*
>> ***Woddy.***

Mon 15/09/2003 17:29
> **Dear Everybodies,**

"Tuesday, Forever!"..........(answered by "Forever,Tuesday!").............No, not a quote from Swallows and Amazons...............merely the contact calls on VHF between two boats, every four hours, during the 260 mile crossing from Madeira,...... keeping within 5-10miles of each other, for company...........very powerful reassurance as a result......both ways.....

The usual pre-voyage fears were much less this time.........both the ship and crew were really quite keen to get out there again......... weather forecasts were being updated several times a day, from a variety of sources, including VHF between the group of boats (we've all met before, at various places and times.....nice!)..............Force 5-6 caused a lumpy ocean swell for the first 36 hours (tiring on your own.....it's all a bit physical....and elbows, knees, hips, and shoulders take a bit of a hammering.....but fewer bruises this time...... I must be learning!).....and more than one yacht was troubled by seasickness ....(surprisingly not Tuesday though)...........managed to keep on top of the sleep a bit better this time, too........

The problem was to slow the boat down so's not to arrive at an unlit rock-strewn bay in the dark.........I overdid it, though, and had to pile on everything but the spinnaker to catch up....really powering along, shouldering the ocean aside ....(that Aries self-steering gear, which I'd modified to work by compass, not just by the wind direction, is a revelation to watch at work, seeming to ANTICIPATE the waves at times!)..............Came upon another yacht, which took fright at the sight of "Tuesday" in full battle-cry, shook out its reefs and took off like a startled rabbit....whereupon I promptly stopped to reef for the night.....turned out to be one of the French aluminium yachts we'd spoken to in Porto Santo and Canical........

Failing wind for the last bit....the others motored ahead, but I was determined not to motor if possible........ idly staring at the swell.........suddenly, white smoke about 500 yards away, just above the sea........Memory clicked, so raced below to get the videocamera...........sure enough, Whales!.........but what sort?.......more than one........probably small, as they're blowing frequently........heading to pass about 150 yards astern of Tuesday..............then, noticed the low, bushy, forward pointing spout from right at the front of the VERY large blunt head..........(GULP!) must be SPERM WHALES!.......(like Moby Dick)........no wonder they're blowing often, there are at least 6 of them!.............the world's largest toothed carnivore...........hope they've been fed recently...........

But they had no interest in me at all.........doing about 6 knots northwards, filling up with oxygen for their next deep dive lasting up to an hour and a half (I believe), for food...............it's 7000 feet deep there........ Although they are still considerably bigger than "Tuesday", they appeared slightly smaller than I expected, but a lot more active.........clearly in a very close-knit group.....................

I remembered how those Fin Whales in Biscay last July had been MASSIVELY big!.....even compared with yesterday's Cachalots, they were SERIOUSLY big!....................I must have done SOMETHING good as a child to get to be allowed to see this kind of thing!.........I captured some of it on video again.........

"Free Spirit" had crossed about 4 days before us, and had taken a pasting in rough seas.......for safety's sake they'd gone to the south end of Lanzarote, so we've yet to meet up with them again.............

Pity.............. and they've missed this BEAUTIFUL Island, with its stark volcanic simplicity and colours................anchored here off a beach in a bay, between GRACIOSA and LANZAROTE............. less than a mile from the village............the water is virtually gin-clear, and warm ....swimming off the boat several times a day, to keep cool, and to scrub the ship's bottom................Old volcano "zits" all around..... .....different colours of ash have caused delightful, totally natural, multilayered "gobstopper" effects in the hillsides....really very artistic......

There aren't any roads on Graciosa at all.......Silence.......Will row ashore tomorrow to explore...... I need to top-up the ship's fresh-foodstuff stores....... I gather there IS a small shop...........I've had real Peaches and real Cream for "afters" for the past 3 days, as they had to be used up before they went "off"....ain't life hell!.....

Past my bedtime....................thanks for all your support and interest (and humour!).....

More soon.......... Stay Well!

Love from,
Tuesday'n'Me.

(RECEIVED) Tue 23/09/2003 18:15

Many thanks for all your highly interesting e-mails, they make excellent reading.

When we did the Tall Ships race the leg from Cadiz to the Canaries finished just North of Lanzarote and we then spent a couple of days anchored up off Graciosa. So it was quite an experience to see Lanzarote and that sheer cliff face where the plate glass window is inset into the face which looks directly down on to Graciosa. Behind the plate glass window is a museum and restaurant. We visited this lookout some years previously when Mark worked in Lanzarote.

Look forward to the next instalment.

Chris and Ruth

Tue 23/09/2003 00:26

Dear Everybodies,

Graciosa turned out to be a really nice anchorage, much safer and more protected than I thought it would be...........crystal clear, warm sea.......swimming/snorkelling several times a day........ the mountains of mainland Lanzarote overlooking it on one side..... the volcanoes and sands of Graciosa on the other.......And so delightfully PEACEFUL....I honestly did not know what day it was once (and nor did I care particularly), and had to be corrected by "Forever"'s crew that afternoon.......(embarrassing!)....

We had two major expeditions, ships' crews combined (ie. 3 people in all)...............After inspecting it carefully with binoculars, I was determined to climb the nearest volcano.........so we did..........hard work, but wonderful views from the top........a bit risky coming down a different route through a pumice-field (nasty if you fall, and rather unstable rocks), but no significant injuries........

39

The second "hike" was to climb The Gobstopper (the mountain with the artistic patterns of different coloured rocks and ash), but it was too dangerous....like trying to walk on ballbearings........a broken ankle/wrist would mean we couldn't work our ships safely, so the risk wasn't worth it..........I managed to get rock samples of the colours though........

So we walked all of the island and back......over 12 miles in all, that roasting day...... over rocks, pumice, lava-fields........ literally talcum-powder-fine red Martian dust (which floated in air like smoke).....lunar landscape......finishing up with a beautiful (if lethal) path halfway up a cliff for a mile, over the sea........... Never was a swim more welcome when back on our boats, simply falling into the sea fully dressed, to wash out the dust..........

Spent ages trying to fix Ron's radar, which had died about 4 weeks ago......fixed all sorts of corroded connections, but even so it won't play....it's fourteen years old, but hasn't done many hours.......needs a trip up his mast to check some voltages at a terminal plug up there (tomorrow?)...... but I think we need an expert's help soon.......VERY frustrating not to have identified the fault yet.......

Then it was time to move on.........a lovely beat out of the channel against the tradewinds between the islands, failing to catch any fish unfortunately..........then a reach/run down the southeast side of Lanzarote in a rising wind, spinnaker pulling hard.......(quite a fight to get the darned thing down again....instead of IT coming down, I went UP.......then reefing before the wind-acceleration-zone (now able to do it in 7 minutes, instead of 35 mins last year)............then total surprise as the wind dropped with a dull thud, instantly.........force 6 only 150 yards astern, but none here at all (just a nasty sloppy sea rolling on).........clearly a local wind-DEceleration-zone!)....never met anything so sudden like that before....

Round the bottom of Lanzarote, and into a delightful bay protected by mountain, cliff and beach......... looking over the side to be able to inspect the seabed for a sandy bit, 30 feet down, before slinging the hook into the middle of a suitable patch........ jump in, fully dressed, to snorkel to check it's bedded in....... then swimming over to "Forever" (still fully clothed) to check theirs too, declining an invitation to supper as I was "improperly dressed"............. then back to "Tuesday" to relax in the evening sun..........(bit different from Thames estuary mud and rain, isn't it!).......

Next day sailed out of the anchorage....... and round to this brand new, very clean and friendly marina (so new it's not mentioned in any pilot books yet)...... usual fears about mooring up, but I don't think I frightened anyone... not even me!...........(a bystander said " oh that's neat...berth 2E for 2'sday")......

Soon met up with Alan and Marsha on "Free Spirit" again, who had such a pounding on the trip from Madeira.......the group is now back to 5 boats...it's fun!..

Strong winds today (Monday...I think)........two powerful mini-tornado's in the sun......got caught by one of them while walking to town.......had to crouch down, bottom to the wind, to avoid damage from the sand and flying debris.......interesting!.....

The town is lovely, clean, tidy, quiet, but with excellent shops.........but I've got to go 20 miles away tomorrow to find the Costumes and Intimidation (Customs and Immigration) to check in to Spanish territory ....
.......(Graciosa couldn't care less WHO we were, and anyway the Customs man was away on holiday!)....

Then planning to enrol in one of several diving-schools here, to learn maybe how to clear a fouled propeller/clean the ship's bottom properly/literally stamp in the anchor/dig out a fouled anchor, etc.......they seem very pleasant and friendly so far......

And all this in good company too!.......can't believe it's all happening sometimes..........A general message to everyone :- "Retire immediately!"......

So, Stay Well, Keep Safe!... More news soon....

Love to all,

Tuesday'n'me.

(RECEIVED) Mon 15/09/2003 21:14

Hello David,

It's been better than you can imagine getting your mail from parts exotic. I've printed them all out tonight - turning into quite a book. Got us thinking - retirement and all that - but not for quite a while.

We've had a great summer weather wise - not wall to wall sun but as near as it gets in Scotland. And another attempt at the island Peaks Race - this time came to an end on Mull (first stop) when one of our number got hypothermia and had to be choppered off the hill. You can laugh - at least our mountains don't blow up and wet forests don't burn.

Sounds such FUN your end - and sociable - and interesting --- he who travels alone and all that - and what a way to travel (one of the few that isn't instant, pre-packaged, world-shrinking and mind numbing - there aren't many real ways left are there).

Keep it coming please.

Bon chance! Love,

Richard and Sue

(RECEIVED)Sat 20/09/2003 14:48

Hello David,

Thank you for your e-mail. I tried to reply in Arrecife, but had bad luck with the Internet. It was cutting off. I spent 8 days in Arrecife in anchor. Had some problems making it hold in mud close to the pontoons with 40 m chain. The wind was up to 25 kn. Have to move 3 times. Finally quite far close to the wharfs. Took the Grand Tour around the Island and worked maintenance on the old boat. Purchased copied charts and 2 pilot books from the Copy Shop on the strand street. Sailed and stopped on front of a beach for a night in a bay on the southern end of Lanzarote. A nice place. Good swimming. Some nudists. We were 3 boats there. Next morning wind rose from the west and have to sail again. Arrived in slight wind to Las Palmas 2 days ago. Very hot yesterday. 33 C inside the boat. Have bought a 45 W fan and will install a wind scoop. Lots of boats here. Some already for the ARC. I am in anchor. 32 euros for 8 days. Pontoon would be 11 euros per day, but only for 2 weeks. Then they start making room for 250 ARC boats. Are you planning to come this way?

Wishing you fair winds and good sailing

With best regards

Matti

Tue 23/09/2003 01:18

Hi Matti!

Nice to hear from you again...Sorry Arrecife was not a good anchorage...it must have been worrying for you, and I sympathise.....

Had a good sail over from Madeira, meeting a pod of 6+ sperm whales on the way (a bit scary, but nice pictures!).........then spent one week anchored in peace and tranquillity in a bay on Island of Graciosa at top end of Lanzarote, before moving to the bay which you found at the South end of Lanzarote,... so only just missed you!

Now in brand new marina on South end of Lanzarote for next four weeks, so that my family can come out for a holiday, in relays........ hope to bumble slowly through the Canaries afterwards, then to Cap Verdes..... ....hoping to head for Recife or Salvador in December, but by then you will be a long way ahead I think....

Stay Well, Stay safe good friend.......Enjoy!

David.

(RECEIVED) Sat 20/09/2003 21:01

Dear David,

Thanks for another great letter. I was very interested to hear about Lanzarote and Graciosa from the sailors view point. We know Lanzarote pretty well as we still have some timeshare on the island and have many time been to the top of the island and looked out at the barren island with perhaps a yacht at anchor. More Whales - you have obviously been mugging up on your fish spotters book - I have never even heard of the majority of names - let alone any have idea of their differences!

Sounds as if your self steering gear is working really well - I have only tried mine a few times with a decent breeze is seems great but there has been a lot of light stuff and it really hasn't helped much - however a trip down the river and round the Bar buoy is hardly the same a crossing oceans!

Happy Voyaging,

Ben (J).

Fri 26/09/2003 23:24

Dear Everybodies,

It's Ron and Bonnie's fault again.........(they deliberately lent me their Instruction book)....

?Remember at the beginning I talked of Highs and Lows of this lifestyle?.......well, today was a new Low, but at the same time one of the highest Highs.............

I explained to Chris, a highly intelligent gentleman, who runs the local diving school, why I was interested in learning more about the basics of Scuba diving, so that I would be safer and better able to dive/snorkel to clear a fouled propeller/anchor etc................he very kindly organised a special two day course tailored specifically for me, with intensive one-to-one teaching.......

So, after spending hours reading "Forever"'s diving training manual, I presented myself at the appointed hour this morning................and spent three and a half hours sitting alone watching training videos about the manual I'd just been reading...............

In fact it was most interesting, as it explained several tricky bits, and I could skip irrelevant areas etc, effectively teaching myself................but I wondered what sort of school I'd got myself into...............

WOW, was I wrong!.............this afternoon I went back for another session...........expecting to sit in the shallows playing with diving equipment.............

Not a bit of it........................I seemed to have retained the right information somehow, so the lesson advanced more rapidly than we'd planned............and the safety "rituals" all seemed to flow sensibly..............the reading and video sessions had certainly worked!......

So, the High was that I was in the water in my wetsuit for an hour and a half with two LOVELY, nubile young ladies (one, the Instructor, is Chris's wife, ...the other is an equally charming English girl doing her Instructor's course)...............the "Low" is that one hour of that time was spent on the bottom (i.e.. really "Low Down") at 25-30 feet depth, out at sea, (having waded out into the surf off the beach...............practising emergency procedures between the three of us with the masks/breathing apparatus etc..............it was all so professional and enjoyable that I barely noticed they were leading me deeper and further out to sea...........

And the life we saw there!.......A tiny blue and black fish which vigorously shoo'd us off his "patch"...... several different shoals of fish accepting us comfortably......... and a large Ray of some form (I thought it was a young Manta, but I now know it was "Stumpy", an individual known to Lanzarote divers since at least last year.....so-called because he's clearly lost his tail in an accident.......and he's known to be 2 metres across his back)................very gently picking up a Sea-Cucumber as it sat surrounded by its own "rabbit-droppings", (surprised by how solid the animal felt)........then equally gently putting him back again......all three of us laughing, giggling, grinning at the wonder of it all...............

I used up a bit more air than the others......... not helped by the instructor giving me yet another fit of giggles, when she released a burst of bubbles deliberately under a male swimmer with voluminous billowing swimming-trunks well above us (naughty, I know, but we couldn't stop laughing into our breathing regulators, all the same!)..............

Then sitting in the shallows in the waves, chuckling about it all while we reviewed each part of it..........It has to be one of the happiest afternoons I've ever had!.........

And I'm due back there early tomorrow morning again for Chapter Two............and Chris wants me to go over their resuscitation procedures with them............it's only 400 yards walk from "Tuesday"..............Life really isn't too bad, is it!........

More news another time, (and there's a LOT of news to choose from here)..

Love to all!

Tuesday'n'me.

Mon 29/09/2003 21:59

Dear Everybodies,

More big Rays, small Barracuda, beautifully coloured reef fish, flatfish, hermit crabs, sea cucumbers, spider shrimps etc etc etc..............a vision of constantly changing colours and movements, without resorting to magic-mushrooms etc............

As from this evening I am a qualified Diver (really Basic, but certificated all the same)....after a professional and very intensive (but hilarious!) few days with tests (practical and written) and several hours spent gliding over the bottom of this bit of the ocean, outside the harbour........

What you see is mind-blowing really,..together with the giggles and jokes and stuff, on the seabed........more blowing bubbles up at swimmers.......blowing not smoke-rings but bubble-rings......waving to a snorkeller 35 feet above us as he fed small fishes by hand..............

I was inspecting a fish closely, turned round but couldn't see the Instructor...turned the other way, still nothing...realised she must be above somewhere, but before I could look, she appeared, her facemask 3" away from mine, hanging motionless, upside down, making faces!...more bubbles of laughter!.............

Something touched my leg......empty sea I had thought..........turned round to find FIVE other divers I had met earlier, from the school, laughing at my surprise, the sea suddenly very full of wetsuits, flippers and bubbles...........

Then sitting cross-legged on the seabed, checking we'd done all the tests and safety-rituals, I asked (by writing on special paper) if she'd remembered to bring the sandwiches, as all we needed was a tablecloth.................

I always wanted to dive...never believed I would, though!........

And remember the little blue and black fish firmly defending his own patch?.........each dive he's still there....same rock....same absolutely clear message from him to "clear off!, this is MY rock!"......................well, the Diving School have decided to name him as an individual fish ....and the name?..........(serves me right I suppose, for making a point of going to check he was OK each time I was down there)........... ...."DOC"!

Stay well, and take care of yourselves,

Love,

Tuesday'n'me.

Wed 08/10/2003 01:24
   Dear Everybodies,
      Need a bigger boat!..............Diving gear takes up a lot of room, and is heavy......trying to bolt it all low down in the ship, so that the weight of it does something useful when at sea...........

      Took a carefully calculated risk yesterday...........was offered the chance of a "deep" dive with my Instructor and three others (her husband Chris (a VERY highly qualified diver), the English girl under tuition to be an instructor, and an experienced Spanish girl from the diving school).........all of them certificated Rescue Divers, all of them up to date with resuscitation procedures
(because I personally checked them and their Rescue Box the other day), all of them personally known to me..........and planning to dive to an area they know well......it seemed as safe an opportunity as I would ever get...............

      To cut a long story short, we went into the open sea, and gently down a sloping seabed to 32 metres (105 feet) down...........then Chris checked everyone's air gauges etc, and directed the three LOVELY ladies to return independently via a scenic route............ He and I continued to a cavemouth 10ft wide by 2ft high, into which we gingerly put our heads......a big cavern opened up inside.......by torch light the place glowed with reds and yellows and gold colours, and two BIG groupers (their bodies about the same diameter as our own) could be seen leisurely eating shrimps off the walls...........apparently only Chris knows of this place, which is the home of this particular pair of fish.........................

      Then very carefully we backed out again.........but my own air supply is getting low now..........there is enough, but none in reserve if there's a problem............so we start back gently, up through a tunnel in the larva rocks, about 20ft high by 30ft wide.........onto a sandy plain with what look like 18" long weeds growing (but they withdraw into the ground as we approach, reappearing as soon as we're past them.......some sort of eel).......

      My air is not going to last.........Chris has plenty........we agree to share his tank when mine is too low.........(and he's watching me VERY carefully indeed now).......I'm staying no more than a foot away from his auxiliary air supply.....watching his gauges.............

      He insists it's time to accept his air now.......no problems, because of the intensive training...........(mind you I've got a good hold of his diving harness to prevent any chance of damaging the air tubes by accident)............very slowly coming up the sloping seabed now, with plenty of time to admire the plants and animals as we gradually decompress.......still watching the gauges very closely.........

      Then he sticks his arm up, and it disappears!........must be just under the surface..........Sure enough, blue sky......then spit out the regulator and blow firmly into the buoyancy jacket to ensure buoyancy..............then I reached into my pocket to replace the mouthpiece with..............................

      ....a BABY'S DUMMY!....big laughs all round from the girls who have been up some time already..........Then a fight against the waves to climb some quayside steps, to squelch back to the car..............But I cannot fly in an aeroplane for 7 hours, and it will be 22 hours before the extra nitrogen I have on board is all gone.............

      Inexperience had led me to use my air too quickly, but we were fully aware of the problem developing........in fact it was a very relaxing dive, dealing with difficulties correctly, calmly........

         But I won't push my luck so far next time..................
            Love from
               Tuesday'n'me.

Fri 24/10/2003 08:53
> **Hi Matti,**
> "Tuesday" and I are still in Lanzarote, planning to leave for Cape Verdes in late November.....but I wonder how you are getting on now?........
> All the very Best to you......stay well!
> **David.**

(RECEIVED)Fri 24/10/2003 10:56
> *Hi David,*
> *Thank you for your email. I am still lingering in Las Palmas. Time goes fast. I have been waitin a spare part from Finland. It should come any day now? Then I leave to Cape Verde. Perhaps I get water first from Gomera? Lots of boats here now from every continent. Already many ARC boats. For other newcommers only 2-3 days allowed in marina. Also the anckering area is filling.*
> *With best regards*   ***Matti Lappalainen***

Fri 24/10/2003 08:52
> **Dear Everybodies,**
> Have had to revise The Plan.............the problem is all these hordes of "ARC" boats coming to the Canaries have wrecked my schedule.............
> Now virtually every harbour is full to bursting, (clogged with yachts)......marinas are charging high fees, while staffed by grumpy locals,............
> And the steady southward movement of the season each day has brought more unsettled weather (I had hoped to stay to the south of it, but it has caught us up)........
> You see, I had originally planned to leave here about now, and spend time exploring each island............but there's really nowhere properly quiet and safe to go, from what I gather from other yachts reporting back by radio.............tales of promised and guaranteed berths not actually being available......having to anchor off in insecure places for a few days while waiting for a clear pontoon................it's not ideal for the singlehander..........
> Except here....... in this relatively unknown (to the outside world) new marina, which is clean, relatively cheap, safe........ with excellent facilities and interests within walking distance........
> So I'd be daft to leave here until it's time to leave the Canaries Isles themselves........all five boats in our loose group have come to the same conclusion.....
> We've each decided, independently, to stay here till later in November, before heading for the Cape Verde Islands.........the others can't go before the end of the hurricane season anyway, (though that wouldn't affect my personal route)..............."Forever's" crew are going to explore the Canaries instead by ferry and aeroplane, staying in hotels on each island, for the next 2-3 weeks.........the rest of us have various interests, and things to fix on the boats, etc....
> I plan to stay only a short time in the Cape Verdes, aiming to leave there for Brazil in the first week or two in December.........(that's going to be a lonely time, as the others are all heading for the Caribbean)...........
> Then the REAL voyage begins............aiming to leave South Brazil around Eastertime, going round the SOUTH side of the South Atlantic High Pressure System ....towards the Jewel of the adventure....St. HELENA! ....but fully expecting not to be able to land there if the seas are awkward............
> And then the longest leg, up to the Azores, in early summer 2004...............
> But all plans in this game are fluid ....so, who knows?!..............
> Sorry the UK weather is cold ......Stay warm!
> Love from
> **Tuesday'n'me.**

(RECEIVED) Mon 15/09/2003 22:43

David ...

Thank you so much for today's e-mail ... it all makes wonderful reading.

Love from **Daddy and Mummy.**

(Incidentally, don't do anything your mother wouldn't do!)

(RECEIVED) Tue 16/09/2003 22:07

Hello,

So glad that at long last you have decided to begin living !!! You see while you think that you are being so extraordinary you are simply doing what some of us humble selves have been doing during the last 35 years. While you were wallowing around the Orford mud we were already having FUN !!!

Still better late than never...........

A female(French 56 years old) I work with has a sister living in the Canaries .She says that she often shows lonely sailors around the place, even a female French single handed one, so if your interested let me know , she said that she would be delighted , her sister not her. I told her that quite frankly I very much doubted that you would be interested

.... well I don`t want to lose a good friend do I? ..

Yours never, **MARY.**

P.S. Don`t forget in times of trouble ......WORSE THINGS HAPPEN AT SEA !!

(RECEIVED)Thu 25/09/2003 18:33

Hello!

I was starting to really envy your voyage of discovery around the world, but with William's arrival we are having plenty of discovery of our own right here at home. And anyway, if we did it all now, we'd have nothing to look forward to!!

Love to you both (you and T),

MOWL

Mon 27/10/2003 22:39

Dear Everybodies,

Thank you all so much for your Emails...I'm sorry I never seem to get round to acknowledging them all, but they are warmly appreciated!

Fin, Ellie and I had a lovely time ...(well, I did anyway!)....the ship was horribly lonely after they left, even though I was ready for it this time...... but I'm getting used to it again now .....a bit.....

The weather is much more changeable now....safe anchorages I'd used only 6 weeks ago are now untenable.....so hoping to head South again,....... but I want to stay with our little group at first, leaving in the latter part of November...........probably going to have to miss out the other Canary Islands altogether I expect, as they are all FULL of yachts.............

Had another Email from Matti, (the Finnish gentleman who sang songs about his reindeer, you may remember? He's sailing solo to Brazil too)........ he's still stuck in La Palma, the westernmost island of the Canaries, waiting for repair parts from Finland...........but he says the harbour is at bursting point, even though he personally remains at anchor......... I hear that boats are being literally turned away back out to sea unless they are part of the ARC or RAC, (both are organised rallies for cruisers).......

You should hear what some highly experienced, high mileage cruising people say about these rallies.....it's certainly not just our local group who are upset by them.........it includes a charming and shy Norwegian

46

couple from Stavanger (we had a lot to talk about!).......and even a hermit-like British couple I was conversing with one evening turned to their 5 year old daughter and asked her, "and what do we call them?" ....instant reply from this little blond-haired blue-eyed angel was.............."ARKY-FARKIES!"

But the other side the coin is "why shouldn't they?".......they each pay good money to those who organise it all, and this is the benefit they gain........but from my side of the fence it seems that they stamp on everyone else........

Anyway, we're lucky here....it's still comfortable, safe, with good friends, lots of interests (playing squash in the basement of the 5 star hotel here 3-4 times a week (for FREE!...I don't think they've rumbled us yet!), diving once or twice each week, snorkelling, tennis, etc....mutual help with ship maintenance and improvements......swapping of Good Ideas between boats.........and I haven't even got the bike out yet!).........so I personally can't complain really, except that I won't see the other islands........

But when I do leave here, it's going to be 6 months of almost continuous sailing, because I have 18,000 miles to cover in all, of which I've only done 2,500 so far.........I'm looking forward to it.........it's going to be "interesting"!.....

Thanks again for all your support, it really does help a lot.........

Stay Well!

Love from

Tuesday'n'me.

Sat 01/11/2003 02:17

Dear Mary,

Hi!...bet you didn't think you get an Email of your own........

Yup, ain't life great!.......I envy you the skiing an' stuff, and I'd love to sail in FLAT water, but this lifestyle is "priddy neat", as the Yanks would say.........(They asked Tot what she thought about her dad hanging around with all these Yanks....apparently she pondered for a moment, then looked up and said that she thought perhaps he should "stick to his own kind"......not sure what to make of that, but the Americans loved it!)

The daft thing is that sailing skills haven't got a great deal to do with this "cruising" ......it's all about being adaptable, getting along with (or around) the local establishment,..........it's all about attitude, "make or mend", lateral thinking, always staying one jump ahead, etc. ....and we've each got our own defensible space in our boats to retreat to......

But I feel I've known these friends here for all my life, or is that the beginning of loss of ....um...er...I....er...um...   ah, yes!.. MEMORY....yes, that's it ......

But when the long-distance stuff starts, well that's going to be "interesting"......going bonkers seems very sensible to me........ but how the hell do you tell you've "only got one oar in the water"? (I like that expression..it implies a frantic circling!)..........I talk to the ship already, even now, but we are just very good friends at this stage....maybe that'll change when I get to the cannibalism-and-urine-drinking bit........

Sorry about the cold weather.......it's getting B cold here too...it's down to 24 degrees centigrade at night now......might have to start wearing clothes again soon.........

Don't work too hard, you poor wage-slave........

"Bye now!"...and "Have a nice day!"..

Love,

David

(RECEIVED)Thu 25/09/2003 21:23

While I was out this morning I met a lady from round the corner who asked if we knew how you were and said she and her daughter were coming out to Lanzarote in about a weeks time and if there was any thing you wanted they would willing bring it out to you, so if you let the family or us know of any thing we will arrange it.

With all our Love and thought's for a safe time,

till we hear form you again

Joyce & oh and him in doors.

Mon 03/11/2003 00:11

Dear Everybodies,

No Boating news, I'm afraid.......haven't been boating for AGES........ we're all wondering if we can still remember how to do it.............

7 metre high swells north of Madeira....gives us a low surge three or four times a minute, even here in the sheltered harbour........Forecast for West Portugal coast was 9 (!) metre seas, and 24 hours later (I gather) seas of a measured 12 metres arrived there.........(gulp!)..........glad I did that bit earlier in the season!......

Serious problems with the weather here.......getting cold at night.....down to 24 degrees centigrade last night........life's a B, isn't it.........

More ship maintenance......it's useful being in a small close-knit group, because we each spot something on each others' boats which the owner already knows he really should have fixed but has never got round to yet......the result is that standards are improved all round!.......and there's always someone on hand to help.....it's all very reassuring and supportive ......new "toys" too (eg. turning an old "bosun's chair" into a properly gimballed, swinging, secure seat in the galley.....probably stable enough to grab some sleep in........ and FREE!)......

The other day, just about to go into a cave, at 68 feet down ...... turned round to see a fish about 18" long, swimming peacefully only 4" from my shoulder.........he turned his head to me, and then seemed to shrug his shoulders and say "well, get on with it then"...........(he was just being curious I think....because we were in a place where the fish rarely see divers) ....but then I realised that he'd brought all his family, friends and mates with him too........scores of them....all formating closely behind him........if I turned left, they turned left......if I went right, they went right, etc.etc ....weird, being responsible for the actions of so many others.........(I'm moderately confident they weren't a people-eating-type-of-fish)............the other three divers were all laughing at the spectacle........

And it's strange to see very nasty poisonous fish comfortable in their own natural environment, too ....particularly Stone-Fish.........leave them alone, and they'll leave you alone.......I learned all about them after my episode in Estapona several years ago, when I got stabbed by a Weever (not nice, that........not nice at all...)

The area where we were diving is in a nudist colony........pity........for two reasons (i) it puts you off your food, and (ii) no swimming trunks to blow bubbles up.............all Germans, I believe...........odd that THEY disrobe, while WE get all dressed up (in rubber etc.) to go into the same bit of water......but it's not always very pleasant to look upwards, at the surface 50 feet above, where they are swimming................

Stay Well!

Love from,

Tuesday'n'me.

(RECEIVED) Mon 03/11/2003 06:45

........*I hope you dry your swimming garb properly or you will catch a cold--or, as they used to tell me , You`ll get what you`ll never get rid of.......No swimming in damp clothes...That`s an order.*
    Mother

Fri 07/11/2003 22:35

.......I forgot ....Mary asked if I still had my old wellies on board ....

Yes.......but I needed a source of rubber sheet (no...not for bedtime) to make new gaskets to re-seal the fuel and water tank-filler-caps.......

So...I cut the tops off the boots and used that, once I'd ripped the cloth-lining off the inside ....was about to throw the rest of the old boots away, when I realised they'd be useful as a sort of Galoshes........

The upshot is that when it's hot but I need to walk over rough ground, I wear them still....but filled up with cold water first......to keep cool..........

Bonnie from "Forever" says she wishes I wouldn't do it, 'cos the sound makes her bladder complain...........
    Squelch,squelch......
      Tuesday'n'me.

Sun 16/11/2003 21:34
    Dear Mary,

      Mother said I wasn't to go swimming in damp bathing trunks.....causes chills etc..........Makes it a bit awkward though, doesn't it.........perhaps I shouldn't wear any, like the Germans.......

Anyway my swimming trunks leak...let the water IN..............

Xmas cards to "Santa Claus, c/o King Neptune, Latitude Zero"....I think......not sure of postcode though.....

High winds here today (Sunday).......so delaying until things improve ......will let you know.....

Don't do anything DANGEROUS, nor play with anything SHARP or pointy, will you........
    Toodle-pip!,
      Me.

(RECEIVED) Wed 05/11/2003 12:18
    Subject: Webbed Feet.

Dear David,

    According to Joe, you looked fit and well when they visited you; this is also supported by your previous e.mails where you seem to be more aware of the ladies in the other crews! If you are uncomfortable with these new and strange feelings may I suggest some Bromide in the Pot Noodles.

    Thats all for now, continue to take care of you and yours, Please keep sending the e-mails.
Regards
    Bob @ Brenda

Chapter 3

Leaving the Canaries

Tue 18/11/2003 01:48

Dear Everybodies, (sorry it's so impersonal, but I'm so slow at typing, and it's difficult to "doctor" each Email).

Well, here we are, ready to go again.........I never expected to spend two months on Lanzarote, but it's been a wonderful time, learning new skills, great new friends, etc...........

Usual pre-voyage-fears...just as bad as before, but I'm a bit wiser now........The other three boats, American, leaving around the same time, freely admit the same flutterbyes in the stomach..........only "Forever" is coming to the Cape Verdes, and Allen'n'Marsha on "Free Spirit" are already in Gomera, another Canary Island.......but they will all be friends for life.......

Been delayed by high winds for a few days.......not necessary to wait, but to make life easier for myself.......Planning to spend a night or two rolling around at anchor in a bay, to try to get some sea-legs again first........

The ship herself is even better prepared than when I left the UK nearly six months ago, and I'm really pleased with her........

My intention is to sail 200 miles due west to have a distant look at La Palma and El Hiero Islands, before turning south for another 800 miles to the Cape Verdes.......the weather is a bit more unsettled now, but I'm not racing.........(unlike all these ARC and RAC boats which seem intent on getting their sailing over and done with as fast as possible.......personally I'd rather spend more time savouring every moment out there, building memories for the future........)

Some Unfair Definitions:-

"ARC" (Atlantic Rally for Cruisers) = 250, mostly brand new, boats cluttering up the ocean with their strong "herding" instincts....some of their manoeuvring skills in harbour are dubious, to say the least....their crews make a lot of noise....some may be in for a rude-awakening....

"RAC" (Rubicon to Antigua Challenge) = Ditto, but fewer of them, and they applied too late to join the ARC. Most seem to be 45' to 70', keen to set speed records, and clearly want their sailing over and done with as quickly as humanly possible....quieter crews...

"NARCS" = (NOT "ARC"s), but hoping to sail WITH the ARC, and get some of the benefits, without the cost.....embarrassed crews.....

"NON Narcs" = Same thing, but not expecting any benefits.

"Cruisers" = Fiercely independent, live-aboards, highly experienced, high mileage, with small (usually TWO person), elderly but very fit crews.........quite some of the most remarkable, intelligent, adaptable, humorous, but polite and modest people I've ever met.....gently deprecating of all the other organisations.......most of them have no other home, but they all know each other, sometimes from YEARS ago.......and their boats are IMMACULATE.... Dick on "Mad River" jokes that he may be having withdrawal symptoms from the smell of varnishing, now he's finished it......even in a boatshow I've never seen such a good finish on wood....makes me embarrassed at my weatherworn deckpaint (which I will remedy in the Azores).....

"Sea Gypsies" = Even more independent, very shy, penniless, amazingly well equipped for repairs, (which they need to be, since their steel vessels are only kept afloat by corrosion, paint and willpower)......it's generally believed that their ships are incapable of making any progress AGAINST the wind.......but they have the most remarkable stories to tell......quietest crews of all.....

That's enough for now......hope my rambling narrative doesn't upset or bore anybody......
Take good care of yourselves.....you are a small but very select group who are important to me.......
Tuesday'n'me.

(RECEIVED)Mon 17/11/2003 17:49
Hello David,

I am now for the second week in Porte Grande, Sao Vicente, Cabe Verde and leaving this week towards Brazil. This place is O.K. The next island (by ferry) is nice to visit 1 day or more. 35-45 boats in anchor 5 in pontoon. A lot of French boats. Most sailing to the Caribbean, many to Brazil, some to Dakar, Senegal. Very gusty place, up to 14 m/s.

Some places holding bad. I have been lucky until to-day when the maritime polis ordered to move further away from the the ferry pier. Have 2 anchors now. Cecar the Mr. Fix has helped me a great deal. What are your plans?
Regards
Matti Lappalainen

Tue 18/11/2003 02:44
Dear Matti,

Thanks for all the most useful info....very helpful.....
Hope to leave Lanzarote this week...but I would like to sail round outside La Palma and El Hiero first, before coming to the Cape Verdes........
Then hope to stop briefly in Sao Vincent and Santiago, before aiming towards Salvador (probably NOT Recife)........then heading southwards........
I will be at least 3-4 weeks behind you, but I do hope we meet again....you may hear of my progress on:-
    Trudi's Net, 21.400 MHz, 1300 hrs UTC,
   and the Italian Net, 14.297 MHz, 1800 or 1900 hrs UTC,
  or the S. Atlantic Net, 14.316 MHz, 1130 hrs UTC........
   or the British Net, 14.303 MHz, 0800 and 1800 hrs UTC
Keep in touch.....take care....safe landfalls, good friend.......
David.

(RECEIVED)Thu 20/11/2003 11:01
Hi David,

Thank you for your email. I will sail today or tomorrow. I will listen the HAM now and then. Probably hear your call sign and voice?? When you come take Cicar as your Mr. Fix. He is very good, very helpful and reliable. Costs around 5 euros per day when serving you.
You don't even need own inflatable.
Regards Matti

(RECEIVED) Mon 17/11/2003 18:28
"Seven days without laughter makes one week." Hi Doc, we miss you.
Allen and Marsha,(on Gomera Island, Canaries).

Thu 20/11/2003 21:46

   Dear All,

   Further delay here.......weather has improved nicely, but with literally hundreds of yachts all leaving the Canaries at the same time, I'm not happy that it's a good time for me personally to leave with them.........yachts tend NOT to show up very well on radar......

   Also, I've had a STINKING cold.......(it was arrogant of me to assume I would be immune)..........so no diving............the last two days have been miserable with aches and fevers, and I'm sure it would be silly to put to sea in this condition......

   And the other three boats ("Forever", "Pendragon", and "Mad River") are putting pressure on me to wait to sail with them...........again, it seems very sensible.......they have been wonderfully supportive to me all the time........truly remarkable people:-

   Allen and Marsha on "Free Spirit" (an Ericson 39, cruiser/racer, 1970s, 8-9 tons) are already out on Gomera Island...... married only 8 months ago.........going to Trinidad.........

   Ron and Bonnie on "Forever" (a Hans Christian, 50' overall, 40' over the deck, 25 tons, 1980s)......been living on board for the last 4 years.....now going home towards Pennsylvania.......

   Dick and Pat on "Mad River" (a slim 44' Canadian design, 15 tons, 1980s) have sailed together for the last 11 years or so........Pat is ex-Liverpool, Dick is American.........married for 30+ years........(Mad River is named after a skiing resort).........Dick bought the boat from a bank for $28000, in an appalling condition, and rebuilt her himself............

   Dave and Sally, married for over 40 years, on "Pendragon" (a Valiant 40, 14 tons, a classic American cruiser of the Rival type, 1970s), have been cruising and living aboard for the last 11 years, now heading home to the USA to buy a motor-home, etc.......

   Another boat, "Tomorrow", (a 38' boat, 1970s, I'm not sure of the designer) is also in our local group..........Ken and Margaret have been married for nearly 50 years, and are now completing their 14 year circumnavigation..... .....but they'll probably leave after us...........

   So you can see that "Tuesday" is about average size for this work, 43'overall, 14 tons, 1975............ but much smaller than most of the boats in the RAC and ARC...........

   Hoping to be recovered and keen to go after this weekend, although there is a possibility of not bothering to stop at all in the Cape Verdes if all is going well..........perhaps just a quick look at one or two of the anchorages, but without formally checking in or going ashore.......I'm worried by reports of thefts etc there, so I don't want to leave the ship unguarded..........Still, maybe I won't like being at sea, and will be keen to stop, as it's about 3000 miles nonstop to Salvador from here........................we'll see.......

      More news before I leave.............

      Love,

         Tuesday'n'me.

(RECEIVED) Sun 23/11/2003 02:43

   David.........

   We do hope your cold is getting better.   "Colds" in hot climates can be a little bit of a worry sometimes. Whatever the weather, don't go until you're really ready..... and we wish you well, and that all will go sailing along in good order.

   We do, of course, give you our absolute full support in everything you do, and you have our absolute confidence. I'm not sure that we wish we were going with you..... but on the other hand we're with you all the way, if you see what I mean.   Goodonyer!   Send us a postcard when you get there.

      *We miss you. **Daddy.***

(RECEIVED)Fri 21/11/2003 09:33

Hi David,

For us desk-bound sailors its a pleasure to read your news letters and recall times past.....I remember leaving Los Christianos in 1979 after a very enjoyable 2 months there. Quite a crowd gathered to wave us off in our 8 metre engine-less (we were on a minuscule budget) catamaran. Unfortunately, after an hour and with little wind we were still only about 600 yards off the beach. There were still a dozen or so well-wishers occasionally waving and no doubt wishing we'd disappear over the bloody horizon......Twenty six days later we dropped anchor in English Harbour –it was Christmas Eve.
Best wishes for a peaceful passage-we look forward to hearing more.

Mike

Wed 26/11/2003 00:04

Dear All,

We're all set, Tuesday and me, better prepared than ever, ready to leave at 0800 Wednesday 26/11/03(in 8 hours time, ie.)........Forecast is good, the swell is down to 3 metres, etc............Will leave with "Pendragon", (the Valiant 40 with Dave and Sally), though they'll be bypassing the Cap Verdes towards Barbados, to see Trudi of "Trudi's Net", the ham radio station helpfully giving me weather reports etc.................

Poor "Forever" was the loser in a battle with the French, who RAMMED their pulpit, hard, while manoeuvring in the marina ("Forever" was still tied securely to her pontoon).....considerable damage to stainless steel, but many witnesses, so the French insurance have agreed to pay.................So Ron and Bonnie are staying here for another 3-4 days while the pulpit is removed from their bowsprit (today), repaired (excellent German welder here), and reassembled.... ...but it's particularly sad for them.......their cherished home, etc.......it hasn't exactly helped the recently strained Franco/Yank relations much, either.... .....But I hope to meet up with them in the Cap Verdes............

The parting from these true friends is really gut-wrenching.......they've become "family".....people I would trust my life with (indeed as I DID with Chris and Natasha while diving)........but thank heavens for modern communications.....it will soften the separating a little.....

Which reminds me, I've "doctored" my Ham Radio so that it will now work on commercial marine frequencies too........a powerful additional safety tool...... AND, it will enable me to keep in touch directly with these wonderful friends going to the Caribbean....

So.......... please expect no news for 14 days......but I'll keep in contact when I can...

Stay Well!

All my Love,

Tuesday'n'me.

(RECEIVED) Wed 08/10/2003 08:01

Hi David, Fantastic, very intrepid of you. Keep the news coming, it brightens up our day stuck in the office, while you are sailing away seeing new sights and having great experiences.

Nick and Denise

(RECEIVED) Sat 04/10/2003 18:08

Subject: Coping with worries.

I am passing this on to you because it has definitely worked for me. By following the simple advice I read in an article, I have finally found Inner Peace ...

The article read: "The way to achieve inner peace is to finish all the things you've started."

So I looked around the house to see all the things I started and hadn't finished.... and before coming to work this morning, I have finished off a bottle of Bacardi, a bottle of red wine, a bottle of Jack Daniels, my Prozac, a small box of chocolates and 2 litres of Stella Artois, a 1/2 can of cider and some cheese ... You have no idea how good I feel! ...

You may pass this on to those you feel are in need of Inner
Peace. **Elizabeth**

14/12/2003 17:53
Dear Everybodies,

So many things have happened!....but here's a synopsis....

Wednesday Nov. 26th, 0800, WONDERFUL send off from all the other boats of our group.....foghorns, cheers, (and yes, even tears).......very emotional it was.....just to make sure I really DID clear off out of it!....

Dawdled outside for "Pendragon" (Valiant 40)to come out an hour later, then set off on diverging courses.......never dreamt that by pure chance we would meet again, for video and photo's, 300 miles off the African coast, four days later...."Pendragon" went down BETWEEN the Islands, then to head West towards Barbados, while "Tuesday" went the long way round the top of them, then to make South, so it was inevitable that our tracks would intersect somewhere.....

Saw Sperm Whales breaching (leaping clear of the water after a deep dive)....several of them...HUGE splashes.......thank heaven they were about 1/3 of a mile away!.......saw other, quieter ones next day, 150 yards away.......

Very windy at times.....I pushed her a bit too hard I think for a while....30 miles in 4 hours at one point.... but the ship complained (one chain-plate began to weep slightly....tightened it up just a bit to cure it...they've already been massively reinforced)....squalls in the Wind Acceleration Zone by La Palma Island were vicious for a few hours...made for a busy night, rounding up to reef and unreef, each time having to remove the preventers, roll the genoa on it's pole and haul the staysail to windward............. b. tired the next day...

Rising seas....big l-o-n-g swell from the north, (from your winter gales).... one smooth 4 metre swell every 18 seconds or so......then on top of that were the 3 metre breaking waves from the east, which made a confused "washing-machine" movement on board....no problem, but it's tiring and jarring after a while...the ship seemed to love it though, goosewinged with a tiny poled-out genoa, full staysail, and heavily reefed mainsail on a shallow broad reach.....between 142 and 154 miles each day, really putting her shoulder to it, surfing diagonally across the seas, even though she's by no means a racer.....

Then came Black Sunday....violent broach in the night (I found myself lying on the cabin-wall) as the selfsteering (Autohelm tiller-pilot on the Aries), radar, GPS, navigation-light etc all "crashed"......probably due to high-voltage-spikes as the towed generator kept leaping out of the faces of the waves......all recoverable and reset soon.......no damage except the masthead tricolour is dead (later found the transmit part of the VHF transceiver didn't survive either)....Then the ropes from the Aries were seen to be fraying at the waterline....... and on top of all that the towed generator kept trying to eat its own string......all of which took time and effort to fix, in the dark and wet, hanging over the transom ....blew a dent in my confidence too......

And then I found a pack of part-baked bread rolls had turned into a pack of healthy flies, maggots and pupae....ugh!....luckily confined to that particular container......NOT a good day....

The next night the repaired Aries rope wore through quicker than I had expected and finally broke, causing another gybe-broach (no problem...the preventers worked very well indeed)...so I said sod it and used an electric selfsteerer (belt drive to the wheel) from then on...

BUT....imagine the dark of the night......the dolphins have come again at sunset several hours ago, to wish

"Tuesday" goodnight......a strong but dry, warm wind..........the ship roaring along, well heeled over, noisy, but fast, mile-eating, sailing down the "moon-path"......the masthead shepherding the stars around....spray-splatters on the foredeck......a ship looking after herself at speed....a personal concert on the tape-player below...a late supper on the stove...and knowing that already 3 flying fish have landed on deck for tomorrow's breakfast...... it certainly makes up for the hard bits....

Landfall at 35 miles out.....strong gusts and big waves....after 1024 nautical miles in 7 days, a restless but safe anchorage at 1630 on Wednesday 3/12/03, in MINDELO, SAO VINCENT Island, CAP VERDES.......and to be warmly greeted by name by a charming chap called Cicar (Caesar) who had been told by Matti (remember the reindeer-singer?) to look out for me....what a welcome!.....Cicar picked me up in his boat this morning and has taken me straight through "Costumes-and-Intimidation", and the "Marmite" Police, and shopping for fresh fruit'n'veg, etc, all within one hour......by myself it would have taken 2 days!....excellent value at 5 euros/day....good thing I politely declined the other, less professional boatboys......

Clambered up the mast today to fix the light.....very safe with the mast-walkers, a climbing harness, and climber's "jumas", even though the ship is moving around a bit......very satisfying, 'cos I was dreading it......

Oops!...sorry it's a long one...more another day...

Thanks for all your moral support...really appreciate it......

Stay well!
Love to all,
Tuesday'n'me.

Sun 14/12/2003 17:27
Dear Matti,

Arrived here in MINDELO on Wednesday 3/Dec/03. Thank you so very much for speaking to Cicar, Mr. Fix.....he met me in the evening and greeted me like a long-lost friend!..... I had refused all the other boatboys as politely as I could.....Cicar has been most helpful and kind.

The sail from the Canaries was rough, wet and fast....but I can't complain at 144-154 miles each day...... I hope to leave here next week, hopefully for Salvador, but I have some maintenance to do first......

I wonder how your trip went...I hope it wasn't too exhausting...hope to compare stories about it later..... (if I ever manage to catch up with you!).

Take care, Stay safe,
(and thank you again about Mr. Cicar!),
Tuesday'n'me.

(RECEIVED)Thu 04/12/2003 02:08
Subject: Well done.

My,my!!! A very remarkable acheivement. Not all that many people have done that, have they! We are so relieved. Though we secretly wish you were not planning to push off again, westwards..... but we do know that if you are going, then you have to do so soon because of future weather conditions.

We are very proud..... and we wish you a safe and happy voyage.

Fantastic! Much love, from **Mother and Daddy.**

(RECEIVED) Thu 04/12/2003 14:21
......Mick and Joe take a very great interest in your travels and worry over the downs and take great delight in the ups. They are enthralled about your ready-to-cook fish breakfast the other morning.Take great care and warn Tuesday I expect her to be ever vigilant. Heaps and heaps of love from **Mother.**

(RECEIVED)Thu 04/12/2003 13:01

Hey you ol'salt,

You made it!!! Yippeeee!!

WOW , what a long strange trip it's been. You really had a mixed bag of sea shit, didn't you? We're glad you made it safe & sound and as usual, you are in our thoughts and prayers daily. We miss you & your great antics.

Why are we out here?????

We've had some strange sailing, mostly we just feeling like a giant salt shaker at a margarita party!

Our SSB reception has been crappy, like rice crispies in cold milk, with lots of overcast skies, we kind of didn't expect it to be this way, but here we are! We'll see how much we motor, we may make it to the Verdes yet.

What are your plans, how long in the Verdes, how is the anchorage there and what about the people and the land? Most importantly, how's the beer? We're teetotal underway, so you can describe it in detail, we'll drink it in our minds!

Don't forget full moon is on Tuesday!

Hope you are well, and keep us posted on your goings on as will we. How did the girls do on their trip, did they come back???

Also, how long can you take stugeron without getting liver damage, because if we're going to get it we want it from alcohol abuse and not stugeron overdose!

*We love and miss you, will keep in touch. Love, **Capt. Ron & Bonnie***

Mon 15/12/2003 11:52

Dear Bon and Ronnie(!),

(Finally got this b*st*rd Email thingy working).

I really felt for you both after the Battle of Rubicon (franco/American war), especially when everyone was leaving and you were stuck in the wreckage....it would have brought me down very low, so how you guys coped I just don't know. You're tougher stuff than I am!

I can never thank you both enough for all you did for me...I feel very humble..... but oh so grateful for all your reassurance. I was a broken man in Porto Santo, with no confidence, and you helped me gradually to regain what I had lost. Nobody can ever take away the laughter and fun we had together, and it will help me in the future as well.

So.....how's you getting on, sliding downhill towards the sunshine? Sorry you had such a b*tch of a start to your crossing, but glad that things are improved a bit now. You really didn't miss a lot in the Cap Verdes...I didn't dare leave the boat to go exploring, so I only saw the surface, but it's not a place where I could relax. "Interesting" best describes it. My worn-out clothes were not out of place there!

Incidentally, if you look at www.mmsn.org and find "shiptrak", and ask it for the position of G0CBE (that's a zero not an o) it should give "Tuesday's" last reported position through the Ham Radio network.........Another way is by looking at www.winlink.org, and then follow your way through it, I believe, using the same callsign......It's all done by volunteers, for which I'm grateful, but it's not always updated as often as it might be, and it relies on my being able to get through on the ham radio...

Yes, my kids had a fantastic time in NZ....it's too early to know if they got any unmentionable diseases, but I'm longing to see their pictures etc..

As far as liver damage is concerned, best bet is to halve the dose of stugeron and increase the dose of Incapol when you can....at least that way the rest of you may fall to bits, but your liver will be pickled for eternity....

You two take good care of yourselves...you're both important to me....and don't let us lose touch

over the years either...
> Thanks again,
> > Much Love,
> > > Fair winds and Safe Landfalls!
> > > > **Tuesday'n'me, (the "token Brit").**

PS. Have a VERY HAPPY CHRISTMAS!......I'll be the one wearing the red-and-white costume and long hat you found for me!......

Sun 14/12/2003 17:55
Dear Everybodies,

I'm sorry the weather has been miserable for you (or at least I gather from radio-hams in Belgium it's been particularly gloomy)......here it's colder again, back down to 26c at night, with a little light and warm rain-shower twice a day.....just right, in fact........

I hear by radio that the other boats have run into flat calms where I was the other day.....and the normal Northeast Trade Winds have collapsed over a length of 400 miles...but no one's in a rush...

Interesting to hear the problems they get....things like an unexplained creak in the rigging, a watermaker not behaving, an alternator not charging, a gearbox failure, etc.....so I don't feel too bad about my frayed ropes and blown bulb...(all fixed now anyway)........

Mindelo has little money, high unemployment, shortage of water......but the people are contented, smiling, very friendly and helpful......and I notice the school kids look healthy and well catered for, with spectacles etc where needed.....no signs of malnutrition........ Almost everyone is African in origin, with European dilution in these northern islands, though the southern islands are almost pure African (the Customs man tells me).......if this place had the sort of EEC help that the Canaries, Madeira and Portugal have had, it would REALLY take off as a tourist attraction.......but I wouldn't like to live here because financially it is a poor place at present, with an exploding population........water is in short supply, but the healthy, smiling faces show that there is adequate to live on at present....

Prices (for what IS available) are very cheap.........fruit and veg quality not bad at all (said to be better on the neighbouring island)......very good fresh fish market.....but watch out for young pickpockets......and a Frenchman I'd previously met in Porto Santo had his inflatable dinghy slashed in five places with a knife today........he must have upset the beach "boat-watch-boys"...........

There are clear signs of Portuguese influence still, (these islands only gained their independence a few years ago)........language is Portuguese......money is a mixture of Euros and Escudos (1 Euro = 110 Cap Verde Escudos).....

As to the harbour itself...... well, it's got to be one of the classic natural harbours ....well protected, good firm sand in about 16-20 ft of clearish) water, although prone to wind gusts coming through the gaps in the mountains.........still some swell in here but very comfortable for a few days....

All in all, "not bad!"........I'm glad I came here.........but I wouldn't want to stay here for long.......
> That's all for now,
> > Love,
> > > **Tuesday'n'me.**

(RECEIVED) Tue 09/12/2003 22:37
Subject: Good Sailing.
David,
Just to wish you the very best of weather and the least possible amount of troubles on this next voyage which

looks a hell of a long way before you arrive in the land of coffee and nuts. No recent Emails received here, but on the third attempt I have contacted Fin and they haven't had an Email either, Ben went to have another look while I was on the phone talking to Fin. This was about eight p.m. It was lovely to have another phone call from you this evening but sad that it may be some time before we hear you again,   hurry up, Salvador!

Anyway, I wish my father were here, he would be bursting with pride of his grandson and be enthralled to hear about your journey. Still, he couldn't be more proud than we are though we wish you were back in Orford.

Heaps and heaps of love,

from **Mother and Daddy.**

(RECEIVED) Tue 09/12/2003 13:25

Subject: *Once more*

Just to wish you well.... once more. Not sure whether you are getting this, as I have not received e-mail from you recently.

See you in Brazil !!! **Daddy.**

Sun 14/12/2003 17:57

Dear Everybodies,

Sorry for delay ref Emails....totally unable to send them by mobile-phone or satellite-phone in the Cap Verdes.............so a lot more than simply 'disenchanted' with modern communications at the moment!.....even the local Internet cafe has crashed!

So....every intention of setting off from here tomorrow morning, 10/12/03, towards SALVADOR, Brazil.......but hoping to sail around and between several of the other islands here on the way....(but not stopping anywhere)........my chosen route is about 2500 miles, (which will make it "interesting").....the ship is full to the gills with green bananas, tomatoes, unripe oranges, peppers, apples, melons etc.......like a ruddy fruit-ship........

Bill on "British Tiger" (singlehanded Contessa 32) left this morning for Salvador......his last words were "see you there!".........he has a 6 month old tom-cat called Buddy on board, but they have a very clear love/hate relationship ....the animal thinks it owns the boat for itself, and thinks Bill is another cat......Bill didn't want the poor beast at all, but it would have died when he found it at 6 weeks old, and he got stuck with it.........I'm taking bets as to who will survive if they ever get hungry......at present Buddy turns his nose up at anything less than premium tuna, and Bill reckons he'll only have catfood for himself soon..........

Please expect no news for 6 weeks (got to cross the Doldrums)......I'm not in a hurry.....please send Xmas cards to "Santa Claus, c/o King Neptune, Latitude Zero"........

Have a Great Christmas everyone!.......

See you next year!

Love to all,

Tuesday'n'me.

Mon 15/12/2003 11:53

Dear Everybodies,

Now running down towards the Equator, 530 miles ahead...(still can't grasp that it's all real!)......December, but cabin temp is 29-30 degrees C, wind force 3/4, broad reach with boomed-out-genoa, staysail and main,, flying fish, bright and new (to me!) stars at night, etc..... MAGIC!.......and it's been like this for the past 4 days.... I know I'm going to pay for this weather soon, but it's been worth it....

Had a wild and fast beam close fetch south-EASTwards from Mindelo...max speed, and taking quite a bit of water on deck....noted a beautifully clear example of wind and wave patterns 20 miles to leeward of one island...waves look chaotic, until you study them carefully, and NOW I understand one of the Polynesian's methods of navigation as described by David Lewis...fascinating!..... down the EAST side of Santiago Island to avoid the squalls in its lee..... and then westwards round the SOUTH end of it ...

Had intended to explore Praia harbour on Santiago Isle, but lighter winds meant it was VERY dark before I got there..... a steep rocky shore 1.5 miles away, variable winds, and I had already noted what I considered "unpredictable" currents and tides between the islands.... and only one pair of (already tired) eyes on board.......it just wasn't worth the risk of stopping at sea there till daybreak.....so sailed straight by it, feeling a bit guilty (I'd suggested to Jack in Pennsylvania that I would look for one particular boat for him there)....

Very solid wind shadow effects that night...nasty steep confused breaking seas and light airs....the heavy boom trying to smash everything in sight as I prepared to gybe the ship, in spite of preventers etc.....Surprised and cross in the morning to note a complete mainsheet winch missing...bolts sheered cleanly....must have gone like a rocket!.....The remaining bits of bolts themselves show clear signs of corrosion, (S/S bolts through bronze winch base), so it's entirely my own fault for not having replaced them.......I have a spare winch here on board which will fit nicely, but the bolts I have in ship's stores are 5mm too short...I had considered the winch itself would break down, not its bolts..........anyway, it's not a problem, and it was a tired old winch anyway (already bodged inside with the base of a Pot Noodle pot as a spacer, to take up slackness due to wear)......

Then westwards for 70 miles, to confirm the other islands are really there....it means I have actually seen ALL of the Canary Isles, and 8 of the 10 Cap Verdes....most impressive of them is FOGO Island, a single massive volcano straight out of the sea to 9280' high....last erupted in 1995/6.....very dramatic!.....

Then the journey begins...a relief to get clear of inter-island effects...trade wind sailing.....like being on holiday.....only two ships in 4 days, but one would have been within 1/4 mile if I hadn't called him up on VHF....heading due south to be sure of keeping up-wind and up-current of the corner of Brazil (it's easy to be set too far to the west)......Two days ahead of me is Bill in "British Tiger" (Contessa 32)... also sailing solo to Salvador.....we'll meet up again there.....he doesn't have a radio transmitter, but I know he's listening on the maritime-mobile networks.....but he was planning to cross The Line further west than I am, as the books recommend for this time of year, but I'm not in a hurry.....

Some bl**dy shark ate my squid-with-a-hook-in-it yesterday..and 18" of line with it....hope it gives him bellyache for a while, as that would have caught my supper.....?maybe he ATE my supper?...

Much, much more, but that's enough for now....

Take care!,

Love to all,

Tuesday'n'me.

(RECEIVED)Sat 13/12/2003 01:18

Subject: Gosh this is getting exciting.......

Well I thought that I would drop you a line , Jonesy is keeping us all in touch , I assume that he is speaking to the right ship or are you really hiding in some house in Kesgrave ???   Now that WOULD make a good story!......

Must say it all seems to be quite an experience ....Don`t forget that the most awful things that happen make the best stories when back at home boozing with friends .Mind you I once told that to JM when we got very stuck in some awful part of Brazil, no Bank , so no money , food or anywhere to sleep safely .......(at least YOU don`t have to worry about where you are going to spend the night) ......he told me to p*ss off he didn`t think it was funny ....

I`m sure that you laughed yourself silly when you discovered that your winch had broken........ I mean the* *whole idea is to have lots of fun isn`t it ?.

Lots of questions I`d like to ask but I suppose that I will have to wait .

Will send a Xmas card to John , I`ll fill him in with the news . Must go ,got a dog show in three hours and I haven`t gone to bed yet.........you see your not the only one who doesn`t get enough sleep ...

love MARY

(RECEIVED)Tue 16/12/2003 11:13

Hello sailor (what a line!)

I just love the name of that boat-"Sutton Hoo"-I thought it was a character from the Dr. Seuz books-like a Feffer Fieffer Feff. It would be great to learn it has wings and 3 ears and a nose with 2 warts on it.

Heard you threw a winch overboard, you moron! What's that about? Hope it works out ok.

We are on Day 13 of our passage. Have had some problems with the autopilot causing us to hand steer-it sounds like a bad thing but hand steering is quite exhilirating. There's a certain freedom of taking the helm away from the machine, it's liberating and actually challenges one's sailing capabilities. Everything is ok now.

How are you managing with sleep/eat scheds? You certainly have enough backers via the ham ssb and regular nets, we are always glad to hear you.

Our down time consists of identifying cloud pictures-like we saw santa and his reindeer flying through the sky with his sleigh full of goodies-that was an awesome one. The sunsets have been disappointing, but the after glow is tremendous.

Why do flying fish only land on the decks at night? With those big bugger eyes they should be able to see better at night, and how far do you think they can fly? They really soar when you hit a school of them.

Did you see the meteor showers on the 13th of Dec? It was really fun to watch, a night show all to ourselves - we made popcorn and watched the stars shoot across the sky and fall into oblivion. It was almost magical.

Hope you are ok, we will talk to you. We miss you a lot and can't wait to get together again.

Stay safe, keep all your parts lubed and use sunblock! (Words of wisdom from the idiot!)

Love & miss you XXOO Capt. Ron & Bonnie

Fri 19/12/2003 00:46

Dear Ron'n'Bonnie,

(Motoring gently for an hour or two, so plenty of Electricstuff tonight).....don't think I'll be able to send many emails at sea though, normally........

Thanks for Email...really "neat" to receive .....(see, I haven't forgotten the language!)

"Sutton Hoo" ....well, it's actually a PLACE, so sorry to disappoint you.......it is the site of a group of ship-burials of around 300AD or thereabouts, where priceless treasures were found in the largest of the burial mounds, (in 1939 I believe)........I happen to know about it, as it's only 6 miles from where I live, and I can see it from where Tuesday spends her cold winters............"Su" means "south", "ton" is where our word "town" comes from, and "Hoo" is a "hill".....these are all Saxon words.................I can vouch for the fact that it's on a hill, and the valley they hauled the ships up is still clearly visible..........It's a lonely but quiet and peaceful place, and I can see why they chose it as a burial place.....it's got good "spirits" about it somehow ....(yet more from The Department of Useless Information!)

Flying Fish and night-flying don't seem to mix, I agree.....maybe they would see a different coloured boat better? ....certainly fewer of them crash on board once the moon is up.......I tried using one as bait......no luck..... should have eaten the bloody thing in the first place!...

Hope all is well with you both......you MUST be due for good weather soon, surely?......

Here all goes comfortably.....I have to improve my cooking a bit, though.....got to be hungry to eat it, and

60

for God's sake don't look at it first!.......the ship is behaving beautifully...her design of hull really fits in the waves well....a real "Lady"......but more details in "Dear Everybodies" Email....

Pity my radio-antenna is so crappy on Marine SSB....I made it for the Ham frequencies, so it's not surprising.....but it would be nice to have been able to keep in touch more.....it receives very well, so watch what you say!.....

May not be able to catch you before Xmas......so have a great time, and be sure to pass on my warmest best wishes to all the doNiMoe-gang when you meet up with them again.......(heck I'm going to miss you guys).....

Take care of both of you, for my sake as well as yours,

Love from,

Tuesday'n'me.

(RECEIVED)Thu 18/12/2003 08:53

Hello mate,

Just one week till christmas-shop early, shop often. or in our case, ship early, ship often!

It is amazing how resilient our vessels are. The squeaking and creaking and bends and twists that Forever has taken in the last week would surely render an ordinary boat unseaworthy. She is a true acrobat, more flexible and reliable than any human I've ever known-and I know some bendy characters!

Last night we finally saw the southern cross, it is like a yellow ribbon round the ol' oak tree to us, like we are coming home and being welcomed by our celestial family. It was a great comfort to see this and ironically the seas seemed to calm and the winds backed down along with it's arrival.

How are your nights? Noises seem to be much more resounding, creaking timbers sound as if they are breaking under great pressure, like a redwood falling in the forest and you are actually there to hear the sound - everybody knows that there is no sound when a tree falls if nobody is there to hear it, after all.

Are you getting enough sleep and most importantly, do you have enough chocolate to make it to the next landfall? We know you plan on spending Christmas at the equator, just make sure you are safe with all the convection activity and the scorching sun-apply your SPF liberally my friend!

As always, we miss you and you are in our thoughts and prayers daily. Today we will actually be able to have a proper cooked meal, roasted chicken with spinach mushroom souffle and lemon herbed broccoli. We plan on sharing a bottle of wine to celebrate our halfway point-we couldn't do this on the actual halfway as ol' neptune had plans of his own. We will, however, make the first offering from the bottle to him.

We will write as we move along and continue to try to talk on the SSB. I am studying the Ham book to see if I want to take my test, it's a bit nerdy, but I'll think about it.

Be safe, keep your spirits high and your bow up. We love and miss you.

Capt. Ron & Bonnie

Fri 19/12/2003 00:46

Dear Everybodies,

There's a brick wall in this bit of the ocean, and I ran straight into it.....MASSIVE thunderstorms (I've never seen anything that big before) with associated violent winds and torrential rain, where the Tradewinds run out of puff and the Doldrums begin......for 6 hours one night I had to tuck my head under my wing and stay hove-to under heavily reefed sails to ride it out........awe-inspiring display of power!......no problems, but I do note it's the only time I've ever put on my Survival Suit while at sea......

Up till then it had been a real "Holiday", and I was loving every moment of it (except for my cooking!)...........boisterous swell, but smooth powerful sailing in a vessel which really sits so easily and comfortably in the waves......you have to watch all the time for chafe and wear though, but the fast reaching from the Canaries to the Cap Verdes had given me some insight into where to look.....

Once having fought our way through the 100 miles of "wall", it's calmed down a bit......still occasional heavy downpours, but it means the shampoo comes out for a tepid but thorough shower and clothes-washing session......It's quite humid, but so far not nearly as roasting as I feared it might be.........got to keep out of the sun, but the deck is double air-gapped for insulation, so the cabin temp hasn't been above 34 centigrade so far........ (how on earth men on open liferafts survived down here 60 years ago, after their ships had been torpedoed, I cannot comprehend.....they must have been supermen)....

Today "Tuesday" is at 4 degrees north, 25 west, (the centre of this zone is around 2 north at the moment)..... so we're getting there, slowly....I've deliberately come more to the east than is recommended this time of year, to see what it's like......most interesting!..........much of the time is ghosting along at 2 knots, but even that is nearly 50 miles/day......variable and shifting light airs..... and to my great surprise the EAST-setting Equatorial Counter Current is running at a full 2.4 knots!.... I expected about 0.5......I wonder how wide it is till we break out of it....

Don't talk to me about fishing........I got one nice big one up to the gunwale and then lost him.......then some nasty PeopleEater ate my breakfast, bait and hook......I even tried using a spare flying-fish as bait......I should have eaten the bloody thing myself.....Then today I caught a large Puffer-Fish .....never seen a football in a bad temper before.....but not sure if they're OK to eat or not, so I put him back.....trouble is that by then he'd filled up with air instead of water, so unless he deflated quickly the poor chap will have got sunburnt.......I have always said that my fishing would allow me to starve slowly, but maybe it would be quicker than that........

Saw two or three Risso's Dolphins today..... they seemed a bit wary, and only came within 30 yards or so, and as it started raining again I didn't get much on film.......I wonder if the towed generator propellor-thingy upsets them, because I've not seen many dolphins/whales around recently......... or maybe it IS that ruddy mouth-organ-music-practice, after all.......there's been an Albatross or two, though...

Incidentally, I note that Bill on "British Tiger" is also trying to learn how to play the Harmonica on this trip..... planning a combined effort in Brazil.....that should REALLY empty the ocean of wildlife!..

When you look up to your night sky, find the constellation of Orion with his Belt......well, at around midnight I'm directly underneath him .....and what I find strange is that "Tuesday" must be upended onto her bow, compared with how she is at Orford.......and soon to become upside-down as we go south....yet nothing's fallen out of the cupboards so far.....

Lots more, but not just yet.....
Stay Well, Take Care,
Much Love,
Tuesday'n'me.

(RECEIVED) Tue 23/12/2003 20:47
Subject: snow

Hi Doc,

When I last looked to the night sky and saw Orion and his belt little did I know that you were directly under it. Just had a look with charlotte to see if with binocks your reflection could be seen, but guess what, its cloudy still.

We've just had the first snow this year. Poo!
All that sun! have a great Christmas!
and keep at it lad
*love **james***

(RECEIVED)23/12/2003 20:42

Hello Everyone,

Please excuse any spelling errors as we are at sea, on a 20-30 degree heel, sometimes I am braced in a 3 point stance between the nav station and the galley sink, sometimes I am hurled from said nav table into that same galley sink, in addition, we are a bit tired and sometimes the capt. is bellowing orders from above as to what else I should include in this newsletter as I am typing (not so well I might add) down below. And sometimes I just don't really care how I spell it, it's the thought that counts! I am not really that stupid-although the jury is still out on that!

We started with 2922 nm from Canary Islands to Barbados. We are now on Day 21 out of Lanzarote, finding ourselves at 14 58N 50 50W with just under 500nm to go to Pt. St. Charles harbour, Barbados.

We want to wish everyone a joyous holiday season, Merry Christmas, Happy Hanuka and Healthy and Quiet New Year.

We will be celebrating Christmas somewhere around 55 degrees West, with about 2 days remaining to complete our transatlantic voyage. We'll celebrate with roasted lamb in pesto?thyme herb dressing, saged stuffing, cranberry sauce, dilled carrots and fresh frozen broccoli. A scrumptious JELLO cream cheesecake with raspberry topping and cafe con leche to follow. At noon UTC we will toast to all our family and friends who are also our family, we hope you will join us.

As we near land, we are grateful for what Forever has taught us, how much we have come to respect each other's skills and weaknesses. We have seen dozens of shooting stars, helmed our way through multiple squalls-the rule that they follow is to occur mainly at night, mostly when the capt. has had minimal sleep and always with an increase in size and fury of swell.

We are still eating off of the 39 inch Mahi Mahi that we caught last week, thank you pink squid, celebrated capt. Ron's b-day with a special rum toast, celebrated our wedding anniversary, we had dancing dolphins on our bow both day and night, we have enough food hurled on the cabin floor to feed a cast of thousands, we've had bags under our eyes big enough to carry groceries in, and, as the capt. pointed out today, the boat down below smells like cheese (he's a little tired!)

Capt's hands are looking and feeling much better-he managed to get himself some severe rope burn while wrestling with a wayward spinnaker halyard-the halyard won, capt. lost the top layer of skin "just a flesh wound" as he says, and he's healing quite nicely thanks to peppermint lotion and lots of protein!

Our big blue backyard is full of surprises, joys and wonder. We wonder when we will see land!

Merry Christmas everyone, thanks for all the great emails, it keeps the wind in our sails.

We will write when we have arrived.

With love to all, **Capt. Ron & Bonnie**

Wed 24/12/2003 20:39

Dear Everybodies,

Crossed "The Line" (Equator) on Tuesday 23/12/03 in the late afternoon....... a major personal ambition achieved......had a slight haircut and got covered in woad (well, hadn't got any, so used baked-beans-in-tomato-sauce), to make absolutely sure King Neptune was pacified, as it's my first time across......sacrificed the rest of the beans to The Mighty Ocean..............It's all crazy I know, but some traditions are worth keeping.......and besides, you get a bit superstitious out here on your own......

I'm intrigued that both last year when crossing the Arctic Circle and this year crossing the Equator, it's been on a Tuesday.....pure chance?..or not?....sometimes I wonder who's in charge here!....

It took seven days to get through the Doldrums, so I reckon I was let off lightly....fascinating weather conditions in that area!....everything except snow and hail.....how on earth they managed to do it in the large lumbering sailing-ships of yesteryear I don't know.......yet it was routine to them......

There's a nice cartoon of a yachtsman finding a split-pin lying on his deck.....that means something's going to fail soon........it happened to me after I put in another reef today as the wind got up ......I cannot find where the HELL it came from....I've checked all the pins I can see by lying on my back with binoculars, inspecting the mast and rigging carefully, so I don't think it's very structural......too small anyway.......we'll have to see what happens............But I'll never laugh at that cartoon again!......

First foray into the construction business yesterday......made some bread.....it's edible, but only vaguely related to what I had planned ....?anyone want any paving slabs for their patio?........Actually, it's not too bad, but it's difficult to tell if it's cake, bread or dumplings, though it TASTES of fresh bread at least................ "could do better".............

Dorado must be one of the best tasting fish around......but the score is averaging 7:2 at present, in favour of the Dorado.......I'm not very successful (so far) at getting them actually on board without swapping places with them ....so the staple diet is still Flying Fish.............Though I managed to catch a massive great FF on the rod-and-line .....didn't know they got such a cruise-missile size.... wouldn't like to collide with it in full flight!......

So, in summary, we're now in the southern hemisphere, with the Southern Cross and the Magellanic Cloud very clearly visible ahead, sailing briskly across the SE Tradewinds and a lumpy sea........ over halfway to Salvador now, but still another 1250 miles to go....it's a BIG ocean, but not in the least bit lonely somehow.......I'm not in a hurry, and the ship seems happy and comfortable...... .... I feel as though I've always lived out here, somehow........(pity my cooking is so "experimental" though!)....

Have a great time over the Seasonal Holiday, and thanks for everything...

Love to all,

Tuesday'n'me.

(RECEIVED) Wed 24/12/2003 16:42

We would like to wish you a very merry Christmas and a happy New Year. Please take care and keep safe. Safety note from Bob!!! Do not handle Puffa fish as some are very poisonous.

All the best

Bob & Brenda

(RECEIVED) Wed 24/12/2003 23:42

Subject: HAPPY CHRISTMAS!

To Daweed,

Post Office ridiculed sending your card to King Neptune. Said he didn't have a postcode. Anyway, it would have fallen off your mantelpiece.

Hope you've got the log fire lit. Wrap up warm!

Woddy.

P.S. N.B. Make sure you cook your turkey THOROUGHLY.

P.P.S. Watch out for the Three Ships.

(RECEIVED) Thu 25/12/2003 14:40

Subject: HAVE YOU GONE CHRISTMAS CRACKERS YET?

Hello........

Well I thought that I`d try and keep you in touch with the REAL world and make you feel more normal ... HAPPY XMAS !!!! Where have you stuck your tree?..and are you sitting comfortably?

Congratulations on crossing the line ......

at least there is only ONE in the sea; when we were in Equator we were told that there were two lines, one real one, and another one for the tourists which wasn`t in the right place but it was more practical for the locals to make money out of them all taking photos etc.

Delighted that you are heading for Salvador known as Bahia Salvador where we were . Fabulous place , funny cos I thought of you when we were there ,sailing conditions looked great from the shore which doesn`t of course mean anything -Some of my best memories of Brazil where in that area, mind you we met up with a Swiss couple and spent most of the time drinking rum and often walked through some extremely rough areas in the early hours of the morning trying to find our hotel ....we must have been MAD !!!! Often wondered why we were never attacked there but reckon that we were always laughing so much that the locals were frightened of us ....worried that they might catch the same disease .

Anyway Jonesie fills us in with all the news.

Do you get ants on the boat ? they tend to eat all the coating around any pills you have so watch it .
ENJOY YOUR FIRST XMAS IN THE SOUTHERN HEMISPHERE !!!
*LOVE **SWISS FAMILY DISERENS***

(RECEIVED)Thu 01/01/2004 00:36
Subject: Happy New Year
Hello David
It's now 12:30am ... we drank a toast to you at midnight. Hope you are safe a well
We love you lots. Keep safe and well, for us all.
Love with happy new year from
Joseph & Joyce

Sun 04/01/2004 02:17
[author's note:- not actually sent till arrival in Salvador]
Dear Everybodies,

(Thank you for all your Emails.....really appreciate them!.....some had me in fits of giggles, some were really nice and cheering, but every one of them was thoroughly enjoyed.......Thank you........)

Xmas Eve night was windy, squally and violent, so I couldn't take the waterproof cap off the cabin-heater chimney.........and the socks which I left out, got up and walked about by themselves.....But nevertheless, Santa appeared (a bit skimpily dressed in a Father Christmas hat-and-matching-apron, and a large "censored" sign at the back), and found the box of Christmas goodies you'd given me before I left the UK.....wonderful!.... very emotional it all was, but warm and comforting......It was too rough to hoist the Christmas Tree into the rigging, so I had set it up in the main cabin, lashed to the mast support, and completed it with fairy lights (all two of them!) made earlier from old LEDs.......appropriate music, with wind accompaniment in the rigging, completed the picture....a little oasis of colour and peace 1000 miles from land.......sounds a bit "sad", but it was really rather nice....(and that day's sextant sight, by chance, was only 400 yards out!)......

New Years Eve was a bit confusing, as ship's time is still on GMT (heard Big Ben on the World Service), but the ship I saw that night was firing serial red flares behind his bridge......I called up on the vhf to say I could see them, (didn't know if it was genuine or not) to be met with a load of loud verbal abuse in a variety of languages, (all of them somewhat slurred), followed by "HAPPY NEW YEAR!".....I recorded it all on video...but that really undercut my confidence in the duty officers on ships at night.....so much so that when a cruise-liner 6 miles away at dawn wished me a happy new year, I didn't dare answer......pity..should have done.........

For 14 consecutive days saw not a single sign of mankind at all...no ships...no planes...not even any rubbish in the water..........managed to read some books ....Ham Radio was incredibly useful, as well as reassuring.....saw Gannets 230 miles from land (I thought they only went about 70 miles off, so I hastily checked the GPS position with sextant sights (the positions agreed, thank heavens!)......caught a variety of very tasty fish, but not enough to survive on (one dorado was caught, dispatched, gutted and cleaned, cooked, eaten, and   washing up all done in 45 minutes .....(I was hungry!)...........)

But it still wasn't lonely, and simply running the ship keeps you very busy all the time......kept trying for the Grand Slam of daytime sextant sights, measuring the Moon, the Sun and Venus all at the same time to give an instant "position fix"....only got good enough conditions once, though..................

Found that rainwater collecting in the folds of the reefed mainsail (wind force 6 most of the time in the SE Trades) leaks out slowly through the sailcloth......a natural Shower for washing!..... but failed to collect enough rainwater as drinking-water to survive on, although I would do better in future with what I've learnt.....

Fewer bruises this time.....and my fears are more balanced now...... one cut finger, one tennis elbow............ and a bit of iron deficiency anaemia (I started a bit low anyway), so I've started some of the out-of-date-free-sample-pregnant-mum's-pills........and the malaria pills too, now I'm likely to explore some backwaters of this area...........it annoys me to have to take tablets, even though I've been peddling the darned things for years!......but I suppose I ought to be sensible......

Time to stop........Once again, thanks for all the Emails.......unfortunately the machine rejects any pictures etc, so my apologies for that........

Stay Well!....... More news soon....

Love,

Tuesday'n'me.

(RECEIVED) Sat 03/01/2004 02:32

David.....

Just to say ThankYou, to you and to your absolutely wonderful family, for all the fantastic gifts you have all heaped upon us for Christmas.

Your family were all here this evening, as you know and I can tell you that one of the most utterly enjoyable things I have seen in a long time was your two daughters each talking to you on the 'phone today. The sheer joy on their faces was something out of this world.

Ben was round here the other day and fixed my computer, which was in an awful mess.   I had lost a couple of programs that I often use, I kept getting error messages all over the place and it was all terribly depressing.   I really thought I would have take advantage of your very generous birthday agreement and buy a new one.

But then Ben came.   We just gave him a mug of tea, and in less than 3/4 hour he had fixed absolutely everything; just how I shall never know.   That man is a wizard.

I cannot tell you how extremely proud of you we all are. Southern hemisphere, eh! Phw4! Makes Norway seem like an afternoon drive round.

Take great care.   You mean an awful lot to us.

Daddy.

(RECEIVED) Fri 02/01/2004 18:21

> *Subject: Boxing Day!*
>
> *David,*
>
> *DELIGHTFUL! It was absolutely wonderful to hear you on the phone on Christmas Day yesterday, especially as it was about the time we usually would have been with you all in your home. Fin and the other two came down .... they grow more and more attractive and delightful; we are VERY proud of being their grand-parents!*
>
> *Rosalie and Gerald have sent a Video in which you and Gerald are heard talking on the Radio.*
>
> *I am glad you aren't feeling too lonely in the middle of the ocean, we feel VERY lonely without you but also very happy for the times that things are not too hard for you.*
>
> *Bless you for all your eagerly awaited Emails and the Radio conversations which Gerald nobley sends us. Tell Tuesday I am relying on her to look after you and bring you home next summer.*
>
> *Heaps and heaps of love,*
>
> > *from Mother.*

Sun 04/01/2004 02:15

Dear Everybodies,

I never cease to be impressed by how much these vessels flex and twist at sea.........I can state quite categorically that I would not want to do this trip in a modern lightweight "plastic-fantastic" mass-produced yacht.......I just couldn't trust the integrity of the hull in these punishing conditions...."Tuesday" is massively built, but even she creaks and moves slightly.......managed to identify one particular squeak to the woodwork built in around the companionway, and if you look carefully you can detect the movement with each wave...........Another worrying groaning noise, in time with the ship's rolling, turned out to be the bottom of the deckstepped mast, articulating on its base, (and I know just how tough her rigging is, as I designed it myself)............three windows began to leak slightly, but were fixed by ramming in some neoprene strip salvaged from another job........Two more chain-plates started weeping a teeny bit, but responded immediately to tightening down onto the sealant by another two "flats" on the nuts (sounds a bit kinky!)......they never leaked at all in Norway gales last year, but this trip is certainly finding any slight weaknesses.....

Fishing rod reel broke too....jammed everything, and it took forever to try to salvage the line.....but I got my own back by reinforcing the axle of the reel by drilling down it and screwing part of one of the broken bolts from the Missing Winch down through the middle.......(nice touch of economy to that, I thought!)......it's tougher now than it was when it was originally made, over 30 years ago......

There's a small leak high up in the starboard bow somewhere....can't identify it yet....it's not new, and not getting worse.....about 2 big-spongefuls twice a day when she's shovelling heavily into seas, (and it never occurs in rain, however torrential).....it must be when water is going UPwards that it leaks ....anyway, to get round it I've today drilled a small hole through the bottom of the shower-tray so that the leak will drain to the main bilge.......easier to get rid of it via the main ship's pumps at the twice daily bilge check, rather than balancing on one leg with a sopping sponge.......

The sails and running rigging take a fearful punishment.......constant lookout for wear and chafe.......... I reckon a month in these ocean conditions equates to 5 years of "normal" sailing, in terms of damage-through-use.......it's the seas that do the harm, not the wind...........the SE Trades blow at force 5/6 all day, and 6/7 at night with rain/wind squalls......seas are 3+ metres all the time, but close together.......double-reefed mainsail (equivalent to 3 reefs on most boats....they are seriously deep reefs on "Tuesday"), full staysail, and a tiny genoa giving 6-7 knots ACROSS the swells on a close fetch, to allow for the current as well as leeway............(it's not at all like running DOWNwind away from the seas).....rolling to an average of 45+

degrees on each wave, every 6 seconds....."Rolling Down to Rio" is dead right!.......frequent heavy jolts and explosions from the breakers.....too wet out "on the patio" to be able to take the sprayhood down.........

But.....it's really WARM and DRY indoors...comfortable 34 centigrade in the cabin....... and ROASTING outside in the overhead sun.................and clothes don't seem to wear out at all, nor need washing ....
...............now I wonder why that should be?..........

All the very Best!.....More news soon........Take Care!

Love from,

Tuesday'n'me.

Chapter 4

Brazil

(TEXT MESSAGE 2/1/2004:
6 miles off Salvador at 1130. Light winds slow progress.
All well, Love **Tuesday)**

(TEXT MESSAGE 2/1/2004:
Dropped anchor SALVADOR 1435hrs. 2384 nm non stop solo in 23 days. All very well, now wiser, calmer (and younger!). more news by email soon. **Love to all!!)**

04/01/2004 02:16
   Subject: Savador, Bahia, Brazil.
   Dear Everybodies,
Dropped anchor here 1435 UTC 2/1/04 after 2384nm nonstop solo in 23 days. Still can't face the thought of going ashore yet, and anyway there's no prospect of clearing-in over the weekend (so I've been told by an Aussie in a rubber dinghy)....probably explore the two marinas on Monday, in the morning before it gets windy....only then maybe face the Natives...

No sign of Bill (and the cat Buddy) on "British Tiger".......I'll wait a few days, but it may well be that he got pushed too far to the west and ended up in Recife (or worse)....there's no answer to my Email to him two weeks ago, so I presume he's still at sea.......

And poor Matti (the reindeer-singer) got caught by violent weather at 5 degrees north (roughly where my "brick wall" was), smashed a hand (which repaired itself), damaged his leg, wrecked both sets of his selfsteering gears, and lost a stanchion wire.... so he turned right, and is now in Barbados safely, having given up the idea of Brazil...will stay in the Caribbean for some months.......

The "Domino Gang" from Rubicon have all arrived at their Caribbean destinations, I think.....but "Pendragon" was caught by a Tropical Storm on the way, which must have been horrible.....Sally said on the radio that they were the worst seas they'd seen in the 11 years of their sailing trip......."Forever" had a nasty rough first half to their crossing as well......and sadly "Mad River" was put ashore by a vicious storm in Barbados.....I was distraught until it was confirmed that Dick and Pat had escaped OK...but I understand that although the ship has been recovered, there are considerable repairs to be done.....

It all makes you ponder a bit, doesn't it.......there but for the grace of God.....

Fresh fruit and veg lasted quite well really, without refrigeration.........melon, oranges (yellow/green in the Cap Verdes.....the orange coloured ones are actually lemons!) lasted 2-3 weeks......onions and sweetpotatoes have started sprouting......green bananas and green tomatoes all ripened together, so had a bit of gluttony that day.......

Apart from the fruit'n'veg, I've now been living on ship's stores for the past six weeks, keeping a record of what needs replacing.......water is pumped into 2 litre containers when needed, so I can accurately monitor what's happening .....I'm afraid rapidly-bio-degradables go over the side, while everything else is chopped up small and rammed through the neck of the plastic fizzy-drink-bottles as they are used........result is eight heavy and solid "pop" bottles, but only one poly bag, to be disposed of ashore (they'll probably just chuck 'em in the sea anyway!)..........one neat touch is that the now filled "pop" bottles can be stowed back where they came from .....ie. no loss of stowage space.....quite proud of that one!...

More details to follow.....

Take good care of yourselves!.....and All the Best for 2004!

Much Love,

Tuesday'n'me.

(RECEIVED) Fri 02/01/2004 23:05

Subject: Joy and Disbelief!!

David, It is unbelievable that you and your own boat have got all the way to Brazil! I bet when you first put the canoes in the river at Wickham Market you never thought you would one day, all alone, sail across the world to South America. We are bursting with admiration for you and I only wish my parents were alive today, they would be absolutely thrilled to think their grandson had achieved so much. A doctor in practice for many years trained at a top world famous hospital; a qulalified micro light pilot; a qualified yacht master certificate; and a lone sail boat sailor crossing the South Atlantic to Brazil!!!!. I cant get over it. And a damn fast swimmer too! COO! Haven't your children something to crow about!

You must be feeling very strange just now. Other boats and people nearby and able, or possibly UNable to sleep all night long. What a beginning for a new year.!

Paul is most impressed with your doings and glad that you found the sextant so accurate. He was very interested in the ShipTrack picture Daddy showed him and he wants to hear about you as much as possible. It was good of him to come all this way and we enjoyed seeing him. We owe him a lot.

It is a great relief to know that you are safely tied up to a bit of real land instead of having it many miles under you. Heaps and heaps of love, **Mother.**

(RECEIVED) Fri 02/01/2004 22:51

Subject: WISH I WAS THERE !

HAPPY NEW YEAR !! WELL DONE !! Of course I never doubted for one moment that you would make it ....well you didn`t really have much choice did you ?? !! Anyway very envious of you being where you are tho it may take a bit of getting used to. To us it was all very civilised having roughed it around for a few months before we arrived at Bahia Salvador. If you go around the old cathedral part, that is where we stayed in a cheap dirty hotel where the walls don`t go up to the ceiling. True about the pick pockets, question of luck I reckon but for goodness sake don`t try to resist cos they don`t give a sh*t about what they do to you . We used to have something handy to give them to bide for time ....and incidently if you do go to the police they usually laugh or ask for even more money but maybe it has improved since we were there. Careful of women who spit on you and while your going" UGH! " their 5 year old lttle darling is busy going through pockets or groveling inside your trousers , they know all about where tourists hide things ....

Anyway as I say I really envy you , longing to hear about your impressions and traveling by yourself you tend to meet some fascinating people . You`re in the pre carnival season , we were there in early December and already there was lots of dancing and music in the streets , we were often so p*ssed we joined up with them !! Goodness knows how we survived .....Are there still those huge coloured ladies dressed in big white dresses selling there curds and whey ...... and young children selling small cups of very sweet coffee (delicious once you get used to it) out of mouldy thermos`s on wheels ? Later on at night we`d see them getting into their cardboard boxes to sleep ...... rather sad but the awful thing was that you gradually got used to it .... Jean-Marc bought himself an old gun in the market which is now sitting on our mantelpiece next to the photo of him sailing Pelican .

Anyway all the best, wish I could nip on an aeroplane and join you .....

Thanks for the phone call at Xmas, really made my day ......Love **MARY:**

70

(RECEIVED) Sat 03/01/2004 11:14

Did you manage to have a decent sleep last night? I do hope your brain managed to get off being on the ALERT! Heaps and heaps of love, we still cant believe it. You really are a red coloured marvel!!!. from **Mother.**

(RECEIVED) Sun 04/01/2004 03:42

Subject: Wow!!!

David....

We are all so terribly impressed, full of admiration and, I have to say, also somewhat full of some gratitude and relief too! Well done, Sir. Though it is a bit of a worry... about your friends in other craft.... but they'll turn up.

Your latest e-mails are just wonderful... thank you so much..... from all of us.

Take care. **D.**

(RECEIVED)29/12/2003

Hi docdavid,

Thank you for your email. Actually I never got over the equator. I encountered bad weather for many days 5-4 deg N. Broke one stanchion wire, had my hand unoperative for a day, got a pump on my knee (still sore), wind wane and Autohelm broke. Turned back N and reached Barbados 12.22. Getting now a new wire and continuing to Martinique in 10 days where my wive is joining for a month and we do sailing in no wind since she would not sail in wind. Things are here 2 x more expensive than in Las Palmas. Saw to-day 20,000 black faces and 5 white. My congratulations to you for reaching Brazil and HAPPY NEW YEAR. Take care.

With best regards

Matti Lappalainen

Sun 04/01/2004 02:14

Dear Matti,

Really sorry to hear about your injuries, and the ship's troubles too.....it could happen to any of us at any stage, but I'm really pleased you got out of it one piece.....

For example, within a few days of a great friend arriving in Barbados, a nasty storm came and he ended up washed ashore....hull damaged, lost rudder, broken propeller, and heaven only knows what damage inside.........I know Dick and Pat on "Mad River" very well, (we were neighbours for 2 months), and I know them always to do things correctly, but it still caught them.......

So I sympathise with your accident in foul weather, Matti...I myself got hammered at around 6 north, in the biggest thunderstorm I've ever seen.....6 hours hove-to under deeply reefed sails...I must have been scared because it's the only time I've put on my survival-suit at sea...actually slept in it too....I'd already lost a mainsheet winch over the side near Santiago Island, Cap Verdes in big seas......

Anyway, we are still alive!........I arrived in Salvador, Brazil 12 hours ago....all well, but I'm not ready to face the "Costumes and Intimidation" (Customs and Immigration) nor the "Marmite" police (Maritime police) yet...........still at anchor behind the breakwater in strong wind, hoping the anchor holds, because there is a concrete wall close to leeward.........

Stay Well and Safe, Matti, and enjoy the Caribbean!

All the very Best for 2004!

Tuesday'n'me.

(RECEIVED)Mon 05/01/2004 17:30

Hey doc

I was monitoring your position on the ssb. You overtook me in the doldrums, I had absolutely no wind and spent Xmas day on the equator!! When I got through the doldrums it was like you said, I should have been further East, I was hard on the wind all the way till almost opposite Recife. Phoned home on Xmas day and found out that my mother is quite seriously ill. She had a fall and a bllod clot has formed next to her brain and they are in two minds wether to operate. since then she has had a couple of mild strokes, they think because they took her off the blood thinnign tablets. It doesn't sound too good so I diverted to Recife to be near an airport sooner. I'm still hear and will stay until I'm sure my mother is off the danger list and will then head back north to be nearer the uk. sakvador will have to wait.Hope you had a great Xmas and new Year and have a great time in the rest of your atlantic circuit. Please keep in touch we may both be in the azores at the same time and I'd like to pick your brains about my boat. she is set up for racing and there are a few things I'd like to change but could do with someone who knows contessa's to bounce ideas off.

safe sailing .. take care

bill

"British Tiger"

Wed 07/01/2004 05:17

Dear Bill'n'Buddy,

WARMEST CONGRATS ON A DIFFICULT PASSAGE!! .....(well, I personally didn't find it at all easy)...

Thanks for letting me know ......and my sincerest wishes for your Mum....I know I would have diverted similarly in the same circumstances......Shame, but I too have learnt how important ones relatives are......

Got to Salvador on 2/1/04....anchored just where we agreed, stayed there 3 days cos I just wasn't in the right frame of mind to meet the Natives yet (paddled ashore briefly once to dump the trash)...bit of a dirty old rathole to be honest, what with diesel spills, and salvage operations to raise sunken motor-catamaran ......so moved round here today (Tuesday 6/1/04) to the main marina.....it's not bad at all, really.... It takes 3 days to check-in, then I'll start exploring....

Hey, you forgot your copy of "We the Navigators" by David Lewis......I didn't realise until later on the day you left, and so I hoped to pass it to you here in Salvador.......never mind..maybe in the Azores?......Yes I'd like us to keep in touch please.......

Not sure when and where with the Azores yet.....don't want to get there while it's still windy and stormy, but neither do I want to leave it too late for a quiet trip back to UK.......present plan is to leave South Brazil around late March/early April.....then Tristan de Cunha (only if the weather is good).... but hope to be able to stop for 10 days at St.Helena, where I have strong contacts.......Probably not stopping at Ascension except to see it in passing (doesn't sound very inviting, according to the guides)...

So, maybe middle of June before I get to the Azores?.......my wife and another couple (very close friends) should come out for a holiday there ....hope about 6 weeks stop there.......and then the girls fly home, and the two boys bring the ship back to the UK.......

That's the rough battle-plan anyway.......too early to know how your own plans will shape up, I know, but it might give a framework to think on?...........

By the way, I've never met them, but three people on a Norwegian(?) yacht called "ROZINANTE" (not sure of the spelling) are heading to Recife from Fernando de Noronha......I spoke to them quite a bit by Hamradio.....his name is Staale.....not sure of boatsize, but I think around 32'....just another contact if you need it...

Incidentally, Matti on "Snoopy" got knocked about at 5 north..... smashed a hand (which repaired itself), damaged his leg, wrecked both of his selfsteering gears, and lost a stanchion lifeline.....sensibly turned right, is now in Barbados safely, having given up the idea of Brazil...will stay in the Caribbean for some months........

Anyway, GREAT to hear you're well.....keep in loose touch if poss?.....

Take Care, Stay Safe,

PS. Tsunamis working very well indeed.....can't thank you enough...

Doc

Sun 04/01/2004 02:15
Dear Ron and Bonnie,

I was really gutted about the news of Mad River ......It was horrible waiting to know if Dick and Pat were OK..........I hope I never have to wait like that again......

Would you be sure to let them know how many of us there are backing them up?.......it could have been any of us...........even Matti, my Finnish friend, got hammered near the equator, and had a damaged hand and foot, broken self-steering, lost a stanchion...so much so he turned right for Barbados, instead of coming here to Brazil........look for a white, steel cutter-rigged yacht called "Snoopy".........

Would you mind passing on my thanks to Sally, please?.....she made some apple sauce for me before we left Rubicon, and I celebrated New Year in style with apple-and-whipped cream......tasted wonderful!.......especially after some of my cooking efforts before............and, does she want the glassjar back again??.....if so, come and collect it!

Loved your Email!......laughed my head off!...............(I'm afraid I only received it this evening when I got time to look after arriving in Salvador 12 hours ago)............any cooking of mine which makes a bid for freedom gets scraped up and put straight back in the pan again (though to be truthful, that didn't happen on this last trip at all......must be my cremating efforts slowing the escapees down a bit......epoxy-substitute, cos it sticks to the pan, like sh*t to a shovel)...........

Sorry about your hands Ron.......spoils your day a bit, that........and the next few days too.......been there...........I sympathise Sir!

Meantime, life goes on.......more news soon....have a cold beer for me!...........

Take good care of yourselves,

Doc.

---PS. By the way, the French Armada to the Amazon (with "Skimmer", Charlotte and Hayward) are here, in a marina, but I'm not in the mood to meet them yet.........

(RECEIVED) Mon 05/01/2004 15:10
Subject: congrats!

Hello our friend,

Hopefully you will get this upon your arrival to Salvador and let us say CONGRATULATIONS!!!!!! YIPEEEE!! YOU DID IT!!!

How was your apple tart (you nerd!) GLad you had a nice New Year's. We had a very quiet one on the boat, but were able to enjoy the great fireworks that went off the beach at about 10 minute intervals, so we had fireworks for 40 minutes straight. It was, again, bittersweet, because we had lunch with the Mad River's...... trying hard to laugh and make things light, but it was difficult.......they are moving on, but everytime you look at Mad River's side it makes your heart sink. It is reparable, fortunately, and the rudder needs to be replaced, but it certainly wasn't how they intended to spend New Years Eve in Barbados.

Anyway, CONGRATS again on your next leg of your journey, you are an amazing man. Did you get to spend

Christmas on the equator? It sounded as if you were below the equator before christmas and went back up again.

We got coal in our stockings!

We love and miss you and are listening to your continued voyage. Be careful and mind your back.

Piss off now, **Capt. Ron & Bonnie**

Wed 07/01/2004 05:17

Dear Ron'n'Bonnie,

And a Very Happy New Year to you two "Bar-Stewards" too! Your Email made me laugh out loud, and so I am comfortably p*ssed off now, thank you!

I dearly wish I could help with Dick'n'Pat's problems, but I would only make it even more emotional and worse .... Please be sure to let them know how I'm thinking of them a lot.....it could have been any of us.....

Really pleased you're both safe......couldn't rest easily till I knew......soppy, isn't it.....

Got to find a doNiMoes set......gone and got withdrawal symptoms from it now!......Raise a glass to "Southern Friends" when you next play?...

Hope you're getting a copy of "Dear Everybodies" ship's updates........if not, let me know.......but they might be a bit long for you, with big words, so if you can't handle them just shout "STOP!"

Hope Ron's hands are better, and that the Shinglythingy isn't being too post-herpetic......

Stay Safe, both of you, ...and don't play with anything sharp or pointed, will you....bad for your eyes, cos it makes them water...........(bit like my cooking).....

Missing all of you lot,

Warmest Wishes!,

Tuesday'n'doc.

PS. What HAVE you done to the Full Moon?........it's upside down..... and it goes the wrong way (to the NORTH i.e.)

(RECEIVED) Mon 05/01/2004 21:00

Subject: BRAZIL NUT

Well thought I`d just pop in and say hello ! Below freezing outside , the tobogan run is going well and when I`m whizzing down the mountain or taking Zap for nice walks in deep snow , I do occasionaly think of you . Brings back lots of memories you being where you are , shame I can`t just pop over for a weekend ....

Is there still a funiculaire ? If there is I will think of you on yours when I`m on mine , although I seem to remember using a public lift most of the time.

ALL THE BEST !! Don`t forget to wear some clothes when you go ashore , otherwise the pick-pockets will have to get very friendly to see where you hide your money ....

Incidently I remember that a lot of the young men had very long nails with colourless nail polish ....maybe it helps them to slip their hands in places easily. **LOVE MARY.**

Wed 07/01/2004 05:25

Mary,

Watcha,

Yup, the funiculthingy is still here..........haven't been up it yet, nor down it even, but I'll try to make a pilgrimage to it before I leave to explore around ARATU (a bay 10 miles NORTH of here, but still in the Bay of Toddy Saints) in a few days....said to speak English there, and there used to be a strong medical complement in the Local IATE CLUB.......might be useful to me, so I ought to have a look really.......

Enjoy the snow!..it's 37 inside the insulated cabin here...I wonder if Mother would mind if I took my thermals off now..I think it's probably safe to do so.....maybe not for the neighbours though.....(Heck, I could murder a ice-cold beer right now!).....

Toodle-oo fer now!,

Fungus-Face.

(RECEIVED)Wed 07/01/2004 09:49

Hi Doc

Good to hear all the news about your trip & adventures, you cannot imagine how I do understand you, having the adventure of your life and enjoying it!!!

Did I ever tell you that I had a solo motorbike trip for 13 month back in 1992/93 through south America? does good to the should and hope one day to be able to sail across the ocean also.

Brazil.... take care it is very dangerous and even the friendliest people will try to rob you, it is common to rob / abuse / take advantage of foreigners. this is more or less socially acceptable, do not forget it is mostly a slave race and some of the whites are descendants of fugitives who fled to a lawless place to hide!

Do try the coconuts (green) they chop the top off them and you get a straw into it too drink the milk, it is quite refreshing and very safe. I used to drink a few daily while in there.

Another thing you might want to try is sugar cane juice, very sweet but works magic, used it as aphrodisiac in my old days!

Mangoes are great, try too buy yourself a big fat juicy one, bite the tip off it and just press with both hands too bet the pulp up the hole into your mouth... well I always found fruits erotic anyway!

What are your plans like? pls let me know what's up and where are you planning to go from there, when etc...

Miss u

Chris & Tashi

Sat 03/01/2004 01:42

Dear Trudi,

"G0CBE"...(Charlotte, Ben, and Ellen...my children...I had to wait quite some time to be allocated this particular callsign....but they themselves insist it's just "Chips, Beans and Eggs!")....

This is just one way of saying "Thank You" for all the support and help you and Gerard and Jack and Tom, and all the others, have given me on my trip-of-a-lifetime....I wonder if you appreciate just how powerful is the reassurance that a radio contact gives...not just for the weather and Shiptrack.....

And this is also just to put a "face" to the voice.....

I've been sailing since before I could walk.....anything that floats.......given a good example by my Dad and an uncle (both still alive and well in their late 80s).....I decided I was going to do this journey even while I was still at school, my sister keeps reminding me.....

I retired in June 2002 after 32years in medicine in the English NHS.....immediately sailed "Tuesday" up the western coast of Norway, into the Arctic, as a shake-down-cruise, to catch the midnight sun .... successfully, crouching under a glacier in bright sunlight, at midnight(!), hacking off ice-samples with a screwdriver to put in urine-specimen-pots to give to friends at home as mementos......(well, they could always re-freeze them, couldn't they?).....

"Tuesday of Rochester" was a Thames Sailing Barge (90 feet long, carried about 120 tons of general cargo, built in 1883), now just a wreck in some saltings on the UK east coast at Orfordness (but even today you can still make out her name on the remains of her transom) ..how she ended up as a wreck in Orford is a story in itself! ....When I was a small boy I used to row my dinghy through her bones at high-water...........and I have incorporated some of her original timbers into the renovation of this present vessel, so that she still lives on........The registered name of my ship is actually "Tuesday of Ore" (from the River Ore, which also gives the village of Orford its name).......There's a whole lot more information which ties it all together, but you get the gist of it at least?....

The present day "TUESDAY" is a single masted sailing yacht....Boomed-staysail-cutter-rig .....centre- cockpit Rival 41 with a small steel bowsprit....British built in 1975.....43ft overall....approx 14 tons displacement......over the last 6 years I've been completely renovating her, including my own redesign of her new mast and rigging (gives her 38% more sail area).......everything is worked manually (no power-assist), so it's all a bit "physical".......only me on board, and I'm not a very big feller, so I have to use my brain a bit... but on the other hand I needed everything to be repairable with a screwdriver and a piece of string........

This present trip has been UK-Portugal-Porto Santo-Madeira-Lanzarote-Cap Verdes-Salvador so far....now hoping to explore the SE coast of Brazil before continuing to Tristan de Cunha Island-St. Helena Island-Ascension Island-Azores, and finally back to the UK and my family next summer.........(I do hope I'm not going to regret missing out St.Peter and St.Pauls Rocks, and Fernando de Noronha, but I was so worried about being swept too far west, like some of the old sailing-ships)..... St. Helena has always been rather special due to our deep family friendship with the Spens family, of whom Teresa was instrumental in setting up the Social Services/Red Cross on the Island ....she's still invited back there every year.....so to be able to sail there has always had a sort of very personal interest for me....

Oh, nearly forgot.....radio here is only 8-10 watts output (I'm severely limited on power (from wind and sun!)).....into a 5 metre piece of domestic wire rammed up inside a plastic 5 metre fishing-rod, the counterpoise being the insulated metal supports for the 4 metre radar mast it's mounted on.....seems to work well on all ham bands between 7MHz to 52MHz with only a small amount of antenna-tuning for each band...........my experiments with insulated mast-stays, suspended end-fed-coax-dipoles, loaded whips, etc, were not as successful as this very primitive set-up, so I daren't alter it!......

Sorry...waffled on a bit...everyone loves talking about themselves!....

Warmest Best Wishes!, and grateful thanks again,

Tuesday'n'me, (Docdavid).

PS. Please feel free to copy this to the others, if you would?..Thanks!

(RECEIVED)Tue 06/01/2004 02:55

Dear David,

Sorry I have not had a chance before to tell you how how very much I enjoyed reading your delightful story about how you came about to be on this trip, especially as it materialized so soon after you had arrived in Salvador, like magic. And yes, I can imagine it took a while to get the "Chips, Beans (why not Bacon? But my thoughtful son ventured that maybe they are vegetarians?) and Eggs" callsign.

You have been doing a fair bit of sailing with "Tuesday" by now, from the Arctic to the Equator is no mean feat, and now I can see that you had good reasons for being at 00° for Christmas Day. "Tuesday" is a splendid name, especially with all those firm ties and memories of some time back for you. And you sound very happy with her, too.

I do hope we can stay in touch with you most of your trip from now on. Gerard probably has the best chance, the Bulge of Brazil tends to get in the way of radio signals from this QTH, unless conditions are excellent, and they have not been. But your signal has always been marvellous, which always shows that power is not everything, and amuses Jack no end! That and the very efficient antenna system you have put together - may it continue to give you good service! I have talked to people at Tristan , so don't give up on us, it will work from time to time, if not always. And yes, I did send on your letter to Jack, Gerard and Doug, you may have had responses by now.

Fair Winds, and best 88 from **Trudi**

Wed 07/01/2004 05:17

Dear Everybodies,

Salvador has its own micro-climate....calm mornings, windy afternoons (force 6)......cleaned the hull up a bit from the "Green Bladder" inflatabubble, and was intrigued to find healthy barnacles growing 14" above the waterline where her quarter wave had been for 4 weeks....quite pleased by it really, cos it shows I'd been pushing her a bit.......

So, at dawn today, Tuesday 6/1/04, moved from the smelly harbour anchorage (much spilt diesel, some from salvage work on a sunken motorcatamaran which was successfully raised....(all on video, as usual!)....also, spring tides are coming, and there wouldn't have been a whole lot of deeps at low-water......)......came into the main marina here, against my ideals, but it's not too bad at all!.....interesting mooring up Bows-on-to-pontoon, stern to ropes from the seabed, but didn't hit nor frighten anyone, with marina staff help (non-english-speaking)......and I'm back on 250v powersupply from crockclips onto overhead power-cables..(well, it makes for a good story!).......Electricity is "free", but water is guarded carefully (lock, key, and meter).........but I feel safe at last!....

Tried to clear with Costumes-and-Intimidation today.....NO chance!.....after walking miles as directed by Pilot Book and locals, spent five-and-3/4 hours queuing in the Police Federal office...was given a number (09, or was it 60?)....met lots of interesting people (a pair of Botanists, a gaggle of American Bible-Bashers (sorry, Missionaries), etc.etc...........eventually to be told (kindly translated by other "victims") I should be presenting myself in another office I'd already been to early this morning......(just like an NHS Casualty Dept I think?)...........actually it was most interesting, studying the faces, etc, and being retired means I've got TIME ......and it's their country anyway....... so stood around patiently trying to find a cooling breeze from somewhere...............and I'll try again tomorrow..............

Found a Bank......it grudgingly gave some Brazilian doodahs (lots of them).....by then I was VERY thirsty and hungry, (plus begging for Vitamin C and Folates)........ so found a street market and bought them out of melons and grapes......two frozen pork-chops from a garage(!)........really BEAUTIFUL they tasted back on the ship.........but I suffered all sorts of nasty muscle cramps and muscle twitches, till it dawned on me it was SALT depletion due to the heat.....(and boy, was it HOT...90% humidity and a cabin temp of 37 C).......cured within 10-15 minutes of taking salt......never had THAT before!........

So......certainly missing all my chums from Rubicon.......a bit isolated at present, but everyone I've met who speaks English has been very kind and helpful.........Planning to refill ship's supplies a bit, then to scratch the surface of this vast estuary for a week or so.......get away from the city etc...

More soon........

Bye for now!

Love from **Tuesday'n'me.**

(RECEIVED) Thu 08/01/2004 03:34

David.....

How wonderful to get your mails.

Regarding the salt depletion.... I have seen this before. We had a chief engineer who got so confused that when they found him he was smoking cigarettes in an empty fuel-oil tank.

Not really any other news, except that Mother and Rosalie seem to be neck and neck in learning about computers. My most often used phrase, and Gerald's I believe, is "Don't ask me.... try it and see!"

Take care. **D.**

(RECEIVED) Wed 07/01/2004 22:40

David,

It was a great relief to look at my flat top and to find the letter from Doc David to Daddy and me. Bless you! Since you hadn't been in Salvador very long I thought you might be feelig a bit lost since the rest of your bunch had dispersed over the ocean and neither of the two you had hoped to meet up with had arrived, so it was good to know you are O.K.-----I hope! I imagined you could be feeling a bit flat and weary when you must have been under stress for so long and then suddenly, at long last, you realised that you had achieved your unimaginable ambition. Probably it would take some time to sink in and in the meantime there would be umpteen official chores to do. When they are finally done it is to be hoped you will be able to really rest and relax and take in what a truly terrific voyage you and Tuesday have done. Just imagine, she was anchored at Orford, Suffolk, England and now you are both in Salvador, Brazil, South America. CRIKEY!!

We are sorry for Bill and Buddy and hope you do meet up later.

Your salt shortage sounds horrid. During the war (WW2) one thing which wasn't rationed was fish and chips and rumour had it this was because the miners ate this a lot and it was a source of salt which they were short of working in heat and sweating under ground. If you have ever been down a pit as I have it was ghastly. The only light was the lamp we each carried and the heat and dust was awful. Seeing men lying flat in tunnels only just wide enough enough for their bodies chipping away at the coal made one realise what we owed to them for our warm fires. There were no pithead baths in those days and the men coming home would literally be coal black. We were used to that sight and never thought anything about it but when we went down the mine we really realised what sort of lives they lead. The ponies were all in small stalls except those which were actually pulling the tubs.

Well, well! How on earth have I got from hot and humid Brazil to hot and humid Yorkshire minefields!

Heaps and heaps of love, from **Mother.**

Fri 09/01/2004 23:46

Dear Everybodies,

Finally managed to get my passport stamped legally......simply by sitting on the relevant doorstep in the baking sun with a good book to read for an hour and a half, until the Federal Policeman arrived...... and then being "sickbag" nice about it....probably thought I was a poof, so he rapidly signed and stamped everything in sight, to get rid of me, quick.....90 day visa....perfect!....all I have to do now is go back to him to check-OUT from Salvador again in 3 days time.......(but maybe it's just the same for linguistically-challenged-foreigners coming into the UK?).....

After precautionary practice with a dictionary("I learn it from a book" as Manuel said to Mr. Faulty) managed to survive my first true conversation in Portuguese.....no doubt some of what I said will have puzzled them a bit, but it produced the desired results....very few people here speak English, French, Maltese, Latin or Morse-code, so I've been a bit stumped at times..... a local lad, working on rich peoples' boats here, likes to practise his English with me each day.............and I'm sure one street fruit-seller thinks I'm dumb.. literally......seemed very sympathetic about it...

Made a mistake three days ago.....gave some grapes to some undernourished streetchildren....instantly surrounded by at least 10 of them leaping and grabbing for more.....ideal time for pickpockets, but I escaped with a small degree of dignity, pockets intact...shan't do that again though, I'm sorry to say......

Ben Johnston's son, Steven, was in Salvador.....I'd forewarned the guard to let him know he was expected, but the note Steven left for me wasn't delivered till long after it ceased to be relevant......great shame, that...would have been really fun to meet up again....

Today met two Belgians (father and son) hauling their french-built steel 39' yacht out for repairs....jammed centreboard....but Salvador is as far south as they're going....they're joining the french rally of 26 boats......Brazilian gunboat escort up the Amazon I gather.........and now another Froggy boat is alongside...nice chap, looking for a crew.....his 46' aluminium boat's not even finished yet, as he had to take it away from the French builders while they were going bust...so his Atlantic crossing must have been "interesting"......he's also in the Amazon Armada.....

Taxi into town today, where bought out the whole supermarket, to reprovision...taxi was airconditioned..(nice!).........the heavily laden ride home was in an older machine.....to keep cool the driver held a 2ft by 2ft curved piece of cardboard out of the window to redirect the slipstream....heavy traffic made him busy, as he kept running out of hands.........

So...she's fully topped-up with water and food again, repairs all done ...... (incidentally, the modifications to the Aries selfsteering gear, and to the towed-generator worked well, as did the swinging seat, and a substantial anti-"crash" rope running fore-and-aft in the saloon) ....quite surprised really.......just need to navigate through the Police Federal again, top-up the diesel tanks, and then I can go out to play.........Planning to spend at least another week exploring this VAST estuary/bay of All Saints, having a gentle sailing holiday instead of all that "butch" stuff.......but it may be a bit too windy to reverse out of here tomorrow.....

Very poor radio signals in here, so no daily contact home........and I've come to realise just how exceptional were the friends I met in Rubicon, and how supportive they were to me.....I dearly miss them now.............I plan to keep in touch by Email, but it's not quite the same..........

All the very Best!

Stay Warm(!)

Love from **Tuesday'n'me.**

Sat 10/01/2004 03:56

Dear Chris'n'Tashi,

Hey, it really did me good to get your Emails!.....you've no idea how it suddenly broke down the false wall of adrenaline I've been living on for nearly 2 months......I'd bought a CD of really lovely gentle BossaNova by Galcosta today (happened to hear it by chance while going past a shop)....after my supper I put on my headphones (it's even better music than I'd hoped).....opened up the computer......then to open your Emails.............result?.......(I ought to be embarrassed to admit it).....sitting here in front of the screen with uncontrolled silent tears running down my face.....smiling too..... happiness?..relief?.....definitely not sadness.......but certainly the first time I've "let go" since I left your beautiful island, for sure.....most unBritish, but honest.............

.......so just so you know how much I value your friendship and support.......

(I wonder if I'll ever have the courage to send this?)

All repairs here finished (I enjoy that sort of work on boats), ship's stores refilled, for the next bit.....but first going to take a holiday by quietly exploring some of the rivers of this vast bay .....at my own speed..... sleeping a lot.....eating red meat and green vegetables and fruit....funny how Mother Nature tells you the right thing to do, isn't it.....

Take good care of you both,

Doc.

(RECEIVED)Sat 10/01/2004 16:04

HIIIIIIIIIIII! Happy New Year! Glad to hear that you managed to make it over the Atlantic safely. Was very sorry to hear that some of the other boats & crew hadn't got away with their trips quite as lightly as you had. Brings it home a little when you hear others haven't had a good time. But hoping that you continue to stay safe.

Keep yourself safe, Ju sends her love (saw her last w/e). We're all very proud of all that you're achieving, but always remember we're here if you want to come home from boating for a bit. Looking forward to hearing more,

LOVE **Tot xx.....**

Sun 11/01/2004 02:02
Dear Everybodies,

The Federal Police chap greeted me like a friend, (though maybe it was because I would be leaving his "patch" and he couldn't wait to see me go?)....it might have helped that I complimented him on his nice new car outside, which made him glow with pride.........so no problem checking out of Salvador at all, much to my surprise......got a nice new piece of paper to show the authorities in Rio......

Didn't bump into anything getting out of the marina, via the fuel-pontoon, even though it involved some tight manoeuvring ......(it's difficult to be at both ends of the boat at the same time.....one of these days I'm going to try doing it with my eyes OPEN)........the ship carries 600 litres of fuel, yet had only used 72 litres since Lanzarote, which pleased me ...it means that in flat water she has a range of over 1400 miles under power alone......a nice additional safety feature...

And only 40 litres of drinkingwater used in the same time.......gives me a bit more confidence for the long trips ahead, after Easter..........the ship has 600 litres in her tanks at present, most of it still the clean, clear, Madeira water.......

Really enjoyed sailing in flat water today, with more shy Harbour Porpoises......... tacking up against the strong wind through a narrow channel fringed with mangroves and palm trees.......to end up at anchor in this land-locked lagoon, 3-and-a-half miles long by 1 mile wide, totally surrounded by low, wooded hills....... water is mostly about 15' deep (except where I VERY nearly beached myself on a TREE....mangrove islands don't show on the echo-sounder till it's too late!....just in time saw the tops of its branches flush with the highwater, when a boatslength away, about 500 yards from the shore......that's yet another thing we don't get much of in East Anglia!)...

Friendly warm greetings by two locals who motorboated out to say Hello, then another visitation, this time from Eduardo (originally from Rio), who is married to an English girl, both now living here for 25 years....he commented that to get a job in this area is like "being given a job in paradise"...he loves this part of Brazil, and I can see why......says he'll come back tomorrow "to show me off to his friends" (but I think I'll try a duck out of that!)....

Still can't believe it...."mangroves", "palm trees", "lagoon", "overhead sun", etc.....how quickly we adapt to accepting new things around us......it doesn't seem possible "Tuesday" is the same boat as normally swings on her mooring in Orford..........no pearl-white beaches yet, but who knows what's round the corner?.......

Best Wishes!

Love, **Tuesday'n'me.**

(RECEIVED)Wed 14/01/2004 14:56
Subject: HAPPY WHATEVER

Hi there our friend,

Good to hear from you, and we are enjoying the "dear Everybodies"-printing them out & sharing them with friends. Sounds like you are getting into the Customs things- I do believe that most customs officers have had frontal lobotamies-a pre req. for applying.

Getting used to life at the dock, sails getting repaired, etc. Even bought a really ugly island made man-animal looking thing, mon!

Free spirit is in Tobago, Hula is in Marigot, Pendragon is here, Mad River still getting repairs done, but chugging along. Everyone says Hi to you and sends best regards.

Capt. Ron growing his hair long and saying things like"Don't worry, be happy!"

We truly miss you and keep praying for your safety.

Hope the portuguese lessons are going ok, we are laughing at the idea of you speaking any other language but proper english.

Have you been diving??

We'll write again later.

*Love, Capt. **Ron & Bonnie***

Sun 11/01/2004 23:06

Dear Gerard,

Very poor propagation to and from Salvador I'm afraid, but I'm doing my best!......maybe things will improve away from the city.......I do hope so, when I start south towards Rio, probably in 10-14 days time, when I've explored some of this vast estuary here.....you've already gathered that I moved from Salvador itself on Saturday 10/1/04, and am now at anchor in a landlocked 3miles x 1mile lagoon, 10 miles up the north end of this huge expanse that is Salvador harbour.....very pretty, mangroves and palm trees, surrounded by low wooded hills......heavy thunderstorms, but always warm......(VERY warm!).......and the flat seawater makes an excellent ground plane for the antenna, too...... I haven't been ashore here at the lagoon, but friendly people all around.......

I'm hoping I can contact Staal (LA7GZ/MM) again, because I thought he said he would be coming this way along the coast.......if you should hear him at all I'd be most grateful if you would let him know I'm looking for him?..........Thanks!....

I thoroughly enjoy the Maritime Mobile Nets...makes a lot of difference to a singlehander....and it's a fascinating way of watching the changes of propagation from day to day...much more interesting than monitoring the beacons!......It seems a long time ago that you picked up my weak signals (for which my grateful thanks) when I was 200 miles off the Portuguese coast last August...I was using a centre-loaded whip at that time..it worked but nothing like as well as the present fishing rod....

Once again, my sincerest thanks to you all for all the time and dedication you all put into these nets.....I'm constantly surprised at the accuracy of the weather forecasts you read..... and they've made quite a difference to my strategy each day while at sea........

Also, it's comforting for me to known that my family and friends are watching Shiptrak, because it gets a bit frightening out here sometimes........I need all the reassurance I can get!....

From all of us out on the ocean, including all those hundreds of listeners (I've spoken to quite a few of them)...we are all very grateful.....

May your shadow never grow less, Sir!

Tuesday'n' Docdavid.

PS.I'm sorry I'm not very good at compressing pictures, but this gives an idea of the ship, at least...fishing rod antenna wasn't up when this piccie taken in Porto Santo.......

Fri 16/01/2004 10:57

Dear Everybodies,

Spent 48 hours at anchor in the very protected lagoon at ARATU...... sleeping, reading, checking and repairing/improving things (found several things which might have failed in due course, all now corrected).....I think the natives were a bit puzzled by my not going ashore and not using any services of the Yacht Club.....antisocial, some singlehanders are......I feel a bit ashamed.......but Tuesday was the biggest boat there, and one of only two to manoeuvre under sail alone...............

Sometimes it's a bit lonely, but only occasionally....... amazing how a language barrier isolates you......(pity I've not learnt enough Portuguese yet).....strange that out at sea it's never lonely at all.........seems the wrong way round......

This Bay of All Saints, Salvador, is an exceptional place.........very glad I came here..........imagine the Walton Backwaters, on the English East Coast, only 30 miles x 30 miles bigger......islands and creeks galore.....and today came across the classical unexpected-deserted-white-sand-beach-fringed-with-palm-trees....total surprise!....and no-one around, either...very pretty indeed............one could easily spend a whole season exploring round here ...it would be a lovely relaxing holiday....

So now Tuesday is at anchor in the shelter of another beautiful hilly island covered with trees, 150 yards off a small white beach......palms and mangroves......no habitation for a mile or two......a little concerned that it's a bit off the beaten track, but worth it I think......(had sailed carefully round an area on the chart marked as "unsurveyed" to get here...didn't have the courage to survey it myself, this far from home......)

When they have a thunderstorm here they do it in style!........4 of them over the last 3 days, each one very big and powerful indeed.......actually measured, in a bucket, 3" of rainfall in 30 minutes yesterday.....almost as much again today.........topped up all the water-containers I could with the stuff (cos it's FREE).........it tastes a bit "bland", but it's spotlessly clean.......used the torrential downpours for showers/washing as well..... pleasantly cooling for when the overhead sun comes out again after the rain.......................I don't know yet if this is typical weather for round here, but I suspect it is........flat calm by the early hours, hot but very still mornings, then all hell breaks loose in the afternoons....."equatorial" weather......

Don't know how I've managed to get through life without eating a really fresh Mango before....... absolutely mouthwatering! ......it puts peaches, apricots, and nectarines to shame..........haven't yet fathomed out how to eat one without needing a bath afterwards, though Chris in Rubicon recommends biting off the end and sucking out the nectar inside............Now looking to try a green coconut, and a drinking straw to stick in it........

All the Best!
Tuesday'n'me.

Chapter 5

Back to Salvador

Text message sent (on a damaged mobile-phone) at 1815 hrs 13th January 2004

"5 mins ago ship struck by lightning. All electrics u/s but ship and crew intact. Strong smell of burning but luckily no fire now. Will need a few days to sort. Love"

(and later)

"Two electrical fires in cabin had self-extinguished. All electronics burnt out. Muscles ache cos I got hit too. Feel shaky but OK. Love"

Fri 16/01/2004 10:58
Subject: Nasty Whizzbang (i)
Dear Everybodies (sorry it's so impersonal, but ....),
Some of you already know, but at 1806hrs 13/1/04, three days ago, while at anchor tucked tight in a bay under the hills of "Cow Island", in another torrential afternoon rainstorm, there was a colossal "CRACK!", so loud it blew your senses, with extreme bright light both in and outside the cabin.....it is impossible for words alone to describe how unspeakably VIOLENT it was ....so instantaneous, so mind-numbing, so disabling.........immediately noticed the strong smell of burning, smoke in the cabin, smoke detector screaming away at me, and grasped that we'd had a direct hit by lightning....

Interesting how logical one can be even when you're very scared .... I remember clearly my first thought was "am I alright?" (answer, "I think, therefore I must be")..........next, "forget the smoke, is the ship intact?", so ripped up the floor boards where the transducers are, to find we're not going to sink immediately (I was going to ram her up the beach if we had been).......then, "kill all electrics, to stop the fire", so threw the two master switches to isolate the batteries, and disabled that bl**dy smoke detector (dammit, I can SEE there's smoke, for God's sake)........Ah, that's better, less smoke already, I can see roughly where it's coming from....wiring locker under the companionway... have a look ....good, no flames now at least.....

"Now what do I do?", (answer, "let them know your safe").....so quickly text'd the family....(never occurred to me to doubt the phone would work, although it's settings were all gone to pot)........ "what do I do now?", as it is obvious the ship has been very badly hurt...........then I noticed the cuts on my feet from walking around in all the bits of glass and plastic from burst fuses etc....picked pieces out of them, and cleaned the floor a bit.....still the foul stink of burnt plastic and rubber insulation material...

I could feel, very close to me, this black well of deep, deep despair, which I knew would disable me unless I was very careful indeed.......nauseating, twists-your-guts-up, worse than seasickness......and I was very aware that I was miles off the beaten track, 6000 miles from home............. but it's remarkable how all those years of Onsite Trauma Care experience surface when you need them.........go back to basics......like, decide what's important/urgent and do that, now......if you can't decide, then don't worry about it, just do what's in front of you, now....you can't do everything, so do what you think you can......And I realised that I'd already bought myself TIME, so that I could begin to plan logically...

So, to cut a very long story short, by assuming EVERYTHING was wrecked, anything that worked was a bonus to smile on.......first found that batteries were still alive (though all voltmeters/ammeters were blown), and a few circuits were still viable.....next was to try to actually replenish the batteries, so managed to get the wind-generator functioning.....found the sources of two separate fires, both caused by shortcircuits from melted insulation or blown diodes ...both would have been very serious if I hadn't thrown the master-switches .....keep checking the bilges....main engine alternator diodes are destroyed, but thanks to Peter's advice there is a spare alternator on board...

Ah, now we're getting somewhere....we have an intact hull, a mast, sails, an engine and (amazingly) two means of producing electricity.......now put some food in yourself even though you still feel so desperately sick ... and you're going to have to make yourself rest soon..... and keep planning the next stages, to ward off that awful, incapacitating, frightening, terrible black hole of despair just behind your shoulder..............

(More to Follow)
Tuesday'n'me.

Fri 16/01/2004 10:59
Subject:Nasty Whizzbang(ii)
Dear Everybodies,

I have to confess that while waiting for my supper to cool that night, before I could attack it, I had a few minutes sitting down with nothing to do.....it totally broke me................sitting at the table, head in hands... heavy tears... guilt...("why the hell didn't I anchor half a mile away" and "there must have been SOMETHING I should have done to avoid it")...it didn't last long, but it wasn't nice............not nice at all...

Then logic takes over...take a seasick pill and a slug of booze (never done THAT medicinally before) to make sure you rest.....kept waking up ("oh no it's happening AGAIN!") as I relived that terrible noise and light, over and over..... painful aching muscles, mainly on my right side, and the annoying shakes I'd had since it happened made it gradually dawn on me that it wasn't just the ship which had been hit, but me, physically, too, though no burn marks found ......so a little doubt for a while about whether I was actually functioning OK ......but how would I know?.....and anyway, what other options did I have?.........Keep telling yourself "'Hope' makes a lousy supper, but a good breakfast", so it will all be clearer tomorrow.......

So, plodded on next day (yesterday), cutting out melted wiring, splicing in new....bypassing switches, meters, plugs, sockets, fuse-holders which had failed........restoring power to things, usually to find the electronics were fried anyway..........replacing bulbs, fuses, connectors...."robbing Peter to pay Paul" by recycling whatever I could salvage.....always trying to stick to the essentials first......anything which will produce a functioning ship...........and now I know why I carry all those spares....

In the afternoon a dugout canoe approached (had only seen 2 boats each day I was there) towed by a elderly single cylinder "African Queen" type boat....I came on deck to talk......they anchored close by, and 3 of the 6 men on board paddled over, and very kindly they took pains to prevent the two boats rubbing together....I handed over my prepared written statement in Portuguese about The WhizzBang .....disbelief, then wonder, then concern... was I personally alright?..are you sure?.. come with us to the village for repairs.. is your motor good?.. we could tow you if you like..Ah, Electronics burnt, yes perhaps it's best to head for Salvador..do you have water?..are you quite sure you have food? ..when you leave here, you know there's a big reef/shallows you must avoid? (I did)..you're sure?.......warm handshakes all round.... "Belgian?" (looking at the Red Ensign).."Ah, you're English..good..OK"....all in Portuguese or mime/sign language........only after they were completely satisfied, about 15-20 minutes, that I was alright did they paddle back, up anchor, and putt-putt quietly away, big waving and smiling, having delightedly posed for a photo.......what WONDERFUL people!...heartwarming.......

(Incidentally, dugouts are VERY heavy, but incredibly easy to push through the water..unsinkable too..instantly, I wanted one for myself!...)

Limped the 21 miles back to Salvador today, ...no compass....no self steering (apart from the Aries, which is only really suitable for the open sea)...the cabin still smelling a bit of old burnt plastics .... and everyone I've met here in the main marina has been extraordinarily kind and sympathetic..I think they're amazed I'm still alive...the word got around very quickly..people come to look at the denuded masthead..people who saw me here last week now greet me as a longtime friend..invited to go to a complete strangers's house for a beer and food (tactfully declined..too much to do here, I said..)..charming English cruising couple came "to commiserate, cheer you up, and have a cup of your tea"...really nice, humans can be.......and like a prat I've gone and promised to climb a charming Frenchman's mast to feed a wire for him in two days time....

And the muscle shakes have finally stopped..... in spite of big thunderstorm with winds over 55 knots this evening......I'm clearly going to survive this episode, but NEVER try it yourselves....it's not very pleasant......it really isn't.......

Thanks for "listening",
Stay Safe yourselves!
Love from Tuesday'n'me.

02:58 PM 1/14/2004

Hi Trudi

Not sure if I will be able to make the net tomorrow as I have to go out and am not sure whether I will be back in time.

I had a call from David tonight (1845 hrs UTC) by mobile phone. He has managed to restore some power and is able to generate a little electricity from both the wind generator and the solar panel, and is now able to run the engine having fitted a new alternator. There was a fire, which was quickly extinguished, but has left all the wiring damaged and a smell of burning plastic. Anything with diodes in it has been smashed!! The little bulbs in the compass were blown out of the compass totally!!

Interestingly he is able to receive on the Icom 703 BUT is unable to transmit - he was on the point of calling me when the lightening struck!!! So he had the mic in his hand!! He is very shaken as can be heard in his voice but is recovering well. He has been working flat out all day to get some running repairs done but will be setting off to Salvador (about 16 miles as the crow flies) at dawn tomorrow in the hopes of getting back to the marina, which is a private one to effect the repairs which look like being enormous.

The lightning took out the vhf antenna and the radio completely but, as the hf antenna is at the stern, it seems that one got off lightly. It looks as though he will have to get the ship out of the water at some stage in order to check the hull - he says it was a helleva bang!!!! He needs to check the steering gear etc.

Hope to talk to you tomorrow.

Kind regards

Gerald

14 January 2004 19:50

Subject: Re: David G0CBE

Thank you so much for all that, Gerald.

The most amazing part is that he can receive on the transceiver, that really sounds hopeful. My son Martin came up with a lightning protection he found in one of his many magazines, but a bit like bolting the stable door.....etc........!

That lightning bolt must have come out of a blue sky, as they sometimes do here, too. Or at least a cloud that did not look very threatening.

Would you like to make a sked for a later time tomorrow, if you cannot make it by 14.00Z? We are quite

85

often still there until a bit later, or I could come up for you at a later time. I will forward your letter to Jack, Gerard and Doug, who are all very interested and send best wishes to David, as do I!
     88 – Trudi

Sat 17/01/2004 01:12
    Subject:Nasty Whizzbang(iii)
      Dear Everybodies,

Basically, anything with a diode or transistor in it, even if it was isolated at the time, is dead.......yet some things survived.....quite remarkable what is damaged and what isn't........very similar to blast damage in explosions, where a china ornament can be untouched although the wall round it has collapsed.......for example, the GPS (satellite navigation thingy), right by the main point of entry of the lightning, works almost perfectly, fuses intact.....just needed a few minutes to re-find itself.....the VHF radio beside it is carbonised........the mobile phone works, but had altered several of its settings......all communications receivers dead (even though isolated at the time), yet the little ICOM HamRadio transceiver (which WAS actually running at the time) works perfectly except it won't transmit...........

The computer, which was within 3" of its 12v charger, is undaunted, though it spontaneously ran a full check on itself first, when I switched it on........the charger itself?..very dead and smelly, zero ohms ie. another hot shortcircuit...........

A solar panel, outside in the rain, survived both the BigBang, and the short-circuit fire afterwards, and is now up and running again, with nothing more than a bit of rewiring in the cabin needed ....the towed water-powered generator diodes, at the very backend of the ship, blew, causing the main shortcircuit fire, again in the cabin..

Main ship's compass had two tiny bulbs in it with only thin wiring to them (some still intact).........the two bulbs have been blasted right through the outer case (two "bullet-holes" and a cracked and burst shell), only prevented from going into orbit by a heavy end-of-a-cutdown-fender resting over the top.....and the compass is inaccurate now, but only by about 10 degrees I think........

Fishfinder, echosounder, Navtex, Radio-cassette player, etc. etc. all dead....but radar still works, although its screen is very dim and its night-light doesn't work....(would you believe it, there's even an unused spare one on board!).....

Some fuse-holders are intact, fuse not damaged, but wiring burnt-out either side of it......others just along-side atomised unrecognisably......several fuses are OK, but most disintegrated violently......I suppose it's a bit naive to expect lightning which has just arced across several thousand feet of wet air to be halted by the melting of a thin piece of wire in a glass tube......

On deck I found only one tiny piece of metal from all of the bits and pieces which used to be at the masthead.......antenna, lights, wind indicator....all vanished..................all lights and wiring in the mast dead.....

Yet a small 10amp ammeter, has survived................. bigger, heavier 60A one beside it smashed ....

Some wires look OK.... but when you test them, the wires inside have melted together, so each piece has to be checked first...

Interesting that not a single one of the 29 old-fashioned circuit-breakers tripped....not even one....yet I've checked them since and they still work.....

A light which used to flash red when the cooker gas is "on", is now a steady red light.....it was completely isolated at the time...............and lots more strange oddities......

Over several years of rough weather she's never managed to shake any soot out of the cabin-heater chimney ... yet the shock wave due to the lightning caused a heap of black powder to fall down .... must have been one heck of a Bang ...

I think several things saved her, (and me!) ....I think most of the amazing horsepower of the WizzBang-Beast went down the stays and over the side because it was raining so heavily....and the fact that I had previously altered the echo-sounder transducers to be INTERNAL, instead of sticking out of a hole in the ship's bottom meant the hull integrity survived....the ship being so massively built paid off too....and it is clear now that the two fires self-extinguished because I turned off the master-switches (heaven knows where THAT bit of wisdom came from!) ......

The overall picture now is a bit more encouraging.....she's slowly coming "alive" again, though battered...quite a lady, this ship is...... makes me proud of her.......but she needs a LOT of work to put her right......

As for me personally?.....well, it's quite obvious now that I received a considerable "belt" from the lightning itself, though I didn't realise at the time......all the symptoms of recovering from concussion, with the added fun of the muscle troubles.....now improving, but I feel like I've been hit by a steam-roller...(I'm hoping my internal rewiring has instantly enabled me to speak Portuguese, but no sign of it so far, unfortunately)..............

Sorry, waffled on a bit again!..

Thanks for being there..it really helped when I needed it....

Love from,

Tuesday'n'me.

(RECEIVED)Sat 17/01/2004 06:17

Hi Daddy,

REALLY hope that you're okay. Sorry, but has brought a tear or two to my eye to hear of all that you've had to go through. Tried to speak to Uncle Jonsey, but not quite got through yet; I'm working nights so don't quite have the same sociable hours that others do.

I'm sure others have been sending you similar messages, but Really do hope that you are alright. Wish I was there with you: feel like I should be YOUR parent & protect you from the sometimes mean world & weather. I'm so glad you are okay, & hoping that as each day passes Tuesday can come back to her original self. She has been a great comfort to all us here, knowing that she is cabable of taking you across rough seas & keeping you safe.

Better go as call-bells starting to ring at work. But sending LOTS OF LOVE and looking forward to hearing from you soon.

With loads'a love **TOT** *xxxxxxxxxxxxxxxxxxxxxxx..............*

(RECEIVED)Wed 14/01/2004 12:29

13 clearly your lucky number. To be struck by lightening on the 13th and live to tell the tale is indeed good fortune. However, it is noted that yet another momentous occasion occurred on board "Tuesday" on a Tuesday.

Suggest renaming ship "Blue Moon".

Woddy.

(RECEIVED)Fri 16/01/2004 23:00

SHIT A BRICK you shouldn`t have taken your thermal underwear off ....

Well of course one often thinks of the worst but personally hadn`t thought of THAT happening .Mind you since living over here I have a lot of respect for lightning, in the mountains you feel very exposed and every time it seems that some house is burnt down, it`s usually the cows that get killed but last summer two teenage boys were struck and killed just walking along a road near Geneva. It always happens to someone else so this is *making your trip even more EXCITING, thank you so much ......*

Daddy thinks that you are MARVELOUS, amazing just what lengths one can go to just to gain parental approval ...... Still we all went OOF!! when we realised that you had made it. Those tropical storms are quite something aren`t they? At least you don`t have all the creepy crawlies getting at you and all the sewage running up to your knees ....

Anyway well done for surviving, personally I would have curled up into a twitchy ball and died.........Mother and Daddy were very enthusiastic, Mother keeps saying "Well even if ....well he has already done what he really wanted hasn`t he??"

Had a long chat with Daddy last night, he seems to be younger and younger ....so you may be a physical wreck but you seem to be doing THEM some good .....so you don`t have to come back yet.

Now do try and be careful , you`re supposed to be having FUN......

Cedric has just bought himself (with my Xmas money) an electronic detector so that someone might find him under an avalanche, (bloody hell what a family.)

Fairly warm over here, only -3° C this evening !

Right F......OFF for now ! Incidently last time I told you to F.... OFF I didn`t mean it in THAT way ....

Love **MARY.**

(RECEIVED)Fri 16/01/2004 21:57

Bugger that, David.......whilst reading Wizzbang [!] & [!!] (!=intentional] the hairs on my neck stiffened - Then I had this sudden feeling.... dammed nigh s..t my self.

Re. your final comment, one does not TRY these things. They are out there waiting for a victim....

Remember--- if you attack life sometimes it bites back; you are, and it did!

Keep ducking and diving & stay strong---you have had worse. (and Hello David, from me too)

*I wish we'd stayed on the internet all day and then we wouldn't have just received your Nasty Whizzbang i&ii........I had a job to read it I'm afraid as my eyes were full of tears for you and what you must be going through and how you must be feeling,...........all I could think of was I hope he still some chocolate left...........
I agree with Josephs comments above though...........but I can't think of worse.........can you?.........for days we have been saying we must drop you a line............. I wish it wasn't with a heavy heart...........you really aren't doing what you were told........look after yourself.........are you reprimanded enough now to do that? ....*

To pick up on the rest of your mail the places you have been to do sound marvellous and am quite envious of the warmth and sun, even warm rain...........instead of cold continual cold rain and gales.........snow promised....next week.

Kay & Broyna are always asking after you they pick up bits of information from somewhere and told us you had arrived........would we send their love and kisses to you ....

He's just told me I've got to keep it short......but is there any thing you need and would like sent out there.........please don't be stubborn or hesitate to ask if you need and cannot get.

All our love, keep well, safe and strong ... we need you back home.

Joseph and Joyce

PS. give Tuesday a pat and tell her she's a good girl looking after you and sorry for the pain she has felt....

(RECEIVED)Wed 21/01/2004 13:24

Dear David,

We are sorry to hear about the lightning strike and the difficulty It has caused you and Tuesday . Brenda had just downloaded your Emails as my friend Neil and I were having a cup of tea.

On reading them we realised just how lucky you were, also I know now, that all the careful planning and squirrelling of spares has paid off.

You were also fortunate that although very badly shaken you were able to reason and operate physically to repair some of the damage and get to a safe base. Well done, well done indeed.

Compared to your news, it would seem that what ever happens here now, will be quite mundane, but I am most certainly not volunteering to change places, I do not have that much courage. God continue to give you strength and ability.

Excuse the pun but your e.mails have rather taken the wind out my sails, so will provide you with info. from this end another time.

Please continue to take the greatest care. If help needed from us use Ben as contact.

All the best,

*Love **Bob & Brenda***

(RECEIVED)Sat 17/01/2004 11:47

Hi David,

We are at the London Boatshow but following your narrative with great interest.

Glad to learn that you appear to be OK (I have dealt with quite a few lightning claims over the years and do not recall any personal injuries although it would seem you had more of a shaking than most).

I do know that you will have some very strange things happening with your electronics now ... some stuff recovering only to die again or malfunction.

Have thought about the Faraday cage principle...for example being in the metal body of a car is quite safe...which makes me think of storing loose equipment in the oven when lightning threatens... or even wrapping equipemnt in metal baking foil(?)

All the best from the team.

***Mike and Julie** et al.*

(RECEIVED)Fri 16/01/2004 21:16

Bill

What a terrible mishap for David - and shock for you and Alex. Thank heaven he wasn't knocked out himself and that he wasn't too far from Salvador. Thank you for all the emails etc. Paul doesn't have email but I am keeping him informed. It is good that so many people are rallying around and I hope that all the extensive repairs that will be needed won't hold him up a horrendously long time (he could have done without that regatta). Just one good thought occurs to me. If David feels moved on his return to write a lucrative book/ article - in true Captain Slocum style- about his adventures, this one will surely have pride of place - at least I hope so!

He seems to have coped with it marvellously. Do send best greetings to him from Paul and myself if you are in touch.

Teresa

(RECEIVED)Sat 17/01/2004 03:41

David...

Welcome back from the brink!

If you HAD to be struck, then you did it with all the skill, and flare, necessary to survive it. Reading your Nasty Whizzbangs (1), (2) & (3) fills me with astonishment, bewilderment, humility, and above all an infinite admiration for the way in which you have dealt with the situation. If it had been me, I would probably have got a taxi to the nearest airport and come home to take up stamp collecting or something.

Your command of sensational English prose is also pretty masterly.....   see Teresa's comments, and she hasn't even seen any of the three Whizzbangs yet (but I have now forwarded them to her).

What we would all do without Gerald I dread to think.   As your agent, connecting you with the outside world, he is superb. (You were talking about the gender of offspring the other day........... just think, if Rosalie had been a Robert then we'd never have had Gerald in the family... (well, I presume not!). We are all extremely lucky.

Your post-concussive and post-galvanic symptoms will no doubt continue to recede and will finally disappear. Just how long that will take is anybody's guess but I would think we are talking about just days here, and not weeks, aren't we?

I repeat.... you are a remarkable person, and you have shown us all some remarkable qualities which none of us had ever really known existed.   Thank you for that.

Sir, I remain, whatever I was before. (I'll forget my own name next).

er, **Daddy.**

(RECEIVED)Sun 18/01/2004 00:09

Hi david

Sorry to hear about all thats happened but delighted that you came through it if not unscathed still fighting.

I expect every wire onboard will have to be checked.its a heck of a task but Im sure you will cope. Vernon sends his best wishes he ran into Fin and she updated him.

I cant think of much to help, you could try sleeping on a rubber sheet prob wont help with a big strike but at least you wont wet the bed... cant realy say " power to yer elbow " anymore,you done that and got the T shirt

I did think that you should have had a lottery ticket. you know the big hand that points and says its YOU. I reckon thats what it was. you just caught it on the wrong day.

I think you did right to refuse a tow dont know what salvage rights are in force you never know dont be to trusting of the natives.

I hope you can sort out the radio. we will still keep listening. all your radio equipment for that matter the marine side being more important, like in the life of Brian always look on the bright side.All that preparation and all those spares we laughed abt paid off.and when you are old and grey well greyer! we can sit you in the pub at Orford and you can top any of the mariners tales told down there. take care glad you are feeling better

John

(RECEIVED)15 January 2004 15:52

Gerald: As I said, I feel that I know you and David personally. I am very sorry to hear about all of David's problems, and I will be happy to help any way I can. I can purchase anything from Ham Radio Outlet in Newark Delaware and they can ship to me by UPS in one day. I can use my VISA and you can repay me later. Then I can airmail to David in Brazil. If David cannot repair his radio; the best thing is for me to airmail a new one to him and then have him return his ICOM to me and I will have it repaired and returned to him as a spare. It is amazing what he has been able to do with that little 8-watt transceiver. I have a Kenwood TS-2000 and an Ameritron AL-82 linear running 1500 watts into a terminated rhombic antenna put up in the trees with a bow and arrow. I have been an amateur since 1939.

Let's hope David has expended all his bad luck!

Jack.

(RECEIVED)15 January 200 15:52

Once again many thanks for your help Jack you have no idea how reassuring it all is.

David is now back in the marina at Salvador but is still awaiting a berth as there is a regatta going on and there is very little space.

Once we have made contact again and he lets me know what he wants, I will contact you again.

In the meantime thanks once more for your kindness.

  Kind regards

   Gerald

(RECEIVED)15 January 2004 14:25

Subject: David and his Problems!

  Thanks for coming up on the net today, Gerald. Copy was bit sketchy here, as I had that over-the horizon-radar signal, which Jack thinks comes from Naples. Jack is a dear and VERY helpful, there is nothing he won't attempt to do to help somebody in trouble.

I hope David makes it safely back in to marina, and then he can assess everything and find help, as well, I am sure. Best wishes to him, and to you –

  Trudi

(RECEIVED)15 January 2004 15:52

Subject: RE: David and his Problems!

  You are so right Trudi – Jack seems to be a wonderful guy and I have just spoken to him by telephone. He has, again, offered to help in any way.

David is now back at the marina but is awaiting a berth with 240 volts as there is a regatta on and so no room at present. everyone is very sympathetic and kind.

We are now waiting for him to contact us and let us know what he wants us to do.

  Kind regards

   Gerald

Sat 17/01/2004 11:30

Dear Trudi,

  I promised to be careful, honest I did!.........that's why I avoided anchoring somewhere exposed.......bl**dy annoying when you really believe you done your best, and it still bites you........

Your comments have been really heart-warming this evening, because after yesterday's elation of managing to crawl back to safety, today's been a bit of a blackhole, as expected....big lonely dangerous city.....I'm "yesterday's news" here, already.....and there's no one here I would allow to do the work, so I'm very aware of still being very much singlehanded...even in here in the marina....no-one can help, no-one's going to do it better than I will, because I know what to do, and in what order, and I know the wanderings of the ship's somewhat "evolved" 30 year old wiring.............. I'm amazed how much has been repaired already (mainly rewiring).......and (hopefully) new bits are on the way from the USA & the UK.....................progress is remarkably good really, now that I can see further round the edges of the catastrophe......

And the moral and practical support from my family.... and you, Jack, Gerard, Doug..... and my wonderful friends from Madeira and The Canaries, (had an unexpected but lovely telephone call last night from "Forever" who is anchored near "Pendragon" in Barbados at present, as they try to help with "Mad River"'s repairs too......we are all very close friends indeed.....) .....

  But the lightning certainly zapped me physically, as well as the ship...honestly didn't think it had, at the time, but it's now blatantly obvious that my problems are considerably more than simple mental shock at the situation.......just like after a head injury, which now explains the deep nausea and the uncontrollable shakes I had for the first two days........but improving rapidly now, if I can continue each day at my own speed.............

So, really appreciated your Email...really cheered me up......Huge THANKS, to you and all in the Family of the /MM nets...

Stay well, and don't do anything Dangerous, like play with anything Sharp or Pointy or Electric will you.................

Really Grateful, I'm not sure I will ever be able to tell you how much,

> from,
> > (um.. er.. well.. who.. er.........ah yes!...)
> > **Tuesday'n'me.**

PS. Thanks about opening an Email box....my family are competing with each other to be the first to release a "bootleg" version of the book from all the vast numbers of Emails sent home since I started on this new career 19 months ago......(not that I'll write a book....too busy making the film from all the hours of video!)....but I've been keeping records of everything, so it's all there if I need to blackmail anyone!.... Perhaps I could include you, Gerard, and Jack in my list of "let's-make-all-my-friends-REALLY-suffer" (ie. in the Dear-Everybodies)?.....but for heavens sake shout "STOP!" if it's clogging up your computer.....

Warmest Thanks again.....

(RECEIVED)Sun 18/01/2004 01:43
> *Dear David,*

> *Thank you so much, I am just glad we can be of help.*

> *I told your brother that there may be some sort of anticlimax for you, when the wave of Adrenalin might collapse a bit. But your positive thinking and keeping busy will get you over that hurdle, too, I am sure. Keep at it, and you are so right - only you should repair the damage, you want to know what and where and why, as YOU are going to live with the results.*

> *"Pendragon" has given up on the eternal rolling and has fled to Rodney Bay in St. Lucia, where they are recovering nicely. "Mad Rivers" I believe are having some problems with getting the rudder put back, as the rudder stock seems to be bronze, and it has stumped the local workmen. It would be a pity to change to stainless steel, which our (Naval Architect) son assures us would be far inferior.*

> *I hope your appetite is returning, and maybe the shock has brought out hidden cooking talents, since it has not improved your Portuguese? Do take care - Trudi*

(RECEIVED) Sat 17/01/2004 20:16
> *Subject: Wow!*
> > *Hi David,*

> *What an inspiration you are! I'm not sure about your latest adventure though. Hope you are feeling better. We really enjoy your emails and follow your journey closely on the map. Where are you heading next?*
> > *With love,*
> > > *Cathy*

Sun 18/01/2004 01:50
> **Dear Jack,**

> Humbled ....yes, that's the right word....I feel really HUMBLE at the remarkable generosity and selfless support you have given me when I was in a bit of a hole these last few days...I could never thank you

enough............we've never even met..yet you've gone out of your way to help pick me up again......

As a singlehander you have to be totally self-sufficient..so it's not always easy to accept help when it is offered..............but I was "knocked down onto my knees" for a little while there, and your offer to help was right where it was needed..

Thank You Sir!...........thank you for being there,

Warmest Best Wishes!

Docdavid

Sun 18/01/2004 01:52

Dear Ron'n'Bonnie,

IF I HAD HAIR, on the TOP of my head, it would be pointing straight upwards still...and pure white!......as I haven't, all I get is a strong "Afterglow" so I don't need a torch   (oops..sorry...."flashlight") ....could run a microwave, even now, I think.......

Bless you for the totally unexpected phonecall in the early hours.....perfect timing when I was in a deep dark hole....tremendous help it was......REALLY appreciated it.....I owe you a lot for that........I hope you'll never have to know for yourself how much............

Still got a few problems with my   er   um   hmm   er   ah!..MEMORY....yes, that's it... memory....................andd wun oar too plobremzs wit mi spellinges an pispronountsiations butt i doant thync theer signifinicant reaalli enni moor, due yoo?

Lots of Big Hugs!

Doc

(RECEIVED)Mon 19/01/2004 19:33

Hi there buzzhead,

You need to rest a little, me thinks though does go on a bit. You really need to take a day or 2 and do no boat work, get your body back to feeling ok, and let your brain relax.

Lightening always has an entry & exit, where was the exit for yours? (were your knickers smokin???)

We miss you and Pendragon sends their regards. We spend the day yesterday relaxing at the St. Lucian yacht club with friends we met in Europe who were racing here. It was quite a bit of fun.

Keep your head above water, my friend, and get yourself better.

We love & miss you & know that Tuesday will be Ok & ready to sail again soon.

*Love, **Capt, Ron & Bonnie***

Wed 21/01/2004 03:10

Dear Ron'n'Bonnie,

Yeah, I've noticed a dent in the middle of my tummy, and a hole in my *rse, and I can't remember if they were there before the WhizzBang......and I still haven't stopped smoking yet............. (though I still have to light 'em)......people still come up and shake my hand to congratulate me......or are they just looking for a Buzz?......

It's all starting to come together here now....some improvements and some "we'll just have to make do without" ....but those four days are still a bit muddled....thank God I wrote it all down at the time!

Thanks for the Emails..........love them!

Stay Safe!

and Love to all the Gang,

Tuesday'n'me.

(RECEIVED)Sun 18/01/2004 22:07

Hi David

sounds as if you are getting on fine with the mighty tasks. Tuesday certainly is tough cant imagine the new gin palaces taking all that.

Had a chap come round looking for you, he was a bit strange had a bolt through his neck said something about needing a start in life ! I said well you got the right person Im sure you could point him in the right direction......top of the mast should do it.

Take care of yourself I lost your mobile number will have to get it so we can speak

love from all here

john

(RECEIVED)Sat 17/01/2004 02:02

Dear David,

I would like you to know that I have just created a new mailbox called "David + Tuesday", which contains all the E-mails you have sent. If and when you decide to write your book (and I think you MUST, when you get back home!), I will be happy to transfer it all to you, in case you have lost any of it, it will be a perfect basis.

The most amazing things are the bits and pieces that survived, and the ones that got cooked, in spite of being completely unconnected to anything electrical. I do remember hearing a story of a boat hit by lightning where some electronic components, still unpacked and in the boxes they were shipped in, were completely destroyed. What strange forces are at work there.

The best part of it is that you not only survived, but made all the right moves immediately afterwards and at the right time. I told your brother that it will probably take a bit more than 2 weeks before you will be ready to move on. You want to make very sure you have put everything essential back to rights, as well as some luxuries! Anyway - in my experience anything to do with boats always takes twice as long as one first thought.

Much as I enjoy getting your E-mails, having you back on the air will be a wonderful day to look forward to, David!

With all the best wishes for a speedy recovery for both of you

from **8P6QM and the Net.**

(RECEIVED)Mon 19/01/2004 01:21

Dear Alex,

We have been reading through David's amazing account of what happened, we are so so relieved that he is safe and in one piece, John was saying if any one could survive such a disaster it would be David, he was so well prepared and his knowledge of all the mechanics of the equipment is astonishing. All the details to me are mind boggling. He must have been well tutored (by osmosis!) by a certain papa!

I got up the web site mmsn etc. with no problems, and as you said the last entry was 2004/1/01 75nm from Salvadore.

Its marvellous that Gerald can be in touch and every one being so helpful. Please send our love when you are in touch by emails, mobile phone or whatever, its a magic world out in the ether!

Congratulations on your diamond wedding by the way, it will be a memorable day now.

love from *Angie*

Tue 20/01/2004 23:42

Dear Bill and Matti,

Looks like none of us got away unscathed..........on 13 Jan 04 poor old "Tuesday" got struck heavily by lightning while at anchor, miles from anywhere, in this very pretty 30milesx30miles bay of All Saints, Salvador.....it struck me personally too, which caused concussion and zapped my muscles and memory a bit, ...but now recovering, steadily, though still a bit confused about parts of the four days after the WhizzBang hit......

It seems there were 3 separate fires inside the cabin, but none took hold because somehow I turned off the master-switches quickly as soon as I could.......transducers are all internal, so the hull remained watertight.....mast and stays still standing, though the top of the mast is a bit pitted now.......but all electronics, radios, lamps, fuseholders, alternators, gauges, many switches and large areas of wiring destroyed ....basically anything with a diode or transistor in it is dead......the stink of burnt plastic and rubber....and you should see the main compass, with its lightbulbs blasted right out through its walls, wrecking it..... it's all very sad.....

It took 2 days of intensive work, not feeling at all well, just to get the ship mobile again, to limp back to Salvador on 15 Jan 04.....

Since then good progress putting the ship together again........everyone here supportive and helpful......... and although as from today she could go to sea again, as the basics are now all done, there's a heck of a lot I want to do still....I don't want anyone else to do the work because I know the 30-year-old wiring, and I know the standard of work I need ....

So, I shall be staying in this area for at least another 2-3 weeks (or however long it will take for replacement parts to arrive)........and I personally need to convalesce a bit, too....

Could have been far worse, I guess, because many people don't survive a personal lightning strike, and often neither do their boats.........but Tuesday'n'me are climbing back steadily now, very lucky indeed..........

I trust all goes well for you both..........

Safe Landfalls!

Docdavid.

Sun 18/01/2004 01:48

Subject:-Tough Old Bird

Dear Everybodies,

Blimey, but "Tuesday"'s a tough old bird!......for the first time since the Nasties happened I've stopped to stand and have a good long look at her from ashore........I'm amazed that after only four days of intensive work, this vessel is virtually legally seaworthy and functional again............and she did it from her own stores and spares!............how many modern "plastic fantastic" boats could do that, after a direct hit from lightning?.........

Obviously there are a huge lot of electronical-thingies still u/s, but none of them are essential....their power supplies are all restored, but they just don't work anymore, or only partially.......it's fascinating how many other bits'n'pieces have been salvaged and then cobbled together somewhere else to produce a good result......tremendous amount to do yet, but she's up and running again!....

Clambered up the mast today, very cautiously inspecting everything on the way........(still haven't been able to find where that ruddy split-pin I found came from!)......couldn't believe my eyes finding the steaming and deck-illuminating light bulbs intact..... and their wiring too!........haven't found any welds in the rigging yet (thank God it was raining when it happened)..........then slowly peeped over the top of the masthead expecting to see a nuclear-melt-down ....NOTHING!....(quite disappointed really)...........five separate fingernail-size pits in the metal, in a pockmarked area which looks like welding "splatter"...........the base mount of the tricolour light is there, burnt and blackened around the Common Earth connection.....and a small piece of the mounting for the VHF antenna is still bolted in place.......a 4" piece of thin black string turned out to be a bit of coax-cable remnant ....otherwise it's just as though the bits had never been fitted............and believe it or not, there is still power to the correct sockets in the tricolour base.................I can only imagine that because the wires run INSIDE the aluminium mast, they were protected....and the masthead bits must have been blasted off by the explosion....or simply vaporised.........(remember that I found a tiny piece of the steel antenna in the scuppers, looking like it had been cut with an oxy-acetylene welder).........

However, it was a different story at the junction-box in the headlining of the saloon, where the mast wiring joins the ship's wiring indoors.........there had clearly been another (ie. THIRD) fire in there, but started by the lightning, not caused by shortcircuits etc..... the common earth wires and the VHF cable took the blast .....wires ripped open...metal plugs and sockets spotwelded together.........charred wood ....sooted metal......................but apart from the VHF cable, it took only 10 minutes to check it all, cut out the rubbish, clean up a bit, and restore all power to the mast lights......have bought a new tricolour light here, which I hope will plug straight into the surviving masthead socket (it looks OK, judging from the digital photos I took up there).....it's a bit "sad" I know, but I confess there is actually a spare one on board, but it's a bit old, so I thought I'll give the tough-old-bird a present......

And me?......well, I'm getting bits of memory back which I now realise had been missing ......today is the first time I know I'm really "me" again......I was sure I was OK...but I was wrong..........got a few new problems spelling....right letters, wrong order... (SpellCheck is a wonderful thing!), and I keep forgetting where I put things down, but how bad was I before anyway?........and my internal "clock" is completely up the spout, but I think that's hereditary......still can't cope with too many things at once though......but tomorrow I'm going to take time to see if I can work out a sextant sight or two, without losing patience.... that should be a pretty good test!.....

Hey-Ho, it's suppertime, so I'd better get out the screwdrivers and spanners ("wrenches" to you ex-colonials) again to eat it!..

Thanks again....you've no idea how much....

Tuesday'n'me.

PS.. Nearly forgot...Mike, thanks for sensible suggestion to keep electronics in the oven to protect them.... especially as it's somewhat under-employed with my culinary expertise......but it doesn't work too well on this particular ship because in this heat the butter melts, and it would spill everywhere if I didn't keep it all in there where it's gimballed...... besides, there's no room for electronics when it thunders now, what with me personally in there already.......

(RECEIVED)Fri 23/01/2004 00:28

Cor you don`t half know how to put the shits up us boy. It would seem to be two tough old birds in one pot. Good news about the repairs that are under way makes one think how right Pongo is when he says Shit happens man. Pick yourself up get things in Order of importance and get on with it. YOU ARE A STAR, full marks. You know all thoughts are with you (feel I can`t do a damn thing to help which is just a fact of life but should you think of anything just shout).

*So how much for a dug out canoe sounds like a good idea to have one, what colours do they do. I did not see one at the boat show so do not know hw much they are here. Hope that the spares that you need arrive soon but you were quite right about all the spares that you shipped onboard. What I do not understand is just how (I know you are a very clever fellow) you are going to fit in the Oven. Just one word of advice when you are in there DON`T SMOKE take care love **james and Liz***

(RECEIVED)Sun 18/01/2004 12:53

Daer Divad,

Thought that I`d better write to you in your new language, well it`s a bit like trying to comunicate with Alzheimer cases, you musn`t tell them they`re talking rubbish but "validate " it .

WOH ARE OYU ?? don`t really have a lot to say , at least not that would interest you. I would say keep your pecker up but I should imagine that that is the last of your worries at the moment .Anyway all the best, remember the Monty Python song "Always look on the bright side of life"... I feel sorry for you in some ways cos your`re going to find life extrememly BORING when things get back to normal !

Just one question often in my mind. Did your hair stick out on end when it went bang ?

J. M.`s comment when I told him about the mess of broken glass etc in the cabin was "When you think how fussy he is about one crumb on the floor ...."

Bye for now   Love MARY.

(RECEIVED)Sun 18/01/2004 15:22

Drea Vidda ,

Me again ! No not YOU you stupid .... Just to say how tactless of me to mention Monthy Pythons song .... perhaps it would be better for you NOT to remember anything to go with BRIGHT ....might set you back in the healing process . Sorry about that . I will try and think of another more appropriate song. Don`t worry I will no doubt think of something to cheer you up.

Meanwhile JM thinks (quite seriously) that you should start writing a book about lightning and it`s effects on people and boats etc , I suppose he is right after all it would help you think about other things wouldn`t it!

Bye !

Love Mary.

Sun 18/01/2004 19:36

Dear Daddy and Mother,

Hmm....the enclosed photo of the masthead is not very impressive, is it.......but does it mean there were FOUR individual strikes or just one?....if four (which would have taken about half a second or so, then I AM missing a bit of memory, as I remember only ONE instantaneous blast.......UGH!

I don't want to harp on and on about it, but it's been a very interesting experience....I have a few minor problems remembering which DAY something or other happened in those first four days, but I can always work out which one it was fairly quickly.......new bits of memory are returning, but only tiny details each time now....for example, I can now recall the visiting fishermen (and the photo shows only 5 men, not 6) being very concerned that I might not be able to raise the anchor, with no electric power, and they were relieved when I explained in mime that Tuesday has a manual winch, worked by a long handle.........

I would be surprised if there's anything significant missing now ......spelling on the computer is a bit worse than before, when I'm convinced I typed it correctly but clearly I didn't......writing is no problem at all, mental arithmetic is no problem, and rewiring boats is obviously dead easy........I still prefer only one problem at a time.....And now I can see that I DID have some of the symptoms of Illuminated Vacant Possession for those four days, even though I wasn't fully aware of it at the time.....(? "IVP" = "the lights were all on, but there was no-one at home")................

Will need to wait here for the bits to arrive from UK and USA.......hope to God they don't get stuck in Customs, but there's nothing I can do about it at present......whatever happens I'm going to have a holiday exploring round this bay again before heading southwards, partly just to be sure of getting some convalescence......

Deepest Thanks for being there when I was in the Sticky-Stuff....words aren't adequate...

Stay Well! All my Love,   **Me**

97

(RECEIVED) Mon 19/01/2004 07:53

    Subject: masthead

        Daddy has just forwarded the picture of the masthead to me - very impressive!

    Jonesey

(RECEIVED)20 January 2004 15:53

    Gerald: I just mailed the IC-703 to David at the marina address you gave me. The cost of postage and insurance was $ 58.00. The box was small enough so that it will go as cargo on a passenger aircraft. The Global express waybill number is ER 685810997 US and the estimated transit time is 3 to 5 days. I will be waiting to hear David's voice on the air; a little more cheerie I hope.

    Jack

(RECEIVED)Tue 20/01/2004 16:48

    FW: IC-703 on it's way to Salvadore I hope you will be able to talk to US ALL in about 5 days time!!!

    Jonesey

(RECEIVED)Wed 21/01/2004 01:10

    Re: um..er..Memory

        Well, Tuesday'n'you, the two of you are doing just fine, I am very happy to see! And thank you for the update.

    David, you have all your priorities right, and those odd memory lapses are getting less, yes, you were very lucky, and are still. And aren't you glad you have a manual anchor winch. Most electric ones give problems sooner or later, anyway - it is a very vulnerable place to put electrics!

    Enjoy your enforced leisure time, you might not get another chance like this for a while. You are so good at looking for silver linings, anyway!

    Take care, and if you go off exploring, make sure there is a tall tree somewhere near where you anchor - or better still, a yacht with a mast considerably taller than yours!

    88 – Trudi

(RECEIVED) Mon 19/01/2004 12:00

    Hi David,

        Have been following your news with great interest. Glad to hear you are both coming through the trauma - Sorry you didn't get your Portuguese linguistic wiring fixed with the strike - If you had I am sure you could have made a fortune fixing gullible guys to your mast in thunderstorms for a 'small' fee!

    I read and gave some of your e-mails to Geoffrey Ingram-Smith like everyone else he was impressed by all you have done - he said the old wooden boats used to hang chains over the side during thunderstorms - should we all now go and buy up old anchor chains?

    Stephen was very sorry to miss you - enjoy your repairs - maybe you should do your own before sorting out the French!

    Cheers,

    Ben (J)

(RECEIVED)Wed 21/01/2004 15:40

So sorry!

Dear Doc,

Bonnie told us of your great misfortune and we are so sorry! But also glad you were not hurt. Hope you are able to get everything back in order soon. Does this have any effect on your plans?

You may have heard we are going on home and will arrive about July. We are enjoying the Caribe while we are here, but looking forward to getting home.

Please let us know how you are doing!

   Dave & Sally

Thu 22/01/2004 05:26
  Subject: Bouncing Back
   Dear Sally and Dave,

How nice to get your Email!....very warming and comforting.........

It's a bit selfish of me, but I'm really pleased I heard you're aiming to take the ship home.....I wasn't comfortable with the "For Sale" sign in Rubicon.....nothing to do with me, I know, but that's what I felt.....

Here everything looks most encouraging......I've been able (slowly and painstakingly) to do all the work myself, as I want to know how and what has been done, and how well...........I really couldn't bear the thought of anyone else doing it ...... we've been through a lot together ....and anyway it would be horrendously expensive and time consuming to get someone to do it for me....and they couldn't do it nearly so well ...... and besides, I'm the one who'll be trusted his life to it ...

She's already perfectly fit for sea again, even now, if she had to....... but I'm waiting to haul her out tomorrow for 24 hours to inspect all the metal bits underneath.......and while I'm there, might as well clean and antifoul her again (all the materials were on board anyway).................then waiting for bits from USA and UK, to put back some of the electric things thought to be essential in this day and age .... oh!, and a main ship's compass replacement, as the existing one was most impressively blown apart by the WhizzBang.............

I'll keep it short for your Pocketmail.....keep in touch with "Forever" for full report......and look after yourselves....you're important to me.......really felt for you both in those awful seas you had....

  And I loved the apple sauce!

   Love,
    Tuesday'n'me.

Thu 22/01/2004 03:03
  Subject:-Life in the Ship
   Dear Everybodies,

These Brazilians are lightyears ahead of us.......this evening I unearthed the "Pan-Galactic-Gargle-Blaster" of Hitch-Hikers-Guide-to-the-Galaxy fame......it has been invented in Brazil, and is already alive and kicking (and Oh Boy does it kick!).....still not sure what's in it, nor what it's called (I've forgotten), but it ranks with the hot pint mug of "Hinterglemmer" from the Austrian Alps as one of the wonders of the universe..........I suspect it's white rum, various exotic fruits, a lot of sugar, ice and lemon, etc.etc.....Oh, and a straw .... (probably unwise to actually DRINK it straight from the glass)......
a beautifully crystal clear and so refreshingly, deceptively, benign-looking drink.........more details to follow, for a fee!.....thank heavens it wasn't more than a few feet to tack back to the boat!..........

The English couple from "Why Not?" , Philippe and Paola, discovered it yesterday......it's constructed in the bar in the marina........if ever I were to become an Incapolic it would be to this stuff..........daren't have another till just before I leave Salvador......

Also found the TINY bar I'd be told about where the boss will slice up a whole fresh mango, blend it, add a few magic touches, and produce a WONDERFULLY refreshing, (but very healthy) cold drink of it......THAT alone's got to be worth coming to Brazil for, on a hot sunny day.......probably it's all old-hat to you seasoned travellers, but to me from rural Suffolk, it was like a new door had been opened.......And now I can begin to see a little of the wonder those ancient explorers saw when they found new plants, new tastes, new scents, new countries...........

Very tired indeed yesterday....fell asleep on the floor amongst all the wiring and tools........but still a successful day, managing to actually REPAIR two ammeters........they're not as accurate as before, but at least they give a useful indication of function..........and interestingly the connections have had to be REVERSED, as clearly the moving magnets have been REmagnetised the opposite way......there must have been some SERIOUS forces at work a week ago........they were both isolated at the time of the WhizzBang...........

Failed to manage to mend a special expanded-range-voltmeter.......in spite of nicking components from one of the broken communication radioreceivers.........couldn't find a voltage-varied-resistor that would work (forgotten what you call the wretched things).......pity......so bought a simple "hot-wire" meter instead......it'll do the job OK.....

The cuts on the soles of my feet (remember the broken glass and plastic?) are healing OK now.....till I trod on the spanners today.....silly thing to do........

Finally tracked down a small leak.........some bl**dy beercans had rotted in the salt air up front in the bilge, and 3 out of 12 had sprung small holes, dribbling slowly into the bilge-sump.......what a relief that's all it was!...........

Intriguing that here all boats are measured in FEET......if you give it in metres they have to get up and walk over to wall-chart to convert it.......just like the Norwegians......beam and draft are in metres......... ....odd isn't it.........

Why is this Email called "Life in the Ship"?..........well, it's a little bit of unexpected magic really........... for the first time the cabin is gently filled with MUSIC again......lovely gentle BossaNova ....local singer.......I've bought a second-hand replacement radio-cassette-player from one of the lads who works here, and it is really lovely to hear the ship cosy, comforting, safe, and my "home" again..........powerful stuff, is music................

Better stop.....hauling her out tomorrow for checks below waterline, and there's a lot to prepare..........
    Byee fer now!
        Much Love from,
            Tuesday'n'me.

(RECEIVED)Fri 23/01/2004 00:28
    Hallo David,
        Pan-Galactic-Gargle-Blasters sound like something to be very careful of! But I like the name!
    Jack was discussing your E-mail and saying he could easily send you all those meters etc from a clever catalogue he has, and save you all this repair work. I told him you considered it a point of honour, to feel you could be self-sufficient and have the satisfaction of repairing the seemingly impossible, but I am not sure if that fits in with American consumerism? And Jack wants his friends to have the best!
    I hope the haul-out went alright, also the hull inspection, and there are no nasty ones, only nice surprises. Your new radio is on the way with many good wishes!
        Take care, best wishes from **Trudi**

(RECEIVED)Thu 22/01/2004 11:46
Subject: "That`s the SPIRIT !!"
Raed Ivadd ,

GOOD ! Now you are beginning to realise that there are other reasons for travelling to other lands apart from the scenery and seeing how other people live....that rum is quite something ....now you know why we enjoyed are travelling so much . I envy you drinking all those exotic juices, one of the first things we bought when we got back here was a mixer for doing our own but they are NEVER as good ....

Byee!!
Love Mary.

(RECEIVED)Thu 22/01/2004 11:01
Hi Doc,

from what I can read you have discovered "caipirihia"!

It is wonderful drink, and beware the consequences, first time I drank it felt like the lightning that struck me... remember it like today even it was 1992, had 5 of them laying on a matt at the beach talking to nice local girl, stood up and fell face down! Thanks God it was only sand.

Mangoes...well another story so I see u enjoy them, they are divine and very healthy, just beware the diarrhoea yes this is the land of new smells, tastes and for some feelings...maybe it was a sign that struck you and not lightning....maybe it was a warning...you'll never know until you live it to the end!

Doc please I cannot stress how much you should be careful where you are, the whole country is very nice and friendly but it can turn into a nightmare within seconds, beware the locals are maybe all thieves, including the police and all the nice people, it is actually ok to rob a foreigner so be careful.....

Have you enjoyed the coconut head off with a straw in it?

Did you try the local lobster and prawn hot pot called MOQUECA you should if not, it is lobster, fish and prawn slowly cooked in a tomato coconut milk sauce and is wonderful....

Well, what else can I say, good luck with all the mess on Tuesday, I am very sure you shall get her back in full shape, by the way what are the plans for the next few weeks? where are you moving to?

Take care and keep safe
Chris

Sun 25/01/2004 01:39
Dear Chris'n'Tashi,

Thanks for your sensible warnings about this place, Chris.....the few times I've walked into town, I've deliberately had on worn-out clothing , and carried NOTHING with me if I can help it....very careful about who is behind me at all times ......and making sure the gate-guards know where I'm going too....and I haven't been willing to take a camera, so no pictures of the scruffy bits of Salvador, which is a pity.......

Haven't eaten anywhere away from the ship at all, either....always concerned to avoid illness, because (just like your motorbike trip), if you get ill then you're disabled......I'll miss out on things, but at this stage it's not worth the risks........

But here in this expensive (by Brazilian standards) marina, I feel a little bit safer.....very tight security..................I know I'm not seeing Brazil itself this way, but to be honest at the moment I'm more interested in the Physical Geography of it, rather than the Cultural side..........

Yes, you're right...it was Caipirinha.....cane sugar booze.....I now have the recipe......amazing but lethal!...."Cocktail of the Gods"....daren't have any more......(actually was persuaded to have another two this evening with the English couple, but spent all evening sipping the drinks slowly (much safer!).....nectar!

...................still waiting to try the coconut and will look out for the Moqueca, but been rather busy here...........

Plans here?.....if the bits arrive, (a Big "if"), aim to spend a gentle week or so exploring the rivers etc here, while fitting them, before heading down to another cruising area 70 miles south of Rio...probably take a full 10 days sailing to get there, staying 100-200 miles offshore to clear any coastal hazards....we'll see how it goes, nearer the time, and I'll let you know......

Fondest wishes to you both!

(Wishing you both were here)....

Doc.

Sat 24/01/2004 03:34

Subject:-Fixed Abode

Dear Everybodies,

"Fixed Abode", for one night at least, because "Tuesday" spent last night up on the Patio (yes, that's what it's called here!)....the smooth concrete area where they store boats ashore....after 2300hrs they put two Hungry-Rotweiler-People-Eaters into the locked compound, so you don't really feel inclined to leave your ship......no-one else around, so you move around the cabin v-e-r-y q-u-i-e-t-l-y, having pulled the ladder up on deck behind you! ....found HUGE dogpoo under the keel this morning..........

Very strange for the ship to be at rest....no movement.....felt all wrong somehow ....unsettling....first time for seven months.......but slept soundly......

Had managed to beat the 3week waiting list for the lift-out, with encouragement from the Boss himself here, by implying that it was an emergency check after the lightning strike......and while she's out for 24 hours, why don't I antifoul her.......

Slightly upset the guy who paints boats here, because he wanted to do the job and sell me his special slippy-bot go-faster paint..... (yes, once again, I'm embarrassed to say, "Tuesday" already had her own anti-fouling paint on board in her spares...complete with roller-brushes to put it on with)......but the others in the yard all rounded up on him to shut him up, with no prompting from me.....I gathered from a broken-English speaker when I asked later what they'd said to make him back off, that they said that I'd survived the Lightning, I'd crossed the Ocean solo, and everyone knows that singlehanders are a bit peculiar, so give the mad fool a break and let him paint his own bl**dy boat if he wants to, while he's still alive...... (genuinely, that's the gist of what I was told!)............now, wasn't that nice of them!......

Getting into the Travihoist was interesting...had to reverse in, between sharp concrete sticky-out bits, in a strong crosswind.......some of you know that this design of boat is said to be unsteerable when going backwards....but she did it, with Phillipe's help, (after a lot of head scratching and a quiet practice earlier)... I was most surprised!)....

While in the Travihoist slings, felt like offering Eugenio (The Boss, a very helpful chap) a decent fee and saying "forget laying the boat up...just drive me straight to Rio!"...........but I expect everyone says that, so I kept quiet.......the operator showed me that she weighed a full 14 tons on his gauge (the books say less than 11......must be a LOT of spares onboard!)...........

Amazingly, NO sign of any underwater lightning damage at all....congratulations from Eugenio and colleagues.....smiles all round ......(bear in mind that all communication is in our respective languages, which makes it interesting)....

I'd started cleaning the bottom of the ship (the scuba diver in Lanzarote who had cleaned her last year had done a pretty decent job, (so thanks for teaching me, Chris'n'Tashi!)) when a gang of noisily laughing youths descended on the boat, seriously armed with pieces of sandpaper.....after the initial fright, I realised that they were a great bunch of lads, the Brazilian equivalent of the High-Pressure-Wash in the UK....and they do a better job too, once I was able to curb some over the over-enthusism (by showing them how I'd just been overzealous myself).....

There was a thin undernourished early teens lad with them, whom they kept ribbing all the time, which he cheerfully put up with while he continued to work........... so when the cleaning was completed I took off my watch and gave it to him as a reward.............

Now, I ought to feel a bit sheepish about this, because it was actually a freebie one (buy three books and you get a free watch)...I only wear that one when there's risk of it being stolen.......but it works, it's accurate, and it's been north of the Arctic Circle......and the effect was immediate....this mad Englishman who got covered in muck and barnacles like us is "alright!"......pats on the back, hand shaking, genuine friendliness, not looking for anything extra for themselves (not like in the town streets) ......definitely NO chance of any friction between the two countries from now on ....but I feel as two-faced as I did with that shopkeeper in Canical, Madeira.........salved my conscience a bit by giving him the box it came in, the instructions, and the extra links for the metal bracelet.............but I sincerely hope they don't think it's a new style of street-pickup!..........

Relaunched exactly 24 hours after hauling out..........most professionally done.....if you disregard that EVERYONE is shouting their heads off giving advice, and casting doubt about the habits of another lad's sister and mother........ .....Eugenio was the only one who said virtually nothing, remaining very calm and collected..........

Then had a little motor-around for 15 mins, waiting for a 41' 2seat speedboat to clear our allocated berth... we practised more serious reversing (confirming that 20 yards is possible occasionally, then you have to give a nudge ahead to straighten things out again).....

So now all moored up again, 99% of wiring completed, waiting for bits from Plymouth to be collected into a single box....earliest date to leave Plymouth is next Tuesday.........

But things are improving well now.......

Be Good!

Love from

Tuesday'n'me.

Tue 27/01/2004 01:18

Subject: "Olidays"

Dear Everybodies,

Took the weekend off ..... reading, sleeping, eating (now nearly regained the weight I lost on the trip down here from the Cap Verdes)....generally "On 'Olidays"...... chatting to other crews (particularly Philippe and Paola on "Why Not?", a Bavaria 37)..........several Danish boats here, but haven't dared try out my newly acquired "Scandiwegian" (= spoof language, sounding like...well.. Scandiwegian, I suppose).....

Several more bits and pieces fixed or fiddled, but very much at my own pace.......made a new Main Splitter Diode out of the old heatsink and two 80 amp diodes acquired locally......totally unable to get the regulator for the engine's alternator unfortunately, (nor apparently an equivalent, which puzzles me...is it because it's made in France?.....B. typical, if so!).....But it only means I don't have a working SPARE alternator, so I'll leave it till the Azores, probably...

There is a species of small bird here.....I call it the "Money Bird", because Philippe pointed out that its characteristic cry starts with "fifty quid!..fifty quid!"......then it changes to an outraged question "FIFTY quid?....FIFTY quid?", sounding really quite upset about it..............whereupon another bird of the same type, perched on someone else's mast answers "yes FIFTY quid!....yup, FIFTY quid!", in apparent stunned agreement ....they have long discussions about this exorbitant fee............and then another one further away joins in, ("what?..fifty quid?...W-o-w!"), and you cannot help but laugh, (or want to tell them to shut up about it!)...they sound so earnest about their complaint......Even when the conversation eventually dries up, they seem to go off muttering darkly about it......"fifty QUID!"......

I'll try to get a recording of it...............They did tell me the name of the beast, but I forget what it was.....begins with a "B"..............

There are three inflatable dinghies on this vessel, in addition to the Liferaft.....all acquired over the years.....one of them is one of these very fragile beach-fun-boats....potentially lethal ... but this particular one belonged to Fin's Dad, in 1980 or so.....it has its uses here as it is so quick and simple to inflate, it's incredibly light, and NO-ONE in their right mind is going to "nick" it.....got to be ready to swim for it if you use it at all.........BUT, unfortunately the plastic it's made of is old and softens in the hot sun .....result?......it's stretching!........needs twice as much wind to blow it up now.............was a 2 seater, but if they're friendly enough it would now seat 3 ....My question is, How big a size will it expand to until one day it goes Bang!? (or more probably a quiet Pop!)......any bets?......

Thanks for all your Emails and messages.....really enjoy them!......sorry I'm not very good at replying to them all..........

Take care ...... have Fun,
Love from,
Tuesday'n'me

(RECEIVED)Tue 27/01/2004 17:42
Subject: "Olidays"
Hi there!

Glad to hear you are relaxing a little, noticing things outside that big hole in the water into which we throw money. Glad you are listening to birds and cruising about in the dinghy. Sounds like fun!

We are still in St. Lucia, mom & dad are coming, mom wanted to know if she should bring anything other than her thong and toe ring! (chip off the ol' block).

Have you been diving?????

Keep your head above water and protective rubber clothing at hand.

Love,
Capt. Ron & Bonnie

Sun 25/01/2004 10:51
Dear David,

We bumped into mother and father (in Leiston Co-op,very high class purveyors of groceries you understand,even got mangos!) and have been hearing of your frightening exploits from day one. It is quite amazing how you coped with such a horrific lightning strike and we are very very relieved you are still in one piece - hope the bits of the piece are coming together in the right order!

Lightning apart, as John is saying, it sounds a very interesting part of the world to be. John would move to Cooktown tomorrow, we loved it, same latitude as you nearly too. Do you look like a proper Aussie ocker??

Just off to play tennis and catch up with Fin ..... snowdrops out, daffs coming through, lovely sunny Sunday morning.Snow forecast.

*Lots luv **John and Angie xx***

Thu 29/01/2004 01:42

Dear John'n'Angie,

What a lovely surprise!......thank you for your nice cheery Email....your book, The Old Man and the Sea, is working well, still keeping itself (and thus ME too) safe from harm*, so once again most grateful thanks!..

I gather the weather is socked-in with snow......I'm sorry, but to be honest I can't really comprehend cold and white stuff anymore......here it sometimes falls to 30c before dawn, but the (heavily insulated) cabin usually rises to 35-37c by day........heaven knows what the temperature outside is....it's too hot to walk on the pontoon, plastic goes all runny, paint and varnish peel in front of your eyes, most normal foods melt..... "mad-dogs-and-Englishmen" type weather...............still, can't complain, as I wanted summer in the northern hemisphere, summer in the southern hemisphere, and then summer in the northern again...

Keep in touch with my Papa for news updates.......you may already know, but later when I'm back at sea again, you may be able to follow the ship's progress on www.mmsn.org, find "shiptrak" at the bottom of the page, and ask it for the position ..... it should give "Tuesday's" last reported position through the Ham Radio network.........Another way is by looking at www.winlink.org, and then follow your way through it, I believe, using the same callsign......It's all done by volunteers, for which I'm grateful, but it's not always updated as often as it might be.......however, it relies on my being able to get through on the ham radio...(waiting now for a new replacement for the "zapped" one to arrive from the USA)......

MMSN (Maritime Mobile Service Network) is an American idea ....and Shiptrak is quite neat really... the deal is that in exchange for them plotting my position on their web-site, I give them a detailed report of my local weather, wind direction and windspeed, temperature, seastate, barometer readings etc, which is then fed into the giant melting-pot which produces our weather forecasts.....in addition, I can have read to me (usually by Gerard in Belgium) a personal forecast, shaped just for me, of my particular area, for the next few days, broken into six hourly chunks, making allowances for my course and speed..............all done by very kind RadioHams, out of the goodness of their hearts............. It depends on the conditions allowing a radiolink to get through, but you can see it becomes a sort of Family, keeping in touch with nearby (= 1000+ miles away!) craft too.......a moving "village" since most of us know each other either personally or by HamRadio.........I find it fascinating, and I'm never really "alone" (unless something goes wrong of course) .... wonderful people.... they really rallied round with support when I got a bit close to The Almighty (or the Other Fellow) two weeks ago..........

No, not looking like an Aussie, I'm afraid............very bearded, burnt, seadog vagrant in worn and patched old clothes, barefoot, etc.....looking penniless....wrinkled and weatherbeaten ...long hair (round the edges).....?ex Hippy?......but capable of fixing ANYTHING!...........mains voltage is 220 volts here.....pure "Playdo" after what I've been through!.....but don't shake hands with me.....might get a Buzz still!....

Stay Well!,

Fondest Best Wishes, **Me.**

*(Author's note:- Angie put this book onboard before "Tuesday" left the UK .. it was definitely NOT a gift, but was to be given back on returning to England, thus ensuring a safe trip ... what a lovely lucky charm!)

(RECEIVED)Tue 03/02/2004 10:08

Dear David,

Many thanks for email, you sound exactly like an outback Aussie, met ones of that exact description in Cooktown, weatherbeaten an'all, just hope you wear the right hat with corks etc. Actually do you get lots of pesky flies?

Thought you might be interested in the check list of "things to do in Brazil" as printed in a Worldwide Travel brochure that I happened to find:-

    -----explore ----3,400,000sq km of Amazon
                    Copacabana
                    Iguassu Falls
                    Carnival
                    Dental floss bikinis
                    Caipirinha hangovers   (???)
                    Samba
                    2,000km of unbroken beach

    Make the most of it before you return to wet old UK - expect to see a photo of you with a dusky maiden doing the Samba, wearing your bikini!
             Luv   **John'n'Angie**

Thu 05/02/2004 02:10
    Dear John'n'Angie,

        No, don't need corks around hat-rim.........a strange type of small bee is good natured.....many small fruit-flies, only a nuisance if you leave opened fruit unsealed.......fewer flies than in England on a summer's day ...

    The List......sod the piranha-infested Amazon, thank you!.....all the others, Yes please!...............will visit some waterfalls near here, by sea..........should see some of the beaches......Pan Galactic Gargle Blasters teshted and found choo bee reellie no' badd, but ish difficul' to 'ememember fer shure...........(Hic!)..............Dental Floss bikinis (nice description!) not as effective as very slightly more substantial ones, in my opinion..(God but I must be getting OLD!)........and Samba not nearly as stunning as some of these BossaNova rhythms, most originating from this particular area of Bahia...........And Carnival is pick-pockets-paradise in my opinion.............Will cruise slowly by Copacabana beach later, binoculars at hand!............

    Victor Meldrew would have been proud of me, I suspect!....

    So I'm doing my best........but wishing Fin were here.............

        Toodle-oo for now!
           me.

Chapter 6

Beginning to recover

Thu 29/01/2004 06:40
Dear Everybodies,

They don't muck about here........"you want a fish to eat, sir?"......KRRUMP!.....bagsful of 'em, dynamited ....I don't know if they need any excuse (like "I was peacefully widening the channel, m'lud", or "it sort of fell out of me hand, gov"), but it seems to happen with no warning, once or twice a day........... (probably a perk of the oil exploration locally, in fact)......

Fireworks..... very rarely do they fire them off at night here, but often in the daylight.........a bit lacking in finesse, though......"don't worry about the order of them, son....just let 'em all off together, saving one single biggy for 2 seconds after they've finished".......by the time you realise it's NOT World War III, it's all over.....

It's very sad, but parts of several bits of electronics still work....can't do anything with them though.....the comms receivers each have deep burns inside round their antenna entry components, but I suspect there is invisible scattered damage throughout them........... I'm planning to produce a self-steering-gear with the best bits of the old Navico (such as its motor, which checks out OK) and the best of the new Autohelm gear from Plymouth...(incidentally, the parcel still hasn't left England yet..waiting for one last bit)...

Repair work on board is getting down to fine detail now.....I've not got quite as far as knitting filaments to mend lightbulbs, but nearly........have been replacing broken indicator lamps with ones made of salvaged pieces and spare bulbs........... I suspect Tuesday's going to come out of this little chapter simpler but a bit better than she was before, in some ways........

There are distractions though....was asked to solder up some tiny connectors for another Frenchman next door, so that he could run his computer on the boat.....it all seems to work OK now ....but I still decline from LENDING any tools (past experience has taught me that invariably they get broken, or never come back again)...."if you want to borrow my hammer, mate, no problem....except you borrow me as well, to work it" ..

(Which reminds me, I still haven't been up that other Frenchman's mast yet)....

Helped take "Why Not?" round to the other, cheaper but noisier and dirtier marina...just for the joyride really...but they've got one of these modern setups,at the helm, with its electronic chart, with you on it as a little moving boat...you see EXACTLY where you are ALL the time, and where you're heading etc, with radar overlay if you so wish...all the other relevant information on the screen too...very tasty piece of kit!... I drooled over it!.......
.......certainly it wipes the floor with my lightning-proof system of baler twine and banging drawing pins into the chart-table (not literally, but it makes a good story!)......... I'm not sure about having all your eggs in one basket like that though...... but when it works it must be SO much easier.......(just think, NO plotting, losing your pencil, wet charts, dropping the parallel-ruler, stabbing your other hand with the dividers while making a grab for your coffee, etc).......first time I've played with one actually installed on a boat.....

By the way.... that TINY bar I mentioned, with the freshly made mango-squashes?.....I measured the distance between the bar and the wall, where the customers stand...14" only!..."customers will remain in a neat row at all times"..(mind you, there's only room for about 3 patrons at a time anyway)......ladies will need to rest above it or below it.....dead level will make your eyes water..........but you'll never fall down if you drink too much!..........

Warmest Wishes to All!,
Tuesday'n'me.

Thu 29/01/2004 21:26
Dear Jack,

My most grateful thanks for sending the ICOM!......it arrived this afternoon in perfect condition....20 minutes later it had been converted to work on the commercial marine bands as well, and 50 MHz unlocked too......(however, you're quite right, it doesn't have the 50 MHz board in it, but I've never used that band anyway)...............PERFECT!

My brother in England confirmed that it transmits, but the noise level in Salvador today is around S8, so it was impossible to hold a decent QSO.......could j-u-s-t about hear Gerard on the Italian net I think, but again no chance of contact yet.....

I won't be on Trudi's net tomorrow as I've been given the chance to go out in a boat to go Scuba Diving on a coral reef at about that time.... couldn't turn it down!.....but I hope to be back on the air again very soon......

I'm very embarrassed that you haven't had the money first, but Fin (my wife) is sending an International Cheque from England (the local bank there isn't used to that sort of thing, and has had to order it in specially).....it really has been most trusting of you, and I can never thank you enough....

I thought long and hard about a 100 watt rig, but the 703 will continue to transmit cleanly at down to 8 volts (but at considerably reduced power), whereas many sets are not happy at less than 12volts.....and the low power output simplified the installation.   ...... having an identical rig also might allow me the option of cannibalising one of them if I ran into more problems (heaven forbid!).....I know it would make it easier for everyone if I had a bit more oomph, but the system works and I'm happy with it........The other thing is that the 703 is stuffed with receiver improvements, a complete morse keyer with memory etc, and the built in ATU is useful just to protect the output stages.......for my particular purpose it's nearly ideal, though maybe I will have to buy a linear for it when I get home (I have an elderly Yaesu 707 as a base station in the UK)......

Every single one of my comms receivers were wiped out (I've really tried to fix them, but I don't have the resources on board....too many separate components knocked out) ...... but another bonus (surprisingly) is the original (damaged) Icom still RECEIVES OK.... so I'm using it just as a very sensitive receiver (for weather-fax's etc).....when I get home again I should be able to get it transmitting again, I hope..........

Here the wiring repairs are finished (some improvements on the original!).....waiting for bits which haven't even left England yet.....when they arrive I've got to spend some time feeding VHF cables down the mast etc, which I will need help with at the mast-base-exits, so I need to stay here until then really....

It's a pity, because I really miss being out at anchor somewhere where I can see all the stars.......being stuck in here with the bright lights and noise is not what I joined for......I want to spend more quiet nights at anchor, watching the masthead rounding up the stragglers again.........and I have to go back to my Electric-Island-of-Cows again to put a few ghosts to rest..................

But first I have to be patient and wait for all these electronical gubbins .....ah well, at least I'm safe here!.......
Warmest thanks again "the cheque's in the post",
Docdavid.

Sat 31/01/2004 00:55
Dear Chris'n'Tashi,

I don't know if I've been wise or not, but this morning I went to the Diving School literally 70 metres from the ship, to make enquiries.......I note they don't use the DIN connections here, and they don't have any adaptors, so I'm pleased you made me take care of mine...........

Met the Boss this afternoon, and he realises I'm just a beginner, thank heavens......so I'm to use their tank but my (ex-"your") gear tomorrow morning on a shallow dive with several others, to a local reef close

108

to the harbour here.......but I'm apprehensive as it will be my first dive with people I don't know and trust completely.....and it certainly won't be the same without my SeaNymph watching over me.....I'm going to feel very alone without you there, Tashi.........

(Sun 01/02/2004)

After considerable trepidation before it, the dive went OK, thanks to you two!.......very gentle relaxed 51 minutes exploring on the bottom along a breakwater reef, no deeper than 8 metres........just what I need for practice......a swell down there still, and a light current so I could just drift along with no effort....(and you'll be pleased to know all that hands-flapping-around has stopped)....

14 of us in the boat, but all experienced except me....so a (male) instructor came with me so just us two in the shallows, while the others went more than 30 metres down elsewhere.......it was MAGIC, sea temperature up to 30c ....how I really wish you'd been there too, to make it perfect.......kept turning round to see if you were following us......soppy, isn't it....

It was very useful too, because I was a bit light, even with 7 kilos (too much bread and eggs?) ...... only neutral buoyancy below 6 metres, so I had to do it all properly by my breathing, not with my BCD, and within 5 minutes it improved dramatically........wonderful!... Found another lead fishing weight to bring back, too........

But when I was back in the boat, grinning from ear to ear, I found all the others (except the Boss and my buddydiver) looked bl**dy miserable.......is that something that happens when you get more experienced?.....if so, to hell with that.. I'm going to enjoy myself!.......so I'm chuckling away to myself feeling really chuffed about it.......

Another shallow dive in two days, I hope........look what you two introduced me to!.....

THANK YOU both.... I owe you a lot,

Doc.

PS. Realised while underwater....for 50 minutes I was completely safe from lightning!.......

Sat 31/01/2004 16:41

Subject:-Back on the Air

Dear Everybodies,

Jack's HamRadio arrived from the USA!.......wonderful!.....it reopens a window onto the world I had lost after the WhizzBang......I had no idea how I was "propped up" by those friends I had met through Amateur Radio, until I lost the electronics....unfortunately Salvador itself is a bit of a "black hole" as far as radio communication is concerned, with lots of interference from other sources too, but when I can get out of here back into my islands things should improve.........it's really nice to be able to be back in the Land-of-the-Communicating again.....a big Thank You, Jack, once again....

Got fed up with waiting for English bits (still not left UK yet).....getting fat and lazy here.......so went for a swim......8 metres down on the seabed for nearly an hour with the local Diving School today, from a 40' motorboat......wonderful, but not the same without my own personal instructress from Lanzarote.....first time I've been allowed out with a stranger-buddydiver, so felt a bit insecure at first....but all that special one-to-one training in the Canaries really worked..... enjoyed the freedom of watching the local fishy-life, which is considerably different from the Canaries .... not as colourful, but very varied......... eg. the "Walking Batfish of Brazil" (honest, it's a genuine fish, which is quite unable to swim properly...it can only hop/walk/jump across the bottom like a rabbit...it's so weird that it looks as though it was designed by a committee)... and I felt calm and COOL on a hot day, too, although SEA temperature today varied between 26-30 degrees c(!)....................(While down there, I realised with a grin that for over 50 minutes I was totally protected from lightning strikes!).......

Brazilian boat-handling, in general, is truly excellent......the Norwegians go in for single large engines in their gasguzzling-powerful-stinkpots, with bowthrusters......here they all use twin engines, no bowthrusters, but just as effectively......I'm most impressed...............(but not by the stinky fumes!)............The owners of the powerboats are not usually as good at close-quarters manoeuvring as the young boatboys are, so you often see them swap places as they come in here..............I'd love to have an afternoon to play with one of these manned missiles, to find out the difficulties and the possibilities with the twin engine set-up...................

Different story with the controls of their on-board entertainment systems.......full belt or nothing..............the usual evening Raves in the local warehouses tend to be African-based rhythms, and brain-numbingly loud, whereas most motor boats tend to have slightly more conventional music.........just as loud, though...........good sound-reproduction systems, very "clean" and undistorted......

I really admire these Brazilians, as I still feel the BossaNova-evolved rhythms to be years ahead of anyone else....really quite complicated rhythms when you look carefully at them, with small and subtle changes every few bars, but instantly foot-tapping, which sound to me "Fun"......they're masters of the chromatic scale, too.........and they seem to really ENJOY their music....... this particular area, Bahia, is said to be the centre of the type of music I came to Brazil to hear, though I have been told that some singers from Rio de Janeiro do a pretty good imitation......

While I was in Madeira I heard a particularly haunting song.....recorded the tail of it.......by pure chance heard it on the radio again two nights ago........quickly grabbed the videocamera, and captured it .....played it back to the English-speaking boattender who stops to talk each day, and eventually he identified both singer and song for me......hope to find it in the shops tomorrow ....(how on earth did we manage before we had videocameras?)........

Enough for now.....must go and construct supper.....

Love to all!

Tuesday'n'me.

Sun 01/02/2004 04:38

Dear Bon'n'Ronnie,

You b*ggers have gone and done it again, haven't you!......you keep leading me astray, so that I actually enjoy myself..........I'd tentatively toyed with the idea of restarting my diving, and your repeated enquiries went and pushed me over the edge again........................(MAGIC!)

You've got a heck of a lot to answer for.... THANK you, once more......... .

How about you...are you diving too?...

Take special care of you both,

Doc.

(RECEIVED)Fri 30/01/2004 03:33

David....

Thank you so much (again) for your wonderful e-mails..... they bring great joy into our lives, except for the striking ones of course.   And great congratulations on the way you have brought your good friend Tuesday up to spec again. And even more importantly, how you have brought your good self (ugh!) up there also.

Reading between the lines I would guess that you are somewhat impatiently looking forward to being at sea again. 'Sat right?   So take care.   And if you decide to anchor somewhere then do so, and get everything neatly stowed away, etc. But then get it all going again and move the ship to a spot 200m to the SE.   That way nothing untoward will happen!

As I said, take care.   Love from us both.   D

Sat 31/01/2004 16:43

Dear Daddy,

You're right! .. ..I miss seeing all the stars.......being stuck in here with the bright lights and noise is not what I joined for..I want to spend more quiet nights at anchor, watching the masthead rounding up the stragglers again.........got to go back to my Electric-Island-of-Cows anyway......got a few ghosts there still to lay to rest..... and I want a sand sample from that deserted white beach as a keepsake.........

Toying with the idea of moving to the other marina after the weekend..........the money saved will pay for my scuba-diving again, and there are other "cruisers" I've met still staying there........English speakers......Danes, English, Italian, Swiss (Geneva), French...... (I think the French Armada to the Amazon should have left by then, so there should be room for a solitary Suffolk Lad) ....

Stay Well and Safe......don't get COLD will you (I can't actually imagine being cold at present!)....

Warmest Love!

me.

(RECEIVED)Sat 31/01/2004 19:46

.. Report, Italian Maritime Network, 31 Jan 04, 1900 UTC

ON6BG on frequency

LA7GZ, Staale (2), on Rozinante, 07-30 S and 34-18 W, headed south from Natal Brazil along Brazilian coast for Salvadore or Rio.

Gerald: Tell/ask David what frequency and time to schedule with Staale, LA7GZ.

Stalle: David is back on the air and will be in the Bahia Marina in Salvadore waiting for parts from UK. Maybe you can stop by and help him retrofit his boat Tuesday.

Gerald, If David wants other parts from here, let me know what parts he needs and I will find them and ship them to him from here.

*From **Jack and Benny**, in the frozen wasteland of Pennsylvania*

(RECEIVED)

…Report, Italian Meritime Net, 2 Feb 04, 1900 UTC

. *LA7GZ, Staale, in Capobello for several days, plans to visit G0CBE, David, at Bahia Marina, Salvadore soon.*

Gerald, they are too close for QSO on 20-meters; maybe you can schedule a meeting between them on 40 or 80 meters. I know David will be very happy to have Staale and XYL visit.

Jack

Mon 02/02/2004 03:58

Subject:- Battle Colours

Dear Everybodies,

Tuesday's Battle Flag.......it's a socking great bright red flag, with a big white disc in the middle (a bit like a negative image of a Japanese flag)....it represents the Panic Button which can be fitted in front of the passenger in a twin-seater light-aircraft....(in the event of an airborne emergency, when it's all suddenly gone quiet up front, the passenger is given strict instructions to press this white-button-on-a-red-background, and keep pressing it HARD........it's not connected to anything, but it keeps them out of your hair while you're trying to sort it all out and decide where the crash-site should be)..........

Well, Tuesday's is now defaced by a large lightning motif, diagonally from one corner right across to the other........(that would have got the Germans and French guessing in Canical, Madeira ...remember the saga of Tuesday's heavy sponsorship by National Migraine Week 1989, with the fender tee-shirts?)........

111

I apologise to those who know already, but there is an unpublicised club (only seven members, entry by unanimous election only) called the Panic Button Club.....(entry is also limited by the fact that I haven't got any more material to make the flags with)......each member has at one time or other done an incredible and wonderful piece of previously unrecorded seamanship, to get themselves OUT of a situation they got themselves INTO through crass incompetence........they each have a PBC flag (the white disc in the middle is uniquely measured by being cut out round Fin's largest frying-pan)......

But very few of them have an un-defaced flag now.....one was blackballed for not attending the meetings (when the boats were rafted together in a quiet anchorage somewhere), because he was out teaching sailing too much, and promptly sewed a black ball onto his flag with pride................another, by dint of virtually pitchpoling his vessel in a peaceful Suffolk creek as the receding tide left the backend of the ship pointing up at the stars, while the deeply immersed front end filled with water through the anchor chain hawse-pipe (he had to bale vigorously all night to save the boat) was awarded a Bar to his membership....sewed the wavy lines symbol onto his flag afterwards........

Well, Tuesday too has joined the ranks of the unclean with her now defaced flag........but it will be worn with pride, that's for sure........

One thing puzzles me a bit though......how come this very select group of skippers, with truly remarkable seamanship skills (and apparently at least one appalling lapse of concentration each as well) all come from a little place like Orford in Suffolk?.......

I reckon it must be something in the water there..........

Stay Well!

Love from,

Tuesday'n'me.

Wed 04/02/2004 00:50

Dear Jack and Gerard,

Really nice to be able to talk to you both again........although I agree it's largely due to YOUR antennas, not mine!.................I've moved about half a mile to a cheaper place, to save money, to be with other cruising boats, to be nearer the heart of Salvador..... and importantly, to enable the Ham antenna to work better, in a clearer space......

Electronic bits should have started their journey from the UK to here this afternoon, Tuesday......I'm going to stay here till they arrive, even though all the re-wiring is finished now, (apart the equipment in the parcel from England)......other non-lightning-damaged improvements to be started now (eg.stitching modifications into the sprayhood and bimini-top), while I'm "parked"...........the company policy is one of constant upgrading!...

Thanks to you both I had a nice chat with Staale today on 7MHz, which was pleasant....it'd be fun if a rendezvous worked out.....

And if you happen to speak to Rudy (VE3KZS/mm), please pass on my best wishes to both him and his wife (a remarkable couple, they are).......

Just for info...... the South Atlantic Net......Alistair (ZM5MU).....I've never heard it clearly yet......virtually nothing until I was south of the Equator......14.316MHz, starts at 1130 UTC, beaming into the Indian Ocean for the first 10 mins or so, then swinging through south into the South Atlantic......usually finished the net before 1200 UTC............I must start listening for it again.......

All the Very Best to you both!

David.

PS. Jack, I can confirm that the cheque is in the Postal Service somewhere..........

Fri 06/02/2004 01:42

Dear Mary,

Just bin going through the post-WhizzBang Emails..particularly yours..........honestly I don't remember reading them ....yet they're ticked as being read in that first 4 days.............

I wondered if I was making a bit of a meal of the whole episode, until I found this bl**dy great memory gap this evening..........so thanks for showing me I'm not such a wimp as I thought!.........

Hey, I love the local music here!..quite amazing rhythms and twisting chromatic chords.........and everyone's been really nice to me......(must be still glowing in the dark)..............and that Pan-Galactic-Gargle-Blaster......WOW!..........

But the examples of poverty alongside the rich........I find it very unsettling...I now realise what a very protected life I've led so far......and I've found that the others here in the marina have quietly been doing their silent "bit" to help, very selectively, the sick and "defeated" kids........(not the kids who ask...they've still got "fight" in them)......never money, only food.....

A fleet of Oppies race and train here in the harbour...one of them is the son of a Swiss chap from Geneva here, who arrived in Brazil in their boat about when I did......lovely family!.....they're really professional sail-repairers, working from their yacht.......they want to make a new sprayhood and bimini-top for "Tuesday".......I've looked at their work and it's fantastic top quality... best materials (not imported, but manufactured in Sao Paolo, Brazil)......so I'm going to agree....................('schpeshly ash weeve orl jusht cum bak from z'boozer, 'arf cutt 'n leglesh agane (!)).....

Good bunch of Internationals here, all really switched on and quick witted, with wicked sense of humour.......five or six yachts moored fairly close to each other..........good company.........

Right, that's yer lot....... (wotever-yer-name-is......I forget)

Byeee! Love to all the tribe!

Me

RECEIVED)Sat 24/01/2004 18:52

Subject: Fixed Abode !david - what an adventure!

Slow up please..... can't keep pace. I'm knackered with all this action--thought you were retired!!!!

On a more serious note, please excuse my cheek etc. but have you checked all stainless steel to alloy connections as there is the possibility of arcing betw.......oh heck! you know what I'm getting at, sorrreee.

Joe

(RECEIVED) Thu 29/01/2004 13:48

Dear David,

Well done on repairs so far and more importantly your last four e.mails have been more positive, you are clearly back in charge again.

Re- Antifouling, knowing that your arms are very short and that your pockets are quite deep, it is understandable why you do most of the work on Tuesday yourself, but please do not start an international incident as we could do with more friends not enemies in this world.

Winter has arrived with a vengance and because of it, it has been necessary to use the car lights etc more often, causing the Jaguar to fail to proceed. It would seem that you had an over abundance of electricity and that we were a bit short of the stuff. Still, my spares were more ready available!

Please continue to take the greatest care of yourself and Tuesday, say hello to your new found friends and try not brass the locals off, HI.

*Love   **Bob & Brenda***

Sat 31/01/2004 00:55
> **Subject: Snow? What's that?**
> **Dear Bob'n'Brenda,**

Thanks for your cheery Email..really brings a chuckle back into the cabin!....

Sorry the mighty Jag is suffering low volts....if I were there with you, there'd be no problem.... a single inquisitive medical digit in the cigar socket and you'd have instant fully charged batteries....

Replacement Icom HamRadio arrived from the USA today..my lifeline!..took it to bits immediately and converted it to include the commercial marine bands too...tested it, and my brother in Yorkshire said he could hear my 8 watts cracking through, (well, OK then, it was rst4,3..but at least it works!)....

I was very fit when I arrived in Brazil, though a bit short of protein and iron, but I'm getting landlubberly again now....got to get some exercise, like a hamster in a cage...but it's so darned HOT here....so got to get underwater again.....

So have been Scuba Diving today with the local diving school here, on a local reef with many fishy-beasts.......I've got to do SOMETHING, cos I'm getting bored now the wiring's finished, and I'm waiting for electronical gubbins from England (still not even LEFT from there yet)....no point me going off exploring again until the ship's properly ready again.....

> Stay Well and Safe......don't get COLD will you (I can't actually imagine being cold at present!)....
> Warmest Best Wishes!
> **me.**

(RECEIVED)Thu 22/01/2004 14:03
> *Hi doc*

> *so sorry to hear about your lightning strike. Hope you are recovering ok. I'm in the UK at the moment visiting my mother. I'll be here till Feb 10th. If there's anything I can do for you while I'm here please let me know. If I can bring you anything out to Brazil I will and then perhaps I can forward it internally from Recife which will avoid customs problems hopefully. I can only imagine the mess and damage caused it must be very disheartening, I suppose you just have to be thankful that it was no worse - another friend of mine was struck off Florida 3 years ago and it blew the sea cocks out of the hull and he lost the boat.*

> *Take care of yourself and again if I can help at all please let me know.*
> *Bill*

Sun 25/01/2004 01:39
> **Dear Bill,**

> Very kind of you to offer to get bits for me, but probably best for me to stick with the existing arrangements I think for now.......I really appreciate your kindness though.....

Things are improving steadily now.....I'm back to "myself" again, and I've done 95% of the rewiring already..........several second hand bits and pieces bought locally too (eg.radio-cassette player from a lad who works in the chandlery here).....friendly people..........so now just waiting for the British and American parcels to arrive...

If you get the chance to come down here, Bill, take it.....it's a good cruising ground 30miles x 30miles, with islands, rivers, creeks, lagoons, shallows and deeps.....mud, sand or clay for the anchor........in another time I reckon I could happily spend a whole season exploring here..........international airport is about 10 miles away.....choice of two secure marinas if you wish to leave the boat........

Do hope your Mum is stable and comfortable....very best of luck!........and how do you cope with suddenly getting back into an English winter after being out here?......

I'll let you know what my own plans are when I know, but still looks like my leaving from the area south

114

of Rio around Eastertime......certainly going to explore round here for a bit first.....it's a very pretty part of the world....

All Best Wishes!,
Doc

Fri 06/02/2004 22:32
Subject: Brazilian Rat
Dear Everybodies,

[I was too ashamed to send this particular Email at the time, because of my behaviour.....but it's still part of the whole story, and should be included really.......]

This morning, 1/2/04, a man in a bl**dy great immaculate speedboat called "Preciosa" rammed poor Tuesday as he backed his boat into a berth.......many witnesses to the impact.......me too......

At first I thought he'd smashed the Aries self-steering gear, (if he had, I would have despatched him instantly)....but luckily he missed it by about 2".........quick inspection showed only some deep scratches and paint damage on the port side of the transom.... but when I looked inside the transom lazarette there was some fibreglass injury....structural damage, ie............the perpetrator was rabbitting on and on (in Portuguese) about the wind, he'd only got one engine, and scoffed at the minor damage to the paint.......showed no remorse at all......I understood him to say "what do you expect if you have a boat?"...... and I got the impression he considered it all my fault that Tuesday was in his way..........

Take my advice..........Don't ever argue with an Angry Dove......

Apart from a single expletive as I saw the collision was inevitable, I was so seethingly furious that I said not a word.......simply, and (I'm ashamed to say) rather physically, frogmarched him up to the office, which surprised him more than a little...(actually it surprises ME now too...it's not my scene at all)....there was NO way he was going anywhere unless I let him...............it is fair to surmise that my feathers had been more than a little ruffled by him..... he knew it too.......

A very QUIET but firm conversation took place, with a translator's help in the marina office.....it's a long story, what happened in the explosive atmosphere in that room, so I won't detail all of it................marina staff very helpful...photos of the damage....did I need to take my boat out of the water for repairs?..........and then they explained VERY clearly to him...not just ANY boat...someone's HOME...Ocean-traveller...thousands of miles...guest in our country...etc.etc.etc.......the little rat was looking a bit more thoughtful now (a bit scared of what I was going to do too, I think..... quiet voices in a latin-american country can be very unsettling)..........finally offered apologies unreservedly, agreed to pay, and to contact his boss who actually owned the boat......marina office had all his and his boss's details.......

By now I'm feeling rather sick of Salvador at this point........so......I finished by saying very quietly, but with obvious and still barely controlled fury, that I, alone, will do the work... MY estimate will be accepted, OK?.....again all agreed.........

Final result?....it's all fixed and repaired now, total cost to me surprisingly only about £8 for glass-cloth and epoxy, one hours' work, plus a full half day tidying and painting cosmetically outside afterwards......
.....obviously I'll not pursue any sort of claim at all, but let the little (unmentionable) stew and worry for a few weeks.....if his boss finds out, he'll lose his job.....I shan't lose any sleep if he does ....

I used to think I was a moderately pleasant chap....not so sure now......this solo-sailing makes you a little more "basic" I think..........but what frightens me is that I wasn't pretending.....I'm so ashamed that I'd "lost my rag" for a while there that day.........if he'd tried to get away I might have got myself into trouble with the law...............................leaves a nasty taste in the mouth.......

Been feeling guilty about the whole episode....(but I've put it all behind me now, and left that marina, to

the declared sadness of the marina staff who had been so supportive).
>Tuesday'n'me.

(RECEIVED)Sat 07/02/2004 20:47
>*Hello David*
>>*.... still enjoying your messages (we look foreward to them) some make extremely interesting reading, others provoke a gasp.. & others solicit a reply, the 'Brazilian Rat' message falls into the latter category*
>*Do you remember many moons ago, you and I were driving off Parham airfield, you in your pillock van and me in my van towing the trailer with the microlight aircraft inside... remember?.. when a learner driver drove into the mudguard of the trailer.. I jumped out of my vehicle & had 'sharp' words with him, you intervened and kept things cool---for which I now thank you, but at the time I wish you had let me kick him in the ......
I now read the Bz/Rt story in the smug knowledge that you have all your testorone working well and no longer have to keep it in total control and can appreciate why I was fired up at the time---anyway good for you*
>>*Joe.*
>*PS ....(Authors's note:- more humour, but unpublishable)*

Tue 10/02/2004 05:44
>**Dear Joe'n'Joyce,**
>>You B******s!......there I was, just about managing to keep cool eating my supper, when I read your Emails and the PS.........food and drink spilled everywhere, as I fell about laughing!.......now I've got to clear it all up!.....you ROTTERS!.......
>>Yeah, I'd forgotten about the mudguard on Parham incident....good thing you reminded me........My episode here shook me a bit, because he really did get up my nose...a real frontal sinus job.....with no-one around I would have flattened him with no warning whatsoever.....I think the local "marineiros" were surprised to see me strong-arming him up the pontoon....but I've been back there since and they all greet me even more cheerfully now....perhaps he had it coming to him anyway.........(was he Royalty do you think?............some sort of Stupid Count, anyway)......
>>Stay warm...it's got cool here today, too.... DOWN to 35c in the cabin...the sun should be directly overhead here this coming weekend, on its way back to you.....(bloody hell, do I REALLY want to spend my dying days in English weather?)......
>>Warmest Best Wishes to you both,
>>>me
>PS..please say howdydoody to DC....tell him I've found the best lightning protection....never failed yet...climb underneath 30 metres of seawater, (wearing rubber if you're into that sort of thing).....take a tank of fresh, DRY (better insulator than WET) air too.....I never heard of a fish being struck by lightning yet.....
>>Oh...and still getting bits of memory back..found some Emails from my little sister, which I had opened and ticked in those first 4 days, but absolutely no memory of having inwardly digested them..I was beginning to think I was making a big meal out of it all, but maybe not.......
>>Byee!

Fri 06/02/2004 22:34
>**Subject: New Neighbours**
>>**Dear Everybodies,**
>>As a result of skilful pressure from the crew of "Why Not?", and the Battle with the Brazilian Rat, and the fact that the French Armada to the Amazon has left Salvador (thus freeing up 20+ berths), decided to leave Bahia Marina for the publicly owned Centro Nautico Marina in the middle of Salvador............

On 2/2/04, just after dawn when there is very little wind, warped Tuesday out of her berth and trundled round to the other marina 2 kilometres away..........it was a real joy, as this is the first time she's moved SAFELY under her own power since the sky fell on her........

Philippe had previously asked if he could catch my ropes for me near "Why Not?", and in spite of cross-currents it all went very well.......bows-in to a pontoon, stern held off by ropes to each quarter.....

It's MUCH nicer here.....Rag'n'Stick boats mainly, not GasGuzzlers, and a very pleasant International cruising community (now that the French have left, and a German semi-paedophile has been arrested from his yacht last week apparently!)......quick witted, highly knowledgeable people...Danes, French-Swiss (top-grade sailmakers, working from their boat), British, "OK" French, Brazilians........high level of security, better showers etc, but at about 35% of the cost of Bahia Marina......not as clean, and a bit more swell, but very convenient for shops etc.....

I'll have to keep walking back to the other marina to see if the Electronicals have arrived, to bring them back by taxi (approx £1) if they have...........The English-speaking boatman from there comes round here to see us British crews from time to time (and to let me know how he's getting on with a medical problem I was helping him sort out)........he also tells me that the dynamiting of fish is an arrestible(?spelling?) offence, but the offenders are long gone before the police (heavily armed) arrive........usually just near the harbour wall.......(puts me off Scuba Diving a bit......unusual entry on a Casualty card in hospital...."Depth-Charged whilst swimming on Holiday")....

Many powerboats here have very weak 5 watt navigation lights......but they all seem to use a single allround white "Photon Torpedo" (a whopping great STROBE light)......internationally illegal, apparently even in Brazil, but effective!.......

Good system in town for eating out, though not tried it yet......you fill up your own plate with food, however much and whatever type you like, take it to the counter, where it is WEIGHED......you pay by the kilo...............(I like the idea!.....not seen it before).......

Many more people speak English than I thought......it seems the way to find out is to have a go at speaking Portuguese, and then they realise that their English isn't quite as bad as they thought (compared to my Portuguese anyway!)......suddenly good conversation opens up, in a mixture of languages, friendly, interested, helpful...... nice!...it seems to help if you tell them what a beautiful area this bay is too..........

A lovely and total surprise yesterday!......a phone call out of the blue from Chris and Natasha in Lanzarote ....couldn't think who on earth it was at first, caught me completely off balance..... but really cheering and warming for me.....THANK you both so much.....lovely!

All the Very Best to Everyone!,

Love from,

Tuesday'n'me.

PS. Oh....and I'm sure you're really glad to know that the soles of my feet have finally healed, after ejecting the last pieces of glass and plastic last week ....well, it's made a difference for ME anyway!......

Tue 10/02/2004 05:44

Dear Jack,

Thanks so much for your Emails...always a pleasure!

I'm relieved that the check/cheque (I'll never get the hang of my own language, let alone anyone else's) is safely deposited....good.....thank you again (you can HEAR how much I have enjoyed the fruits of your labours!)....

Telephone message today at some ungodly hour of the morning, for me to phone the Brazilian office of the carrier of the English parcel of electronic goodies....it's already in Brazil, and should be here at it's destination by 6pm local time (9pm UTC) tomorrow Tues 10th....at some vast expense I'm sure, but I intend to need this package only once in my life......I'll believe it when I see it, but it sounds hopeful at least...will let you know....

Glen and Nita, KJ7NN/mm, on "Rapture" arrived safely in Salvador in the early hours of Monday 9th....terrible tale of vicious storm in Namibia, which they survived but with considerable damage (intending to do repairs here)...they're both well, great company, nice to meet them...

Pleasant chat with Staale, LA7GZ/mm, today on 40 metres...steady progress, but it's probable he may go straight on to the Rio area without stopping here...not decided yet.......I know exactly what he means about getting into (and out of) "sea-going-mode", especially for singlehanders, so I fully appreciate the decision when he makes it.......I hope we'll meet up, somewhere or other, along the coast this Spring...who knows?..

Sorry about the cold weather both in the US and the Europe .....still can't really comprehend it though.....much cooler today, DOWN to 35c in the cabin.... the sun should pass directly overhead here this coming Sunday, on it's seasonal journey northwards, so I confirm that it's slowly on its way towards you again!.......

All the Very Best to all on the nets....it's really "neat" (see, I CAN speak American) to be back on the air again..........

David on "Tuesday".

(RECEIVED)Sun 08/02/2004 20:12
Subject: "Free Spirit"

Just a quick note to let you know we are well and hanging out here in Grenada. It is nice here but would be better with you around. You made the right choice by going the way you did. You will see so much more of the real world. It is not real here, too commercialised for me. These islands has been walked on too much.

Hope all is well with you and family, give them our regards.

Allen and Marsha

Tue 10/02/2004 05:48
Subject: Time Flies!
Dear Allen'n'Marsha,

Just realised, it's nearly 3 months already!.....

Have looked high and low for DoNiMoes which go up to more than 6 dots...cant find any here, though they play a lot of "ordinary" dominoes.....been busy anyway, as you can imagine.....hopefully, big box of replacement electronical gubbins arrives tomorrow...I've finished the rewiring already.....(you should see the wrecked main compass, split right open...new one should be in the box)....

Nice place here.. still don't feel safe out-and-about, but probably safer than in London or Paris in fact ...nice happy and really friendly people, the vast majority, ...but the contrast between the obscenely rich and the obscenely poor is vast...bit of an eye-opener for me...

But it's good that virtually everyone in this closely guarded marina, in the middle of downtown Salvador, gives food to those kids who have given up...never money, just any spare piece of meat, bread etc......not to those kids who run around asking for food.... they still have some fight in them...only to those who are "defeated"......

Everything is ridiculously cheap here.....a full meal for seven of us costs around $15...beautifully cooked too....anything can be fixed/mended here too, except electronics....welders, carpenters, fibreglassers, sailmakers..etc.......sad bit is that I haven't needed any of them...that's all stuff I'd rather do myself...

And the nearby playground of islands are really lovely..unspoilt, deserted, quiet..some white sandy beaches....bird-wildlife I've never seen before...fishermen use dugout canoes and sails....charts have quite reasonably large areas marked as "Unsurveyed"...it's a pity I can't spend a year here, just exploring THIS particular area.....

I'm fairly well recovered now...quite respectable bits of missing memory of those first 4 days have returned, or are surfacing still, though still jumbled up a bit, so there was perhaps more damage to me than I had thought...silly thing is that I was totally unaware they were missing........(I thought it was impossible to get brain damage if I hadn't got a brain!)....

Still planning to be south of Rio, ready to start the major part of this voyage, around Eastertime....that should be interesting, because it's going to be 2-3 months at sea....quite looking forward to it really....

Keep trying the odd sextant sight...wins you no end of "street-cred"!....

I'll pass on your best wishes to Tot and the family.....thanks!

And Stay Well, both of you!...

      Doc

Wed 11/02/2004 01:37
Subject: "Having a bit of a Moan")
Dear Trudi, Jack, and Gerard,

Once again my thanks for your support, because I'm gently going up the wall with frustration at the delays here....I thought I knew how to be patient, but clearly not at present!...

Being tied to a big city with all its noise, smells, lights and bureaucratic complications is most definitely NOT what I came here for....I can see the fun of the place, but I'm a country lad, and Metropolis is beginning to wear a bit thin here now.....

Daft, isn't it......to spend most of your sailing life longing to get back into harbour, and the moment you do, you can't wait to get back out there again!

No earth-shattering news from Salvador, I'm afraid....we know that my parcel is in Brazil (presumably in Salvador Customs) and we know that Customs have said they want to return it to its point of origin because the total value is said to be more than $3000 (if so, it's by a few cents only.....must be small dollars I think).....(I had wondered whether to split it into smaller lots, but decided that it would invite suspicion)......now the carrier has said they've lost track of it, although we specified that the package's progress would be monitored at every step of the journey........the only ray of hope at present is that the carrier has advised me to do nothing while they try to sort it out from both here in Brazil and from the UK end......"just wait" she said....sensible advice........I think they're used to this sort of problem......but I will continue to be a very polite nuisance to them, enquiring very frequently as to any more news etc........that way they'll have to sort it out, just to get rid of me........

It sounds awfully like what I would call a "Scam" ....I've seen it happen in the past to other yachts in other poorer countries .....hoped Brazil might be a bit better than that.......we will see....

Meantime, found evidence today of yet another small plastic-insulation fire on that day, in the compass binnacle itself, below where the main steering compass blew up.....that makes FOUR separate fires in all........(I find it incredibly lucky that I wasn't "out" for long, and that by some reflex (maybe from my flying days?) I had killed the master-switches)......so, more wires replaced today (at least that's something I CAN do!)....

And I've started contingency plans to continue this voyage with the bits I have with me now, just in case.....sort of 1950's style of sailing....primitive, harder work, using the sextant as a tool, rather than as an interest etc....self-steering will be a bit more vague....allowance will have to be made for the broken main compass (there are small spare ones)... the kitchen timers I use as alarm clocks (critically important for me, singlehanded, otherwise I can't rest) are all purely mechanical ones, for this very situation.....and sails and ropes, the stars, the sea and the weather are timeless.....

Family, friends and other yachts' crews here have been most sympathetic, which has helped a lot.....

Sorry to sound so wrapped up in my own problems....I know it will all work out for the best whatever happens!..

My sincere thanks to everyone on the Nets, including Doug, Tom and Des...it's most supportive just hearing your interest.....sorry radio signals to and from Salvador City are so rubbishy at present....

Stay Well!

Tuesday'n'me.

Fri 13/02/2004 04:36

Subject: Climbing up the wall.

Dear Everybodies,

Rapidly going crackers here....waiting for the package of electronics from England .... there is so much I could be getting on with if the bits were here ..... very frustrating ......

Believe it or not, it already arrived once in Brazil (Salvador Airport), only to be returned to Brussels (head-office of the carrier) by the wisdom of Brazilian Customs.....(certainly these components are clocking up a lot of miles!).......unfortunately, the comments I would like to make about this total mess-up are frowned upon in polite society........

Maybe one day I'll look back on this example of bureaucratic idiocy and laugh about it................but not today........

There is a fridge-magnet on board.....it says "Never trust a doctor whose office-plants are dead!", a gift from 2002's Retirement Bash ......I've found it has absolutely no magnetism left in it at all, since the lightning.....won't even deflect a compass at all ....

And found a striplight in the engine-room had blown the end out of its bulb, and wrecked its inverter.....but it's nowhere near any obvious path of the strike.........

Also, had discovered evidence of a FOURTH fire in plastic insulation inside the steering binnacle, underneath the main compass (which was itself wrecked)...............

Imagine the sheer SCALE of massive electromagnetic forces around in that elemental instant, to cause all these extraordinary effects at some distance from the actual electrical path........makes me feel very small indeed..............

A handheld GPS, right alongside the lightning's entry into the cabin, survived completely intact, even remembering all the track of last year's Arctic trip.......probably because it was in an aluminium-foil-lined Cool-bag, specifically for this eventuality.....

It's Friday 13th tomorrow.....it was 13th January when things went all chaotic......now, I'm not really superstitious, but if it weren't so hot (38c in the shade today) I think I would stay in bed all tomorrow and read a book....................

One lighter moment...in the evening, it abruptly started to rain heavily....instantly the pontoon was full of scurrying wet figures, frantically leaving the boats they were visiting to return to their own, to shut all the open hatches etc................so, when it begins to rain here, it appears that everyone swaps ships.....

Very Best Wishes!

Tuesday'n'me.

Sun 15/02/2004 02:07
   Subject: Repairing "Tuesday",(and me)
      Dear Bill'n'Buddy,

Just a simple update on progress here.....Still in Salvador itself, gently going crackers waiting for electronic-bits to arrive....they arrived in Salvador Customs over a week ago, who promptly refused them entry because they were "too valuable" (?!)....so the shippers took them back to Brussels, via a delay in Amsterdam (crazy, ain't it!), and we hope they'll set off again, repackaged, in the next few days.......

Meantime I'm going SPARE here, in the heat, the sun passing overhead here tomorrow, on its way northwards......I can't do anything more till they arrive, so I'm thumb-twiddling....it's like being in jail, sitting out your time.......

There's a whole long list of weird things damaged throughout the whole ship...eg. magnets reversed in ammeters....a fridge magnet has lost all trace of magnetism......compass blown apart....etc etc...I keep finding new bits of peculiar damage each day......

And obviously, a major rewiring exercise, now completed......

As for me, pretty well recovered now, though still some residual memory problems, particularly for those first four days which are still rather "muddled".....bits of missing memory returning, which I was completely unaware of having lost...... each day something new comes back......strange, but not painful!.........but I can still work out a sextant sight OK!....

What news of yourself and Mum?...it must be very difficult, when there's not a whole lot one can do......Mother Nature is definitely in charge......

If you think I can help/advise/explain in any way, Bill, do use me....I still find all things medical fascinating, (and I've been quite in demand here on the pontoon in Salvador, which has been interesting.....diseases seem fairly international!).....

Still hoping you might be able to come to Salvador, but I appreciate the difficulties...

         Stay well!
            Doc'n'Tuesday.

Monday 17/2/04 02:40
   Subject: " SNAFU"..a little disenchanted perhaps?..
      Dear Everybodies,

Just about managed to crawl out of yet another bureaucratic mess today.....it was quietly pointed out to me that although I had imported ME into the country (as my passport has been stamped to that effect), I hadn't actually finished importing the ship herself, through Customs.....

Luckily for me, Customs employ humans with brains .....(unlike the Police Federal here ....the guy looked at me standing in front of him and said very grumpily that he was refusing to sign me in to Salvador again as I was still in Rio.........that baffled me, too........ till I realised that HE was the one with the problem.....OK, so I'm still in Rio, if he says so....he's clearly a Very Clever Man and knows about these things....)

Customs understood the problem of a "dumb" Englishman, and neatly got round the paperwork by backdating my ship-importing-papers to when my passport was stamped .....(even the passport itself had been incorrectly stamped by the Police Federal, as they showed me, obviously quite used to it!).......

It's a bit like that Karaoke in Oleao, Portugal.......it's so AWFUL that at first it's amusing, then annoying, then infuriating.... and finally back to funny again, as you wonder just how bad and disorganised and chaotic the system can get, without actually grinding to a standstill...

The saga of the electronics package from the UK continues.... the shipping agent (Brazil) says its now arrived back in Brussels again, to have its paperwork corrected...... ....their office (Brussels) told me today confidently it's in Brazil.......neither of them seem to have any record of it since 13th Feb '04......... "Carnival"

121

(a week-long public holiday signifying the beginning of Lent, they tell me, though they seem to have little in common) begins in two days time.....the country comes to a shuddering halt, I gather...... so not a lot is going to happen with this package, I suspect........my plans at present are beginning to exclude its arrival on board at all......

On top of all this, the agents (Brazil) say today they will only take it as far as Sao Paulo airport....Wow, thanks, that's a REAL help....it's only 900+ miles from here, and inland too......makes it a little bit awkward though, if they want me to pick it up personally.....

IF it ever arrives, before my 90 day visa expires, I wonder what will be the contents, compared with what left the UK on 5th February.....and if this is "Express" Delivery, I'd be intrigued to know what the Ordinary one is like?......

I thought only a computer could really foul things up...... .....WRONG!...come to Brazil where they are REAL experts at "SNAFU"!.....it takes a great deal of skill to mess things up as well as this.....you have to grudgingly give them credit for it......

Anyway, enough griping about it for now...I trust all is well with you, at least......
     Tuesday'n'me.

(RECEIVED) Wed 18/02/2004 17:50
     just checked the status of Waybill 9980393485 on the DHL tracking page. It was received this morning at 0808 in Viracopos and at 1236 it says "Clearance Delay". Here we go, AGAIN! I hope David is following this by phone in Brazil. **Jack**

Thu 19/02/2004 03:31
     Dear Gerard, Trudi, and Jack,
          I don't know how you did it, but things are happening at last!...my daily phone call to the shippers (Brussels) was obviously completely misinterpreted as being aggressive (I really tried to make sure it wasn't at all, but that's how it appears it must have been received).....and Gerard's amazing ability to smooth troubled waters then got things moving... then Jack's follow-up call reinforced an International Concern about my electronics-in-transit, which helped too....

So much so that I gather the agent would only talk to Gerard and nobody else about it....(how on earth did you manage that, Gerard?....VERY impressive!....)

The combination produced a much clearer picture of what was happening..suddenly we know where it is, and what to do....

So today, with Paola as interpreter, I went to Customs here in Salvador, who helpfully produced a list of Brokers for finding a way through the Importation Customs maze at the airport 900 miles away..... by pure chance, our conversation was overheard by a very helpful chap in the office who said HE was a Broker too, and could he help?....doesn't speak English, but his understudy does...

Across the road to his 9th floor, spotlessly clean office, where suddenly there was sympathy, support and interest in the problem....humour too....two telephone calls (in Portuguese) later and we're getting somewhere now...... very reasonable fee agreed, but likely to have to pay a hefty import tax, in spite of international Yacht-In-Transit rules........

The outcome is that Paola and he composed a letter appointing Eduardo as the agent for "Tuesday" for Customs, while I went back to the ship to bring back the Official Ship's Seal to give more weight to it ...(this seal was put on board as a "spoof" stamp, as a joke.......never dreamt it would actually be useful!...it looks very important on the letter, though!............the only copy is 4' high, painted on the harbour wall in Porto Santo, with the Port Police's positive encouragement....the design includes a medical-rep's-free-sample human-body-outline shape on it, advertising something or other pharmaceutical).........

There's a lot more to the story than that, but you can get the picture, at least..... Now we wait and see....

Meantime I'm going to do what all the locals do at Carnival-time.....sail off to the nearby, but much quieter, islands, to avoid all the chaos in the city...together with two other boats "Why Not?" (Phillip and Paola) and "Sailmaker", (Ivan and Christina from Geneva who are making the new bimini and sprayhood for "Tuesday")......will keep in touch with Eduardo by local phone, for progress reports....

You may not have realised it at the time, but I think the International interest in this saga must have helped considerably....THANK you, gentlemen, most sincerely....

(I'll believe it's all finalised when the bits are physically BOLTED into the ship, though)...

　　　　Very Grateful!
　　　　Tuesday'n'me.

Fri 20/02/2004 00:49
　　Subject: Island of Itaparica (i)
　　　Dear Everybodies,

White sand beaches, palm trees, clear smooth seawater.... and gentle, pleasantly relaxed, smiling and friendly people.......it's very quiet...soft cooling wind (temperature is still 35c indoors, but it feels comfortable because of the breeze)........the drinking water tastes better too.......VERY different from Salvador!....

What a crying shame the replacement parts never turned up when they should have....could of had this present environment for the past two to three weeks if they had..............Ah well, poo happens sometimes...

It wasn't all that easy to get here, with no self-steering gear and one or two other problems...but it was well worth the effort to see this very beautiful place...the two other yachts are already here, and everyone is comfortably "mellow"...even the "Fifty Quid!" birds sound calmer and less agitated here too......

Planning to spend a few days around hereabouts, keeping in touch with the importer-brokers by phone (I have a local mobile-phone number now)....expecting no news till later next week I gather (Carnival)....we will await developments....

Once again, most grateful thanks to all on the Transatlantic Net for their support, which I am sure was instrumental in gently getting the shipping agents to concentrate a little harder.......

Some people are good at finding ways of making a living.......one young lad carries cheese around with him.... on sticks like kebabs....dips them in seeds and herbs in a polythene bag....produces from his backpack an already LIT charcoal stove made of pieces of tin...and cooks the cheese there and then on the pavement....good "non-touch" technique too.....they are MOUTHWATERING!.....cooked to perfection....and cost a few pence each....

Another idea I've not seen before involves charities collecting your receipts at the supermarkets....they then go to the supermarket and say "we KNOW you sold this value of goods, but how much did you actually declare for tax purposes?"......the supermarkets are then for some reason(!) keen to donate the missing amount straight to the charity.........neat, isn't it, although it relies on widespread corruption continuing....

Chain-mail clothes, made from aluminium ring-pulls from beercans.........watch out for thunderstorms though!.....

Ivan and Christina, from Geneva, are professional sail repairers etc...not allowed to advertise in Brazil (nor Madeira I understand)....changed the name of the 18 ton yacht they live on to "SAILMAKER", now written in great big letters on the cockpit dodgers etc....and it's right where their market would see it too, in every anchorage they go to........

Oh it's such a relief to get away from the city! Stay Well! **Tuesday'n'me.**

(RECEIVED)Fri 20/02/2004 14:42

CONGRATULATIONS! on finally moving on, what a nightmare trying to get parts, guess the family will say "should have stayed home, you bloody fool!"

Glad to hear the anchorage is as it should be, peaceful, fun, colorful and without hassles.

We are still in St. Lucia, mom & dad finally arrived and stayed 9 days too long, but it was fun. St. Lucia is celebrating their 25th anniversary, so we are staying for jazz and music and free food (yum).

Mad River made it to Trinidad in time for carnival.

Pendragon is 2 days out of Panama and Free Spirit are still honeymooning!

Miss you and glad things are underway again.

We'll write again soon.

Love, Capt. **Ron & Bonnie**

Sun 22/02/2004 02:40

Subject: I can see the stars again!

Dear Ron'n'Bonnie,

Thanks for your Email, full of news....GREAT to hear how everyone is!......

Here still not resumed the main voyage, but diverting to inspect some more of this lovely bay ...it really is very pretty, with no end of secluded anchorages in sheltered waters.....Tuesday'n'me explored all of a very charming river today......another tomorrow ....lovely people on the islands too....... (still not recovered from watching all the dancing maidens at Carnival last night.... ....(purely Medical/Anatomical interest, you understand, of course).......... mobile sculpture........poetry in motion.......)

But I have to return to Salvador itself for the next few days in the ongoing Saga of the Shipping Agent, the Package and Customs.....oh POOEY!

There is still a bit of damage from the Big Zap annoyingly.....still can't "multitask" (I think it's called) as I did before, and p*ssed off with forgetting where I just put something down ....everyone does it, I know, but it's a seriously significant problem at times........I don't think I'm quite back to "me" again yet .... but Tot pointed out that it's still very early days in the recovery process, like with concussion....

Still wondering if your Mum really did bring a thong with her........!

Warmest Best Wishes to you both, and Greetings to the Gang when you contact them!,

Stay well!, **Mad Doc.**

(RECEIVED) Fri 20/02/2004 08:09

Subject: News

Hi Doc

Finally I get time to write in peace, so here´s our news...

It´s Friday 20th and our last day in Nice, we have managed to pack everything in our van so now it is overloaded and I have to drive very slowly the 1875 kilometers back to Cadiz so as to board the ferry that will carry us to Las Palmas, where we have to spend a full day waiting to board another Ferry to Lanzarote arriving there on Friday in a week.....bloody long trip, too many hours driving, waiting...

Nice and I guess all of France is so different once you have lived in the Canary islands, we do not like it any more and could not think of living Here. People are so aggressive, traffic jams, dirty etc.... what a small piece of paradise we have at Playa Blanca...

So this is mainly the news from our side, we shall not be able to read any mail before next Friday but will try to give you a call on your new Brasilian phone just to check if it works and to hear your voice, you know we also miss your presence, believe it or not!

Have read all what's happened, the Shippers hit etc....have patience....you have the luxury of having time, and everything is an experience.

Life in Brasil is so different, I once tried to settle there but could not manage to, the nicest part for me was the south, almost near the border to Uruguay, the more south you go the whiter people get and the more it looks like Europe! .... a totally different Brasil.

It is so funny because I think I am the only one who knows what you are talking about when you mention the food by the kilo or the grilled cheese etc....wish I was there with you there are so many things I could show you that you go near and do not even notice they exist...but I am sure you do
make the most of it anyway.

If you get the opportunity do go with some other boat people to a CHURRASCARIA this is a place where you pay a fixed price, have salad bar and the different kinds of meats are braught on a skewer to your table for as long as you can eat! it is a real treat and I used to love it.....just take it easy when you start eating and let time go by, you can stay as long as you can and eat as much as you can so no rush... by the way it youou see small skewers with little blackened things they are chicken hearts, a delicacy in Brasil nd actually do not taste that bad.

You take good care of yourself, and remember you have a friend if you ever need anything!
   Chris

Sun 22/02/2004 02:39
   Subject: Nearly starting to smile again, a bit.
      Dear Chris'n'Tashi,

Really enjoyed your phone message and the Email with all its interesting news and info this evening! .... WONDERFUL!.....THANK YOU.........(it's done me good too, because I was so wrapped up in my own gloom and problems I was failing to remember that everyone else has difficulties to climb over as well)......GREAT to keep in touch and follow your progress!....

Lots of useful information about Brazil in your Email....thank you!....gives me things to look for, though being afloat and tied to guarding the ship limits me a bit..........

Every cloud has a silver lining they say....(B*LL*CKS, I say)......but I HAVE seen things and met people I wouldn't have otherwise, so all in all I suppose I've gained out of his maddening waiting.......the river I explored with "Tuesday" today is particularly beautiful........another tomorrow....

I've not been diving again, although I really miss it.......I was put off by the fish-dynamiting near where I had been down that one time, and the amount of diseased sh*t and cr*p that goes into the sea there gives me the shudders....how I long to be under clean water again.....I don't know if Tashi remembers, but I recall saying to her once that after each dive I felt calmer, walked a little slower, spoke a bit quieter............I need my "mellow" fix!...

The Agents now say the parcel has arrived at its destination ......but it HASN'T though!........

All this hassle was what I came sailing to get AWAY from, dammit............

So I had to get out of Salvador to restore some degree of sanity........it's difficult because I don't have suitable self-steering-gear, a proper compass, etc etc, and I'm knackered today after some hard sailing with no aids to help ease the workload..... but we're getting there, Tuesday'n'me........

I've still got a few problems myself as a result of the "Zap" ....they would have been seriously problematic if I were still at work, but I can bumble my way round them usually......short term memory weakness, can't cope with too any problems at a time yet, etc......it'll be interesting to see how I cope at sea again, but I don't think it will make a whole heap of difference as long as I "pace" myself......we will see...... (my daughter pointed out that it's still very early days in the recovery process).......

   Thanks for "listening"... Safe Journey! Missing you both... **Doc.**

Tue 24/02/2004 03:56
> **Tropical Islands**
> > **Dear Everybodies,**

These rivers and islands are very beautiful indeed.....such a contrast from Salvador itself!....beaches of different colours (reds, yellows, orange and white)....cliffs and rocks of a variety of hues....and the contrasting light and dark greens of the palm trees and forests behind.......all under the deep blue sky.........

After sailing through a gorge in one river, with its swirling crosscurrents, came into a vast lagoon where the chart shows large areas as "unsurveyed".... three more rivers run into it, and there are more little islands.....delightful!.....

But there's a sting in its tail........I tried to round one of the bigger islands where it looked as though it might be OK, but kept running out of "deeps".......never hit any, but shoals everywhere, some rocky, some softer (judging by the ship's spare echosounder returns), a real nest of vipers....(no wonder some of it wasn't surveyed!).... eventually decided a safe retreat seemed sensible and, in a rising strong wind, struggled against wind and current to beat the way back out of the trap again....it took ages, and I ran out of daylight.........so groped my way in dense darkness (I still have no main compass) to a place I'd spotted earlier in the day, close to a red sandstone cliff, and anchored for the night, not keen to explore uncharted waters in future........(the moral is that some charts are like some newspapers, telling an interesting story loosely woven around the true facts).........

To my great joy, the next morning dawn-light showed it to be a stunningly entrancing place, with a small golden beach, the forest beyond it, and undercut cliffs each side......silence except for the crickets, and the dawn chorus of birdsong (including the "Fifty quid!" birds)...........then soon after sunrise, was surrounded by a large school of 30+ River Dolphins (I think they are... NOT Harbour Porpoises).............still can't believe it's all real!.....

It's been hard work, with none of the usual support from self-steering-gear, etc..... having to do everything the old-fashioned way....steering by fine-tuning the sail balance etc, which is not easy in confined waters and variable winds.......but I've been gradually pushing the ship harder and harder, to check that the rigging etc is still up to scratch after its electric-shock-treatment....all OK so far....

But I have to return to the stink and sweat and noise of Salvador City tomorrow, partly to collect a replacement alternator-regulator from the UK by "other means of transport" ....

Still finding unexpected effects of the Whizzbang.....a photoelectric switch that doesn't anymore (switch, ie).....a diving compass giving crazy readings, (till I moved it with a view to binning it....turns out that it's OK, but the cupboard behind it is now heavily magnetised....must be all the Baked Beans tins in it....they certainly weren't advertised as being Magnetic Beans when I bought them!).... It's going to take quite some time to set up the new Ship's Compass to balance out these effects (if it does ever actually arrive on board)....

Oh, and the sun now swings to the NORTH of me at noon...that's another "first" for ...

> > ...Tuesday'n'me.
> > Best Wishes!

Thu 26/02/2004 06:16
> **Subject: Back in the smelly old city again...**
> > **Dear Everybodies,**

Coming back to Salvador, after the beauty of the islands, felt like going back to school again after a lovely holiday ....smells, power cuts, water-supply failures, taxi-drivers trying to overcharge, shops all shut, pickpockets, the infernal racket of brain-killing drum beats playing African rhythms........many bands of enthusiastic musicians competing with each other....... Carnival in full swing (the musicians are really enjoying themselves, although all playing different tunes!)...................and the worries of diplomacy in a foreign language still to come (hopefully to gain the release of The Package).........

Actually, I shouldn't dare to moan......it's quite a sight (and sound), which I wouldn't have seen otherwise.........the ship's deck actually vibrating with the mega-decibels..........everybody on shore very cheerful and happy, although a bit "spaced out"..........a myriad different coloured lights ....all the way through every night till dawn......(also gangs of half-a-dozen-or-so heavily armed police, only occasionally leaping into the crowds and forcibly arresting someone.....usually perfectly justifiably too)...

But it's really not my cup of tea.........

Got stung by Fire Coral yesterday, handling a rope to help someone moor up... I took care to avoid it, I thought....obviously not carefully enough.....won't do THAT again!......

Another yacht was visited by real-life Hobbits (or were they Goblins?).........nonsailing friends from their own Mother-country ....Di   sastrous!.....weird behaviour, apparently almost ASKING to be robbed......even being told off by the police to be more careful......drove the crew crackers......When they finally left to fly home, left a parting calamity behind them by accidentally pulling a reefing line through the boom so that the single-line-reefing system no longer works..... I suspect I nearly witnessed a murder at the time!......

A singlehanded sailor I've met here saved a drowning Brazilian man's life three days ago......it seems the nonswimming chap was persuaded to cross a river supported by his two swimming friends.....one got cramp and abandoned him (nice to know who your real friends are!)......the victim was unconscious and full of water when he was dragged ashore, but with my friend's help they got him going again......life seems cheap here methinks.....

I thought the best ice-cream came from Mallaig in Scotland.........wrong again!......on the Island of Itaparica you wander round the shop collecting many samples of different mouthwatering ices, dropping them into a bowl.....you pay by the kilo.......a kaleidoscope of tastes, tuned to your own personal specification! ....WONDERFUL!....

Watching the dancing maidens on the island during Carnival was watching pure poetry in motion.....relaxed, totally at ease with the beat of the music .....so elegant ....if I were younger I might have been tempted to get into trouble, but thank heavens I'm older now and can simply observe, as I know they can all run faster than me ....

Yesterday, a Brazilian guard had got dressed and started to leave after having a shower here in the marina ...Philippe runs out after him virtually naked..."Oi, mate, you've left your gun in here!"...embarrassed guard, very grateful, beats a hasty retreat.............................Welcome to Brazil!

But....... Dear Brazilian Bureaucracy, PLEASE, let me have my electronics soon...............

All the Very Best!

Tuesday'n'me.

Thu 26/02/2004 06:16

Dear Gerard,

Nice to hear you again, though radio signals into and out of Salvador itself are very poor, I'm afraid....

Just to confirm, my present plans are stay here until I can collect the much-travelled-electronic-package (though heaven only knows when and where!), then to spend another week or so in the lovely islands fitting the bits, and knocking the ship back into ocean-going-condition again, before heading off southwards....intending to stay 150 to 200 miles offshore until somewhere south of Rio...then hoping to explore some estuaries in South Brazil.....

I have to leave Brazil by early April, planning to go to St.Helena, (possibly via Tristan de Cunha Island if the weather is kind).....then to the Azores.......(a l-o-n-g trip!).....and eventually back to the UK, perhaps in

127

August.........

All is well on board, apart from the maddening frustration of waiting for these essential parts..... individuals in Brazil are really lovely people, but the moment anything requires organisation, or a uniform, the system falls apart...........but it's their country, and I don't suppose the UK is any better in reciprocal circumstances anyway......

Yet again, thank you for all your efforts and support, and I promise I will let you know the moment I have the electronics checked and actually on board the ship.......

Warmest Greetings!

Tuesday'n'me.

PS. Sorry about the misunderstanding ... the "7 3" referred to "best wishes", NOT to the "7th of March"!.....poor radiosignals confused the picture!....

Sat 28/02/2004 02:23

Subject: Doing "porridge".

Dear Bill,

Still furiously kicking my heels here...still no replacement electronics yet...stuck in Customs at Sao Paulo we think, but helpful Broker, and Customs in Salvador, working on my behalf.....

The Bay here is very lovely .... I rebelled and spent a few days out amongst the islands and rivers, before having to come back to Salvador itself to continue the diplomacy again.....unlikely I'll be able to head south again for at least another 2 weeks, but hope to do most of the final work on board at ITAPARICA ISLAND, in the bay here, (if I ever get me bits out of Customs).....peaceful there, friendly and safe.....there's a good sailmender, sprayhood-maker, with his charming family, working from his boat there, so I'm getting a new pramhood and bimini made while I wait....

Keep in touch!

Doc

(RECEIVED) Thu 26/02/2004 14:40

Hallo David,

AS Gerald said today - (I had lovely copy on him, we also called you, but I don't think you were there) - we are all living in hope, firstly for you and your electronics parcel to get united, and for Gerald a start to springtime temperatures soon, it sounds very cold in Europe.

Thank you for your E-mails .The change from your paradise island to Salvador sounds quite a shock. We were in Honduras last month, and the South American "ambience" is a bit overwhelming, I know. Colourful and - very, very noisy. Fireworks at Christmas parties, usually those noisy crackers. One wonders why not everybody is prematurely deaf. And we thought Barbados was too noisy, it's sleepy here in comparison!

We are off on holiday from Saturday, 28th Feb. - again, I suppose everybody is saying, but we have had a very busy two months with non-stop house guests - for a week's cruise on the "Royal Clipper" (largest sailing ship in the world today). I am sure Jack and Gerard will keep things going on 21.400.

Here's crossing fingers and thumbs - love, **Trudi**

Sat 28/02/2004 05:55

Dear Trudi,

Thank you yet again for your nice comforting and supportive Email...I always enjoy them...they cheer me up!....

I'm most embarrassed at how much time and effort you've all put in to help me, especially when all my life it's been drummed into me to be self sufficient and independent...but it has really helped enormously..

128

Have a lovely time on "Royal Clipper"...I'm very envious indeed, and looking forward to hearing all about it on your return....I hope it's FUN as well as relaxing..you certainly deserve it!..
Very Warmest Wishes!
David.

Thu 29/01/2004 19:03
Great news that all is going well with the repairs. Graham sends his best wishes to you. He has returned from his transatlantic trip which went well but not without some problems, the worst of which was a charging problem resulting in no means of charging the batteries. So hand steering for half the trip (lesson is don't have all your eggs in one basket.. we know this doc, don't we, he says from his warm home)..
When I told him of your slight hiccup he thought his was well down on the rictor scale.
I know you will be just fine when you get under way again. Trust me I am not a doctor.
Take care,
love james and Liz

(RECEIVED)Sun 22/02/2004 12:21
Envious that's me, bloody envious, we have 4deg C and wall to wall grey, at least 10 days of grey, then there's the N/E wind ......
Regards, Joe.

Tue 02/03/2004 02:30
Subject: STILL, Shipping Agents, Customs, etc etc
Dear Everybodies,
(Just to keep you updated with this miserable business of the replacement electronics..)
Three days ago some paperwork from the carrier arrived at the delivery address, about the package... within one hour I personally put it into the hands of the Broker..
The helpful Broker in Salvador managed to be granted a conference with the headman of Salvador Customs, the same evening.. the Customs Boss is a highly intelligent but blind man called Fernando, who rapidly grasped the situation, quietly asked a few very sensible questions, and produced a plan of action..
So today I have been sent to the civilian permit place, then the Police Federal main headquarters, and finally to the British Consul himself (an excellent man, who told me in no uncertain terms that I have done exactly the right things all the way along)........ Apparently it's for more proof of who I am (I'm beginning to wonder myself now!)......The Consul says categorically there should be NO tax to pay, and Customs should personally see the goods are placed aboard the vessel, as they are technically "Bonded Stores".......he's not seen this sort of mess up before, and wonders what's going on.....however he is not completely certain about the Broker, or finds him naive, (although I explained that somewhere along the line I had to trust somebody local to help)...suggested I phone his friend to check him out (I've done so, and all seems OK)....
So I am to produce the paper from the Consul, the ship's documents, and my passport (for the umpteenth time!) tomorrow, so that copies can be faxed to Sao Paulo to prove (yet again!) I am the lawful recipient of the package..
Then Customs have to decide how much Tax they will charge me (it seems everything is "adjustable" here..paying a Tax is not legally required in this situation they say, but they tell me that it would take months for the package to be released otherwise, because of twists and turns of Bureaucracy)....
Then, hopefully, I pay up and we start the package delivery process yet again..
The sad part is that I only have 90 days visa in Brazil.. already 50 of those are gone, and so far I've seen

129

very little except the zits on the backside of Salvador city..and the seasons are marching steadily on towards when I must be leaving this continent anyway...

You may remember that the package arrived in Brazil on Feb 10th, originally, (and by the time the shipper's paperwork was sorted out and it arrived back in this country for the SECOND time, everywhere had shut down for a week at Carnival)....... that one error by these agents has cost me nearly three weeks delay already, and a lot more besides time...I am not impressed..........and then for them to say it had been fully delivered when clearly it hasn't, seems a bitter pill to swallow.....maybe their contract is merely airport-to-airport?...

It seems so upsetting to me that all the success in managing to save both myself and the vessel, and then being as resourceful as possible to rebuild her again, count for nothing, and cheapens my efforts .....

And remember also that the Police Federal here are still insisting I'm in Rio (he refuses to take in the fact that the disaster meant I had to limp back to Salvador for repairs)........ so that I have to actually go to Rio before I can clear out of the country..

I keep feeling, in my gloomier moments, that I'm being punished for something, but I just don't understand what I've done wrong....

Sorry to go on and on and on about it... and once again, my most grateful thanks for all your help..
Both Tuesday and me.

(RECEIVED)Tue 02/03/2004 09:36
You ARE being punished - for your freedom!........
Best of luck with your package (and I hope the delivery reaches you too).
Jan

Wed 03/03/2004 11:50
Subject: A ray of sunshine!..
Dear Jan,
(You wicked girl!..loved your Email..brought a chuckle into the cabin, right when it needed it!)

Thanks for all the news, especially as I was wondering yesterday how you were getting on...I confess I do not regret retiring before you did/do...it would have been very difficult for me the other way round..

Still doing lots of medicine though, ...just giving a personal ("nonmedical") opinion unofficially, when asked by other crews for advice....so far seen one pneumonia, one frozen shoulder, three separate pairs of otitis media, one arthritis of the neck vertebrae, one tropical ulcer in an embarrassing place (and no, it wasn't syphilis!), one peptic ulcer, an asthma, several warts, and countless other ailments and injuries.... definitely no stitching (pity, I enjoy some of those, but unwise to do any ACTIVE treatment here I think), but several splinters removed...I LOVE it, and now I know why I studied medicine in the first place.......and so far, I'm amazed that every single one has recovered (or are they just saying that to avoid me?)...

It's a slight worry that one boat came 30 miles back here, because I knew them already and they needed help (the Pneumonia)...in fact they had decided on the right treatment from their own ship's supplies, but wanted reassurance that they were correct before starting it...did my ego no end of good!, but I felt unworthy of it......but 30 miles sailing, against the wind and waves, to see the doc...would NHS patients do that?..

And it's so refreshingly simple to get medication ..just go to the pharmacy (several all in tight competition nearby) and ask for (almost) anything..cheap too!.......so I go with the victim/patient... they ask for, and buy, the drug required, but under my watchful eye....

Also found the various crews are very keen to have their first-aid kits and medicine chests reviewed...I must have seen more than 20 now, all different, and I'm proud to say that "Tuesday's" own kit is not quite the

130

worst (though it's a bit close to it!)..

Isn't it a shame that the NHS overload kills off that enthusiasm and interest in many of its doctors and nurses...

Enjoy part-time work while you can....'cos you're going to be damn busy when you retire, I can tell you!

Warmest Love, Jan....and Stay Well!

Me

(RECEIVED) Tue 02/03/2004 12:14

subject: War and Peace

Daweed,

Seems to me, now would be excellent time to read (and finish) "War and Peace". Could send copy by any means except the dilatory haulage league...looks like that French lone sailor chappie will have sailed round the world in a shorter time than it takes dilatory haulage league to deliver package from Plymouth to Salvador. Alternatively, you could "Teach Yourself Finnish"...a horrendously difficult language to learn (even the Swedes can't manage it). You would be fluent when you leave Brazil.

Woddy.

(RECEIVED) Sun 29/02/2004 21:58

Subject: Darwin Awards 2003

Dad,

Thought this might make you laugh and help cheer you up a bit. I doubt if any of these are true but they are still funny nonetheless. Darwin Awards 2003:-

1. When his 38-calibre revolver failed to fire at his intended victim during a hold-up in Long Beach, California, would be robber James Elliot did something that can only inspire wonder. He peered down the barrel and tried the trigger again. This time it worked.....

2. The chef at a hotel in Switzerland lost a finger in a meat cutting machine and, after a little hopping around, submitted a claim to his insurance company. The company suspecting negligence, sent out one of its men to have a look for himself. He tried the machine and lost a finger. The chef's claim was approved.

3. A man who shovelled snow for an hour to clear a space for his car during a blizzard in Chicago returned with his Vehicle to find a woman had taken the space. Understandably, he shot her.

4. After stopping for drinks at an illegal bar, a Zimbabwean bus driver found that the 20 mental patients he was supposed to be transporting from Harare to Bulawayo had escaped. Not wanting to admit his incompetence, the driver went to a nearby bus stop and offered everyone waiting there a free ride. He then delivered the passengers to the mental hospital, telling the staff that the patients were very excitable and prone to bizarre fantasies. The deception wasn't discovered for 3 days.

5. An American teenager was in the hospital recovering from serious head wounds received from an oncoming train. When asked how he received the injuries, the lad told police that he was simply trying to see how close he could get his head to a moving train before he was hit.

6. A man walked into a Louisiana Circle-K, put a $20 bill on the counter, and asked for change. When the clerk opened the cashdrawer, the man pulled a gun and asked for all the cash in the register, which the clerk promptly provided. The man took the cash from the clerk and fled, leaving the $20 bill on the counter. The total amount of cash he got from the drawer...$15. (If someone points a gun at you and gives you money, is a crime committed?)

7. A thief burst into a Florida bank one day wearing a ski mask and carrying a gun. Aiming his gun at the guard, the thief yelled, "FREEZE,

MOTHER-STICKERS, THIS IS A **** UP!" For a moment, everyone was silent. Then the sniggers started. The security guard completely lost it and doubled over laughing. It probably saved his life, because he'd been about to draw his gun. He couldn't have drawn and fired before the thief got him. The thief ran away and is still at large. In memory of the event, the banker later put a plaque on the wall engraved with the words, "Freeze, mother-stickers, this is a ****-up!"

8. Seems an Arkansas guy wanted some beer pretty badly. He decided that he'd just throw a cinderblock through a liquor store window, grab some booze, and run. So he lifted the cinderblock and heaved it over his head at the window. The cinderblock bounced back and hit the would-be thief on the head, knocking him unconscious. The liquor store window was made of Plexiglas The whole event was caught on videotape.

9. As a female shopper exited a New York convenience store, a man grabbed her purse and ran. The clerk called 911 immediately, and the woman was able to give them a detailed description of the snatcher. Within minutes, the police apprehended the snatcher. They put him in the car and drove back to the store. The thief was then taken out of the car and told to stand there for a positive ID. To which he replied, "Yes, officer, that's her. That's the lady I stole the purse from."

10. The Ann Arbor News crime column reported that a man walked into a Burger King in Ypsilanti, Michigan, at 5 a.m., flashed a gun, and demanded cash. The clerk turned him down because he said he couldn't open the cash register without a food order. When the man ordered onion rings, the clerk said they weren't available for breakfast. The man, frustrated, walked away.

11. When a man attempted to siphon gasoline from a motor home parked on a Seattle street, he got much more than he bargained for. Police arrived at the scene to find a very sick man curled up next to a motor home near spilled sewage. A police spokesman said that the man admitted to trying to steal gasoline and plugged his siphon hose into the motor home's sewage tank by mistake. The owner of the vehicle declined to press charges, saying that it was the best laugh he'd ever had.

    Ben

Tue 02/03/2004 02:31

    Dear Favourite Son and Heir (um...forgotten your name though),

    Your Email ref Darwin Awards ..... perfect timing!... as I'm getting SERIOUSLY p*ssed off here...thank you very much indeed....it's the first time I've laughed for several days!..

    Hope all well and stable for you, and all the menagerie at the Rendham Road Zoo House...

    And don't worry about the Tax thingy..it'll all come out of the inheritance anyway...

        Warmest Love,

        Dad.

(RECEIVED) Tue 02/03/2004 17:25

    Subject: Condolences!!

    David,

If I were not such a well brought up person I would say your Life at the moment is a right little ladybirder, but I will just think it instead. How on earth you manage to keep cool, calm, and collected with all the incredible earthquakes you are having to undergo, beats me. In ordinary circumstances I would say "hiccups" but that is far too slight a word to describe all your trials and tribulations.

Honestly, and seriously, Daddy and I are full of more and more admiration for the way you manage to hang on. The only good thing is that in the years to come, when you write your diary and read it, you will be astounded at all the so and so problems you suffered and overcame. And I suppose it will make your diary even more fantastic to read!!

I tried to ring you today but my Portuguese wasn't quite up to what a nice lady was saying but thanks to Latin at school I did manage to guess that she was repeating your number --or was it my school Greek? Anyway, you had said that you would be using a local number for a while so I expect she was telling me you, or the number, were not available.

In case it is still unbearably hot and humid in Salvador you should know it is just above freezing here, perhaps that will make you feel a bit cooler!

Like you, we cant wait for the package to turn up and hope to goodness it is what you ordered and not an electric blanket and woolly bed socks or something equally N.B.G.   GOSH!! Wouldn't you be furious!!.

Heaps of love and take care!! **Mother.**

Wed 03/03/2004 11:51
   Subject: Thanks again!
      Dear Mother and Daddy,

Loved your Emails!....very cheering when life is a bit upsetting here at times.....supportive advice from two other singlehanders here has helped too...

But now definitely thinking along the lines of sailing with what I have on board here now, and not raising any more hopes....one or two other avenues to try to get the bits, but just for fun really...and I'll try to buy a small handheld satellite position thingy here, a cheap one, as a backup....anyway there's no sensible alternative but to cancel the order with Plymouth, and get the shipping agent to take it back to England.....probably have to pay the carriage again though, even though it never got to me....

I still think it's pretty despicable of the Customs here though, even if I ignore the agent's muck up....don't even know if I have time to go to Rio anymore, so I may have to leave the country illegally from Salvador itself......HONESTLY, what a crazy system!....and yet the individual people here are really nice and friendly...such a shame...

The main purpose of this Email is to thank you so much for the money you gave for the telephone bill, even though it was far too much and I will never be able to use it all......it's been a tremendous help, as it has meant if I have to call shipping agents, or the British people in Plymouth who sent the bits in the first place ,for example, (as I did a few minutes ago) I haven't had to start fretting at the cost if there's some delay getting the right person etc.....that alone has been a real godsend....And the support from all the family has been truly wonderful...your other offspring and their entourages are really LOVELY people!.

And please remember that through all of this since I crawled back to Salvador, I myself have been in no danger at all, and neither has the ship (apart from Brazilian "rodents")... the problems have been only frustration etc, but no danger....so I'm perfectly safe, (apart from when crossing the road here!).

I omitted to confirm you are both well when I phoned last night....I hope you are?...

   More news soon,
      Thanks for being there!..
         Me.

(RECEIVED) *Wed 03/03/2004 00:03*
   Hi David.

   Sori to hear of your tribulations with the spare parts .I guess there must be somthing to say for europe after all.

   Anyway dont despair Im sure there must be someone with a bit of common sense.
I should try screwfix they promise to deliver the next day.

   Missed the sked time over the last two days but find that 14.150 usully occupied so will try between 140 and 150 I havnt had time to try out the vertical but will make the effort next week ,will have done all the tiling and grouting stuff by then.

Ok old son take care and remember monty python always look on the bright side .
you start with nuthin and yer leave with nuthin so what yer lost , nuthin!

godbless **john**

Fri 05/03/2004 06:34
Dear Bill'n'Buddy,

Still partially disabled here, even with the help of the British Consul...unfortunately the British press got wind of the story too, which would have made it worse, but my brother in England deliberately managed to make it sound so boring that we think we may have stopped them, luckily..

So have pretty well scrapped ideas of exploring south of Rio...maybe leave from Salvador in 3-4 weeks time, going south-about round the South Atlantic High......autumn will start soon, and I want to be in the Azores by mid-June, but giving myself some time in St.Helena with friends there..... it's going to be a l-o-n-g trip, going round the traditional sailing ship route....it will be an interesting experience!

Take care, stay safe, and maybe you will get to Salvador before I leave....

Best wishes!
Tuesday'n'me.

(RECEIVED)Wed 03/03/2004 04:48
Subject: Greetings from Santos, Brasil.
Bon dia!,
David:

You are not longer the only one stroked by lightning in Brasil! Friday night last week there was a heavy thunderstorm passing by and some strokes where realy close. I thinked about you and turned of all the electronics/switches/fuses and released the cables to all the batteries. Rozinante shaked by the thunder in some of the attacks. But there was no direct hit, but some was really close. I could feel the energy in the air.

The next day I understood that my stereo amplifier was destroyed. I fixed that one and checked everything else I thought. Today I understood that my central unit of the autopilot was also destroyed as a result of the lightning. It's just reporting some error message when I try to turn it on. I have a spare older model and the compass and engine for it is ok. It was only the central CPU unit that was killed.

The next thing I learned from your stroke is that i will not get any package sent to Brasil! My friend needed a vacation so he comes down with a radar/gps and new autopilot unit. The GPS and Radar is new and supplementation and I really need a Radar after been sailing in the shipping routes along the coast of Brasil. I only hope he gets well through the customs, but I've understood by people working for the same company as I used to work for before I left for this trip that they never get stopped in customs by air when travelling to Brasil they have an office in Rio de Janeiro.

I don't now what your plan is but if you go down to Ihla Grande area let me know and we catch up! I will listen to 21.400 and 14.297.5 for you and the progress on your equip. Good luck! Best regards,
Staale, on "Rosinante".

Chapter 7

Bureaucratic delay

Sat 06/03/2004 19:37
  Subject: Return to Itaparica
    Dear Everybodies,

It's so refreshing to be back at anchor in these calm and beautiful islands again!....usually no sound of infernal combustion engines....... no heavy beat music...... the sounds of birds ("Fifty Quid?!..w-o-w!") by day, and nightjars, with crickets accompaniment, by night.....dug-out canoes under sail....fishermen silently at work, on the sandbanks at low water.....children playing....hot sun, but cooling breeze.....and the white sand, palm trees, the darker forest behind.....the different hues of blues and greens in the water....and the fluffy cumulus fair-weather clouds on a deep blue background ...some days there is a heavy but warm rain shower, for a few minutes only..... relaxed, friendly islanders, smiling black faces with bright white teeth ....and swimming too, but underwater visibility is only 1-2 metres....

Yes, this is definitely the other side of Bahia, Brazil....

Met an English-speaking German the other day .."Ah, you ze English jacht "Tuesday" have, ja?" ..... apparently I was seen sailing, about 3 weeks ago, when I was knocking seven bells out of the sails and rigging, checking all was intact by sailing absolutely flat out, creating a massive rolling wake, with more canvas up than would be thought prudent in normal circumstances....."you usually like that go sailing?" he asked in awe...... I didn't want to let the side down, and said "..well..er...depends...um..."...........I think his view of English solo sailors has been shaken a bit, but I'm not sure whether beneficially or not....

Nick, the Aussie ex-Rhodesian solo sailor, on "Lala Salama" (means "Peaceful Sleep", and not what I translated it as ..."Rest in Peace"..!) has spent the last four years sailing...his vessel is a really sensible, well laid out S&S 34, but specially built in Australia, with a vastly superior cabin and deck-moulding and layout...much better than the European ones, and more heavily constructed too...very nice boat indeed ...

He has been in Salvador before, and has picked up much of the language (though I'm starting to understand a little more now too)....showed me several areas of Salvador where they sell the fabrics and materials that are useful for making repairs to boats...top quality, Brazilian made...and very cheap indeed.......and during our journeys was able to see a little of the off-the-beaten-track bits of Salvador which was very interesting....only once was there any possible threat of being watched and followed, and that turned out to be a false alarm....I suspect some protection from his ability to swear fluently in the local dialect, and my salt-stained overalls and worn-out agricultural worker's cap, suggested that we wouldn't be rich pickings anyway..........(incidentally, several times I have been asked, during general conversation, about where I work in Salvador....Compo would be proud of me!)...

So, more repairs and strengthenings achieved on board....

As far as the Magic Package of Electronicals is concerned, ("magic" because it keeps vanishing), I've done everything I can from this end, and am now rather bored with it all....so, working on the principle that if I ignore it then it will turn up, I've agreed a deadline with Peter in Plymouth (very helpful chap) of around the 13th March..if no package by then, we ask the carrier to return it to Plymouth (as it should know its own way by now!)...........

Meantime, I'm having a holiday in the islands here, near Yvan and Christina, the French-Swiss sail makers, while they make my new bimini and sprayhood.......

I've been looking at what we still have on board, and with a bit of lateral-thinking, have come up with one or two modifications to help me....it won't be an easy trip, but I'm lucky in having a "special relationship" with this boat so that we can help each other.....the ship is full with stores, food, fresh water, fuel etc......... but slightly depleted in "spares", obviously....

By the way, it dawned on me the other day that this ship recovered from a full "belt" from lightning ......ENTIRELY FROM HER OWN STORES! ....(apart from a masthead tricolour light better than the spare one, a voltmeter which wasn't essential, and a backup handheld GPS machine (only a backup, now wrapped in cooking foil and hidden away)....quite a ship!..

And, to take the pressure off ME, I've virtually abandoned the idea of seeing any other bits of Brazil.....it's a crying shame, but it means I can relax and do things at my own pace before setting off into the ocean again .... and anyway I have actually gained from the unusual experience of this whole Whizzbang-thing (which most definitely was NOT in the original script!)....

Still got a few short-term-memory problems though...quite funny really at times....bought the really basic spare backup hand-held-satellite-position-finding-thingy two days ago (about 40% more expensive here)..then promptly LOST it!....PANIC!!....then slowly worked out the only place it must be, if not stolen...... and there it was, of course, tidily put away with the newest salami's in one of the food lockers.............. perfectly logical really......um....I think......

Hope the Spring Season will start for you soon..

With Best Wishes from,

Tuesday'n'me.

(RECEIVED)Tue 02/03/2004 19:41

Hi.

I am Cathy's husband in NZ, we have met briefly at or around Sax surgery. Just want to say that your emails are a real inspiration and is great to hear of your adventures. Despite the hold ups you are doing amazing things. In a year or so this will be funny.......maybe.

Dave

Tue 09/03/2004 04:20

Subject: More random ramblings from Itaparica.

Dear Everybodies,

(No order to these scattered comments, I'm afraid)

When food goes "off" here, boy it does it quickly!...some bacon the other day didn't survive the heat, but the beasts growing on it (some I've never seen before) were breeding to take over the world...UGH!

Cockroaches...I've taken great pains never to let any cardboard into the ship here (the insect eggs live in it), but I have seen the not-so-little fellers calmly walk up a mooring rope ..so they'll get on board eventually anyway ..... found three aboard 14 days ago, so declared chemical-war with local cockroach "hotels"...they really work!...none seen since..

Climbing on board over the bow is fun..."Tuesday" has to moor bow-to-pontoon, to avoid damage to her fragile selfsteering gear...having to "tight-rope" walk up the ropes themselves in the pronounced swell in Salvador, and carrying heavy provisions, calls for a degree of blind faith for a few seconds...only fell off once, so far, but luckily landed SITTING on the ropes by sheer luck....(much to everyone's amusement!).....if you time it wrongly a wave suddenly tightens the warp, neatly catapulting you into a low earth orbit...

Very heavy thunderstorm overhead the other day...I was interested to know how I would react...only one tiny bit of deja-vu, then no problem...just curiosity......it surprised me that I wasn't upset, but I was reassured

136

by this too........mind you, can't see or hear much curled up in a ball with head tucked between knees, arms wrapped round the back of your head, can you.....

The "fifty quid" bird is about the size of a starling...a brown bird with a bright yellow waistcoat...here they call it "Bem ti vi" (not sure of the spelling) meaning "I saw you well" (ie, its cry is "I REALLY saw you", or "I CAUGHT you!")......I prefer the "Fifty Quid", though, personally....

Music ....they say that to get a Bahian to dance you simply drop a saucepan lid ..they LOVE their drums and rhythms!...

The ground Spring water here is beautifully clean, and said to make old ladies younger than their daughters...I await with interest its effect on me.....

I was introduced to a wonderful tasting Pizza the other day...the owner of the tiny establishment here in Itaparica ("Tinho", a big man with a quiet chuckle to his voice, and a bandaged toe (ingrowing toenail removed in the local Casualty that afternoon)) explained that his house isn't big enough for the customers to sit indoors, so you eat in a walled-in area outside, a lovely peaceful and restful place.....halfway through the meal (he's sitting with us while we eat, chatting with us quietly) he points out two big metal rings in the wall...it seems that slaves were chained there to be whipped and flogged to death..their bodies were thrown into the ground where Yvan, Christina and I (the only customers..only two tables anyway) were sitting eating our pizza's...but, to my surprise, somehow it didn't detract from the mouthwatering meal, and it did seem to fit with the air of calm in the place...a sense of gentle relaxed respect for those men and women who died not so very long ago...

I wondered if I was being given tourist bulls hit...but no, it's genuine, I've since found out....a Slave Cemetery....

And the Pizza secret?..seems his wife won't tell anyone outside the family, but there are rumours of quite a bit of cognac going into the "mix"....

Not much said about boats this time, I'm afraid...but I'm enjoying this 'oliday away from the self sustaining bureaucracy of Salvador... eat yer hearts out!..

Stay Well, Stay Safe!

Tuesday'n'me.

(RECEIVED)Wed 10/03/2004 03:01

Subject: March at last (but still freezing)

Dear David, and Tuesday,

All is well here, that is to say that Mother and I are as well as can be expected considering our age!

Your latest mail (9/3/04... rambling) has cheered us up no end. The humour is strongly evident again, and there is a sense of a return of that confidence that you get when at last you know exactly what you are going to do. By the way, I have sent copies to Angie and Paul/Teresa.

Have fun, and keep 'em coming.

Much love, as always..... M and D.

Thu 11/03/2004 03:28

Subject: Reasons for the "LONG WAY" round

Dear Everybodies,

This is just to explain why the safest and simplest route is also the longest one...

There are two routes back from here, both constrained by the strong prevailing winds and currents....the first is to fight one's way back north along the coast, then towards the Caribbean, Bermuda and round the top of the Azores High......but the risk of hurricanes in the western Atlantic starts to rise again in late May......

The other is much longer, but (hopefully) kinder, and that's round the bottom edge of the SOUTH Atlantic High in a big arc towards St Helena, Ascension, across the Equator, maybe as far east as the Cape Verdes if I'm lucky, then in a clockwise arc round the South side of the Azores High to approach the Azores Islands from the west again ....a huge letter "S", going from bottom to top...

Either way it's dead easy to get stuck in the middle of the high-pressure-systems and becalmed for weeks, or get too far out and blasted by westerlies.... "barometer-sailing" is used (if the pressure rises turn away from the high centre..if it falls, then turn towards it) to preserve a reasonable sailing breeze...

That's the theory at least, and it's what the square-riggers used to do.......

The second route is the one I want to take, but it involves a trip of nearly TWICE the number of miles I've done to get down here....

It's sad that I won't have time to explore this vast but beautiful coast (because of the dubious parentage of the shipping agent and the Brazilian Customs Dept.), but I have met many interesting people I would not have known otherwise.....

Whatever happens, the 9000+ miles journey home the "long" way round via St Helena is going to be interesting, particularly with the minimum equipment I have left after The Big Bang...(it looks unlikely I will receive the replacement bits, and so they'll be returned to the UK.... assuming they've not been stolen already!)...

But at least I can now receive WeatherFaxes at sea again, (courtesy of the Brazilian Navy in Rio).....so in the right conditions I can get hold of weather information quite nicely, as long as I have sufficient electricity.....those special diodes I'm waiting for are made only in England, and are a bit critical for that reason, so I've asked for another two complete sets to be sent out, in two separate parcels, but by POST this time....we will see if anything arrives!...

But I'm not planning to leave until the end of this month anyway....

Very Best Wishes!...... on a starlit, calm, still, and warm, Tropical Bahian evening,

    Tuesday'n'me.

(RECEIVED) Thu 11/03/2004 16:18
    Dear Tuesday'n'me,

      Jack is telling everybody that you will be in dire danger if you leave without all the bits and pieces you had hoped to be busy working with by now. But I hope your explanation will re-assure him somewhat. Let's hope at least those diodes you would like will get there, and the rest will be returned intact. This carrier is normally very reliable and should know the ropes in countries they function in. But South American buerocracy is a pretty slippery area, it seems.

    Enjoy the islands while you can, and good luck, David, sorry copy seems very sketchy these days.

    88 – Trudi

(RECEIVED) Tue 09/03/2004 08:29
    Hi Doc

      Have been reading ur mails and know for sure you are doing ok, enjoying a dip into local culture and having a lesson in patience.

    Sorry I did not write much lately but the fact is that I am a little stresssed with all the opening of the new Dive Centre. It is almost finished, still the tiny little bits to be fixed.

    Ok, I leave you here must rush to Arrecife to buy 1001 stupid things that are still missing in the Centre.

    Chris

Thu 11/03/2004 20:51
> **Dear Chris'n'Tashi,**

It's always a real pleasure to receive your Emails!...... and I appreciate your taking the time to let me know what is happening, when you're so rushed off your feet......thank you so much...

I can deal with Mother Nature dumping me in the sticky-stuff, but the over-important, self-opinionated, senseless bureaucracy with all their paperwork, apparently deliberately being obstructive to justify their own jobs, gets right up my nose...I hope you're not getting TOO much of that?........

You will have gathered that over here things are much more relaxed again...the people on this island are really nice, helpful and tolerant of my inability to speak much Portuguese...they seem to have found a comfortable balance between pleasure and money, only doing enough work for what they need, and no more than that.......they seem good and healthy people, and it's a pleasure to listen to them and observe..........very different indeed from Salvador!

I think of you both a lot, and I'm really pleased you have let me into your world............. remember to "pace" yourselves if you can..............I now realise that life is all too short, otherwise.........

> Take Care!
> > **Doc.**

PS..No more diving here yet, but lots of swimming....

Mon 15/03/2004 02:59
> **Dearest Tot,**

It was really SMASHING to speak to you again yesterday...THANK you!..

All well here, helping with other peoples' boat problems, and even helping clear an overgrown garden (if you can credit me with doing any gardening!)....Yvan and Christina have bought their first house ever, only two days ago, so we've been chasing out the beasties in the house here on the island by burning the garden-rubbish by the doorway, and letting the smoke percolate right through the building...different, isn't it!..

Tomorrow back to battle in Salvador again, with chasing these electronic bits....it's so unfair... particularly as they seem to have totally lost the package altogether now....sounds like theft to me, to be honest......maybe we can claim on the insurance....but I'm still partly stuffed without the bits.....

You sounded quite a bit more confident yesterday....well done!...but, PLEASE use me if there's absolutely anything I can help with, won't you.......you know I would love to be involved, so don't you ever think it would be a burden, will you......

Not much else....planning to leave here at the end of March, with or without the bits........

> Look after yourself well, Tot, won't you.....
> > All my Love,
> > **Dad.**

(RECEIVED) Mon 15/03/2004 12:04
> *Subject: Entry St Helena*
> > *Dear Bill*

Just a quick one. If David has visa problems, and is seriously worried about not being allowed to land on St Helena, please let me know with details of reason and I'll email the Governor. I can't promise it will work but think it might.

> *Teresa*

(RECEIVED)Wed 17/03/2004 11:23
> *Subject: Entry St Helena*
> *Dear Bill*

St Helena is a British Overseas Territory and British nationals do not need a visa, only their British passports, to land on the island. So unless there is some special requirement for ships - perhaps requiring confirmation of their last port of call?- David should have no problem. I should have mentioned that in my earlier message. Anyway, this afterthought needs no answer!
> **Teresa**

Wed 17/03/2004 06:32
> **Dear Daddy and Mother,**

Thank you for all your Emails, which I loved!.. Comfort, support, encouragement, and lots of local news items, with comments about Fin and all at home, whom I dearly miss.......THANK you both!....really cheering when it's sometimes a bit difficult here........

Would you be kind enough to give Teresa my sincerest thanks for her interest and support please?..... I hope I won't need her help, but it's really nice to know it's there......

And, hopefully, I should meet up with TOT in a few hours time!.....how about that for a WONDERFUL SURPRISE!!...I get the impression it was all a spur-of-the-moment decision a few days ago, someone else's cancelled trip, and I do so hope it works out!.....more news to follow soon, I hope...

It's some ungodly hour of the night here, after a tiring day, much of it spent deep under Tuesday's bottom, removing barnacles and such...... so must stop..... but please be sure to stay well........hope Spring comes for you soon!....
> All our Love,
> **Tuesday'n'me..**

(RECEIVED) Wed 17/03/2004 11:38
> *David,*

Just turned on my flat top not expecting to have anything since when Daddy came to bed after four a.m. in answer to my usual sleepy question he said "Nothing". It seemed unlikely there would be anything from you, and to my great joy there was your EM sent very recently and with news about Charlotte!!! Looking back, either Fin last Sunday or even Charlotte herself had mentioned something vaguely that in the distant future there might be a remote chance of someone going out to Brazil but it was all so unlikely that we didn't take it in ----- I now cant wait for Daddy to wake up and tell him! Obviously, we worry and worry about you, though it must be even worse for Fin, Ben, Ellen and Charlotte, (cant imagine how it could be worse, but it must be!!). You seem so cut off from us all stuck without the bits you are hoping will turn up that Charlotte's visit will be a tremendous morale boost; though goodness only knows how you manage to keep sane with all the frustrations which keep on occurring. Daddy and I dont know how you stop yourself from smashing something up------- You really are amazing! What a father your children have to boast about!! And aren't Daddy and I proud of our son!.Mind you, we always have been, but never imagined we could have produced such a b-----marvel!

Dont bother to think we will welcome the Spring....Spring comes before Summer and they predict heatwaves and I, at least, LOATHE the heat and always have done. It is NOT because of my hippopotamos shape because my mother was horribly thin and she too, couldn't stand the heat.So I feel even more sorry for you stuck where you are when you are in dock!
> *Heaps of love,*
> *Mother.*

140

Thu 18/03/2004 03:59

YIPPEE!! Just a quick note to say TOT HAS ARRIVED SAFELY ON BOARD,(needless to say NOT by the firm I tried to use!), and we've had an excellent meal ashore this evening....it's really LOVELY to see her again, and a great surprise that it was all organised in such a short time!...I went over to Salvador by ferry today to meet her, to bring her back here to ITAPARICA Island.

She can only stay four days, sadly, but it's done me a power of good already!

More news in a few days...

Tot'n'Tuesday'n'me.

(RECEIVED) Thu 18/03/2004 12:15

Subject: Wonderful!! Wonderful!! Wonderful!!

Absolutely thrilled that you are together.!! Cant wait for Daddy to wake up to tell him.Heaps and heaps of love to you both and congratulations to Charlotte for a terrific achievement.Haven't Daddy and me got an amazing granddaughter?! and aren't you and Fin clever for producing her!

*More love to you both from **Mother/Gran.***

Sun 21/03/2004 00:56

Subject: Checking the inheritance is still safe!

Dear Everybodies,

Truly WONDERFUL surprise three days ago...out of the blue, my elder daughter announced she'd booked a flight to Salvador, via Sao Paulo, with only 14 hours notice from the airline....FANTASTIC!..

She arrived apologising for not having raided the Customs Office in Sao Paulo....

And then we had a really special three days, exploring, meeting friends here, observing the local culture, tasting the local foods etc etc.......up the Funicular railway, and down the Elevator in Salvador city .... fascinated by the most guilded church I've ever seen (complete with tortoise wandering around the cloisters)....seeing all the places I've mentioned in these "Dear Everybodies"... the tiny Bar with unique Mango drinks...the by-the-kilo cafes...the ice-cream-multichoice-parlour....PanGalacticGargleBlasters.....(and even the kind, but sadly unsuccessful, people in the Customs Agent's office)...ie., most of the places that Phillipe and Paola so kindly introduced me to when I was still glowing from the Whizzbang....

And she enjoyed the dancing in the square last night in Itaparica (first time I've ever seen an English girl moving with the Brazilian-dance-hip-movement without even leaving her chair!)......

I hadn't realised how many local people around here recognise me (probably "that weird Englishman"?) ......really warm friendly greetings ....and I hadn't noticed how much more Brazilian Portuguese I must be understanding now (but it's slightly easier after a beer I've found!)...

Everything worked out well ...even the taxi-driver, Luiz, arranged to come back specially today, to take her to the airport ......he's cheaper than most of them, too....

And in the midst of it all, one of the three sets of special diodes arrived (I only NEED just one set of them)....unfortunately it was accompanied, in the post, by a tax demand form from England too, which could have spoilt things a bit if I'd owed them money...but just for signature only .. then to be returned to England "By Hand", because Tot took it back with her when she left this morning.....

To get back to Salvador early this morning was unusual too ....very low tide stopped the ferries running because they couldn't get through the rock/sand/coral reef to Mar Grande.....luckily we managed to catch the very last one out, and even then the boat grounded (but never stopped) several times ....we could see in the clear water that we were rolling boulders and shredding mud and seaweed... the keels are made of "iron wood", which is so solid it sinks in water, and when it hits a boulder, the wood wins....amazing material, it is....

141

So "Tuesday"'s cabin is a lonelier place tonight, since she's gone back to the UK ....but I know I will get used to it again in a day or two, and the cheery comfort she brought will last for a much longer time.... Thanks, Tot!...

Hope the weather improves after your present gale in the UK,

with Very Best Wishes!,

from Tuesday'n'me.

Sun 21/03/2004 00:56
Subject: What a WONDERFUL three days!
Dearest Tot,

Can never thank you enough for having the sheer guts and tenacity to come all the way out here!.....What a girl!!...

From a purely selfish point of view, it's done me a tremendous amount of good, in that my Little Whoopsy was pushed into the past where it should be, and now I can start moving forward a bit better.....THANK YOU SO MUCH!......

I got the impression that you had a good time too... certainly an unusual and memorable one!...... Nick was sorry to have missed you, but appreciated that we were a bit pushed for time this morning ... he knows we tried, anyway... he says you are a lovely girl, but that you must have got it from your mother ...

Incidentally, that WAS the last boat out of Mar Grande this morning...the next one that ran was the one that I caught back there again, so we were pretty lucky!......

Do hope the journey home wasn't too much of a trial...that, in itself, must have been an adventure even on its own....

And I warn you, you may get grilled by the rest of the family for details of life here...do us a favour and wind them up a bit will you, just for a giggle!...

Thanks for taking the tax form back with you....I gather it's a bit fundamental for me staying out of Clink....

Hope the piccies come out!..

Bless you Tot,

All my Love,

Dad.

(RECEIVED) Tue 16/03/2004 10:49
Subject: Yacht insurance
Dear David,

We continue to read your e-mails with interest (and amusement). I note you are intending to take 'the long way' home and therefore we had better extend your cruising area to include Atlantic waters not south of say, 45 degrees south. I have lost track of exactly where you are with repairs-I assume you will have a fully functioning radar and proximity alarm prior to departure? (Please excuse these impertinent questions).

Let me know if the Atlantic coverage is sufficient.

All the best.   *Mike.*

Wed 17/03/2004 06:31
Subject: Extending "Tuesday"'s cruising area
Dear Mike,

(I had been a bit concerned that the "Dear Everybodies" would be boring for you experts, but I'm really chuffed that they might be brightening up some gloomy winter mornings in the office!...thanks!)...

I have on my list of things-to-do to phone you about the possibility of agreeing to extend my cruising area, as we discussed last year, and I'm grateful to you for pre-empting me..

If it can be agreed, down to 35 degrees south should be more than adequate, but I realise I'm coming to you "cap-in-hand", begging!.....I hope to leave around the end of the this month...

In answer to your question, the repairs I've done have left me with/without the following :-

(1).....I have no MASTHEAD vhf antenna nor Windex.........(but I have a deck level VHF 1 metre antenna rigged up, checked and found to be functioning well..........only one of three marine VHF sets works (an old 1982 one with all the channels except M2).. but I've managed to make one of the broken one receive-only again now...................an additional hand/held 5 watt VHF is working OK, too..)

(2).....One of the four(!) self steering gears on board is u/s....another works, but I can only alter course with it now by setting off at a brisk trot across the aft-cabin to press buttons near the transom, where it works on the wind vane arm of the Aries .... the Aries itself is fine and fully functional.......and the fourth one is an old "AutoPilot mk 2", an American electric machine in a big alloy case, which works by a belt onto the wheel (it's old, but fully checked and working, and bl**dy powerful, although a bit awkward to use in confined waters)...

(3)......there are two handheld GPS machines on board now, both fully functional....in addition there is an unreliable fixed Garmin 128, as clearly it has been upset by the Whizzbang and refuses to send any NMEA data any more...(so although its basic functions have behaved fairly well over the last two months, I'm not certain of trusting it)...........Anyway there are two sextants on board, which I enjoy using, together with two sets of 2004 tables.......And the next bits of this trip will be in wide open water anyway ....

(4).......down to my last two Seafarer echosounders now, so not able to sound depths of more than about 50 metres.....the big, powerful fishfinder died....(pity..it was very useful in Norway, reading happily down to 550 metres)

(5).....Radar...it's a bit over-the-top, but I had on board a complete, and new, SPARE JRC radar, and it survived the lightning, (probably because it was surrounded by other metal bits and pieces)....the original scanner is OK, but the control-and-display-panel was wrecked....all I had to do was to swap them over, set 'em up, and bingo!...fully functional radar with proximity alarm all checked, calibrated, and aligned!......

(6)......Radio receivers...... all FOUR(!) died...but a ham radio set, although it no longer transmits, now receives well, as you saw from the weatherfax.........incidentally, the replacement identical set arrived on board only five days after leaving the USA, by post.......(pity all those English bits got stuck in Customs!)..... I've altered the replacement set so that it too acts as a full range receiver, and now will transmit in the commercial ssb bands as well as in the ham-bands.....it's been a godsend being able to keep in touch with my friends on the Transatlantic, Italian, British, and South Atlantic MaritimeMobile nets.....wonderfully supportive people, as well as giving me personal weather information each day....

(7).......EPIRB survived ok..... its self test cycle behaves as it should....

(8).......The spare wind generator, solar panels, and spare alternator are all working again now, but I need those special diodes to make the towed, water-powered Aqua4gen generator OK again...it's a very useful piece of kit, still producing electricity on cloudy days when there's not enough wind for the wind-generator..but hopefully at least one of the small packages coming through the ordinary postal service will get here in time...

There's lots more, but you get the idea of what I've been cobbling together out of the broken bits ....I used to be very embarrassed to be carrying around all this spare rubbish I've acquired over the years, including all that electric wiring etc .... (simply that I can't throw anything away, especially once I've repaired it)....... but by pure chance it's really paid off this time..... I reckon "Tuesday" was a floating second-hand chandlery when I left England, thank heavens!....a bit "nerdy" as the Yanks would say, but I'm glad, now!....

Sorry, it's another long Email, Mike, but thanks for all your interest and support.

Very Best Wishes! **Tuesday'n'me.**

(RECEIVED) Thu 18/03/2004 14:00

    Subject: Yacht insurance/cruising area

      Dear David,

Many thanks for yours of the 17th.

You seem to be extremely well-equipped even after the 'whizz bang'.

We will extend your cruising area to 35 degrees south at no additional premium and with immediate effect.

(I know it is not in your plans but please be aware that we do not cover African waters- apart from South Africa, Morocco and the Med coast countries).

The 'long way' is indeed a very long way and I trust you will have a peaceful passage.

Policy documents showing the extended cruising area will be mailed out in the next few days but, as mentioned above we will extend with immediate effect.

     All the best **Mike**

Sun 21/03/2004 13:27

    Dear Mike,

      I'm most grateful to you for arranging to extend the cruising area for Tuesday'n'me, and I appreciate what an unusual step it is in the present insurance climate.....thank you indeed...

Things are looking better with the success yesterday of one of the three strings to the bow I used to get these diodes...some bits of the ship are actually BETTER now than before the Whizzbang, by simplifying and streamlining various circuits....and also the enforced delay has given me the chance to have specially made for me, cheaply but in top quality, the new sprayhood (and bimini).......it seems to me that Tuesday's job is to protect ME from all the nasties, so that I can look after HER better while at sea, and simple things like a decent spray hood are very important to make that contract work .....sounds a bit "heavy" I know, but that's the way it seems.....we've been through quite a hammering, together, she and I.......

Planning to leave around the end of this month, trying to find a good weather-slot to be able to get at least 200+ miles offshore comfortably first....this is most definitely NOT a good coast to have as a lee-shore in a blow!.....(large areas of unsurveyed coral, close in, etc.)...

Warmest greetings to you and Julie, and all in the office in Plymouth who were very kind to me last June/July, (when I was suffering pre-voyage nerves before this 15 month solo-Atlantic-wander-about)...

    Tuesday'n'me.

Fri 26/03/2004 01:28

    Subject: I owe you a drink!

     Dear John,

Before I start to set out on this biggest leg so far, (and the REALLY big one after it), I wanted to thank you for all the cheery Emails you sent during the nasty bits of this adventure....really appreciated comments such as "when you are old and grey well greyer! we can sit you in the pub at Orford and you can top any of the mariners tales told down there" .....at the time I was still 'not-all-there', but it made me realise that I WAS actually going to survive, and be able to talk about it...I can't thank you enough for all your moral support, old son!..

Radio signals near Salvador are pretty crappy with QRN, but I hope to be more audible once I'm out at sea again (hopefully end of next week)....I try to be on:-

Trudi's Net (Transatlantic MaritimeMobile Net)	1300 UTC	21.400MHz
Italian Maritime Net	1900 UTC	14.2975MHz
British Maritime Net	0800 or 1800 UTC	14.303MHz
South Atlantic Net	1140 UTC	14.316MHz

These are all just for MaritimeMobiles only, actually AT SEA, covering a vast area, but sometimes it's possible to start a personal chat AFTER the Net....if not, then it's still interesting to hear what's going on, and get an idea of what propagation is like.....

A whole lot of people are involved in running the nets to try to get worldwide coverage........sometimes I can only get through by Tom in Toronto, sometimes Des in Port Elizabeth (South Africa), sometimes via Gerard in Belgium etc etc, but they are really well organised to try to pick our weak signals out of the background..

Like you, I've found 14.150 MHz useless...there's always QRM round there...

Oh, and I'm still only using 8 watts output (10, if the batteries are fully topped up), and the 8 Euro fishing-rod antenna ......

OK, that's it for now....Stay well.... Love to Maggie (cook'n'bottlewasher position still available!).... and Very Best Wishes to Vernon when you see him, please.

> See you in the Autumn!,
> **DocDavid.**

(RECEIVED)Fri 26/03/2004 17:10

> *Hi David*
>
> *Many thanks for the e-mails certainly do look forward to recieving them.*
>
> *I will look forward to the pint at Orford. I expect you could murder one in that heat. I will upset you even more we are gonna have fish and chips tonight full of grease and all thats bad for one.*
>
> *Just think when you get back after being exposed to all these bugs you should be immune to everything .... and fire proof too!!!!*
>
> *Sorry haven't got the hang of this texting lark. The phone wants to put its own words in, and it takes me ages .*
>
> *Ok take care and hoping to make contact soon*
> > *John*

Fri 26/03/2004 01:27

> **Subject: Yet more random thoughts from Itaparica**
> **Dear Everybodies,**

Just recovering from the second bout of food poisoning I've had since arriving in Brazil....and before you ask, NO it wasn't my own efforts at cooking on either occasion! ....nasty though, with violent fevers, confusion and waking up earnestly shouting complete gibberish, disorientation, immobilising pains, and very severe galloping-gut-rot......the worst of it only lasted 24 hours, but it was quite frightening during that time, even though I'm supposed to know all about it .... I note that others have had it here too.....

Nick, the Rhodesian Aussie, had a vicious influenza-like illness, which bowled him over for a few days... several of the local workers have had the same..... seen more tropical sores here too.... it seems that even Paradise has it's down-side.....

During a meal out, the beerbottles tend to accumulate, so they put them under the table....that way there is no argument at the end of the evening over how many there were in all...simple and neat!.

I've been quite busy the rest of the time.....mending a cassette-player... some local lad's bicycle ..... Yvan's Yamaha generator (tricky, that was...had to fathom out how it worked first)... sewing covers for the echosounder etc out of old sprayhood material...... gardening (don't laugh!..I know you consider gardening most unlikely for me..... but, as I have only done the Basic course, I'm in charge of the wheelbarrow at Yvan and Christina's new house) .....wall-plaster removing too ...

And skin-diving under "Tuesday" to preserve her Slippy-bottom, Go-faster antifouling paint finish ......(as I approached the propeller from one side, a substantial sized fish appeared through the propeller aperture from the other....not sure which of us was more startled ..... we both backed off cautiously, trying to preserve our dignity.....I had always considered the propeller was mine, but this particular fish seemed to disagree).....

The Aqua4gen towed generator is up and running again, thanks to the arrival of those special diodes.....I'll find out tomorrow if the spare set arrived in Salvador city as well....

And I've managed to resurrect the old Autopilot Mk2 selfsteering gear, built in Fort Lauderdale in the 1970's or 80's ....it's a bit primitive, but very powerful, and I've managed to improve it a bit, and mount it better, to make it easier to use ....

As an extra bit of fun, I'm negotiating to buy a second-hand Autohelm 4000 from another yacht....seems they couldn't get it to work properly.....but we shall see....

Remember the Police Federal guy who insisted I was in Rio?....well, he's out on strike, I gather......seems the ordinary Police are not as well educated as this chap and his mates think THEY are....but the pay is similar....so it's a demarcation dispute, in other words.... I hope he stays on strike, then I have a cast-iron excuse for being unable to check out of Brazil.....

Since Tot left for England, the weather became hotter and changeable..... so I'm back to sleeping on the floor again, where it's cooler...

There's a potentially aggressive Low, stationary near the coast 200 miles south of here, and I hope it will decide what it's going to do before I leave ..... it might be useful to me to try to follow it out across the Atlantic, if it eventually goes that way, to shorten the route to St Helena...

Have a look on http://www.rubicondiving.com/en/training.html, and tell all your friends! Due to open shortly, I can personally give it my very highest recommendation, for obvious reasons....

Enough for now... it's late, and I have to get up early tomorrow to take the Combi (a beat-up old VW van) the four miles to the ferry to go to Salvador (hopefully the last time!)...

More random waffling soon!..

Very Best Wishes!

from **"Tuesday'n'me"**

(RECEIVED)Tue 30/03/2004 07:37

Subject: Re: Gut Rot

Hello, now you have at last become a real traveller you know that if you f*rt you have to accept the consequences ..... that awful warm feeling that lingers... Still if you haven't had that wanting to die feeling sitting on the bog (if you can get there) you haven't really been to South America. At least you've got water, in most of the places where we stayed there wasn't any , the locals all put the bog paper in the plastic litter bin (no lid) next to where you squat so you're surrounded by very wet brown flies. We did have water on the boat going down the Amazon (thats where I understood what violent cramps where all about) but unfortunately it disturbed the giant turtles which were transported live in the toilet originally in sacs but over the 9 days they got them selves out. One person I met felt sorry for them being on their backs so she turned them over, not only did she get hell from the captain but also got bitten!

Thank goodness that you've seen the isolated beaches side of it . We met a Brasilian called Zeca (we called our dog after him) who showed us around.

Still remember that lovely warm wind , not the one I mentioned in the beginning of this letter ...I suppose warm wind sums up life in Brasil ....

Incidently JM and I also went over to Iparica by boat just for the day, didn't have time to explore it much so the little we saw was a bit touristy, remember we were by foot and trying not to spend money. Somebody told me that it has changed completely around the cathedral at Salvador .... used to be very rough, the chap at the tourist office didn't even want to tell us how to get there. "This is a terrible area !" he said when we said that we had an address of a cheap hotel there.

Wonder what happened to all the young children sleeping in cardboard boxes in the streets, or are they still there?

Anyway envy you, tho must admit we have a different type of paradise over here ......the skiing is fantastic these days , the sun is now hot up at 2800 metres and even after all these years I can't believe that this is real.

Afraid not surprised you didn't get you parcel . When Mother calmly told me all those weeks ago that you were just waiting for it , I said out loud (not in front of her) "You must be JOKING !!" Still that's all part of the FUN of the adventure you're having isn't it ?!!!!!!

Now I must go and start practicing those sea hymns again . I like doing that!

Take care !!

Love Mary.

(RECEIVED)Thu 25/03/2004 10:13

Subject: Homeward bound

Dear David,

We do not fully understand the difficulties involved in selecting a route home but as always regarding nautical matters, we respect your judgement knowing that you will give the matter considerable thought and research.   If the journey takes longer that first envisaged we do not care, just come home safely.

I mentioned earlier in your journey that I had damaged my port wing in fall. Well after five months of discomfort I saw a doctor at Saxmundham who offered up after careful thought a cortisone injection. This I accepted and only cried for a short while afterwards, and, as he advised, the pain disappeared in 36 hours (approx) (what a star).

I am puzzled though as to how someone so young can become a doctor, he looks about fourteen years old! His name is the same as the chap who left the tent during Scott's expedition and said " I may be some time" .

Please take great care,

love **Bob & Brenda.**

Mon 29/03/2004 01:34

Dear Bob'n'Brenda,

Always nice to read your Emails!.... also sad your limbs are falling to bits....yes, those injections of "go-faster-juice" work OK, but they are a bit bad for the eyes, I know......makes them water for a while.....

You'd be proud of me, all the cobbling together of bits here etc...... And with some of the parts of a 15year old selfsteering gear I bought off another boat today, I've got a decent chance of having a good backup system working by the time I get to St.Helena, I reckon.....

Off the record, not looking forward to the first three days of the trip, what with finding my sealegs again, wading through the fishing fleets and shipping lanes, getting knackered again, (suffering my cooking again!) etc..

But once I'm more than 200 miles off, I should be able to drop back into the routine once more.....now THAT I am looking forward to!.....

Kindest Wishes to you both, and thanks for all your support,

Docdavid.

PS. By the way, the story of Capt Oates is misquoted, I'm told ..... it's true that he left the tent saying "I may be some time", but they say he took the bog-paper-roll with him as he went ......not enough roughage, you see...

Mon 29/03/2004 01:33
Subject: Preparing to leave Itaparica
Dear Everybodies,

All in all, Salvador, Bahia, Brazil has evoked strong emotions in me, not all of them pleasant.....(but what a BEAUTIFUL place once you're away from the city!)......

Elation at the scenery in the vast bay here, with it's beautiful islands and rivers, plant and animal life, and it's scents and tastes, sounds and colours...the constantly changing skies and clouds ....the tropical thunderstorms.....the tropical sunsets.....feeling at first hand the burning overhead sun and the roasting temperatures........... seeing what I've read and dreamed of seeing since years ago.....

Delight at meeting the charming local people, who kindly tolerate my lack of knowledge of Brazilian Portuguese in a manner I cannot imagine most English people doing if the situation were reversed..... wonderful people, but they couldn't organise anything except Carnival ....only met one nasty Brazilian (the Police Federal gentleman, who clearly has a Big Problem).....not counting the crooks, robbers and thieves of Salvador city, of course.....

Wonder at the local attitudes, beliefs, and culture .... thought-provoking music and dancing ... arts and crafts, and local produce ....

Contentment at the pace of life here, and the trust that builds up between like-minded but international sailing folk, communicating in a variety of languages....

Pleasure at the tremendous amount of knowledge I've gained since I arrived here....a lot of it applies to life in general, not just to a lifestyle of travelling afloat....I am now acutely aware how little I knew when I started this trip.....

Worry that the multiple insect bites (from night mosquitoes) might go septic and become tropical ulcers (seen several victims here)....same applies to those glass and plastic injuries in the soles of my feet, which took several weeks to heal, leaving scars...

Frustration at how Bureaucracy often seems to be entirely self-protecting, self-sustaining, self-opinionated .... seemingly useless at doing its self-proclaimed but apparently senseless job at times....it looks like it actually hinders Man's wish to advance, in its efforts to preserve a record of transactions so they think they know whom to blame when things go wrong...

And Disgust at one of the shipping agents' apparent attempt to tell me indirectly that it is MY fault that the Magic Package was never delivered, by misrepresenting (or if I'm really charitable, misconstruing) the facts....... coming on top of the remarkable repairs that "Tuesday" and I have managed to achieve, it feels like a total and very personal deprecation of our efforts to survive.... (and leads me to believe that there are two types of Human Animal on this planet, namely those who have an glimmering of where we stand in Nature, and those who do not....the latter live in a very artificial world indeed)....

However, some more little snippets to brighten the mood:-

I've been promoted! ...from Wheelbarrow-Driver to Scyther...well, it's not really a scythe, more a long-handled flat shovel, sharpened on all its edges ... had to learn how to work it, but everyone stands clear while you wade into the long vegetation, flailing around violently with golf and hockey shots, thinking of shipping agents, Police Federal and tax collectors... and lo-and-behold the place looks MUCH tidier after clearing away the blood and wreckage.... but I'd prefer a real scythe, to be able to do a better job of killing things....

Slight interruption in the middle when a large BULL ambled in through the gate to eat the grass....Yvan advanced gently towards it and asked it very politely if it could possibly mind leaving if it wasn't too much trouble?..please?....... whereupon it lifted its great head, took two heavy decisive steps towards him, and growled a deep, rumbling, "P*ss *ff!" in a manner which could not possibly be misinterpreted .....then dismissively returned to its grass-eating ....

However it instantly gave in when a small boy and an emaciated old man, each armed with only a thin stick, silently came in....nothing was said, but the bull knew it was time to go.... only then did we realise the colour of Yvan's bright red shirt....

Hot and bothered after the exertion of shredding the grass into confetti.... but suddenly buckets of cold water straight from the well were thrown all over me, amidst howls of laughter, with the unexpected but desired effect....

The last trial of a trip back to Salvador city is behind me now....Police Federal is still out on strike (with no public support), so I can't get my passport stamped......because of the passport I cannot re-export the boat.....but I have to leave because of the visa...... I'll be adding "Illegal Emigrant" to my CV ......

It's classical Brazil.....funny, as long as you're not personally involved....

But it did give me the chance to go and see those Brazilians in Salvador who were especially good to me.....Francisco (the English speaking boatman, whose medical problem is much better now thank you)....the English speakers in the office at Bahia Marina who were supportive in the fisticuffs with the Brazilian Rat......the man (the father) who makes the wondrous-nectar-mango-drink in the tiny bar (another long chat in Portuguese-and-Mime)....Luis the helpful taximan (who greeted me like a long lost brother, much to the surprise of the other taxidrivers!) ... several others, including the guy who still thinks I am the personal friend of Gary Newman ...

Pity that Phillipe and Paola aren't here as well..they were a godsend in those first few days especially...

And I have collected the last of the FOUR packages sent here through the ordinary post...all arrived in undamaged condition within between 5 and 9 days (there's a moral there somewhere!)........so I have a spare set of diodes for the Aqua4gen towed-generator...excellent!

More snippets in a day or two...

Stay Well!

Tuesday'n'me.

(RECEIVED)Tue 30/03/2004 17:57

Hi doc

just thinking about you and I guess you are about ready to leave on the BIIIG PASSAGE!

Have a safe trip, I´ll be thinking of you. I´m still in Recife,

repainting the boat and waiting for an old girlfriend to fly down for a 2 month visit from the states. We´ll probably hang around the top end of Brazil here, maybe as far as salvador, but I´m wondering about heading for Venezuela and then Cuba maybe eventually. If all goes to cock and I´m still in Brazil in November then I could be tempted to head for South Africa. It´s a hell of a life when you just can´t decide where in the world to go next!!

Safe sailing **Bill and Buddy** *{and Shusha, a Brazilian kitten that followed Buddy on board and seems to have adopted us!!}*

Tue 30/03/2004 23:31

Subject: Leaving for St.Helena

Dear Bill'n'Buddy,

Just so's you know, Tuesday'n'me should be leaving Brazil (illegally, as the Police Federal are all out on strike here, so you can't check in or out.....Suits me fine, as it's much easier this way!)......probably in the next 72 hours or so....

Towards St.Helena....Ascension... Azores....

It'll be a l-o-n-g trip.....but hopefully ending up in that new place we marked in the Azores on my Tsunamis...........intending to leave from there towards England before August 1st,....

Enjoy your stay here....I really like the local people, as they've all been very kind to me, here on the Island of Itaparica. ..... If you have a fraction of the fun I've had, you will be a happy man......

Stay Well!

Fair winds and safe landfalls!

Tuesday'n'me.

Mon 29/03/2004

(TELEPHONE TEXT MESSAGE to Phillipe'n'Paola on "Why Not?")

"Are you both OK? Only just heard of the cyclone in your area, by the photo and article in the paper. No answer to your phone so naturally concerned for you both.

Doc."

(Answered by voice-phone, ..."all well..took appropriate precautions..no problems, thanks!")

Tue 30/03/2004 23:30

Subject: More useless bits of information

Dear Everybodies,

Hurricanes never happen in the South Atlantic, they say .... hmm! ....Well, there was certainly one heck of a Category One Extra-Tropical Cyclone around 35 south, 45 west two days ago...that's south of Rio, and just about where I would have been if I hadn't had to change The Plan when I couldn't get the repair bits, after the sky fell in ......beautiful satellite picture, but serious waves and weather... a few deaths, a lot of injuries, a great deal of damage......and they're not used to that sort of event on that coast...... it's very sad.... but luckily quite localised, I gather.....

Extreme rain in Salvador itself about two weeks ago......spoke to someone who got caught in it..said the water was too deep and too fast moving to get around, so just had to cling on, wait and hope........I saw the damage to the roads and the top-of-the-water-level-mark, when I went to meet Tot the next day....

A delight to speak by phone to Philippe and Paola today....they tell of an amazing tale of total bureaucratic idiocy ...days of delays.... being removed from the Customs office under armed guard .....about an idiotic Tin Hitler who had to back down later anyway............(could he be related to our striking friend, Agent de Policia Federal, Salvador, do you think?)..............

I thought they drove on the RIGHT side of the road in Brazil..............not so in Itaparica town!....either side is optional, depending on who the driver wants to chat with, out of the (glassless) window as you go past, but the right side is used when there is doubt, it would seem.......sometimes EVERYBODY drives all on ONE side, but that's usually because the other side is in the sun, and too hot......or often there's a dog asleep there..... or occasionally because there's a HUGE deep hole there, where a loose manhole cover used to be....

Bicyclists usually ride on the LEFT, even on fast roads and in Salvador city itself , which puzzled me at first..............it may all sound a bit vague, but it WORKS and it seems so refreshingly sensible, simple and honest, at the time...........they don't have motor-accidents here on the Island.....the vehicles simply blow up, for lack of maintenance (like the Combi I was in three days ago).....

Fuel for vehicles is usually heavily doctored with alcohol, but I don't know what type (not seen anyone drinking from their own fuel tank yet)....... it certainly makes engines go bang though! ....Diesel for boats is heavily doctored with sediment, water and corrosives....the problem is not the making and distilling of the fuel, apparently.....it's the poor quality of transportation means they have.......rusty road-tankers and dirty storage tanks .....Luckily I've barely had to buy any, and I filtered even that as it went in.......

Bought the old selfsteering gear I mentioned, from another boat yesterday.....it looked tired and grubby

150

but functional......set it up in the cabin to check it today....very disappointed to find it wouldn't work...... but if a man can build it, Tuesday'n'me can usually fix it....

So, CHAOS in the cabin again as it's out-with-the-tools-and-wires-and-meters-and-soldering-irons-and-stuff again.....anyone would think we'd just been struck by lightning.....

We won again!....beat the little beast into submission after quite a bit of head-scratching (caused by there being TWO separate faults with the field effect compass modulething ..... once again, cobbled different bits together, to make a PlastimoNavicoAutohelm-electric-concoction-thingy, which actually works!....(quite proud of it, rather conceitedly... but also a little concerned in case this was the way I did my job for 30+ years, before I retired!)...

Wiring spread out over everywhere like healthily thriving brambles .....so I tried to fit it all INTO the ship....panels off, ceiling down.....haven't quite finished it yet, but I'm winning!.....I hope it all fits back together again before I leave....

The end result should be that there are several methods I can use to try to make life as easy on myself as I can .... I'm going to need all the help I can get, but I'm much happier about setting out now than I was four weeks ago....

Waffled on for too long again.....my apologies....please blame my son, for teaching me (eventually) how to work this darned E-mail-computer-thing....

Hope Spring is well on its way to you by now!,
Tuesday'n'me.

(RECEIVED) Tue 30/03/2004 11:53
Dear David

I read your last email and feel you have really enjoyed your stay in Brazil..........given the ups and downs...............but hope you feel better now........

This morning we were sitting in the conservatory having coffee ......

........when I commented that you seem to have enjoyed yourself.......... himself replied of course............. it's an experience + + + +.................even if he banged his finger..... it would be an experience, he'd enjoy it.....

..........I'm not quite so sure about that bit................. but the reason for this mail is to say the same as everybody else will be saying ....PLEASE look after yourself.................take great care and no risks............... and of course Tuesday without whom this adventure would not have been possible.

Make sure you have a good supply of chocolate on board before you leave..................that's if you can get good chocolate over there.............

Keep safe look after you both
Lots of Love
Joyce and Himself

Wed 31/03/2004 02:01
Dear Jo'n'Joyce,

I promise to take it.......

....Care, that is....and VitC....and pregnant mums' pills.......(all out of date of course!)....

After the b*ll*cking you gave me with the Whizzbang, I KNOW I have to be careful!...

It's going to be a l-o-n-g passage, but we think we're ready, Tuesday'n'me, so going to take it easy .... Comfort first....

No news is good news...radios may fail, electrics may die, rigs fall, engines seize etc., but they won't stop us....... the ship and crew are both designed for this sort of thing, so the odds are heavily in our favour ......there

151

will be some awful times, a lot of miserable times........ and a very few wonderful times, which will outweigh the others.....

But knowing there is all that support from the family (and that includes friends, as you taught me) makes a tremendous difference.... feels like a real physical support (no, not THAT kind of support!)...

Take good care of you both, too...you're very important to me...

See you on the other side of the pond!

Byeee!

(PS. Chocolate MELTS here....but yes, Brazilian stuff is good, and plenty on board, thank you!)

Tuesday'n'me.

Wed 31/03/2004 02:02
Dear Mary,

I'm ready to leave this place, but I've been really happy and contented on this island.... the locals are smashing people, with a great sense of humour and bonhomie....and the sailing friends here are great....you would have loved to stay longer and got into the local world.... tourists are only here at the weekends....

The ship is prepared...just need to finish the new sprayhood, pile in the green veg'n'fruit, and eggs and bread, and we're away out onto the Pond again....

Off the record, not looking forward to the first three days of the trip, what with finding my sealegs again, wading through the fishing fleets and shipping lanes, getting knackered again, (suffering my cooking again!) etc..

But once I'm more than 200 miles off, I should be able to get back into the routine .....now THAT I am looking forward to!.....got lots to do while I'm out there away from the shipping routes etc, really out into the open and free ocean...back to practising the harmonica, too...

No sun tan on the back of my neck...hair's too long.....pony tail, sometimes....or pile it under my hat if I have to look tidy..... typical has-been-hippy-type..... but I must be the only singlehander who's not on wacky-baccy....one guy grows his own, on his ship! ....fascinating people though.....

Should be another Email to the family before I leave, so I'll quit now while I'm ahead.....but I could murder a cold beer right now!..

Byee fer now, and stay safe... there are big risks in your lifestyle too...

Well, p*ss off then!,

Love, Me

(RECEIVED)Tue 30/03/2004 19:17
Subject: Wondering.

David,

Lovely to have your EM yesterday --- two of them identical in case I lost my new glasses no doubt. For the last four or more years the annual eye check-up has been all right with no need for new specs. However, this time I got ones which are just that much better and I can now keep up with the Docdavids (and I think, Ben) and have a pair which I think you can bend like yours, you showed us one day which made me cringe, but you said it was OK. However, I have no intention of experimenting with these although the man did all sorts of contortions with them, but it does seem that next time they get involved with a rosebush or something they may be able to twist themselves out of trouble.

Fin and Ben came on Mothering Sunday (Bless you for your call) it wasn't until they had gone that I turned on my flat top and found musical greeting cards from your family on both AOL and Freeserve. They are delightful and made me laugh aloud so thank you for your share in them and the lily bulbs---I hope the cards will still be on the screen when you come home.

Needless to say, Daddy and I keep wondering what you are doing at various times during the days and nights. PERHAPS by some magic the package will turn up even at this late stage though we realise it is almost an impossibility. Also we know that at any minute you will start the LONG VOYAGE. It would be amazing when you get to St.Helena (weather permitting) you should get in contact with someone who knew about Rosalie's Pen Pal when she was a teenager in the Guides. They would never have expected to meet up with the writer's brother!

Daddy is at work at Aldeburgh cinema again; on Sunday, David Shepherd (the wild animal painter) gave a show at the cinema and Daddy did the videoing and the chap was most impressed with the quality of everything, which was nice, especially as there was very nearly a disaster with the film but your father managed to sort it out. Not up to the standard of your amazing work on Tuesdays Whizzbang damage (which leaves Daddy gasping at your brilliance) but left Daddy feeling quite pleased.

Dont forget, you have succeeded in achieving your aim in sailing to Brazil and NOTHING can take that from you. If ever you decided to leave Tuesday and fly home we would be delighted!! However, in the meantime we will hopefully monitor your progress on Shiptrack and rely on Gerald to pass on any news from you and Tuesday. Your tropical D&V sounds horrific, for god's sake be careful!!

If you see any more sperm whales tell them we were all so sorry when one of their relations grounded the other day and despite all efforts she died. Can't remember whether it was somewhere in Norfolk or Scotland.

Heaps and heaps of love and longing for when, from a discreet distance, we see you sailing up to Orford, God Bless you, from Mother.

(RECEIVED) Tue 30/03/2004 02:46
   Subject: With great respect for both of you, and for your achievements....
       David,
Thank you once again so much for all your wonderful mails.

As you will be heading east very shortly, this is really just to wish the two of you an extremely bong thingy, which I am sure you will have. It is particularly pleasing that you have now got plenty of diodes and will be able to use the towed generator. I was thinking, with the way the ship is now you have still probably got, inspite of everything, more navigational aids and a higher safety factor than Chichester had. Is that right?

So there yer go. Well done, Sir! Take care..... and come back soon.
       With much love from all the family....   **Daddy.**

Wed 31/03/2004
   Subject: Thanks, even more!
       Dear Mother and Daddy
So much news... I'm missing out on it, and it's going to be difficult to adjust when I get home again.... and for everyone to adjust to ME, I suppose....poor Fin having to put up with me under her feet again....

And congratulations on getting the Rubbery Specs....the truth is, of course, that they bend further before they break....nothing more, nothing less than that... I managed to break mine, I remember, on at least two occasions, but they were repaired under guarantee each time as they were "indestructible"....

You mentioned Sperm Whales.... it is most definitely NOT one of my intentions to get anywhere NEAR a whale... I'm happy to film with a telephotographic lens, but the damage they could do by accident does worry me.... not much I can do about it though...except keep the cameras running (which I omitted to do during the Whizzbang...it was all a little too serious to think of it, at the time)....

You're right, Chichester did not have the advantages of many of the things I've mended...and I have

153

satellite position navigation (if the GPS sets continue to work), and (after 30 years of evolution) better self steering than he had, (although still worked by the wind)......better weather forecasting.................I have a much better ship as well........

But on the other hand, he was a very professional and polished navigator, with vast experience in that field....and he was a remarkable pioneer and a trail-blazer....................

I'm just me.....

So it's still a whopping great mountain for me personally to climb.....I can do it, I'm GOING to do it...........not to prove anything, but just to have a brief look, listen and feel at what men saw, heard and felt 500 years ago.... but in my case from a position of considerably more safety.....and to see for myself the things I've read about for so long.....

And also to see just how tiny this "big blue marble" really is......(at 5-6 knots!)....

Time to stop...it's late....more "letters from Tuesday" before I leave.....

Stay Well.... Don't worry ...I've already shown I've got a good sense of self-preservation, and I'm much more experienced now than when I left England.... and I'm doing something I've always dreamed of doing....

Love you both,
D

(RECEIVED) Sat 03/04/2004 10:07
David,

Just read your EM on my flat top.It is a wonderful last message from Brazil with an exciting heading. We will try to obey your instructions not to worry but it wont be easy. I wish there weren't so much water in that b----- ocean and you could keep to the shallow end, but then Tuesday would complain, no doubt. As Daddy always says,you cant have everything!! Anyway,we pray that you enjoy the voyage and that it isn't too long before you come sailing up to Orford. I know Fin is longing and longing for that day. In the meantime, if weather permits, in their wildest dreams Paul and Teresa would never have imagined that the boy they saw as a tiny baby would one day sail his own boat to St. Helena!!! But TAKE CARE!! Daddy and I love you very much and need your moral support-------and so does Fin, and Charlotte, Ben, and Ellen and all your Dear Everybodies.

Bon Voyage! Heaps and heaps of love, **Mother.**

Sat 03/04/2004 03:48
Subject: Start of 2nd Transatlantic
Dear Everybodies,

We're ready to go again!.....(at last!)

It's going to be a l-o-n-g but steady trip..."comfort" is the watchword for this next leg of "Tuesday's Travels"....no drama if I can help it...no records to try to beat...nothing to prove....

The actual course will be dictated by the winds, so the little dots on Shiptrak may meander about a bit...looking for the EASY route......lighter winds if I can...

Don't know the total distance it will be yet, nor how long......depends how far south I have to go to find the winds I need........but approx 3000 miles in an arc to St.Helena, so possibly around 4-6 weeks or so (but prepared for a lot longer, if necessary)....

She's loaded like a ruddy fruit'n'veg ship again.... food and water for 6 months if I'm careful with it.....

NO NEWS MEANS ABSOLUTEY NOTHING!..

Please do NOT read any disasters into a lack of news, as a thousand and one things can cause communication failure, and many of the electrical circuits are still "on probation" as a result of the Whizzbang.....but Tuesday'n'me know well how to manage without these things, even though it would be a great shame....

Not really looking forward to the first 2-3 days, to be honest, what with re-finding my sealegs, avoiding other shipping etc, and having to be closehauled to get offshore.... but once well offshore the risk of encountering ships and fishing boats should be much less.... and by then I should be settling in to "sea-mode"....... there should be a nice moon for first few nights as well...

This evening I had a full lesson in Bread-Making-at-Sea from Yvan....(I know, I can hear all my family falling about laughing at the idea of me being successful at it, but just you wait...this could possibly be my new career!..)

That, and the harmonica playing..

They are GOOD people here.....

Tinho (the Pizza-house-in-the-slave-cemetery) absolutely insisted on giving me a free lift to the shops in his Combi, when we met by chance today....

And the lads who are rebuilding Yvan and Christina's house had cutdown and prepared two big Mamoa fruits for me today, and they didn't even know I was leaving...

Then I wanted to spend the Last Supper at Tinho's Pizza-Parlour...mouthwatering food again!...but afterwards he insisted on driving Yvan, Christina, and me miles out of the way, in the dark, to try to hunt down really fresh eggs for my trip ....(the guy with the eggs was out, though..gone to church....we'll try again very early tomorrow morning)..

I noticed, while in the Combi, a really heavy looking piece of wood shaped a bit like a baseball bat.....with a wrist strap on it ...... "oh yes" he says " that's Consilio" (which I gather means the "Advisor")..I'd heard talk of Consilio, but I thought he was a friend or something... I never realised it was actually a very effective means of deterrent.... (another side of Paradise I didn't expect!)...

During supper Tinho gave me his Email address.....looked me straight in the eye, pointed his finger at me, and said firmly in English (I didn't know he knew any), "Write!"...........it was NOT a request!....

Yvan and Christina have insisted that I take several little bits and pieces that they found useful at sea, since they're not going to be sailing again for a while...(an example is a thermos, but one which needs only one hand to operate)...I'm not used to accepting gifts, but it has been most heartwarming to observe their interest in this voyage ....(even though they themselves been travelling for the last 20years, living on their boat, and raising their family, while doing so....)

Fatima, a normally very business-like and mature woman, who owns and runs another restaurant here, called me in Portuguese, loudly, to "Stop!" as I passed her place....I worried what I'd done wrong......"heard you were leaving....do take care, won't you?"..was all she wanted to say.... kind words, genuine words, ...leaves a warm glow....

Sprayhood is finished and fits PERFECTLY...I don't believe I've seen that standard of professionalism put into any British sprayhoods ...top quality...very pleased with it.......

So...Stay Well, and Stay Safe yourselves.....I'll keep in touch as best I can....but remember, NO NEWS is still GOOD NEWS!

Love to all!

from **Tuesday'n'me.**

(RECEIVED) Fri 02/04/2004 12:35

> **Subject: Bon Voyage !!!**
>
> **David,**

Wonder what you are doing at this moment! Have you ever thought of what could be going on in your stomach? No doubt the butterflies have sent the kittens into labour. When you finally cast off tomorrow,(Saturday?),it surely will be with many mixed feelings; wish we could do something about it but we cant. But dont ever forget, you have achieved the incredible feat of sailing from Orford to Brazil in your own boat and alone. Never, in your wildest dreams could you have really believed this would happen one day. I wonder what the vessel lying in the Orford river, or rather whoever named her, would have thought!

When we go through Wickham on the rare occasions we still think Chris T. should get an award for the lovely houses he built, which, incidentally,are much admired by Chris Craggs,. The three small garages are still there and the Aunts garden untouched but otherwise the area looks delightful, and it means all the dogs haven't been dug up. Which reminds me, the three bits of Rosemary I pinched from the layby are all growing nicely here so if you want some for your house when you come back you will be able to grow your own.Oh!, and if your promotion to Scyther in Chief hasn't made you too swell headed then perhaps when you come home you could empty my small wheel-barrow which is full of dirty water but cant be moved because it is just under a blackbird nest which might be in use.

This EM is really meant just to wish you and Tuesday a safe and mainly enjoyable trip to St. Helena. What a wonderful self-medical post lightning treatment you have undergone and terrific DIY you and Tuesday have performed to repair the boat.Daddy and I are bursting with the knowledge of your utter brilliance--must be the result of making you go and pick the kale in the aunts' garden and then eat it (you HATED it) when it was cooked for dinner. Poor David!!

> Masses and masses of love, from **Mother.**

RECEIVED)Fri 02/04/2004 02:40

> **David and Tuesday,**

I'm not quite sure what my true feelings should be ... about your pending departure I mean. Should I be relieved that you are still in Brazil, and virtually safely on land.... or shall I be happier once you've set sail again. On balance I am rather inclined to the latter.

That country (and a bit of fate thrown in) does not seem to have treated you very well and there always seems to me to be a small degree of legal threat. No...ignore this last thing.... it's probably just in this mind of mine.

So yes.... I can't wait for the news that you have finally pulled it up and gorn orff, and hopefully will be reappearing on ShipTrak. All things considered, I really do think that you will be safer once you're at sea again. Anyway, take care.... and don't do anything that your grandmother wouldn't do.

It will be fine... you'll see. **Daddy.**

Chapter 8

Leaving Brazil

Thu 08/04/2004 22:36
   Subject: Back in the Pond again
      Dear Everybodies,

The other day I knew a child of a family on another boat was unwell ...needed a certificate to explain absence from school...didn't have a local doctor who knew the child, as they live afloat...... it occurred to me that I could solve the problem for them....

Found one last piece of personal headed letter-paper on board, so I knew I only had one shot at it........wrote out a Medical Certificate mentioning a "feverish illness" but no diagnosis (as per normal) etc etc., signed it, dated it, and then stamped it with the ship's stamp (like the four foot high one painted on the harbour wall in Porto Santo).....

Felt a bit guilty for doing it, but later learnt that the School Director was absolutely delighted with it, proudly showing it around his colleagues ("from an ENGLISH Doctor!") before sending it to the Education Board..... as a result, the missed exam will be held at a later date, and the child has earned a lot of "street cred" with his schoolmates..... I still feel a bit guilty about the ship's stamp, but the certificate itself is morally, ethically and legally correct....

Just before I left Itaparica, doing last minute shopping (like 60 eggs, which have been preserved by Yvan and Christina's method), I finally managed to see the long-tailed monkeys living wild in the trees here.... I watched them play as they ran along the power lines and leapt into the trees, behaving at first sight like squirrels, but about the size of a cat..... then I got a good look at one of them in a tree, before it turned it's back on me to pick its ears (and worse), while muttering to itself in monkey-Portuguese..... it has a most fascinating face quite unlike any other animal I've seen in the wild... there was clearly someone in there, looking out at me!....

What a treat to see them at last!

SO, WE'RE UNDER WAY AGAIN!.....Worries and fears, but in correct proportion now, and glad to be finally starting the main adventure of the whole trip ......

A frustrating slow beat away from Salvador, in light airs and trade-wind seas .....began to think I'd have problems getting clear of this unforgiving, coral-infested, lee shore ..... what with dodging ancient fishing boats with (and without) internationally unrecognisable lights as well... soon got short of sleep...

One night I only covered 7 miles, and only 1 of those was to windward... but then the rainy squalls started, and we were back to working each windshift as it arrives...very like the Doldrums in some ways....

Finally reached the Trades, and we're now doing 5-6 knots, just cracked off hard on the wind, punching into a 2 metre swell, heading south-easterly .... it's a bit wet out on the "patio", but the new sprayhood works very well........At night she only needs a staysail and single reefed mainsail (ready for the frequent 25+ knot rainsqualls) to keep that speed, but by day I add a bit of genoa as well... a balance between good progress and comfort..

I FOUND WHERE THAT SPLIT PIN CAME FROM!! .. (It had been nagging away at me these last three months)....Three nights ago I heard something stealthily rolling around on the deck... only intermittently though.... finally cornered it......a Clevis Pin which fits the old split pin!.... (so now all I had to do was find where the h*ll the clevis pin itself had come from).....

I worried all night...... at first light I was out with the binoculars again, inspecting everything in the mast rigging.....nothing wrong seen, which didn't make me feel any better, either ....

It was like the sun coming out on a gloomy day when I finally nailed it .... simply a non-essential part of the reefing system on the staysail boom .... not particularly structural at all...

And the reason it came loose?.... not enough room in the design to allow the split pin to open fully... (there is now, though!)..

Each day I've been in radio-contact with Nick on "Lala Salama", who left at the same time as "Tuesday" did... he's heading north towards Trinidad.... (Poor chap, he's had more engine "V-Drive" problems, in spite of our combined efforts to sort it once and for all... but he knows what he's doing, although it must be infuriating for him when it lets him down)....

Ham-Radio is incredibly helpful and reassuring, although I'm embarrassed at times by my (deliberate) low power output... Thank you once again Jack, for so successfully finding the replacement rig and sending it out to Brazil!..

Already the bananas have ripened... in spite of choosing different aged bunches, they all hatched together.... ate the lot!....and the apples, too....

Half the potatoes rotted... I chose them carefully, so it must have been my error in packing them..... ditto a quarter of the oranges...shame!.........Melons, onions, tomatoes all OK, so far...

Apologies, but I'm not likely to be able to RECEIVE Emails, I'm afraid, till mobile phone works again .. sat-phone link is too unreliable down here..

Meantime........ !HAPPY EASTER!......(I confess there are two big chocolate Brazilian Easter eggs hidden on board here somewhere, if I can remember where the heck I put them!)....

Warmest Wishes!,

With Love from **Tuesday'n'me.**

(RECEIVED) Sun 04/04/2004 18:04

Dear David,

Presumably you are now on the high seas en route for St Helena...

We have reached Rio/Niteroi where we are staying in a very nice and cheap club.

We miss your company when knocking back the pangalactics so drop us a line if you find that they have got electriciy in St Helena.

Ciao

Philippe and Paola
SY "Why Not?"

Thu 08/04/2004 22:38

Dear Yvan, Christina, Thais and Jeremie,

Warmest Greetings from near Trindade Island!

This is just to say a deep and sincere Thank You for letting me share your thrill of the new house, and for all the help and advice (and gifts!) you have given me... it's been really FUN, which was such a refreshing change after all my difficulties in Salvador itself....

And, thanks to you, Yvan, as a result of our late evening conversations, I've learnt a lot more about ME, and maybe I'm not quite as crazy or as wrong as I thought I was....it's given me a bit more confidence too.... I will let you know what happens when I get to England!...

The sprayhood is GREAT....only lets in a few drops in torrential rain, or if it gets a direct hit from the sea (hard on the wind at present)..... wonderful to have light under it... and when it's folded up, the windows

158

roll in a smooth, even semicircle...no creases...Delighted with it, thank you!...........(But I think I'll reinforce the INSIDE over the hatch, when I get home, to protect it from constant abrading from my head and back each time I climb in and out over the washboards.....probably use spare window material I have, but not stitch through the outer coat, just to the Zip edge, to avoid any new stitch holes, and so I can still remove the whole sprayhood easily....I'll think on it further).....

You are altogether one of the most pleasant and ordered families I've met... and for Thais and Jeremie to put up with a boring old f*rt like me, and still retain perfect manners, is a great credit to all of you.....

It's been a real treat to meet you, and I wish you all the very best you could wish for yourselves....but you don't get away that easily, because I will keep in touch!....

HAPPY EASTER!

Tuesday'n'me.

Fri 16/04/2004 22:25

Dear Y,C,T & J,

Bread-Making!.. It works!...... (OK, I admit it needs a little fine-tuning, but thanks to you it's opened up a new world while afloat)...THANK YOU!

The thermos works excellently too, held in its little alcove by velcro-straps which were originally made to hold up the leg-bags old men use when they have to have a catheter (rubber tube) for their personal water-works...(NOT second-hand straps!..these were unused)...

Please would you be sure to thank the lads working on your house for the two Mamoa/Papiao(?) fruit they gave me? I ate them on the second and third days, and they were absolutely delicious!....most grateful to them...

Meantime, still plodding along closehauled in variable conditions (everything between 1 and 42 knots windspeed), still trying to get a decent slant (wind angle) to St.Helena...... slow progress, but in civilised comfort....

Hope all continues well with the house, and that there is sufficient Trade to finance it....

More news when near St.Helena I hope....

So, Stay Well and Happy, and may your shadows never grow less!

Grateful thanks,

DocDavid'n'Tuesday.

Fri 16/04/2004 22:25

Subject: South, out of the Tropics now..

Dear Everybodies,

Greetings from the Southern Ocean! .....it's already a lot colder at night, but what beautiful night-skies!.... Southern Cross high in the sky...the Clouds of Magellan...and can still just see part of the upside down Plough on the northern horizon....

Still pounding/plodding closehauled southwards, at present under a double-reefed mainsail and staysail only.... trying to find the balance between reasonable progress to windward against the Tradewind seas, and comfort... hoping to get a decent "slant" at St.Helena.... (I'd tried to follow a small Low which cut into the South Atlantic High, but the gamble failed.....couldn't keep up with the darned thing, so it's back to Plan A)....

A bit limited at times by a re-sprain of the right elbow ... was literally singlehanded for a day or two... but you just have to plan ahead a bit more carefully, to protect it ... it is improving slowly I think....

How many lunatics do you know who have crossed the Tropic of Capricorn at sea, THREE times in one day? .... (in my case my excuse is that it was due to tacking to work the wind shifts, on 14/4/04)....

159

There are a lot of singlehanders down here in the South ....I've "met" nine of them, two by radio only ... all of them seemed very sane indeed to me ..which is a bit worrying!....maybe I'm not fit to judge?......(ah!..except two French solo-sailors, who were definitely "peculiar", one of them certainly due to "wacky-backy") ....

One long-experienced solo-sailor had a terrible time off Uruguay in a gale, and we were all rather worried about him..... he sounded so old and exhausted on the radio.... but he made it to Tristan de Cunha Island, where they came out to look after his boat while he was whisked off to the doctor for a checkup.... it was too rough to anchor so they just jilled around in his boat till he was brought out to it again .... (they are GOOD people on that island, also supplying him with stores of island potatoes and Tristan mutton too... it really restores your faith in human nature).....

He's back at sea again now, recovering and fit .....(but what a wealth of experience he has, after his many years and scores of thousands of miles of solo sailing.... we spent quite some time chatting on the radio)....

Had one or two fights on board here.... one time Tuesday wouldn't let me get the mainsail down to reef, but I did it eventually, after a very personal battle.... the problem is alloy sailslides in an alloy track.... only the top two, but they jammed very firmly..... they're smothered in grease now, until the next time....

Tradewind squalls can bite!.... 42 knots seen during one of them, but luckily I took fright when I saw it coming, and Tuesday'n'me rolled ourselves into a tight ball before it hit.....no damage....

Disappointed at my latest bread-making efforts.... I've really given it my best shot, so I'll delay trying again until I can get some healthy yeast (mine is old)..

Problems with the ship's main water supply.... some precipitate in it, in spite of checking it before I left Salvador.. I'm already using charcoal-and-silvernitrate filters, so I'm not sure what's causing it.....tastes reasonable... but it's a nagging worry I could do without....

Anyway, even IF the ship's tanks were poisoned (which would be a great pity, as there's half a ton of the stuff in them) there's another six weeks of totally separate water in a variety of containers on board, and a hand-operated watermaker, so I'm not in any difficulty ...

Meantime the ship is heading resolutely straight at the Antarctic, until we can get a favourable wind..... now been bashing away on the port tack, closehauled, for two weeks (apart from a few hours chasing the Low), so it's a bit wearing on fittings and crew..... but Tuesday'n'me are nursing each other along in moderate comfort..... let's see what 30 degrees south brings!..

More news when I can... Trusting you are all fit and well,

> With Love from,
> **Tuesday'n'me.**

(RECEIVED)Thu 22/04/2004 11:41

> *Subject: Homeward bound*

> *Dear david,*

Simon and Garfunkle once sung a very nice song called Homeward Bound, and being truthful, it is nice to hear that you are doing just that.

You once sailed Toots backwards with Fin in the Orford river, showing off of course, but do not make a habit of it, especially now. So on your knees old son and request of him on high for favourable winds.

Well done on getting Tuesday and yourself shipshape, ready for the return journey, on reading your recent emails it is clear that you have got your head right to face the difficulty of the return trip.

We at this end are bracing ourselves for the holiday snaps viewing , normally this amounts to perhaps a couple of folders but we fear this time it might involve putting you up for the night and running into a second day, the trip being so long and eventful.

Spring has sprung here , and mostly now the weather is good.

Please continue to take the greatest care of you and yours, I myself am now on a diet (approximately One week) and I believe I have gained two pounds, catch you later .

Love, **Bob and Brenda.**

Sun 25/04/2004 23:16

Subject: 25/4/04..South Atlantic High (high pressure, that is!)..Day 23..

Dear Everybodies,

S-l-o-w progress for a few days, as I got a bit too close to the High Pressure area here, trying to predict where it was going to move to next....but no problem...all calm and peaceful, warm and restful....quite a bit of potential chafe in sails and rigging though, so there's lots to do to keep on top of it...

Good winds since 24/4/04 again though....lumpy seas, wet "upstairs", but good progress eastwards......enough wind to fill up the batteries again, just using the wind-generator....

It's colder now, bearing in mind that it is the equivalent of your October down here at present...down to 25 degrees C.....have to wear overalls to go out-of-doors at night ...

There's more rubbish in the water here than anywhere else I've seen in the Atlantic so far.... fish-boxes, large fishing buoys, plastic containers etc... makes me wonder if this area is the southern equivalent of the Sargasso Sea, where everything collects in the centre of the ocean circulation....(I hope to heaven there's no plughole in the middle!)....

I cannot get over these wonderful skies down here!... Gorgeous sunsets and dawns, deep reds, orange/ yellows, golds of all hues, with a surrounding background of purples, mauves and deepest blues .... the sun comes out of the ocean itself, a little earlier each morning as we head eastwards, and it sinks back into it again each evening, with no obstructing cloud....

And at night....Wow!.....even the stars set by slowly going pink then red, before they abruptly disappear below the horizon .... more than once I've sworn there was a port navigation light visible, until it suddenly disappeared....

It never gets dark as the Milky way is so much brighter in the southern hemisphere this time of year, because we are looking towards the Galaxy centre (though the middle itself is obscured by dust clouds in space, unfortunately)...

Thousands of diamonds sprinkled overhead, continuing into the water below as phosphorescence ... sometimes it's difficult to see exactly where sea and sky meet.......I spend probably an hour most nights just roaming the sky with binoculars...a bit "nerdy", I know, but.......

As a result, Tuesday'n'me have discovered our own COMET, (yea OK, I bet someone else found it first, but WE didn't know about it).....it's almost due southwest of the Greater Magellanic Cloud, and I've now found it's still heading towards the sun...so it may get more dramatic, I hope...it's already become a naked-eye object, as it heads westwards.....

I've called it "Tuesday Comet" .. one reason is because it was on a Monday/Tuesday night that I confirmed that it had moved each night (and so it couldn't be a nebula)...... nice long but faint tail...(wonder what its real name is)...

Other bits'n'pieces:-

Lost 60 metres of fishing-line to some big People-Eater.... then another lure the next day, when the fish was just TOO powerful for me...... last night I managed to retain all the gear, but what ever it was it straightened out my fishhooks and bit some of the tentacles off the plastic squid lure......probably would have needed a bigger frying pan anyway, (MUCH bigger!)....

Position sights by sextant, using the meridian transit of the planet Venus, in the middle of the day, are consistently within 1 mile in latitude and within 7 in longitude.... quite chuffed about these results!... real old fashioned stuff, but quite challenging at times...

Only had two dolphins come to play, (Bottlenose, or bigger I think...it was in the middle of the night)..... no whales at all so far......... several albatross's, (and they are VERY BIG birds indeed!)...remarkably manoeuvrable, taking off from the water even though there was little wind, by using the motion of the 3 metre swells to give an artificial "wind"......VERY neat indeed!.....so elegant....took some video of them...

Ham Radio has been a absolute godsend!.....most days I'm able to talk to Jonesy at home, so I can know my family are OK .... it means I don't feel I've been alone at all...... I look forward to the radio-nets each day, with discussions and reassurance and mutual advice from other solo-sailors nearby (ie, within 2000 miles!), constant updates of weather predictions to help plan the route, and the company of really pleasant and cheerful people giving me confidence and support .....very much appreciated....

Interesting the route some radio position-reports have to go to be heard at the right destination....one the other day originated on a boat in the Red Sea, received by me in the middle of the South Atlantic, then to Belgium, and on to Pennsylvania, finally being forwarded to Canada... depends entirely on how the conditions at that time allow the radio-waves to bounce around inside the ionosphere...I still find it magical, even after all these years....especially with so little power required.....

The other night, completely becalmed in calm water with fishing-line vertical, noticed that apart from the occasional creak from the ship and her rigging, there was complete and utter SILENCE.... very rare these days.... and under such a stunning starry sky too.... I feel really lucky to have seen these things.....

More news soon, I hope... only a little over 1000 miles to St.Helena now (less, as a bird flies), so I'd better start getting ready soon(!)....

Stay Well!,

Love, **Tuesday'n'me.**

(RECEIVED)Tue 27/04/2004 11:30

Subject: Tuesday's Comet = Comet "C/2001 Q4 (NEAT)"

I've had a look to see what I could find about the comet David mentioned. The Internet is an excellent resource for global information like this. I've just tried to abbreviate most of the articles down into this e-mail. There's much more information available via the web links if so desired. Things rarely go as planned so some of the details will change slightly. I hope this helps, once again my e-mail has turned into an essay.

There are two comets due to be seen soon (one of them only in the northern hemisphere). With no light pollution that could be quite a special sight:

The "Tuesday Comet" is actually called the exciting name "C/2001 Q4 (NEAT)" and was discovered in August 2001 by the Near Earth Asteroid Team at a distance of 10 astronomical units from the Sun. It appears to be NEAT's first and only passage through the inner solar system. This comet is predominantly a southern hemisphere object until May. For southern hemisphere viewers, from about 16th May, comet LINEAR will join NEAT in the evening sky putting on a double comet show.

Closest approach to the Earth occurs on 7th May at 0.32AU (48 million km). At this time, the comet should be at peak brightness of around 1st/2nd magnitude and prominent to the naked eye. It will be located high in the evening sky for southern hemisphere observers in the constellation of Puppis. Northern hemisphere observers will also pick it up during this time as the comet heads northwards.

Closest approach to the Sun occurs on May 15th at 0.96AU (144 million km) in Cancer, very close to the Beehive Cluster M44.

The other comet David should be able to see soon is called C/2002 T7 (LINEAR) and was discovered in October 2002. It is thought to be LINEAR's first and only passage through the inner solar system. It should brighten to 2nd/3rd magnitude (may become visible to the naked eye) in mid May, being at its brightest on 17th May.

It will not be visible from mid latitudes in the southern hemisphere until the middle of April. From mid April to mid May it will rise before the Sun and so be in the morning sky.

By 20th April LINEAR will rise 2.5 hours before the Sun, and at least 3 hours before the Sun between 25th April and 15th May. The comet will be between east and northeast some 20° above the horizon 1.25 hours before sunrise. The full Moon on 4th May and the presence of the waning Moon in the morning sky after that is likely to make seeing the comet difficult during the first half of May. After mid May LINEAR will rapidly disappear from the morning sky to become visible in the evening.

In the evening sky, LINEAR will set about 1 hour after the Sun on 15th May. Each following night it will set about 0.5 hours later as the comet moves higher in the evening sky. On 23rd May the comet will be less than 3° from Sirius. The Moon is at last quarter on 11th May and new on 17th May. By the end of May the waxing Moon is going to make observing the comet more difficult.

The two comets, LINEAR and NEAT, are both likely to be visible in the evening sky from about 16th May until the Moon makes observations difficult about 10 days later.

(Finder Charts and Orbital Diagrams:
http://encke.jpl.nasa.gov/charts.html
A nice animated gif of the orbits:
http://antwrp.gsfc.nasa.gov/apod/lib/koehn_threecomets_2004.gif)

So I must have learned something at University after all!
Ben

Sun 02/05/2004 19:54
Subject: Comets
Dear Ben,

I'm terribly impressed!.... Thank you very much for all the research about these things, and yes the moon has b*ggered up observing for the moment.....and I'm now heading north too, which doesn't help...

No, don't try to send pictures, thanks.....I'll see them later....... the problem here is that the signals to and from the Iridium satellites are so unreliable that it takes literally an hour sometimes with connections breaking down in mid message etc. just to send and collect my plain text mail alone....

It's been fascinating trying to predict where the darned thing will have moved to by the following night..... not easy without drawing it, or photographing it, each time, but I was gradually narrowing it down when I ran into clouds and the brightening moon....I wouldn't want to be a professional astronomer unless I could work in one of those specially chosen areas, such as the Canaries....too frustrating otherwise!....

I hope all is well with you....I've rather lost track of what everyone's up to these days....

Warmest Love, Ben, and thanks again.....
Dad.

Sun 25/04/2004 23:18
Subject: "Lembrança"
Dear Tinho,

Greetings to the King and Queen of Pizza-Makers, from the middle of the South Atlantic Ocean, 1600 miles from the nearest mainland....

This message comes to you by a satellite-link, direct from my small ship while she sails across the ocean's

163

seas....Some days the winds have been light and the progress slower than I had hoped, but very peaceful, warm and calm...

I thank you for your kindness and help while I was staying on your beautiful island...it made a great deal of difference for me, in a foreign land, not speaking your language, and so soon after my catastrophe of being struck by lightning at Ilha das Vacas...

Pizza's will never be the same for me again, now that I have tasted THE BEST!...many people all round the world now know of the wonderfully calm atmosphere of your Pizza-House-in-the-Cemetery-of-the-Slaves, and your superb food... please would you be sure to pass on my very best wishes to your wife, and congrzatulate her on her cooking?..

I hope neither of you are suffering any more from your feet!...(your toenail, and your wife's burns from hot cooking-oil)...

Stay Happy and Well, Tinho, and thank you again...

> **From David-the-Doc, on the yacht "Tuesday",**
>> (at present at position 28 degrees south, 14 degrees west).

(RECEIVED) Sun 20/06/2004 14:10

> **Subject: RE: "Lembranca"**

>> *Meu amigo,*

gostaria que você me dicesse como vai, estamos querendo saber como vai este amigo muito querido, como esta indo a viagem ou como foi esta viagem, aqui continuamos todos bem e as nossas pizzas continua esperando pela tua volta a esta cidade, lembranças a todos os seus familiares.

> **TINHO.**

Mon 26/04/2004 00:35

> **Dear Bob'n'Brenda,**

Warmest Wishes from the Southern Ocean!....at 28 south 14 west...over 1600 miles from the nearest mainland....but now only 1000 miles to get to St.Helena.....

Tonight there is sufficient wind to make enough electricity, but it's calmed down a bit outside so I can work this machine....still doing 6+ knots though...

As a result, I managed to get your Email ...

Here all is well .... plodding along at good speed into a 3+ metre sea, just cracked off close hauled, on the port tack, wind force 5, with a small genoa, staysail and single reefed mainsail, under this amazing night-sky....still a hell of a long way to go, but so far Tuesday'n'me are enjoying it well.... constantly concerned about crashing into something solid, but it's too dark to see anyway at the moment, so why worry?... the last ship was over 2 weeks ago, but several bits of flotsam seen in the last few days....

Don't worry about prolonged sessions of holiday snaps...I can be easily bribed to stay away...

Stick to the diet!.... here I'm eating a lot of things which are really BAD for us (we're told), but I've lost a lot of weight and feel very well (if you disregard the rheumatics and sprains).... you certainly burn up calories out here ......

Lots of sun here...but the back of my neck is white because my hair's too long .... don't know whether to ponytail it, plait it, or tie it in a bow, (I've actually tested two of these), but no doubt Fin will have firm views on that in the Azores.....surprisingly, a long beard turned out to be a darned nuisance, so I had to get the mower out in Brazil to tame it.....and an uncontrolled moustache gets caught in the slider of the harmonica, which stops you dead, in mid symphony, as the wretched machine clings painfully to your face like an angry rat.....

Lovely to hear from you... Stay Well and Safe.... more news next time conditions here are OK....

> Love from, **ExDoc.**

Sun 02/05/2004 17:15
    Subject: (30/4/04)...A Day in the Life, in the open ocean...
      Dear Everybodies,

At first glimmering of dawn, clamber out of bed, checking GPS position, heading, and course made good, while pulling on overalls..

Check bilges dry with the pumps..

Main batteries voltage check..

Nav lights off...

Up 7 steps into the cockpit, firmly hanging onto handholds and the rope lanyard....the first of 37 times that day.....

Yawn, and sniff the weather..

Look round the deck and rig, and all round the horizon....

Watch the seas, while slowly waking up, cursing the sprained elbow which continues to be debilitating...

Adjust sails and steering for more power, now that it's daylight again...

Down stairs again...down the tunnel under the cockpit, to turn off the wind-generator which interferes with radio reception when it's producing electricity.....

Tune into the UK Maritime-Mobile Network, to check in with Bill G4FRN, (if radio propagation is good enough)..

Back down the tunnel to turn the wind generator back on afterwards...

Kettle on... refill the Thermos, putting yesterday's (and now cool) unused boiled water into a daytime drinking container first... and make a LARGE mug of hot tea with the extra left in the kettle, balancing the mug on a wooden tray on the cooker, where it won't spill because of the gimbals....

Fill in the log, plot the new position onto the chart (and join up the dots to show the actual line of travel) ......tot up the miles in the last 24 hours (ah well, maybe tomorrow will be better)...

Then upstairs again, to drink the tea s-l-o-w-l-y, while having a morning "stare" at the ocean....

Music practice (learning to drive the Harmonica)...

Final look round, then back to bed for 30 minutes, to read a book or to get more sleep....

Mid-morning, tune into Alistair on the Durban /MM net....note other boats' positions as they report in, too...update weather forecasts....greetings all round...sometimes relay their reports to the Net Controller if signals are poor, (and vice versa if mine is bad)....burrow down the tunnel again before and after, of course.....

House-tidying, more music practice, general maintenance to reduce the jobs-to-do-list to a manageable length....

Lunchtime is Trudi's Transatlantic Net, the main one of the day.... always interesting and reassuring, together with more weather reports....

Back to bed for another short snooze.....

Afternoon sextant sight, (I confess not every day, in the open ocean).....more maintenance (a never-ending task), after more checks around the deck and rigging...

Maybe Breadmaking.... (Success again the other day!)...

Perhaps Fishing, when the light starts to come off the water a bit (more likely to get a bite then)..if we're not going too fast.........bilge-pump checks again....

More radio work to download weatherfax updates from the Brazilian Navy on shortwave, via the computer...

Back to bed, every time I can do so...

Evening chat with Jonesy on the radio (hampered by weak radio signals often), followed by the Italian 'MM Net...

Evening star-sights (sextant), but maybe I'll work them out tomorrow........Then settle the sails for the expected winds for the coming night.....

Meantime supper is being suitably constructed, and then cremated, as dusk falls....nav lights again....

The evening meal (the main meal of the day) is usually eaten straight out of the pressure cooker, while sitting in the swinging chair in the galley.... so it doesn't spill, you see...

Minimal washing up (it's still my ambition to have no washing up at all... I believe the Texans sometimes eat out of bowls made of bread....seems to me a definite step in the right direction)....

Evening concert, both active and passive....

More reading, mending, etc...

Bed around midnight, to sleep for a maximum of an hour each time before waking with the clockwork alarms, to check all is well upstairs.....radar is keeping watch for me too, but so far I've spotted ships (only ONE in the last three weeks) before it did....it is VERY good at seeing rain squalls before I do though....

In areas where there is any shipping likely, I never sleep more than 15 minutes or so, but that's in every hour, day and night... the Norwegian trip taught me that it is possible to get into the routine of this, without going totally crackers..... mind you, I haven't got a clue what time of day or night it is, or even WHICH day it is, unless I check my watch first.... you often think you're not getting any sleep, but then you realise you've been dreaming, so you must have had some, at least....

So, awake several times each night to go and sit in the cockpit upstairs.... just what I was doing the other night (cloudy and very DARK), when suddenly I got the fright of my life when an express train steam-engine suddenly flushed out its cylinders, close alongside (and I mean CLOSE!..) .... didn't know whether to stand up, sit down, or jump overboard ... so I stayed very quiet indeed!...I never saw what type of whale it was, but it was bigger than a Sperm Whale, but smaller than a Fin Whale..... probably a Humpback, or possibly even a Southern Right whale (very rare!) ......tried to film it but it was too dark, although I did get a good recording of the noise it made..... very kindly it did its breathing on the LEEward side, so I didn't get covered in water stinking of fish......it stayed at exactly Tuesday's speed for about 10 minutes, got bored and then vanished..... (but you should have heard the sheer POWER of just its normally breathing .... a long single explosive "FFFFfffff..!!!" every 90 seconds.... mind boggling!).....

During all of the above, there is the constant adjustment of sails and steering, the fights to do the reefing and unreefing (heavy work on this boat), watching the weather like a hawk, planning ahead to work the wind changes to best advantage, striving to keep a continuous lookout on deck, struggling into and out of oilskins and life jacket/harness etc many times a day.., desperately trying to keep any saltwater out of the cabin...all the time being thrown around in a washing machine by these 3+ metre waves....

Sounds fun? ...well, I'm not sure I'd want to do it for life, but it's less terrifying than when I was still at work.....

More ramblings to follow, I'm afraid..... I hope they're not too boring, but you can easily delete them!...

Stay Well!

Tuesday'n'me

Sun 02/05/2004 19:55

Subject: (2/5/04)..Back in the Tropics again!

Dear Everybodies,

Seems strange, but realising that we're within 400 miles of the Island of St.Helena now is making me nervous of actually hitting it...seems awful close to me!..

The journey eastwards at around 28 south was really rather fun, apart from the becalmed bits..... it was warm, comfortable, smooth and mostly sunny.....beautiful fish to eat....noticed the (electronic) barometer swings with each passing wave, and was able to measure height of the l-o-n-g swells coming up from Cape Horn by this means.........salvaged a wandering fishing float and its heavy nylon trace gear, taking great interest in the deep ocean barnacles attached to it......by allowing them to rot down in the fresh rainwater I had collected I was able to separate the cleaned shells (5 per barnacle), and then reassemble them with double-sided sticky tape and superglue and small pieces of Monel rigging wire, to make matching pairs of earings for my family ... it worked quite well! ... Mid-Southern-Ocean barnacle-earings must be exceptionally rare ....

Then wondering which day we'd be able to tack when the new wind would arrive....would it be next Thursday, as in the classical cruising joke?.....(no, it was at 0330 on Friday morning in this particular instance)....

Then we hit the longed-for easterly winds.....dark threatening cloudy sky, relatively cold (a new sensation for me!), damp, and a steadily worsening swell with the normal waves on top from a different direction.... aggressively nasty squalls, mainly at night, lasting hours at a time, with exceptionally heavy rain.....thankfully no whizzbangs though....

I was pushing the boat quite hard at first (42 miles in 6 hours at one point)... but the seas got steeper, more violent, and within 24 hours, in the middle of the night, I had to protect the ship a bit more.....dropped all sail except the staysail..... and as it was too dangerous to try to stow the mainsail properly on the boom without two fully functional elbows, I left it lying in the lazyjacks, with the boom nailed out sideways on its preventer (the sail thus remaining head-to-wind on the boom).....felt guilty about it, but it worked well with no chafe, and we still averaged 6 knots on a close beam reach under staysail only for several hours ..... uncomfortable but safe....

Last night was a repeat performance, with staysail and a fairly deeply reefed main at first (but I soon had to drop the main again) but this time the seas were worse..... only three-and-a-half to four metres on average, but steep, and every so often there was a much bigger b*st*rd with a breaker on the top.... when one of those hit they just knock the ship around like a toy, and you realise just who's the boss round here..... when 14 tons gets thumped about like a Mirror dinghy, you have to start nursing the boat a bit more carefully....I'm very glad she's solidly built and remarkably sea-kindly...

The heavy rain blinded the radar by its echo, so I switched on a powerful (but illegal) Brazilian masthead strobe light.....it may be sinful, but at least I've done my best to make myself visible, although I would only use it in these special circumstances....

But progress was still good, in almost the right direction....today I haven't even tried to put any mainsail back up again, even though the wind is down to 20 knots, because we're still doing 5-7 knots with two small jibs in awkward seas.... but the waves are gradually lengthening out a bit now, and I hope for better conditions tomorrow....

But the big bombshell today was when the Ham-radio transceiver abruptly died.... it still receives OK, and everything works except it won't transmit anything... not even CW....it's a bitter blow for me, as it was a significant part of my daily life here...... I'm going to miss it deeply, as I rely on it so much for weather info and Shiptrack (which incidentally I've never seen yet)......but I'll ask on St.Helena if there's anyone who might be able to help me fix it, as I already know which component it is which has failed (a cracked pre-driver transistor in the output stage) ..... (Why do I always think it's my fault when something goes wrong?.... never grew up I guess)..

I am embarrassed to admit it, but I do have on board another (old) 5 watt output 10 metre set, as well as a 5 watt 2 metre one, but they're not going to be much use for what I want.... we will see....

OK...you've suffered enough.... hopefully the next Letter-from-Tuesday will be from St.Helena?...

Stay well, Stay safe! **Tuesday'n'me.**

(RECEIVED)Sun 02/05/2004 21:40
   Subject: Radio Problems
      Hi David

I'm sorry to hear of your problem IC703...yes I'm sure you must be really cheesed of!......anyway, regarding your question on the problem, although we don't have to many people here how is qualified in repairing radios of this tech on such equipment can help you out and to try and cure your problem. We don't have any electronic shops that sells spares in relation to Ham radio transceivers but I'm sure he might be able to come up with something should the fault be a simple diode or something minor which we hope it is.

Incidentally, we have been without Mains Power for last 3 days so only got it back yesterday PM (Sat) since there was some unstable rocks about the Power Station underneath causing a danger so it had to be dislodge.

I have a friend on Ascension Island who could receive spares if they were to be flown in and then put on the Royal Mail Ship 'St Helena' but the timing has to be right and not sure how long you planning to stay at St Helena, unless your travels will be via Ascension?. Lets first of all wait until you reach St Helena...unless you feel you can have something flown in then let me know and I will come back to you with the timing of the ship to and from Ascension and I can also send you the address for Ascension.
      regards Barrie

(RECEIVED)Wed 05/05/2004 18:43
   Subject: RE: Free Spirit
      Hi Doc,

We are in St. Martin at the moment waiting for good sailing weather to sail to the British VI. At this point I am tired of the Crib. A well worn wake where they have little to offer except for the sunshine, clear warm water and beaches, the things that should be free, except they want you to pay them for it. I enjoyed the Med more. You picked the right direction, and you only have to put up with yourselves, which totals 3 of you, ME, MYSELF AND I.......

   Hope all is going well with you.
      Let us know how you're doing,
         you're in our thoughts and prayers,
            Allen/Marsha

Fri 07/05/2004 22:55
   (Subject: St.Helena)
      Dear Everybodies,

WOW!...what lovely people here!....lovely warm welcome from the Port Authority on the VHF...(able to meet Bryan himself later and tell him how grateful I was)...but he suggests not to swim today as a large shark was seen in Ruperts Bay (about 400 yards away) yesterday.... said to be a bit unusual on this side of the island......

Able to arrange with Barrie (by 2 metre VHF, using John's old 5watt IC2E fm handheld set and a ribbon-wire SlimJim antenna propped up in the cockpit) to meet up today...

Really nice welcoming smile, and so helpful, (even though I may have messed up his day by being late).... showing me where the relevant shops, stores etc were, all the things which one needs in the first days of landing in a new place.... even showed me where Gladys H. lives, so that I was able to give her the letter and small parcel from Ros, personally (they were penpals 40 years ago)..(that was a nice moment!)........THANK YOU Sir, you are true gentleman!

Everybody seems happy to greet you, chat, smile and laugh.... they are curious to know more about you, but in a quiet, polite and delightful manner....... none of the Latino armwaving and loud voices of the Brazilians..... it's a fascinating contrast......

I LIKE this place!...no "fifty quid" birds, but wild Minah birds strolling around mimicking EVERYTHING.....

But first, a bit of recap, (and I'll have to leave out great chunks 'cos there's so too much to tell......) :-

After the rough stuff, it calmed down a lot and settled to a very pleasant swinging ride at 5-7 knots, in comfort and peace..... still 2-3 metre seas, but kinder....

The stunning view of the eclipse of the full moon when it reddened and dimmed, allowing the myriads of stars of the southern sky to come out in their full glory, on a cloudless, crystal clear night......... very beautiful indeed.... that's a night I could never forget....

Then, as the sun set on Wednesday 5/5/04, j-u-s-t managed to see (at 30 miles) the mountains of St.Helena ....so hove-to at about 1 knot overnight to make sure of approaching in daylight.....

It gave me the chance to dismantle the faulty radio yet again, and work on the exact component which was faulty .... I took it out, cleaned it and replaced it here on board that night, in case it was simply a dry solder joint, but the transistor itself is cracked, so I think it's had it......it worked for a while and then died again........... it's possible we could find a substitute, as long as it is a simple switching transistor ...... however, if it turns out to be the pre-driver transistor then maybe we can cannibalise the old whizzbanged set..... but unfortunately I have a nasty feeling that the older radio has the same fault ......we shall see, with a friend of Barrie's here on the Island, tomorrow.......

Nearly overshot the anchorage here...bowling along at 6-7 knots, I didn't realise how much ground we were covering and how tiny the island is ..... and Jamestown is so much smaller and more hidden away than I expected........

Hove to again to sort ourselves out...... then tacked in, very s-l-o-w-l-y under mainsail only, to anchor (under advice from Bryan, Assistant Harbourmaster, by radio) in 19 metres (= 62 feet) of amazingly clear water, 200 yards off the rocks at 1430hrs, 6/5/04.....60 metres of chain to get back on board again next week sometime, but I'll remember a story I was told by Yvan, and do it in stages....

3137 miles in 33 days, although not quick, was mostly comfortable........ in spite of over 90% of it being closehauled.....

One other yacht here, a charming American/Canadian couple ....been here two weeks, and love it too much to leave!.......

And the rocks of the headland themselves are sighing and whistling every 10-12 seconds, like a sleeping giant, as the mighty ocean breathes in and out........ it is due to a small "blow-hole" in the rocks here where the air gets trapped and compressed with each swell, to make a noise like a vast flute .....fascinating to listen to, as it seems to dream in its sleep!.......

Getting ashore at the landing place is fun..... have to time it well, with the swells.... get it right and it's easy and elegant..... get it wrong and you're going to break something, while getting VERY wet! ....

And the Royal Mail Ship "St.Helena" came in this morning.... anchored close in...... everything (except the passengers of course, who do it by motorboat) comes ashore by lighter, using the ship's derricks........... and you should see the skill of the crane operator ashore, plucking large containers out of the lighters at the peak of each wave ....one container per lighter....... very professional indeed!......

There's so, so much more....... but enough for now!...

Much love to all,
    from,
      Tuesday'n'me.

(RECEIVED) Sat 08/05/2004 18:49

> *Subject: from an envious wimp!*
>> *well done, bloody well done!!!*
>>> *Joe*

(RECEIVED) Sat 08/05/2004 19:51

Dear Tuesday'n'me,

You are right, David, the two of you sort of belong together, and I have to address my letters to both of you! thank you so very, very much for including me in the Everybodies, I feel very honoured, and have enjoyed them very much. I do hope it is alright to send a reply now you have access to a computer ashore, maybe. What a blessing that phone of yours has been, I must say. I shall never say anything negative against an Iridium phone again! And I am so glad, that Barrie is looking after you so well. Maybe he will even talk to me one of these days!

Good Luck with the repairs, we are crossing fingers and toes, but Jack is itching to send you another set, I know!

Still, apart from the difficulty getting to and off shore, I think you will probably stay a bit longer than you thought, it is a very unusual island, I believe. Here's a little story, David:

In 1986 we met a delightful young lady from St. Helena. Veronica was then in her early thirties, had never been away from the island, when an elderly American singlehander (in his 80s) was looking for a crew to help him sail the boat back to the States and complete his navigation, mostly to give his family at home some peace of mind. So Veronica signed on with Joshua on the boat "Comitan".. Apart from Barbados (she said she had never been to such a big place before!) she did not see much of the world on that occasion, as when she reached Miami, she had an urgent message about a death or illness in the family, and returned to St. Helena immediate;y. If you should come across Veronica, David, do give her our love. She just might remember. I just looked up her entry in the visitor's book, as I could not remember the year!

Here's hoping and sending lots of very best wishes from Barbados,
>> *88 – Trudi*

Mon 10/05/2004 01:38
> **Subject: Veronica**
>> **Dear Trudi,**

Thanks for your Email..... always so positive and encouraging!....

I would be delighted to try to find out how and where she is.... everyone knows everyone here (not necessarily biblically though), so if she's on the Island we can be sure.... I'll let you know as soon as I find out...

Lovely little 2 metre net running here now ... they're absolutely delighted to be able to talk to a non-ZD7 callsign, and are so grateful.... I quietly pointed out that the delight was probably even more mine than theirs... how many G- hams have four ZD7's in their logbooks on 2 metres?.... they hadn't thought of it that way!......

Very nice people indeed.....
> Warmest Wishes!
>> **David.**

**(FOOTNOTE:- I found out that Veronica does still live here, but she is "offshore" (ie. away) at present)

(RECEIVED)Thu 13/05/2004 01:57

Subject: Congratulations!
Tuesday and David...

Well done. Fantastic! Your voyage from Brazil to St.Helena was truly remarkable and we are all full of admiration... for you, and for your skipper David. What an epic!

Gerald, as you know, is absolutely marvellous... in his communications with you and with his forwardings to us. You make a good team. I have got some of your most memorable e-mails ready to send to Teresa and to Chris C but they will have to wait until I can get through to them. There is no answer from Teresa, probably because she may be in the $tates helping Paul.

We don't envy you when you are at sea in bad conditions, but we would give the Earth to be on St.Helena with you. What a fantastic place... I had no idea. I have printed out the photos taken of you two on the island. I presume there's a doctor there somewhere, and I presume some sort of cottage hospital. And I am intrigued by the water supply... is it derived directly from rain or does it just come up from the ground somehow? If the latter then where the hell does it come from?

We wish you all good luck for your voyage up north. I must say, it seems a pretty formidable task. We all desperately miss you and long to see you back safely at anchor at Orford. Bring David safely home!

With much love, from all of us. **Daddy and Mother.**

(RECEIVED) Mon 10/05/2004 15:18

Dear David,

If the Whiz bang did not do to much damage to the gray cells, you may remember Ben very kindly sorted out for us a security piece of software after he resolved our computer virus problem, this seems at the moment to keep our (sorry, HER) computer clean.

I have looked in my Readers Digest Atlas (lovely it is) and sure enough a St Helena UK. is marked on a blue bit, but since there does not appear to be any land how on earth did you find it?

I think many of us will envy you the experience of whale sightings,sunsets and heavenly bodies etc, but will never have the courage nor ability to undertake such a venture.

As usual April was very wet but now the sun is shining, the trees, hedgerows and grass are lush and green, England in all her glory.

Please keep the e.mails coming advising us of your progress and current position, even if I am not very good at finding your location in my Atlas.

Continue to take the greatest of care.
Love **Bob & Brenda.**

Sun 09/05/2004 23:35

Dear Everybodies,

This Island is a jewel!.....such a lovely relaxed atmosphere, even though the quay is busy as the RMS "St.Helena" is still unloading.....there is an air of sensible "safety-consciousness" on the quay, which was noticeably in Brazil by its total absence.....

Just to sit in Castle Park, with its squirrel, snail and birds (all made of shaped ornamental bushes) in the warm sunshine... everyone greets you, and usually stops to talk to you..... even visitors to the Island from the ship ......

And round you, quite unflustered, walk Indian Minah (?spelling?) birds looking furtive (I gather they were imported to remove ticks from the livestock)..... and a nice type of miniature grey pigeon with a pleasing pattern to its feathers which won't stop to talk as it's busy right now thank you very much, (or so it

171

seems, as it mutters quietly, as it walks past your feet, head down, concentrating on its own world)...

Using the inflatable to get ashore, with acrobatics to get safely on the landing place in one dry piece, additionally trying not to lose the dinghy or break your arm...... powerful swells here, and tidal currents too (as I noted today while skin diving to check and clean the ship's bottom)..... the water is as gin-clear as anywhere I've seen before, though not as warm as at Graciosa.....maybe be the cold current running up from Capetown? ...

At night the dinghy is hauled aboard, across the aft cabin, as Tot and I did in Porto Santo......stops seals etc lying in it during the hours of darkness ....

Water from the tap on the landing place is excellent quality..... dinghied out to the ship in the jerrican..... only needed 40 litres to top up the tanks .....

Cravings for the essential foods of life are now satisfied (namely fruit, fresh bread and chocolate).....as usual, my eyes were bigger than my stomach.....it's a great relief not to have to keep a constant eye on how much food and water I'm using, as I have to do when at sea....

Good Spar supermarket with all the stores I need to restock ......and the check-out girls are friendly, smiling and helpful......mind you, the prices (for obvious reasons out here in the middle of the ocean) are about 5-6 times the Brazilian ones....

And have met up with John and Bruce (both radio-hams here).... charming, friendly people...John is very kindly reviewing my findings with the radio, to explore the possibilities I mentioned earlier....... I hear by VHF tonight from Barrie and Bruce that so far he has been very successful..... more details soon I hope.....

Good company from the crews of "Sangreal" (Ken and Gail, from Washington), and "Novina", a large Taiwan-built yacht registered in Ipswich (Ken and Pat are based at Shotley ...isn't it a small world!)...... expecting "Cloud Nine", (a South African 37' catamaran with 5 people on board) to arrive tomorrow am.... I was in contact with Deon on board by radio for many days, till the set died)...

Then to start exploring a bit more, I hope......

(Yet more comments to follow....)

Tuesday'n'me.

(RECEIVED) Mon 17/05/2004 18:03

Subject: Where some of the coffee comes to...

Sorry for another short one....But I promise, I had written a fairly descriptive letter during the trip....But my computer, amongst other things, shat itself and I have lost it all. Also it refuses to work again....

Safe and sound arrival,Chagaramus,Trinidad,Thursday.. 2300mls,17 days,not too bad for a little fella in a little boat..About 300 mls more than the direct route but I went on a more Northerly course to avoid traffic and try and get through the ITCZ sharpish..

As usual Lala went like a dream with mostly No3 jib and 1/2/3/Reefs in the main, but the trip was bit of a rough rock n'roll ride with lots of water in the cockpit,on a broadish reach most of the way with 20 odd knots SE eventually slowly turning NE at about 6'North, gusting 35 and dropping to 5 when it felt like it..

As usual the seas were the hassle, very Confused. Hot humid and very squally through ITCZ, but fortunately no doldrums, which was just as well as I now have a transmission problem. (I am too bored with it all to tell U all about it...)

Had a smallish whisky or two with my old mate Neptune at 6 am, crossing the big 00'00, and I've got say it was a little early even for me but what the hell..You got to keep the old boy sweet.......After pushing hard for the last 36 hrs managed to pick up a mooring 30 minutes before sunset. Lala, U little Beauty, you!...I love It...Love U's all..

Take lots of care U hear....God Bless... NICK...

Sun 09/05/2004 23:41
   Dear Everybodies,

Great News!! (for me, at least)... John (ZD7JC), by applying some lateral thinking and skill, has managed to produce a working radio for me!.... we now know my diagnosis was right, but instead of trying to fix the individual component he simply took a gamble and swapped the whole board (virtually half the radio) with its stablemate from the lightning-damaged one.....I had assumed it was dead, but very wisely he assumed nothing..... and it works!........and, remarkably, the one which is now full of diseased components will still act as a receiver for weatherfax etc........I'm VERY impressed, and I'm so glad we asked for his help.....

I think we've been very lucky to get away with it, and the setup is still not to be trusted yet because of its previous "zapping", but I'm very pleased indeed that I'd chosen an identical model as a replacement, to enable this cannibalisation...... once again, Jack, I'm indebted to you, sir!....

As I'm not aiming to stop at Ascension Island, I'll wait till I get back to the UK before chasing repairs to the spare radio..... my experience with electronics and carrier has deeply imprinted me, and I'm not going through all that worry yet again.....

(Incidentally, that parcel of electronics is still in Brazil I gather, and it would appear the shippers are quite happy to do nothing at present...after all, they've got their money for the mess up, haven't they, (which leaves a filthy taste in the mouth)..... it may catch up with them when I get back to the UK though, but they have been fairly and clearly warned.......)

Onto lighter things:-

"Jacobs Ladder".... all 700 steps of it.... looks straight forward to do, but it's not at all easy!.... I understand the record is around five and a half minutes, but nonstop it took me a full 14 minutes today.... at the top I could breath or talk or walk, but strictly only one at a time........ if that's what it takes to get to heaven, I'm definitely going the other way!........Smashing view from the top though........at night it is all lit up, when as well as being practical it looks very neat too.....

A very pleasant group of people on the 2 metre VHF net here .....really nice and friendly chats on the radio...

Great fun today when Barrie and his son Shane came out to inspect the ship, Shane valiantly trying to row the heavily laden dinghy.... he did very well.... I wish we'd had more time for me to show them more on board, but duty called them away .....

Driving the empty inflatable "Green Bladder" dinghy back to the boat with the 2 horse-power Suzuki engine running flat-out, I discovered with surprise that it will plane very well, so I've suddenly got myself a speedboat for nothing........

The mail ship has left, but a huge great 90' ketch flying the White ensign has arrived ..."Thalassi".... she's a boat I know well from my books... met two of the crew, but I don't think they're allowed to talk to us mere mortals......nasty thing to say, but I'm not alone in being secretly delighted that their vessel is rolling around in the swell just as much as the rest of us are......

Sparrows.... very pretty birds with brightly coloured heads and red beaks.... much more elegant than ours back home.....

Enough for now......
As they say in Brazil, "Tudu Bem!"...All is well.....
And as they say here, "Go Well!",
   Love from
      Tuesday'n'me.

Fri 14/05/2004 23:09
> **Dear Ron'n'Bonnie,**

You'd love the local broadcast radio here!.....it's on medium wave AM (they don't have FM nor VHF)....two sorts of music throughout the day ..... namely Country, and Western (as a local told me, with a sly grin) ...... interspersed with details of the recent crime wave, where they THINK someone may have stolen a garden-tap-handle............. clearly the work of a crime syndicate we believe.........

Trust all is well for you ....please give "Forever" a gentle pat from me.......

> Fair Winds and Safe Landfalls!
> > **Doc**

(RECEIVED)Sat 15/05/2004 07:34

Have been trying to call for the past week with no result...

Is anything wrong with ur British cell phone (except it being british!)

We both miss u so much and I would have loved you to be here. Guess I´ll have to wait a bit!

Maybe you want to send me your phone no. again? ....

Sorry must hurry, have a group of 12 dives to take out this morning.
> > **Chris**

Mon 17/05/2004 23:54
> **Subject: Telephone numbers**
> > **Dear Chris,**

Sorry .... not your fault, but mobile phones only work when within range of repeater-antennas..... and there ain't none out here!!

Unfortunately St.Helena doesn't have a cellphone system either, so it didn't work here either..... maybe in the Azores perhaps?....

This Email comes via satellite, but it's very slow and bl**dy expensive, so the sat-system is only switched on very briefly to send/receive, occasionally, when I have enough electricity power etc.....

The Telephone number you have is perfectly correct....

Meantime, thanks for all the news..... and I hope you've been taking your extra vitamins and orange juice and iron the way every expectant father should?

Miss you both, but glad you're here with me in spirit,
> > **Doc.**

(RECEIVEDTue 11/05/2004 09:20
> *Subject: Guess Who?!*
> > *Dear Uncle David*

What a merry dance you lead us on with firstly the radio working then it not working somewhere in the middle of the ocean, then it working again! Do you do this sort of thing on purpose just to see how many nervous wrecks you can make us all over here?! Glad to hear that you have finally got two good radios working again.

Daddy sent us a few photos of you and I am afraid to say two things:

1) Two of them now adorn our fridge for everyday peering at and

2) You so do look like Ralph as I remember him! (Sorry - must be the beard and the sailor's hat!) What ever happened to him? Is he stillwell? I bet he would be proud of you now (or call you a silly old fool!).

Matthew is suddenly shooting up but he does look like Boris a lot these days with his very white blonde hair all over the place! His speech is coming on. It was lovely last week in that when I woke up I could hear him calling "Mamma" which is the first time he has said it -now it is non stop!

The weather is getting a little better now so they love to play out in the garden all the time - it's great we don't see them from one hour to the next! Are you still unable to receive pictures?

Anyway, enough of my ramblings. Glad to hear you made it to St Helena in one piece and all the very best to you crossing the Atlantic to the Azores. If I didn't have commitments I would have loved to come and seen you there.

Take care and happy sailing.
Lots of love
EDAM XX

Fri 14/05/2004 23:08
Dear Everybodies,

Maintenance, repairs, reprovisioning, several improvements to make things easier for myself, etc....stupidly trod on a sailmaker's needle with my full weight when it was stuck vertically in the carpet, but managed to remove it all ...daft thing to go and do, but if it goes septic there are all the facilities on board to deal with it.........

Another 60 eggs preserved by Yvan and Christina's method (10 seconds flash-boiled in vinegared water) .... it's been quite busy on board, but at my own pace.... still miss those electrical bits stuck in Brazil, because they would have made a considerable difference to simplify things at sea at times .... ah well, we'll use what we have......

Went to see Gladys H. again (the lady Ros used to write to over 40 years ago), to give her Ros's new address ... although I am a complete stranger to her she insisted that I stay, sit down and have tea and cakes (which she had made herself ...they were especially delicious as I haven't eaten any pastry-things for months...mouth-watering!)..... Photos of her trip to England ...I felt so guilty sitting there in my (clean) overalls with nothing to offer in return at all, but it was a lovely afternoon, which she seemed to enjoy too... I'll see her again before I leave, to thank her......

She's given me a letter to deliver by hand to Ros..... probably won't receive it till September, I suspect, but even that may be quicker than MY shipping agent.......

Grand tour of the island two days ago, in the open back of a pickup truck .....there were ten of us, all from the yachts which have accumulated here now...... local chap called Robert was excellent, and had all sorts of details on hand to answer our questions .... Barrie's sister took us round Napoleon's living quarters, and made it all sound "alive" and interesting .... not even a bit like a history lesson.....

This island is a very pretty place, in many ways reminding me of a cross between Lanzarote and Madeira, but in a gentler manner than either....multicoloured dry volcanic areas, but very green in the highlands.... great range of tree-types with the altitude changes, peak height being about 2,700ft ..... with all its ridges and valleys it seems a much bigger island than I had thought........ ....and we were lucky with the weather, as it's rained on and off since then with cloud covering the hills......

I've never seen tortoises as big, nor as old ...... I muttered quietly that I hoped I'd be as fit as the oldest one (over 170 years) at that age.....Ken from "Sangreal" said "Oh, you will David...you'll be crawling around slowly on all fours if you live that long, too!"

It was a Good day... and Barrie and Val very kindly invited me to supper with them afterwards, and we had a very pleasant, relaxing evening in their lovely house perched on the top of a hill..... he has a radio and antenna-mast setup which made me feel ashamed of my own efforts......... outstanding view from up there, too ......fascinating conversation made me completely forget the forthcoming voyage..... Thank you both for a very memorable evening!...I had forgotten what it is like to eat PROPER food instead of the "catfood" I've

175

been living on for the past 6 weeks!.....very much appreciated.......

Then yesterday I spent about 90 minutes in the public library researching (with friendly help from the librarians) more information on the Geology of this island, a subject I've always been hooked on..... found all the information I wanted, and it was quiet and peaceful in there to let me absorb it all..... good timing too, as it was raining fairly all afternoon outside...

The Plan at present is to try to set sail tomorrow Saturday 15th May, all being well, (particularly if I can get all that darned anchor-chain up again, since it got hooked on a rock for a while today).....the ship and crew are ready..... the intention is to break no records but to travel in comfort at reasonable speed.....

Then to head for the Azores nonstop, by a path similar to the one from Salvador (but opposite handed for the Northern hemisphere)...like a big left-handed, (ie. mirror-image) question mark..........

It's the main voyage of the whole trip, with all the previous legs being mere practice for the real one ..... looks like being between 4000 and 5000 miles, and expecting 6-8 weeks by the time we've got through the Doldrums again, and round the North Atlantic High (into the Horse Latitudes once more)..... by then we will have found out whether I really do like sailing or not!.....

More news when I can....

Stay Safe and Well!

Love from,

Tuesday'n'me.

(RECEIVED) Thu 13/05/2004 17:55

Subject: Wishes!!

David,

Wishing that you may have a peaceful voyage home; wishing it didn't look such a hell of a way twixt St. Helena and the Azores; wishing that the time may pass quickly for you when you are out of reach of Emails; but wishing that you and Gerald are able to keep in touch; and above all, wishing and longing to see you and Tuesday at anchor at Orford. That sure WILL be the day!

We loved the photos of you at St. Helena and the fairy tale news that you have met up with Rosalie's one time Girl Guide correspondent. I hope Rosalie writes to Mary Morris who would be delighted to know about it.

Daddy and I keep wondering several times a day "wonder what David's doing NOW" and we pray that you are happy and not too worried at the time. Come home soon!! We love you very much and I only wish my father were alive, and Gran, they would be so very proud of you.

Heaps and heaps of love, from **Mother.**

Chapter 9

Northwards from St.Helena

Mon 17/05/2004 23:04
Subject: Getting warmer as we head northwards..
Dear Everybodies,

The ODSC BURGEE HANGS PROUDLY, and permanently, in ANN'S PLACE, (the famous restaurant), on ST. HELENA! ......

It's a modified, REEFING version of the flag (for strong winds) with reef-points sewn into it .... there is only one other similarly altered ODSC flag in existence, which has been on display on the ceiling of Sixhaven Yacht Club, Amsterdam since 1983 (which is when I donated it to them as a peace-offering after the aborted Orford to Amsterdam race).....I saw it was still there 3 years ago, at least....

Had watched HMS "Scott", Naval Oceanographic Survey vessel (described as "the most sophisticated bottom-scraper in the business") came in for an informal visit.....pleasant crew, who appreciate the island ...

And I watched with interest how the Saints gathered on the sea-front to watch RMS "St.Helena" depart for Cape Town ....you have to bear in mind that the "St.Helena" is the island's lifeline, and I could get a glimpse of what emotions it must stir in the islanders to watch her disappear, hoping she will reappear in 6 weeks time again..... everything coming onto the island comes by her, to be craned ashore from the barges which unload her out in the anchorage........if what you wanted wasn't on the ship then you don't receive it, fullstop ....

It was sad to leave St.Helena, the "Emerald Jewel"......and sad to say farewell to Barrie and Val who went out of their way to be so kind to me........ for Gladys some flowers, and a thankyou letter .... what a wonderful place, and remarkable people!.... the experience I will always remember with a smile.......

Gentle rain washed down the dinghy nicely before it was stowed below....... getting the anchor up took forever, but was not a problem..... and Barrie and Val will be pleased to know that the St.Helena explosive grapes have worked very well!.....

Leaving was made easier and gentler by some VHF range experiments we did, as the island receded in the distance, for which I thank you Gentlemen (Barrie, Bruce and Garry).... we called it a day at 42 miles, though the loom of the lights was still just visible at 50 miles.......there was no contact next day at 92 miles ......

So here we are now, rolling fairly heavily with the wind a little aft of the starboard beam, a medium sized genoa poled out flat to windward, and a staysail to leeward (no mainsail up)...... trundling down the Tradewinds at around 120 miles/day at a leisurely pace, very much "on holiday", in radio contact with another English yacht 50 miles ahead......nearly halfway to Ascension already, but another 1000 miles to the Equator.....

Some moderate squalls each night, and it's quite cloudy ....but each day is a little warmer, the sun in the north a little higher, sunset a little later...... each night the Plough is higher ahead, and the Southern Cross and Magellanic Clouds a bit lower in the south ......

So I'm now fairly confident that the Earth really IS round, and not flat........

That's all for this one ..... more when I can....

With Love from,
Tuesday'n'me.

Mon 17/05/2004 23:04
Subject: On the move again..
Dear Y, C, T, and J,

Just an update..... "Tuesday" left St.Helena Island at noon Saturday 15/5/04, towards the Azores, nonstop, expecting to take 6-8 weeks by a roundabout route skirting the West side of the N. Atlantic High..... approx 4-5000 miles.....should be interesting, cutting across the various latitudes of weather....

Loved St.Helena .....so friendly and peaceful! ....but I was aware all the time that the (rather rolly) anchorage was only secure in the prevailing wind..... like in Porto Santo...

New, fresh yeast on board now for some bakery masterpieces on this voyage! ...could be my new career?....

Thanks again, because I learnt so much from you two.....as I said before, it was a real pleasure to have met you, and I'm sad that we may not meet again....

Hope all is well with you still ......Stay Safe!...

Fondest Wishes,
Tuesday'n'me.

(RECEIVED) Mon 17/05/2004 22:08

Hi David you must be a couple of days out by now. I am listening but I am not sure if you managed to get the rig fixed. I dont know if you will get this email whilst mobile so will resort to the twisted pair if we dont hear you soon.

All well this end .The barbie season is upon us so have a word with Tuesday see if she cant squeeze a few more knots and get you back in time for a sausage or two
take care .luv from my lot **John**

(RECEIVED) Fri 21/05/2004 00:09

Hi David

Hope all is going well with you onboard!.

Sorry its taken me so long...have just got off those evening and night shifts, so looking forward to 3 days off now as I took an extra days leave....and of course its St Helena's national day tomorrow being 21st May (St Helena's Discovery) there will be a small function I believe in Jamestown....last night was the Miss St Helena Contest and Valerie she went to see the sights which was very nicely performed...followed by shome shots by the digicam. The 1st prize for Miss St Helena by the way is 500 pounds and free trip on the 'RMS' to Capetown so....not bad for St H standards I suppose!...

So, hows things with you .... and wonder whereabouts are you now, assuming you must be quite near Asc? haven't listen in for a while...must do that hopefully tomorrow Fri., although I know Jack and the net are well in touch with you!.

Anyway, Val and Shane send their regards.....explosive grapes has been well taken care of and nothing more heard!!....there is however few left in the fridge...must admit I do nibble at em time to time!.....again it was great to have you at our home and wish it could have been at a more relax day of preferably a Sunday, and then a bit more outings would also have been nice...never mind, we will count on next time!.

Must close now, and look forward as always to those rather interesting "Everybodies" letters .... In the meantime go well and keep safe.

All the very best,
With Love from your friends that sits on the 'Emerald Jewel'...
Barrie, Valeire & Shane-Simon

Sun 23/05/2004 18:26
    Subject: Thanks, more than I can express.
    Dear Barrie,

You and your friends on The Emerald were really wonderful to me, a stranger out of the sea ...... just can't begin to thank you enough..... and it was a great pleasure to get your Email today....I'll send a few of the piccies from home (?September?) when I have access to a decent phone link....

I wonder, would you be kind enough to personally thank the others, please? .... especially John who stayed firmly in the background even though he was the one I owe a deep debt to ... don't tell him, but I intend to find some suitable equipment in England, and quietly post it to him .... I'll keep thinking of what would be most useful to him on the Island .... So far the Icom 703 continues to work as it should, thanks to him..... Maybe also he would like to see what I said about him in the "Dear Everybodies"? ....

Yes, like you, I wish I could have had more time, but the Seasons wait for no man, unfortunately .... there was a lot of work to do on the boat while at anchor there, so I didn't get to do many of the things ashore I would have liked to have done .. I felt I was remiss in not having made more time with you, for which I apologise ... I had so much to ask you about the Saints themselves, as well as about the Island .... but "Tuesday" comes first I'm afraid, especially when setting out on the longest voyage I will ever make, probably.....

I'll keep in touch after this voyage as well, I'm afraid, so you're not going to get away that easily!..anything I can do, even from England, please do ask, including medical stuff (you know I find it fascinating!)..it would be a pleasure to help... you know our home telephone in England....

Anyway, more Dear Everybodies to follow,
        Do take good care of yourselves,
            Warmest Love to you and Val and Shane,
                Doc David'n'Tuesday.

Sat 22/05/2004 16:13
    Subject: Staale
        Dear Trudi, and Alistair (of the Durban maritime mobile net), (and ONLY to the two of you),

I wonder if I could ask for your help for Staale (LA7GZ/mm), at his request please, as he doesn't have Email facilities on board?... it may require a bit of tact and diplomacy though...

Staale has been without selfsteering for two days, but HE IS DESPERATE THAT HIS MOTHER AND FATHER DO NOT FIND OUT, at least until he is on land again. He says the reason for secrecy is because his parents are fully aware of the additional risks it puts on him, and he fears they will become ill with concern for him. I believe they co-own the boat too. As Staale knows his own parents better than any of us, I thoroughly respect his wishes.

He has 3 processor units, 2 fluxgate compasses, and 2 electromechanical rams for the tiller. Manufacturer is Autohelm/Raytheon. The problem is a mechanical one in the rams, the same fault in each. The first one had worked perfectly well for 35,000 miles, and when it failed he did not imagine the spare one would collapse within 10 minutes.

He has been doggedly trying to repair his broken autopilots, both of them, but he has reluctantly reached the conclusion that he cannot fix them with the equipment he has on board, even by cannibalising for parts and materials. Staale is an expert at fixing things, but sadly he has had to admit that this has eventually defeated him, unfortunately.

The boat is difficult to manage without selfsteering, but he and I have put our heads together to come up with some possible solutions. His main worry is how the boat will cope with another gale like the last one, without exhausting him by requiring him to steer manually all the time. We have discussed it fully today, and will talk more later.

179

His plans include seeing what might be possible on Tristan de Cunha (he will contact Andy himself), but otherwise to wait till the end of a necessarily slow passage to Cape Town to sort it out. He is naturally quite concerned about how he will get on when close to land.

What he would like you to do please is :-

(i) be aware of his difficulties, so you understand his slow progress,

and (ii)make ABSOLUTELY SURE NO MENTION of this incident appears on Shiptrak, nor should it be mentioned on the nets, for fear his parents will hear of it. This is clearly very important for Staale.)

On a lighter note, we both wish it put on record how much we have valued your help, interest, and support. It has made a great deal of difference for both of us.... it's a big empty place out here on your own when things go wrong.

Thank you for all the work you do... much appreciated....

Best Wishes!

from David on "Tuesday".

(RECEIVED) Sat 22/05/2004 18:58

Subject: Staale

All perfectly understood, David, and I can see Staale's concern.

Please give him my best wishes, I hope between the two of you, you can work out something.... and I won't mention a thing, and I am sure Alistair will do the same.

There is a high going Staale's way, he will be without wind for a while, and it might give him time to work on the problem.

Thank you for your confidence, David!

88 to both you and Alistair – **Trudi**

PS. David, what sort of a boat is "Rozinante"? I have no description in my notes, fell down on that one, sorry. I am wondering why he has no windsteering? Maybe we have better copy tomorrow.

PPS - just discovered your previous "dear Everybodies", and got my question answered, thank you, David!

But I still wonder - why no windsteering? No point asking him now, but it would be good if he could do something about it in Capetown, before he heads north again?

Sun 23/05/2004 18:26

Subject: Staale (ii)

Dear Trudi,

(While I've still got electricity!)

Many thanks indeed for your tact, and for forwarding to Alistair.... I feel very bad about doing things behind peoples' backs.

As far as wind vane steering is concerned, yes I agree.... but I haven't talked windvanes over with Staale yet because it must have been a ghastly time, when you're kicking yourself for what's happened .... the last thing you need is someone telling you what you SHOULD have done, when you already realise it yourself now.... so I'm waiting till he's more settled, and preferably for him to raise the subject, before I wade in with my own views...

I suspect the reason "Rozinanthe" doesn't have a purely mechanical selfsteering gear is because she's not totally Staale's boat ... I believe she belongs to the family, on loan to him, so it's a bit tricky to start cutting the boat about and altering her appearance...... especially when the first Autohelm had been perfectly reliable for 35,000 miles ....

Interesting that the first piece was made by Autohelm when they were still independent, but the second

180

when they'd been taken over by Raytheon ...... many of the metal pieces in the first had been made out of plastic in the second .... ?moral?....

Had a nice chat with him today....he's a lot happier now that he's made some decisions about what to do ...... he said he just needed to tell SOMEONE about it (something most singlehanders can't do) ... I only found out how important that is in the last few years.....

I've got a lot of time for Staale... he's obviously an intelligent and clear thinking man, with feelings like the rest of us ... he fits the mould of the majority of singlehanders I've met... a tough and resilient bunch, and it's been a real privilege to meet some of these remarkable people during this trip ... I'm an amateur at this, but these guys are true professionals....... most interesting..... helps restore one's pride in being human!....

Oops! .. turned out a bigger "quick" note than I planned!...

Warmest Best Wishes, Trudi, to you and all your family..... and thanks for understanding....

Tuesday'n'me.

(RECEIVED) Sun 23/05/2004 16:03

*   **Hello David,** *really wonderful to read your Emails, makes us (me any way) feel as though I am there with you !*

*   *Had an interesting occurrence last Wednesday (19 May) Joyce and me decided to go to Le Touquet for the day, left Parham at 10.05 - in the aeroplane that is - just about to cross the Thames at 10.050 when the oil pressure went up, like off the dial, after a minute or so of bumbling about, you might know- what do I do now etc? so called 'pan pan' "cripes I've done it now" bugger! not able to hear the lady at the other end of 121.5 so her transmition was relayed to us by a passing airliner and we were diverted to Southend Airport, seven miles distant, we were asked to 'squark' 7700 the distress code (this is getting serious) as we approached to land I noticed a jinormouse fire engine lying in wait for us, we totally disappointed them by making a textbook landing but they wouldn't go away, they followed us until we stopped just to make sure we were ok. We spent 3 hours at Southend having the engine checked by the resident aircraft engineer, a kindly man - who knew Bob Hammond, he eventually declared that the problem was a faulty oil pressure sender which could be disenabled so that we could fly home. So it was lunch at Southend on Sea - not in France, never mind will try again soon.*

*   **Joe**
*   (And keep looking after both of you*
*   Lots of love,*   **Joyce)**

Sat 22/05/2004 16:12
   Subject: Approaching the Equator again.
      Dear Everybodies,
              You can tell a lot just by listening.......

The wind humming and whistling in the rigging, changing it's note with each passing sea and with each roll, as the apparent windstrength alters....a groaning from the mast-step on deck, as it moves in its seating very slightly ....the occasional clank of a spinnaker-pole-car on its track on the mast itself ....the groan from a taut rope to the poled-out genoa as the load keeps changing, where it passes round a fairlead pulley........ the wind-generator has a "chipping" sound because one blade is minutely different from its two neighbours (in spite of all my efforts at polishing it), but it's useful as it does give a moment-to-moment idea of how hard it's blowing outside.....there's the hiss of breakers approaching ......and all the time the rumble of running water along the hull, which varies in texture with speed, with turbulence and bubbles under the hull when doing more than 7 knots.....................all of it interspersed with the thump or crash of waves breaking against the outside ....

The water tanks in the keel echo as the freshwater in them sloshes about (in spite of internal baffles), and you can get an idea of how full they are from the type of sound.......there is creaking of the woodwork in the companionway, and the cabin-panelling, and the floorboards, as the ship flexes slightly......rarely something rolls about in a cupboard, but those are soon traced and silenced.....the tray inside the pressure cooker moves with a tinny squeak, in spite of the cooker gimbals.....a groan from the cooker gimbals themselves sometimes....

There's a pulley on deck which squeaks occasionally........ sounds just like a human voice almost out of earshot....... wondered if I was beginning to crack-up, even though I haven't reached the urine-drinking-and-cannibalism stage yet, until I found what caused the sound.......... as it's a Tufnol block I'm rather loathe to lubricate the pulley with anything other than water..... so it continues to mutter to itself every so often..... it's now an accepted part of the ship's vocabulary.........

Had to give myself another talking to the other day...... poor Staale has been in the most appalling weather down at 40 south since several days ago, and when talking to him by radio at the time, his description of what it is like in a shrieking 45 knots of cold wind, with short and steep 5 metre waves breaking clean over his ship, made me feel very insecure for a while..... had to remind myself that it's not ME down there...... Empathy can be a darned nuisance at times.....

He sounded quite confident and tolerably comfortable in his wooden 34 ft Colin Archer type yacht .... he said, (when I quipped "Rather you than me, mate!"), "Oh, don't worry, you'll get yours between the Azores and the UK..... think on THAT while you're drifting backwards towards Brazil again in the Doldrums!".......

It's nice to know "Tuesday" is designed and built to cope with that sort of situation, as long as I attend to her correctly ..... personally, I'm still very much in "holiday mode", whereas Staale says he's now definitely "back at work in 'gale mode'!" ....

Ascension Island came up as expected (which is always reassuring!), the day after Ascension Day...... closest approach was 33 miles, passing to the East of it ..... it became visible at 40 miles, very vaguely at first..... strange, but I had absolutely no urge to call in there, now I'm back in "seagoing mode" ...... all the complications and worries of anchoring and official paperwork, etc, and the wrench of having to leave again.... so it's not for me at present, thanks.....

Nice chats by radio with Ian (ZD8I) on the island though, who told me more about conditions there ..... I note he is fully aware of the "Guinevere" (?spelling?), the landing craft at Orford, as he's working for the same company here on Ascension..... small world!.....

So, we're now reaching along at good speed under a single-reefed mainsail, staysail, and a nearly-full genoa poled out to starboard, a swinging ride in a 2 metre swell, force 4, in the warm nights and warmer days ..... getting cloudier though as we approach the mixed-up climate of the Doldrums ....400 miles from the bit of the ocean where I want to be when crossing the Equator ....it's 25,355 ft deep there, and I'd rather like to have visited that particular spot over the Romanche Gap .....(not sure why, though, really.... just because it's there, I suppose, and I remember reading about the Gap when the Continental Drift Theory became accepted) ......

Enough waffling for now..... All is well on board...... Stay well and safe yourselves!...

Love from,

Tuesday'n'me.

Sun 23/05/2004 16:09

Subject: A voice from your past

Dear Philippe'n'Paola,

Really great FUN to hear you on the phone today!.... have been wondering often how you were getting on, and then it suddenly dawned on me that you wouldn't have received the Emails I send when I don't have access to an ordinary mobile-phone service ...... don't bother to reply, but the address you have is still the best one to send TO ..the other one is simply so that I can successfully send OUT by satellite phone (which is infrequent because of the expense, and the crappy signals these past-their-sell-by-dates Iridium satellites put out)....

On the phone I was only receiving 2 words out of every 3, but I gather you are both pregnant, have sold the boat, Paola's working the streets again, and Philippe has sold his body for medical research but no-one wants it yet ..... delighted to hear you've both settled down to a proper career structure in Brazil .....

In so many ways I'm sad that I'm going back to England when I only saw a glimpse of what real life is like ..... lifetime friends I barely had time to meet properly, especially yourselves who helped pick me up at a time when I had been driven right down onto my knees ....but on the other hand I have a heck of a lot to go back home FOR.... can't have it both ways at this stage of my life, but who knows what the outcome will be when I've had time next (northern) winter to reflect on what I've learnt ...... we will see how I adapt to life ashore, and how my family and friends put up with me living at home again ...... (so far, this trip has brought the family even closer together than it was before, which I didn't expect)......

Enough of this serious stuff ...... I hope you're impressed by the follow-up service available through the NHS, even from 200 miles south of the Equator!....

The story of what I've been up to is in the other Emails, so no need to bore you with it twice .... but I warn you there is a written multiple-choice exam afterwards, to check you've been paying attention......

When you return to the S.Atlantic, do call in at St.Helena.... I loved it there! .....not stuffy and British at all ..... and the natives speak "broken english" between themselves, a sort of pidgin-english, but not quite ..... with what you taught me, Paola, I found it fascinating, and I got them to talk about it to me, and explained its origins on the Island...

Take very good care of You, both of you, won't you... you helped me rebuild myself ..... I owe you.....

(And Love to Yvan and Christina when you speak to them, as I haven't been able to contact them except by Email)....

Look after your bits!....
Docdavid'n'Tuesday.

(RECEIVED) Mon 24/05/2004 10:20

Dear David,

Horribly long silence from this end I'm afraid. Which isn't to say that I (we) haven't been reading all your emails with anticipation and pleasure. The more you describe and do the more I'm both envious and admiring. The envious bit tends to kick in when I'm driving down the motorway to Edinburgh or some such place and imagining where you might be - what you are doing, who you are meeting or what place you are exploring. The admiration kicks in when I wonder what the view's like to windward or I remember what it can be like to be out there and feeling a tad vulnerable.

Out "there" is generic of course but it was helped last week when Lacushla made it to St Kilda. It's a mini crossing but going west of the Hebrides does feel quite committing with dodgy sea legs, a lumpy sea and the knowledge that if it really blows up, going back through the sound of Harris is not a good option (we'd end up going round the Butt of Lewis and heading for somewhere south of Cape Wrath) - so I was full of empathy and admiration and all those other social-worky feelings as we crashed westward. I was thinking - don't think I could do what David's done. Lacushla's in her element going to windward and we kept between 5.5 and 7 knots with first one, then two, then three reefs. Clawing to windward without going too fast was a bit of a compromise and she was having to work hard - so there was plenty of water down below but God knows where from. Not built quite like your ship. A bit flimsy and flexible. I liked your description of how Tuesday talks to you about the wind and how she's moving - haven't yet got that level of shared language with Lacushla!

You've certainly been through it with the Wizz Bang and all the aftermath but it must be great to know that you can cope with that sort of event independently and that you have a sound vessel however low tech it might become. Have to admit I'm still ludite but GPS was rather nice coming back from St Kilda finding the right passage through the sound of Harris with a 6 blowing, a 7 forcast and that lovely West Coast dreich drizzly atmosphere - it's weird (also a little dissapointing and lacking in spice) being told exactly what the leeway is in a lumpy sea - I think I might have known (near enough) in Icterus but I'm still getting used to Lacushla. St Kilda was good - second time there but first under my own steam (last time Village Bay was untenable and we made a brief landing at the base of the southern cliffs). Strange contrast between remoteness, a sense of long history emphasised by the thousands of stone Cleits (store shelters for peats and drying seabirds) and village street, the wild vertical landscape and the satelite TV and bar in the radar base. We were the only boat in for the first 24 hours - the ranger said we could use the buoy in the bay which was reassuring as the wind went into the West and squalls came off the hills driving tumbling curtains of spay in front of them. The downside was that as she spun, the rope riser got wrapped around her torpedo keel. It took as 2 hours to clear and in the meantime the gusts were hitting broadside, she was tripping on her keel and leaning over almost to her gunwales - a little scary because I wasn't sure of the physics and how far we could go (so the washboards were in!). In the end we unspliced the buoy and let the whole thing feed out on a floating line.

We're all OK here. Wondering what to do with the next 20 years or so - kind of mid life quandry - working on it. Lucy now at High School and Angus coming up to his last year of primary. Sue teaches 3 days and I work away for Barnardo's. Hope all's well with you and yours.

Anyway - enough of this little domestic news. Thinking of you now on your longest passage.

*Enjoy! Love, **Richard.***

Wed 26/05/2004 00:10

Subject: No, no... I take my hat off to YOU, sir!..

Dear Richard,

What you have done takes no less guts than my trip, I can assure you .... all those rocks, spray, rain ... rotten visibility ......that cold, when nothing dries..... fills me with apprehension immediately, just to read about it! ......

I'm not being polite, nor condescending, I promise you .....what you did in Icterus was very special indeed, and I know I wouldn't have had the guts to have done it ..... and what you have done to St.Kilda, when you have a set timescale because of family and work as well, is no different from what I'm doing, except that in this climate down here it's a heck of a lot more comfortable.....(don't need clothes, for example) .....even thinking of that trip makes me have to steel myself towards that sort of sailing ......

The only thing that's different is not the wind, nor the weather, nor being a long way from anywhere and all that sort of thing ..... it's the WAVES ..... they can be f-ing Gy-normous, and I hadn't seen anything like that in the North Sea ..... you have an advantage, because you've already seen them before in Scotland I expect ......

But for heaven's sake DON'T TELL ANYONE that what I'm doing is 90% perfectly normal sailing .. keep the story alive that it's all eating barbed wire and nails, wearing hair shirts, close to The Almighty, sheer hell, blood, guts, and gritted teeth, etc etc..!.... Otherwise none of us will have any street-cred left ....

And PLEASE can we arrange to meet up in the winter .... time specially put aside for it? .... because I'm sure there is a vast amount of information we could swap which would be useful to us both for the future....I'd be most interested to hear of any possible plans you have for future trips, then maybe I can do them "by proxy", as it were.......I don't just mean sensible plans, I mean the wildest-dream type plans that you daren't tell anyone about in case they laugh....when-you-win-the-Lottery-type plans, eg .... because I'm coming to realise that almost all things are possible if :-

(i) you really know what you want to do,

(ii) you know what you're willing to give up, or to risk, to do it,

and (iii) you are prepared to actually stand up and go and do it (and you've shown you're fully capable of the last one)......

Thanks for letting me know of your trip ... really enjoyed reading about it ... Keep in touch!

All the Best!,

DocDavid'n'Tuesday.

RECEIVED) Tue 22/06/2004 20:26

David,

It was great to get your Email - and very flattering but I'm still not convinced that popping out 50 miles west of the Hebrides is quite the same as 4,000 miles alone with the ocean.

What is so amazing to me is the range of new sites and experiences you've managed to get at sea - seems like a good enough reason to spend all those anniversaries out there!

Yup - it would be very good to sit down near a warm fire with a pint or so of Adnams over the winter - and a blank sheet of paper! Of course you could always come north if you haven't got fed up with travelling by then and do the same thing here - Lacushla will probably be out of the water this winter (I can only take every other year of listening out for NW Gales and ampathising with the old girl dipping her forstay into the waves), it's still not bad territory around here. I for one need some mid-life counselling - sound like you might have some answers!

Have a good landfall if you haven't already - and another good stop in the Azores.

Love, Richard.

Tue 25/05/2004 22:56

Subject: I quite like this sailing thing I think....

Dear Everybodies,

Smooth but empty sea, warm wind, good speed.... adds up to free electricity and another Letter from Tuesday ....

Wanted to watch 10,000 miles (since leaving Orford last June) come up on the log, but missed it by a few minutes through not paying proper attention .... didn't matter, as it happened, because the lightning-damaged GPS machine crashed again at that point, so I wouldn't have seen anything special .... I've reset it, and it's behaving as well as it can again now ...

The Romanche Deep is where the sea depth almost doubles, in a vast, east-west crack in the earth's crust ......it's a knife-cut 250 miles long by 15 miles across, and 2+ miles deeper than the normal ocean floor ......makes the Grand Canyon look like PlayDo....

I expected it to be just another bit of ocean to plough across, but to my surprise the sea was absolutely teeming with fish for about 10 miles (nearly two hours).. mostly tuna I think ..... jumping out of the waves all round the ship, almost like a fish farm at feeding time..... and flocks of flying fish, both sides of the ship, suddenly appearing and vanishing again 50 yards further out, as though they were clearing a path for "Tuesday" to pass through .... then some birds (?type?) waiting to pounce on them when they appear ....

Disappointingly, no BIG animals seen though ....

Was it due to nutrients coming up from active volcanic sites on the seabed? ..... or perhaps just due to the immense canyon down there stirring up the prevailing current, and wafting food upwards? .... don't know,

185

but certainly unexpected ...

Some of the best sailing so far, from Ascension to The Line ..... broad beam reach, poled out small genoa, staysail and single reefed main... very little heel, maximum comfortable hull-speed, mile-eating pace, with very little wave noise ..... covering 160 miles per day (and remember, "Tuesday" is certainly no racing boat!), touching 8 knots at times.... a lengthening 6-8 ft sea, giving a smooth but swinging ride .... and getting warmer every day under the (still northern) sun ... all in all, really a very civilised form of transport.....MAGIC! ....

I promise I did not manipulate it to be so, but I crossed The Equator again today, at 18 degrees west, at 1 minute past noon, in "Tuesday" on a Tuesday ... I do not understand why this boat keeps saving Special Occasions for Tuesdays .... it's almost becoming embarrassing! (I'm not superstitious, but.....)

Since it's Tuesday'n'me's second time, we didn't need to have such a big and messy celebration this time ...... just a token haircut, and a small bottle of bubbly ...... Ran into problems though..... with half of the bottle for King Neptune, half for the ship, and half for me, I ran out of halves ..... luckily, good old Suffolk-Anglo-Saxon logic came to the fore, and no-one felt they'd been sold short as I was able to quarter it into three equal halves successfully ....

So now we're beam-reaching northwards, back in our own home pond, expecting to fall into the weather-melting-pot of The Doldrums in the next two or three days..... usually massive thunderstorms, strong squalls from every direction, very heavy rain, interspersed with humid flat calms .....not looking forward to having to break through The Brick Wall again that I ran into on the way down, (the only time I've put my survival suit on at sea) ....but we will see what has been allocated to us in the next few days ....

Then, once we're through, to start the long curve that should hopefully give us the winds we need towards the Azores ... it may be days or it may be weeks, who knows? .... but we're prepared for both ....

It's a lovely warm night tonight ..... the Southern Cross astern ...... the moon with it's glittering moonpath ..... and four "contrails" of phosphorescence behind us, one each side from the wake of the bow waves, one from the keel and rudder in the middle, and one from the propeller of the towed generator off to one side ..... reeling off the miles like a jumbo jet in slow motion.........and ahead The Plough is calling.......

"Homeward Bound!"

Stay Well!

Love from

Tuesday'n'me.

(RECEIVED) Wed 26/05/2004 18:39

Hi David

congrats on crossing the line already and on a Tuesday.

Still not sure if you have HF or not.I have been calling in vain on 14.150 and 14.303 when its not being used by anyone. I think 14.300 to 303 is a much better spot. I will be in France next week so will try out the vertical from there.I will try at midday.but also will be on most evenings from about 8.30pm .Sun still out over Sax but a bit cooler today 16% C. Ok will keep it short will keep looking for you

If all else fails catch you on PO on the way in.

John

(RECEIVED)Fri 28/05/2004 15:57

Subject: news from Brazil

(From Philipe'n'Paola)

Dear everybody,

Time flies and WOW we have just realised that we have not given any news Anyway, we are writing this from

186

a place called Parati (or Paraty) in the state of Rio de Janeiro, in Brazil (our position is 23º13'73S 044º41'75W). We first arrived in Brazil over five months ago, just before Christmas, having made landfall in Recife.

Our Atlantic crossing, from the island of Brava in the Cape Verde, has been a fast one – only 12 days– and without major problems – if one does not count a 2 days long tropical storm and the fact that our autopilot broke down just outside Recife. Still, we had time to get even more tanned, read a few books and sight the occasional whale.

Christmas 2003 has definitively been one of the best ever, spent in Recife in the company of fellow sailors from all over the world: Norway, Poland, the UK, France and Brazil. In order to make everybody happy and follow all different traditions we started celebrating on the 24th with a Norwegian breakfast of porridge and mulled wine and finished several days later after various national meals and barbecues, not to mention an early morning tea (heavily diluted with rum), courtesy of the British MOD crew on board the joint services yacht "Adventure". Any weight we had lost during the crossing was sadly put back during the festive season.

Since early January we have then slowly travelled south to our present position. Along the road we have stopped in Suape, Tamandare, Salvador (for a loooong time), Itaparica, Morro de San Paulo, Bay of Camamu, Ilheus, Cumuruxatiba, Vitoria, Buzios, Cabo Frio, Rio de Janeiro and Ilha Grande.

The more south we go the more the place has a European feeling and there seem to be a more friendly atmosphere, especially as wealth seems to be a bit more equally distributed with the consequent fewer guns to defend the rich and their possessions (i.e. their motor yachts).

In February we have had two sets of guests coming from the UK. Mostyn and Margaret from Wales and than Sue and Martin from the Isle of Wight. Mostyn is Philippe's great childhood friend and they had not really seen each other for almost fifty years, so spending time together was really precious to Philippe.

It was M&M's first yachting experience and we really admired their courage. They have since told us they would consider coming to see us again at a later stage of our cruise, so we can only assume they were not too put off by the experience. Martin and Sue, who last visited us in Portugal, flew into Salvador and spent a couple of weeks sailing southward with us. It was good to see them again and have some experienced crew to share the load, not to mention the drinks.

More recently we have had a two weeks visit by Dan, Philippe's son. They had not seen each other for a long time and it was good for all of us to have the opportunity to do things together. First we sailed with Dan in the Ilha Grande region for about a week. Then, having taken the boat back to the marina in Paraty, we went by bus for a couple of days in Rio de Janeiro, to do a few touristy things, like walking around Copacabana and Ipanema and climbing Corcovado. Dan had been sailing with his dad before and though he is not an experienced sailor he was excellent crew. We are now waiting to see which of Philippe's other children will come and visit us next. In the the meantime we have a vague "reservation" by Graziella, Paola's mother, to come and see us in November. We have not yet told her WHERE she will be able to come and reach us. By the way, all our visitors have been introduced to caipirinha, the local – lethal- drink and we envisage a sharp rise in the importation in the UK of its ingredients.

We had planned to keep on going south and get to Buenos Aires, via Uruguay, before the arrival of the southern hemisphere winter and before our visa expired. However, we have been a bit slow, the season is changing and more cold fronts are making their way up the southern coast of Brazil (not to mention the first ever southern Atlantic hurricane). Along this bit of coast there are no harbours of any type for hundreds of miles and the charts clearly show lots of wrecks… So, as we got to beautiful Parati, we decided that we might as well join the number of sailors who leave the country and continue our southbound journey only towards the end of the year   Watch this space!

Love Paola and Philippe

P.S. You may wonder why we have not said anything about the famous Brazilian carnival. Well, to be perfectly frank it was not really our scene in Salvador, where it has become (like in Rio) a huge commercial enterprise. We thoroughly enjoyed instead the celebrations in Itaparica, which were more friendly and family orientated, with people of all ages dancing together in the village square.

(RECEIVED) Wed 26/05/2004 18:24

Dear david,

LOVELY to talk to you the other day. we have now added this address to our safe list... so maybe if you have the time and inclination you can send us the bits of the story we have missed so far. hope you are safe and well and not eating too many m&m´s....

love

paola and philippe

Sat 29/05/2004 15:40

Subject: 29/5/04) ICTZ

Dear Everybodies,

"First, send ten men forward!", say the instructions in a Victorian sailing manual I have at home, when describing how to hoist a spinnaker ..... they'd have been useful on board, two days before we hit the Doldrums ....It was entirely my own fault ..... silly really, but I wanted to have a go, but I chose the wrong day ....I've put the sail up often enough before, but I still blame the wind for suddenly getting stronger at the wrong moment that day....

It was nice and warm, with an apparently predictable sea and wind, so I thought this would be the best opportunity to experiment ...... broad reach, nothing to bump into, lots of time etc, so I decided to give "Tuesday" the full Monty of absolute maximum sail area in a decent wind ...... Mainsail, Staysail, 150% Genoa, and Spinnaker ..... 2,200 square feet, all working hard ......should be fun I thought, (particularly as her rig is to my own spec and 38% bigger than the standard one) .....

WRONG! .... she HATED it in that wind, took off like a scalded cat, dragging half the ocean behind her, and I was very rapidly made aware that she was in charge of me, rather than the other way round ....she still behaved impeccably, but it was abundantly clear she was not happy about it....... it was one heck of a fight to get it all under control again, especially as everything is manual on this ship .... then manhandling heavy armfuls of colourful sails below again undid all the improvement with the damaged elbow I'd managed to achieve .... I felt rather foolish and somewhat humbled .....(But we did cover a lot of miles in that half hour, though!) ...

Incidentally, the rig I use when running dead downwind works well for damping out any rolling ..... mainsail one side, boomed out genoa the other, and staysail pinned in flat fore-and-aft to kill the vortices coming off the two bigger sails ..... two weeks ago I had tried running downwind with twin foresails only and thought it most uncomfortable ....

Temperatures in the 90s, but there's been a nice breeze to keep life comfortable ..... it's cooler to sleep on the cabin floor, and there's less motion down there ..... an added bonus is that if she leaks I'll know a bit sooner .....(puts a new slant on wetting the bed, doesn't it).....

More bent fishhooks from the fishes that got away .... wish they wouldn't chew the tentacles off my pink plastic squid lure though .... it's only got one arm left now ..... But I did manage to catch the propeller of the water-powered-generator with the fishing line a few days ago .... took forever to untangle THAT mess, I can assure you! ...

The St.Helena fruit is keeping very fresh indeed ..... even in this climate .... I wonder if it's anything to do with the fumigation process they all go through, that Barrie told me about ......(there IS a fridge on board, but I never use it as it takes too much electricity) ....

Then on Friday 28/5/04 we crashed into the ITCZ (the Doldrums) at 5 North.... abrupt change in the sky, with a very marked amount of "mixing" up there (as my flying instructor used to say) .... nasty vicious squalls with no particular pattern and from every direction, thunderstorms, and absolutely TORRENTIAL rain (talk about calling it "falling water"!) ...... and a chaotic and untidy sea caused by several different wave trains ...... if you watch carefully you can begin to separate them in your mind, but the overall effect is irregular lumps and deep holes appearing and disappearing apparently at random, sometimes 3+ metres from top to bottom .... "moguls" ....the times when there's little wind it's not very comfortable at all, quite frankly ...... and it knocks seven bells out of the sails as they slat and bang about, even with the booms firmly prevented from moving ......

But we're getting further north all the time, (about level with Sierra Leone now), trying to stay to the East so we can get a decent slant across the NORTH-East-Trades when we get through this present entertainment .... Today the ITCZ has moved further north, ahead of us, so we've had a "borrowed" day of good progress in the last of the SOUTHERLY Trades as they punch a big dent into the Doldrums .... fingers crossed that it lasts!....

More from The Department of Useless Information soon.....

Stay Well!

Love,

Tuesday'n'me.

(RECEIVED) Mon 31/05/2004 20:41

Subject: LA7GZ – Staale

Sorry, David, I have to send you this one!

This is what I sent to Alistair, in case he does not know:

"I have just been talking to G0CBE - David on Tuesday.

He tells us that Staale is safely at anchor at Tristan de Cunha, wind down to 10k.

He has had a 90° knockdown, which flooded his main batteries. Also his spare battery got cracked, and is now leaking acid. Otherwise the boat is undamaged and Staale is unhurt. He managed to dry out the main batteries, which are now being charged again, but he is still short of power. He is hoping to leave for Capetown tomorrow.

David says that Staale is very impressed with the design and building of his boat, and with himself, as well, for both of them to come through this unscathed."

And this is what I got from Jack:

"LA7GZ, Staale on Rozinante, Relay from G0CBE and ZD7MY I think. At anchor at Tristan da Cunha, boat and Staale OK. Rozinante knocked on side and took on salt water. Main battery will not start engine. Aux battery lost electrolyte but Stalle hopes to recharge aux battery when he leaves for Capetown tomorrow and will contact us by radio. Wind< 10 Kt. Remember, Susan went on side there also a year ago."

I wonder who is right?

Main thing is, that he is ok for now. And we hope will make it safely to Capetown. The next low is a small one, let's hope the seas don't build too much with it.

88 – Trudi

Thu 10/06/2004 01:18

Subject: Snippets, from the NE Trades.

Dear Everybodies,

So many things to describe .... but here are a few of them ....

Saturday, May 29th, 2145 GMT, would have been sunk by an oilrig supply vessel ....had spotted him before the radar did, but eventually had to stop completely to let him trundle blindly (and deaf too) across right where Tuesday would have been .... how can they possibly call themselves professionals when they behave like this? ....and he wasn't showing a stern light either ....

We were very lightly let off when getting through the Doldrums (aided by the weather information from the Maritime-Mobile radio nets, for which most grateful thanks!) ... it was almost as though a door opened, we went through, and then it closed behind us.......only one day of calms ....had stayed close to the African coast, but paid for it by getting thoroughly covered in red sand, under a pink sky ...

A Tropical disturbance caused odd winds and seas for a while, but we were on the northern edge of it, so no problems .... the barometer didn't like it though! ....

Beware of high flying flying-fish! ..... they can gain a surprising altitude .... one brained itself halfway up the spinnaker pole the other day, poor little chap, so I ate him ... most mornings I have flying-fish for breakfast these days....deliciously fresh! ....

Dolphins .... many schools of them round here, many different sorts ....complete "villages" of them .....old battle-scarred bulls, mums with their young babies, family groups, tear-away adolescents darting around upsetting the others, etc... fascinating to watch! ...... so gentle and so near under the bow on a calm day that you can smell their exhaled air (seawater and fresh fish) ... the Bottlenosed dolphins are quite a bit bigger and heavier, and the breath-sound is different too .....

Then a pod of 3 or 4 Sperm whales cruised leisurely by around sunrise three days ago, between 50 and 100 yards astern ....(I'm frantically winding in the fishhooks and lures trailing astern ..... certainly don't want to annoy one of THEM if I can help it!) ...it's the first time I've HEARD them clearly, as they're quite quiet breathers for their vast size .....if I hadn't managed to capture all this on video, I'd still be thinking it was all a dream! ...there was also a marlin or sailfish jumping repeatedly, but the moment I pointed the camera at him he stopped, so I got nothing unfortunately ....

Managed to film the Venus/Sun transit through cloud on Tuesday .... tried to use the end-point of it as a means of checking the ship's clocks, but couldn't do it accurately enough to be useful ....pity! .....However, I was surprised to see that it was all upside-down compared to what I expected, until I realised that of course I'm still having to look NORTH at the sun .....the moon is to the south of us now, and at long last at least that's the "right" way up again!......

Suddenly noticed last week .... (couldn't think what was different at first, until the penny dropped) .... for the first time since the lightning strike on January 13th, the sudden stabs of localised pain I'd been getting in my right arm and leg have faded at last! ...(they'd been a nuisance as they had been waking me up sometimes, and during the day they would suddenly and painfully distract me .... I hadn't expected symptoms to continue as long as this , and I assumed I was stuck with it) .....whether the neuralgia was produced in the peripheral nerves or in the brain itself I can't fathom out, but let's hope that that's the last of the health problems the Brazilian Whizzbang causes me ...

Nasty wind variations in the lee of some of the Islands of the Cap Verdes ....flat calm for some hours behind Fogo (the volcano 2800 metres straight up out of the sea) ....then we went within 5 miles of Brava, the only island I actually SAW in the hazy visibility, with only a moderate wind acceleration zone afterwards .... but we were impressively knocked about by 28-30 knot squalls caused by Sao Nicolau, Sao Vicente and Santo Antao islands, even though they were 50 miles to windward ... most certainly I had not expected so dramatic an effect at that distance at all .... quite unpleasant for some 5 hours or so, though progress was good ....another lesson learned! .....

And now we're bowling along at 6+ knots, slicing diagonally across into the 2+ metre Tradewinds seas, just off closehauled, with (as the seagull flies) only 1200 miles to the Azores ....I tried pointing up a bit higher to the wind, but it got very bumpy and noisy and uncomfortable ... the ship didn't like it either .... I'm not worried about the strength of the hull itself, but one or two of those heavy 14 ton "slams" into the holes between the waves might weaken or damage some of the internal joinery in the cabins .... double-reefed main, staysail, and a tiny genoa give adequate speed .... more than this and she starts jumping the crests a bit, which is not lady-like for a 30 year old girl, tough though she is ....

I'm surprised how cold it is here .....down to 26C at night .... yet the sun should be overhead again in the next 2-3 days as we pass underneath it again on the way northwards ... maybe the sea temperature is much lower here, or something? .... a puzzle ...

So much more to tell you, but that's enough for the moment ...

Love to all!

Tuesday'n'me.

(RECEIVED)Thu 10/06/2004 08:12

Subject: Re: Snippets, from the NE Trades (reply to).

David - hello.. Re. your comments about 14 tons dropping 2 meters, I wondered, have you any way of measuring the 'G' forces - say with a spring device? (I ask because David Cook has recently been testing variations of the Shadow undercarriage, the fully loaded aircraft was dropped from 10 inches-this, I understand, produced a factor of X2 and permanently distorted the U/C.)

Amazed at your speed! it would seem that you could be in the Azores in just over one week - do you now like sailing?

Best regards Joe.

(RECEIVED) Sat 12/06/2004 01:30

Subject: whats up doc??Again!!

Hope this finds you well and safe!!

I am in London with my still busted CVJ, arrived this weekend..Hasnt changed much apart from its very expensive..I am not sure how they can say inflation is very low, a pint of beer is £3,20 fags nearly a fiver..I am staying with a mate in Hammersmith,which is great.

Left Lala,the old girl on the hard in Trinidad 23 US cent per foot per day,not cheap,hope she is OK on my return..

Take care,give me a shout when you get back to Blighty or before it would be good to know you are safe and sound.

Soft seas and fair winds..

God bless NICK..

PS>>Your mate with the crewing agency,big surprise I left his contact details behind..So if you get a chance to send them to me I would very gratefull.. Got to get something to do quickly..

(RECEIVED) Thu 03/06/2004 09:51

Subject: Radio propagation

Hi David,

Nice to be able to still make that HF QSO whilst on passage North.....didn't think for one moment it would work, and after a week too....we would have either lost the HF connection........BUT, 'Tuesday' and her Skipper knows that such treasures was left behind and that was of course the 'Emerald' !!......so, who knows one-day there might be a return!.

However, it was kind of you and to QSY for the first time at 1,820 nautical miles from St Helena, made 10m came alive!..not knowing for one moment there was going to be propagation....but again, with 'Tuesdays' HF comms.....the IC-703 with approx 8watts had with-in seconds pounded a 59 signal into ZD7MY QTH, how amazing!.   I was also amaze David and to hear the Tri-Star (which you brought to life after approx 10 years) and with 5watts how well it was Rx at my QTH with a 57 sig. It would be interesting again to do another test on 10m with the Tri-Star and see what the RX is like...maybe by now you would be able to copy sigs from Europe or ? on 10m.....Let me know how it behaves?

I'm quite certain that 10m QRP should be poss for both of us to work each other quite further North, anyway, we'll see how it goes!

Incidently, the RMS 'St Helena' is now on her way South to the island, having safely off load her passengers & cargo at Ascension, since it was held up for 2 days of very rough seas that made landings impossible at the Pier......All goes well, the RMS will leave St H on Fri PM and then procede North to Portland via Asc & Las Palmas.....hopefully, if the timing is right she might pass you along the way. No doubt visual of her may not be poss...but who knows! it might be poss on a Tuesday hi!!.

Go well.....and take care out there.

Best Wishes

Barrie, Valerie & Shane

Sat 12/06/2004 01:30

Subject: The missing Brazilian package.

Dear J,

Thanks so much for continuing to chase up about this messy business ...

To recap. :- (so you can pass the information on)

- The paperwork alone was delivered to the correct address at the marina in Salvador on 20th Feb.

- Carnival then started (a week-long bank holiday, in effect), and everywhere was shut, so I wasn't able to collect the paperwork till 27th Feb., when I personally delivered it to Martins & Azevedo the same morning, following advice I was given by the shipper's representative in Brazil.

- Nothing happened, as it appeared that they said the package had been delivered.

- Finally, countless phone calls etc later, I was told by Martins & Azevedo that they had eventually, after persistence, received confirmation (on 19th March), from the shippers themselves in Brazil that the package itself was still in Sao Paulo.

- I had to leave the country only a few days later when my visa expired, never having received the parcel.

- You already have the name, telephone, fax no., Email address etc. of Eduardo, the helpful Customs Agent who communicated with the carrier to get this confirmation.

- Eduardo is not a senior member of the firm, but he's the only person in the office who speaks a bit of English, and even then very little of it. Everyone in that firm was charming, especially Eduardo, who is a very pleasant and helpful chap, but I think it would be best to speak to him in Portuguese for satisfactory communication. I'm confident he will remember the whole business (particularly as he knows that in my flying days I met his personal hero, Gary Newman.) The firm have copies of all the relevant papers ... I made sure of that, before I left.

Jonesy, on a personal note, I find this whole sordid affair most distasteful, and it's quite difficult NOT to say to these shippers what I would really like to say .... But it would be counterproductive, and I hope they get the message that I'm trying to HELP them sort out their own sticky mess.

Just out of interest, today has not been a cheerful one, as one of the main genoa fairlead pulley blocks abruptly exploded violently last night with one hell of a BANG.. the broken bits then smashed around dangerously in the dark until I got it all under control again ....I've got a spare old and weaker one, but the exploding one was a top quality American one, only three years old ... it should not have failed ....

And there's an unexplained irregular "thump" from the rudder area which has been worrying me for the last week, so today I've been feeling a little more insecure than usual ....

6000-7000 miles in 2 months may be beginning to tell on the old girl a bit, particularly since 90% of it has been bashing to windward, so I'm "nursing" her a bit at the moment ...

So you will imagine how much I appreciate the radio-skeds .... continuing thanks are due to you, sir! ....

Byee fer now!
Toodle-pip!
T'n'me.

Tue 15/06/2004 01:08
Subject: (14/6/04) Farewell to the Tropics
Dear Everybodies,

On Thursday 10th June, we finally caught up with the sun again, and so it is now in its rightful place to the south of us again .... still virtually overhead, it is just beginning to shine into the cockpit from astern, most of the day ...... and the weather is getting warmer at last ....

Overslept a bit during the next day, so missed the moment of crossing the Tropic of Cancer .... pity ....

Three nights ago I heard a single quiet "click" (it amazes me that one can detect that small sound in amongst all the other racket going on) ... went on deck to investigate and thought it might be the genoa sheet tightening on its winch (it's a massive rope under about one ton of load when sailing hard) .... idly dismissing it, I was still sitting in the cockpit ten minutes later, in the dark, when there was a colossal "BANG!" 3 feet away, followed by a violent crashing on the side of the hull ...... once I realised it wasn't a big multi-armed animal trying to get aboard, it took a moment or two to work out that the 3 year old Harken main genoa fairlead pulley-block had exploded, with the thrashing sheet and pulley remains trying to smash their way into the cabin through the ship's side .... not very nice in the darkness ....

It wasn't easy to tame this mess without being sideswiped myself, but the only damage appears to be to the paintwork (which I repaired today while it's calm) .... and by rummaging through the ship's stores (yet again!) I found a 30 year old original fairlead as a replacement ... it meant I couldn't put much pressure on it, so we had to slow down a bit ....

But a Cunning Plan evolved ... by putting TWO fairleads in series, close together, (plus a bit of modifying of one of them) the load is now almost halved on each (because of the layout on this particular boat), so we're now back up to full potential again ...

All this was somewhat disconcerting ..... together with an increasing concern about a steadily worsening "thump!" from the rudder lower pintle at the bottom of the skeg, which must have worn a bit with all these miles ..... it made last Friday 11th June a bit of a "bad hair" day .... it put me in my place, reminded me that I'm very much on my own out here ..... had to make an extra cup of tea to get on top of it again ....

Saw my first aeroplane since leaving Brazil today ... that, and a grand total of five ships since St.Helena 31 days ago, are the only signs of humans on earth that I've seen .... (oh, and one empty plastic Coca-Cola bottle) ....

No birds and no animals recently, except a beautiful Dorado (caught today for food, I'm ashamed to say) ....and huge numbers of Portuguese-Men-of-War very evenly spaced every 100 yards of so ... they don't seem

193

to like being near each other very much.....mile after mile of them .....

They're quite active, using their tentacles to rapidly twist their bodies one way or the other, to adjust the angle they can sail downwind .... fascinating to watch them in the light airs while Tuesday'n'me were drifting around going nowhere fast, effectively becalmed ....only noticed them since the wind dropped today ......Gerard reminded me (on the radio) that they come in two shapes, left-handed and right-handed, in equal numbers .... but not a good place to swim, here today .....

Up till now I've had flying fish for breakfast every day .... I wonder if I'll ever get fed up with them .....or if they'll disappear now the Men-0f-War are here ....

Busy most of the day, constantly checking and improving .... a bit of chafe in a staysail sheet here, a weeping window frame there, a fresh slight seep from a deck fitting, a seacock needing adjustment and reinjecting with grease (they're fitted with grease-nipples so that it can be done without taking the ship out of the water) ..... a loose cupboard door catch which started squeaking etc etc .....it's actually quite fun, especially as the ship seems to be a real living entity much of the time .... it's a definite partnership .... strange, but that's how it feels ....

Up till today we'd been so long on the starboard tack that there are small barnacles growing on the port topsides ... only noticed them today when the wind dropped and that side came up out of the water again .... not very big, but I hope they come off easily without taking the paint with them! ....

So, tonight we're temporarily under engine power (first time since leaving the marina at Itaparica, Brazil) because the batteries are low and there's no prospect of useful wind for at least 24 hours .... at dawn we'll start drifting again and see where we get to .... 31 days and 3,200 miles since St.Helena, with another 800 or so to do, but probably in light airs only ..... further progress may be s-l-o-w ....

One final comment .... magnetic beans do not upset the compass! ..... so I don't have to stay at least 1 metre away from it (which would have made using the hand bearing compass a bit awkward) ... it seems it's both the tins and the lids which were the problem ... maybe they should now be stored alternately upside down and right way up to cancel any effects?....

Stay Well!

With love from,

Tuesday'n'me.

PS. Wind has just arrived! .... but yes, you've guessed it ...... bang on the nose, from the north .... ah, well .....

(RECEIVED) Thu 17/06/2004 21:59

Subject: Happy Birthday!

Dad, Happy Birthday from everyone here in Sax.

Have fun in the sea.

Fin is going to book a flight, currently from 6th July to 20th July unless these dates aren't ok with you. Could you phone/e-mail to let her know whether to book these dates or not. Thanks.

Ben

(RECEIVED)Fri 18/06/2004 15:24

Subject: Happy Birthday

Hi David,

*Happy Birthday to You, Happy Birthday Dear David, Happy Birthday to you. Well I hope you are having a good day. Just thought I would wish you well on your Birthday. Do hope you and Tuesday are having fun, I have enjoyed reading your e-mails, your adventures sound very brilliant I look forward to all the photo's and stories. Anyway must go as Rebs is calling me! Take CareBest Wishes **Ginny***

(RECEIVED) Fri 18/06/2004 20:24
> **Subject: Happy Birthday, David!**
> **Dear David,**

Sorry I was not there to wish you a Happy Birthday today, so I hope this does not jam the works. You should be getting a nice sou'westerly, not strong but good direction. I hope they did not work you too hard, thanks and fair winds
> *from* **Trudi**

(RECEIVED)Sat 19/06/2004 03:57
> **Dear Daddy,**

know you've got loads of e-mails so will make it short. HAPPY BIRTHDAY and also HAPPY FATHERS DAY for this Sunday. Hope you're well. E-mails are now getting through from Grandaddy via phone calls from Jonesey whilst they are away, so all aware of your progress. Wondering if you have rough ETA. Have 2 weeks off from 21st June-4th July & wondering whether we'll be able to meet in the Azores. Know Mummy has flight booked & that's Great.

Stay well & look forward to your daily progress north,
> *Loads a love*
> > ***Tot x......***

Sun 20/06/2004 03:09
> **Subject: 'Olidays'n'Azores**
> **Dear Tot,**

What a lovely surprise to open your Email tonight! ... really liked that! ...

Still 400 miles to go yet, and not sure what the weather's doing ... hoping to visit Flores (westernmost island of the Azores) very briefly ... maybe not even stop, cos time's pressing a bit ... then 140 miles to Horta, Island of Faial, the capital ... big marina, very crowded indeed I expect as everyone's on the way from USA/Caribbean to summertime in the Med ... hoping to be there in a week's time, if not before (as I'll try to speed up a bit more) ...

Mum's planning to come to Horta around 6th July, for two weeks I dearly hope ... I really miss your Mum ... very special ...

Would LOVE it if you can come out! ... but sorry not to be able to give definite date yet ... I will let you know as soon as I know ... so don't stop looking at flights! ... (and buy ear-protectors for mouth-organ) ...

> Take good care of you, won't you ...
> > Fondest Love,
> > > **Dad.**

(RECEIVED) Sun 18/06/2004 03:09
> **Subject: Sh*t......57 !!!**

Don't know if this is going to get to you but at least I can say I tried......we've had computer problems. HAPPY BIRTHDAY!! Have you got 57 candles onboard ??

Yes Dany`s made it........ he's been selected to be one of the five boats from Switzerland chosen to take part in the European 420 Junior Championship in Dublin in August !! Has to do some more sea training (compulsory) so has to take time off school. As for me I get hotel , accommodation at Quiberon etc. all paid by Swiss Sailing since I`ve been engaged as driver to help get the 6 boats + motor boat up there . Shame it would have been nice waving to you from the motor boat as you sailed passed France .....maybe some other time.......

195

Cedric took part in the famous Bol D'Or regata this weekend , (biggest one on a lake in Europe) they b*llsed it up a bit he said, so only came 79th out of 500 boats(!)

Sounds as if you're having lots of FUN again , did you manage to get the pulley fly off on video ? Sorry I completely forgot to sing the hymns lately tho' I did look them up in the book ......fascinating reading ! Interesting cos just after the " For those at sea " section you go immediately into the "In times of trouble" section...now THERE`s some really interesting stuff but of course that wouldn't concern you at all would it ....?!

> *love **MARY***

Sun 20/06/2004 03:09
> **Subject: Genes, & 57 years**
> **Dear Mary,**

Delighted that the sailing genes have really surfaced at last! ... please give my proudest congrats to my Godson, and I'm so pleased all that religious instruction I gave him has paid off(!)... and Cedric's doing great too ... well-dones to him too ...

And, just out of spite, when we come and visit you, I'm going to play my favourite piece of Brazilian music again'n'again'n'again'n'again'n'again'n'again etc so you'll be sick to death of it ... and then, when you're at your most exasperated, I'm gonna play the harmonica to you ... very very badly indeed... painfully badly ...

So, if you want to stop me, you'd better start being VERY nice to me ... cos I've been struck by lightning you know ... um ... er ... yes ... I think perhaps ... um ...damn, forgot it again ...

Don't know who you are, but thanks for the wishes regarding reproduction and travel ... Mia Farrow said it was the nicest thing you could wish anybody, in her (unsuccessful) defence in court for saying it too loudly in public, ... lots of Travel, but none of The Other out here though ...

Hey, you remember that ELDERLY guy, a Brit, who got trapped under his boat when the keel fell off a few years ago, during a round-the-world singlehanded race? .. and then amazingly got rescued by the Aussie navy, 5 days later ... Tony B.... ?

Well, he was 57 too, at the time ... so there ...

> Toodle-Pip!!
> > **SunburntWeirdyBeardyBaldy.**

PS. Oh Heck, I've got to learn to start wearing clothes again ... still having problems getting me trousers off over me head ...

(RECEIVED) Fri 11/06/2004 21:57
> *Hi David,*

> *We are continuing to read your mail with great interest. It makes the little world of Orford seem rather mundane!*

> *James Robinson left yesterday to go and join Richard Roberts homeward bound from Denmark. He expects to get him into the Frieslands before coming home. Sue and I leave tomorrow for Ijmuiden and then working our way into the Frieslands and expect to be away for about 5 weeks. Have spent a few hours mapping out information and spares we carry for a few weeks and so start to appreciate the fantastic amount of work you put into your preparations - not only to have all the right gear to do the most extraordinary repairs - but also the knowledge of how to do them.*

> *I shall look forward to catching up on your e-mails when I return.*

> *Cheers,*
> > ***Ben (J)***

Sun 20/06/2004 03:07
Subject: 36th day at sea (and 3,700 miles) since St.Helena
Dear Everybodies,

Low battery voltage again, and virtually no wind, means having to run the engine again unfortunately .... but at least it means I can play on this laptop while the ship's batteries are being recharged ....

Still mile after mile of Portuguese Men-of-War, every 100 yards or so ... I had absolutely no idea there could possibly be so many of them! ... very elegant opalescent pinks, mauves and blues, almost transparent ... when a wave knocks one over, it promptly turns round so that the wind flips it upright again ... neat! ...

And they're not stupid either ... they readily detect the presence of the boat when up to 10 feet away, withdraw their tentacles, and get all agitated about it .... same thing when the shadow of the sails falls on them, (just like you described on the radio, Trudi) ... pity they're such vicious little brutes .... I wonder if the sudden absence of the flying fish is anything to do with them? ...

The spare alternator on the engine, which I fitted at The Electric Island of Cows near Salvador, failed suddenly two days ago and wouldn't charge anything ... it was an awkward job exchanging it for the repaired lightning-damaged one while the ship was rolling around heavily in no wind under the overhead sun, but the result was worth it ... I'm so grateful to those friends who smuggled into Brazil the bits to mend the original alternator, otherwise I'd be seriously short of volts at present ... maybe those who know them could pass on my thanks to them once again? ...

I realised the other day that I have spent the last Christmas Day, New Years Day, Easter Day, my wedding anniversary, and now my birthday, actually AT SEA in these last few months ... not sure what you can read into that, but it's another Useless Fact ...

I had hoped for a gentle wafting warm breeze from a favourable direction on my birthday, and the forecast was for 15 knots wind from the port quarter ... yippee! I thought ..... trouble is, it all arrived in one lump ...(either that, or those knots are seriously big ones) ... a full blooded Force 6+ for several hours, which was uncomfortable as I was carrying a little too much sail, and getting thrown around fairly, before the seas sorted themselves out a bit ... but we covered 36 miles in 5 hours, so I can't really complain ...

One benefit of that wind was that it has retaught me the definition of the time you finally decide to reef ... it's invariably 15 minutes BEFORE the time the wind drops again, having proved its point and got its way ...

So, we're now 400 miles from The Azores, in light winds still (but that should change in the next 48 hours) ... we've got through into the Westerly airstream for the moment, at least ....

Not sure which Island we're going to at first as it depends how the weather looks, but hoping to settle for a short holiday in Horta by the end of this month ... several bits of maintenance to do ... and I want a good long unhurried look at that lower rudder bearing before pressing on to England ... looks like a good excuse for more diving, if the Portuguese Men-of-war will allow! ...

Meantime, take good care of yourselves too,
Much Love from,
Tuesday'n'me.

(RECEIVED) Mon 21/06/2004 02:48
Subject: 'Olidays & Azores
Dearest Daddy,

Enjoy the rest of your time at sea. And viewing the Azores islands as you pass. Know Mummy's looking forward to coming out too see you too. Stay safe... keeping my weeks free, so let me know. But don't stop enjoying YOUR time.

*Loads a love **Tots x.**...*

197

P.S., my excuse for no Birthday/Father's Day present is that I definitely sent it, but was in that Brazilian package. Well that's my excuse & I'm sticking with it,... until that ruddy package is found & then I'll have had time to think up another excuse....

Chapter 10

North of the Tropics again

Fri 25/06/2004 01:48

Dear Everybodies,

Dropped anchor inside HORTA harbour, FAIAL Island, AZORES, at 1410 GMT Wednesday 23rd June ... 4,092 miles in 40 days, which includes crossing the Doldrums, and cutting straight through the Horse Latitudes ... and the ship and I are still on speaking terms too ...

Mind you, we've been very lucky with the weather ... considerable help from both the TransAtlantic and the Italian MaritimeMobile networks with finding our way round adverse or light winds ... using every opportunity as it presented itself ...

It wasn't all sweetness and light though :-

First there was a worry with the fresh water quality ... a nasty sludge appearing in it, apparently getting worse after initial improvement ... I took several samples of it and gave them every opportunity to grow some bug or other, and was able to confirm that it wasn't due to a still living organism ... boiling the water didn't help ... and experiments with very fine filters helped only very slightly ...

But I found that if it was given a chance, the sludge could be made to precipitate out if the water could be kept still enough, ... but as soon as I tipped it up to pour it, it all mixed up again ....more lateral thinking was required, in a boat bobbing around everywhere ...

Whirling a bottleful of water on a string, round my head, (to make a centrifuge) worked, but was far too hazardous (and wet!) ....

But as usual, the simplest answer is the best ...

Certain small bottles of fizzy drinks have a sort of valve on them, instead of a cap ...found it fits standard 2litre bottles too ... so, cut a small hole in the bottom of a suitably fitted bottle (leaving a small rim so that it still has a sort of bendy "lid" to it) ...up-end it ... fill it through the new hole and hang it upside down in the cockpit for 24 hours, in a place where it's free to swing ... then briefly open the valve at the lower screwcap end ... all the gunk falls out onto the cockpit floor ... leaving beautifully clear water fit for drinking, still in the bottle, ready for draining ...

... and that's the stuff I've been living on for the last 5+ weeks ... all the water I've used has gone through this separation process, successfully ...

The second problem was a worry that really ate into me, and disrupted sleep ... even made me collect all the video film I've been making of this trip and add it into a waterproof container in the Panic Grab Bag (for use in sudden sinkings) ...

A gradually increasing "clunk" had became more and more obvious ... at first it could only be felt occasionally, but in certain seastates over several days it got worse, until it could be physically heard right through the length of the boat... seemed to be in the very tail-end of the ship somewhere, and eventually it revealed itself to be coming from the lower rudder bearing at the bottom of the skeg, about 5 feet under the seawater surface ... no possibility of inspecting it (and consider all those millions of Portuguese Men-of-War in the sea anyway, even if I had felt adventurous) ...

Had to nurse the ship carefully over the next 10 days, to avoid straining it further ... the worry was that if it failed, the whole rudder would be wrung off sideways, with a distinct possibility of taking part of the hull

199

with it ... instant big hole in the ship ... it certainly concentrates the mind a bit, I can tell you, with this chance of disaster hanging over you for 24 hours of each day ... suddenly several hundred miles seems an awful lot bigger ... you have to be quite disciplined to make yourself get some sleep ...

So, regretfully, decided to give Flores Island a miss, and diverted 130 miles more downwind to Horta, to ease the strains on the rudder ... a foul night in 25 knot winds, grizzle (grey drizzle), then heavy rain blinding the radar, visibility less than 1 mile, awkward steep uncomfortable 3metre waves, and a dramatic temperature drop, all caused a miserable few hours while approaching the island ... real culture-shock! ... not much rest for me that night ...

But things improved just before dawn, and the final landfall was sunny and clear ... and what a dramatic landfall it was too! ... the first sight was the top of the volcano of Pico appearing ABOVE the clouds ahead ...

Couldn't face the thought of marinas etc, so anchored in the old traditional place in the harbour itself, near a thin scattering of other foreign yachts ... local official in a powerful rubber boat politely said that I shouldn't really anchor out there but should go into the marina to check in ... but he responded (only slightly reluctantly) when I said I'd come a long way and was feeling a somewhat tired, and I didn't want to make any mistakes now did I ... he agreed ...

It's lucky I didn't have to explain how I quickly made a miraculous recovery in the next half hour, and was able to spend nearly an hour and a half swimming in the cold water, scrubbing the topsides and knocking seven bells out of that rudder bearing to try to reproduce the "clunk" again (bruised my foot as I karate-kicked the rudder, and on one dive I got so involved with it that I stayed down a bit too long .. I suddenly realised I'd got to go up to the surface again, in a hurry ... banged my head on the propeller in the rapid ascent ... that's one stupid mistake I won't make again) ... I'd got too cold too, like a fool ...

The hot cup of soup afterwards tasted wonderful! ... but got only moderate sleep in a rising wind, with the anchor chain grinding away at the rocky harbour bottom ... unused to the gentler motion too ...

And so today we up-anchored and came in to clear Customs etc (very friendly and pleasant officials here), but because it's so crowded at present there's no berth available ... so for the next two days Tuesday'n'me are rafted up with other boats against the marina wall ... nice neighbours, very friendly and quiet, Americans and English ... good atmosphere though it's been cold, grey, rainy, and blowing hard ...

Ship's water-tanks now emptied, flushed through and refilled ... took a long time ...... minor maintenance and cleaning since ...

Even though it feels so COLD, I'll sleep well tonight! ...

Stay well!

Byee for now!,
Tuesday'n'me

(RECEIVED)Fri 25/06/2004 12:02
*Nice one Doc......God Bless......**NICK**..*

(RECEIVED) Thu 24/06/2004 08:46
Subject: *Re: Su 'n bur 'nt weir dy bear dy bal dy.......? Is this some sort of nude dance you do round the mast ?*

Welcome to where ever you have arrived !!!
*Love, **Mary**.*
(P.S. Cedric's passed his driving test last Monday , so stay on the water when you get back to Europe .....)

Fri 25/06/2004 12:02

Dear Y,C,T & J,

Safely in the Azores now, rafted against the marina wall, with pleasant American and English neighbours ... arrived Wednesday 23rd June, after 4,092 miles in 40 days from St.Helena ...

Two worries during the trip ... (i) poor quality freshwater in the ship's tanks, and (ii) steadily worsening wear in the rudder lower bearing at the bottom of the skeg (the ship needed a bit of nursing through the last 10 days ... quite worrying at the time) ...

Had to go easy with the breadmaking ... I started to put on too much weight!

And the selfsteering gear I made using your old Autohelm and the bits of my old Navico system has worked excellently, so I owe you more thanks yet again ...

Staying here for 4 weeks, and first Tot (you remember her?) and then Fin (my ladywife) will be coming out to join me here on board for a holiday ... I'm longing to see them both, but I remember your comments, Yvan, and I'll let you know how it goes ...

Hope you are taking good care of my two transparent tiles in your roof ... I fondly think of you all often, and I trust all continues well for you ... hope the Avacado plant is growing successfully? ...

Take good care of yourselves,

and if you see Tinho, please say Hello to him too for me?

Warmest Wishes!

DocDavid'n'Tuesday.

(RECEIVED) Fri 25/06/2004 13:49

Subject: RE:Free Spirit

Good to hear from you and know you made it ok. I enjoyed Horta when I was there, I could have spent a lot more time there. Don't forget to check out the volcano crater, watch where you step, there is a lot of cows in the area.

We are settled in here in Luperon, the Dominican Republic and Haiti has alot to offer if you have the time to spend here. It takes little money. We have volenteered to help build some houses in the area in hopes of getting to meet some of the people who smile a lot but have little reason to. I'm sure they have a secret to share.

Free Spirit has held up well. Did have to replace the head that was leaking and the stove that caught fire. Did I tell you we had the standing rigging replaced in Trinidad!

The boaters here are planning a hog roast on the beach and a mooning contest during full moon, I'm sure you would enjoy that Doc and I could see you standing in line to be the first contestant. We sure do miss you and your beautiful personality.

May the seas and wind be with you my dear friend.

Allen and Marsha

(RECEIVED) Mon 28/06/2004 16:38

Subject: RE: Azores

David

Welcome back to the northern hemisphere. Bet you're missing that southern night sky! Looks like a reasonable average given the route. Now you have the chance to relax and enjoy the Azores for a while. It'll make quite a change for you.

I took my Yachtmaster practical exam last week which went very well and was quite enjoyable given the circumstances - took it on a school boat and had three competent crew candidates for crew - one of which was deaf in one ear and over 70. The examiner was also in his seventies, blind in one eye and wore a monocle!

Having a ticket at last will be no bad thing I suppose and could open up some new opportunities.

I've been wondering what to do next in the training line and thought I might pick your brains. I have long thought about getting an Amateur radio license and I was very interested in what you had to say about how the ham network had supported you. I already hold a marine HF radio license from my merchant navy days (not GMDSS). Do you think its worth it?

Have a great time in the Azores.

Best wishes.

Eric

Fri 02/07/2004 02:22
  Subject: Ham Radio Ticket
  Dear Eric,

Thanks for all your news which I enjoyed reading ... Excellent news ref Yachtmaster exam ...well done! ... I wonder if your Yachtmaster examiner was THE "Monocle Jim", who is a true native of West Mersea? ... he's a remarkable seaman, and I remember meeting him many years ago ... always interesting to talk to, was Jim ...

Yes, Ham radio has been exceptionally useful to me over the last 20+ years, and as my brother is a radio-ham as well, I have been able to keep in touch with my family all the time too ... it needn't be very expensive, and as an example it's worth noting that my antenna only cost £6 to make, and I've managed perfectly well with only 8 watts output for worldwide communication all this last year ... I believe the licensing rules have changed in the last three months, to make it easier for everybody, so you may find you need only minimal Morse to be able to get an HF ticket ... certainly, I recommend you investigate the possibility, maybe by starting at the website of the Radio Society of Great Britain? ... (sorry I don't know the exact address, but a search engine will find it for you) ... you don't NEED the ticket, but it does open up all sorts of possibilities for you (not only when at sea but during the rest of the year as well) ...

On UPPER side band, these Nets might interest you, to hear what goes on:-

Trudi's Net, 21.400 MHz, 1300 hrs UTC,(Trudi in Barbados)

and the Italian Net, 14.297.5 MHz, 1900 hrs UTC,(Jack in Pennsylvania, Gerard in Belgium)

or the S. Atlantic Net, 14.316 MHz, 1130 hrs UTC,(Alistair in Durban)

or the British Net, 14.303 MHz, 0800 and 1800 hrs UTC (Bill in Cobham,UK)

Meantime, make time to ENJOY yourself, and I'll be in touch again soon ...

  DocDavid'n'Tuesday.

(RECEIVED)Fri 02/07/2004 08:30
  Subject: Ham Radio Ticket

Good to hear from you and thanks for your advice. I have got as far as getting the manual for the first part of the ticket so I think I'll go ahead.

Yes it was THE 'Monocle Jim'. I did think you might know him as he is obviously a bit of a local character. I certainly learned a lot from him though the biggest lesson from the whole exercise was to realise just how much more there is to learn.

Very impressive to achieve all that on an 8 watt output. I do have a receiver and dipole antenna set-up at home so I'll try some of the frequencies you suggest though I've often found difficulty receiving the UK Maritime Net on 14.303 - I assume I am too close or that they somehow beam their signal south.

Good sailing

  Eric (Aliz Motte)

(RECEIVED) Wed 23/06/2004 15:06
Subject: Newsletter
Hi David,
Trust this finds you well.
We are producing a Newsletter and I would like to use some extracts from your cruising log. May I?
Good sailing!
Mike

Sun 27/06/2004 00:37
Dear Mike,

I'm delighted if there's anything you can use out of the "Dear Everybodies" etc for the Newsletter. Please do go ahead, and I consider it would be an honour if you do so.

Various family members have kept copies of all the Emails, no doubt to produce their own bootleg editions of the book!

In truth, I have absolutely NO intention of writing a book, I assure you, but there's a good chance I may not be able to refuse all the requests I've had to go and give talks about it all, when I get home .. I have 15 hours (!) of video to prune already .. people I DO like will get a 30-60 minute version .. those I DON'T like will have to suffer at least 2-3 hours of it .. that should put them off a bit!

I'm deeply indebted to you for all your support for this trip .. it's really made a difference for my confidence .. Thank you! .. We're not home yet, but at least now I can give myself TIME, for weather windows etc, before setting off for home again in the second half of July ..

I'll keep in touch meantime, through the Letters from Tuesday'n'me.
Very Best Wishes!
David on Tuesday.

(RECEIVED)Sun 27/06/2004 23:11
Subject: Staale
Hallo David,
Jack just sent me his Italian Net Report, and included this:
LA7GZ, Stalle on Rozinante, Gerard just received email from Stalle; arrived safely in Simonstown, False Bay South Africa, after 69 days at sea from Rio except for 4 days in Tristan da Cunha. Thanks for all the help and weather received from the Italian and Transatlantic Maritime Mobile Networks. Will send an email with photos. **Trudi.**

Mon 28/06/2004 01:57
Subject: WELL DONE! (both you AND the ship!)
Dear Staale,

ABSOLUTELY DELIGHTED to hear you are safe and secure again! Very well done indeed, sir!..

It will take some time to adapt, I warn you, but it's not at all painful, judging from my own experience!

The biggest difficulty is when people ask you what it was like, and you know they will never really understand what you've been through .. it's almost easier not to try to explain to them ..

You said we will never be the same again after this last 2+ months .. you're right! ..

I salute you Staale .. you are a remarkable seaman!
Warmest Best Wishes!
DocDavid'n'Tuesday.

Mon 28/06/2004 01:58
   Dear Everybodies,

   Good news today! .. a Norwegian friend, Staale, has made it successfully to Cape Town from Rio, after 69 days at sea (disregarding a few hours stop at Tristan de Cunha) .. South Atlantic midwinter gales, a 90 degree knockdown, broken selfsteering gear .. he's certainly a fine seaman and a tough chap after that little lot .. Well Done! ..

   I cannot get over how COLD it is here .. it's physically quite upsetting .. but the thermometer says it's still 22c even now, at midnight .. I suppose it was arrogant of me to think I would be immune to the change, but I really thought I had mentally allowed for it ..

   WRONG! .. I find great difficulty adjusting my temperature, particularly during sleep, almost as though I had lost an automatic reflex .. (well, I suppose that's what it is really .. a forgotten reflex .. wonder how long it takes to regain it) ..

   And of course, every thing on board is DAMP, because of the condensation due to the lower temperature .. hope to be able to successfully ventilate everything in the next few days, otherwise it's going to be like sailing in an English late-autumn again ..

   All in all, it's an interesting side-effect of this lifestyle that I had under-estimated ..

   Another thing which I can't readily adjust to yet, is not having to ration the water and the food .. putting on weight again rapidly! .. and it seemed very strange today doing the clothes-washing without a care in the world .. splashing water everywhere .. all I need now is a really good wallow in a hot bath! ..

   And I haven't stopped talking yet, since I arrived here ..

   I got fed up with carrying the broken alternator round the town for several days trying to find someone to fix it .. so in frustration out came the spanners and screwdrivers and soldering irons etc again to see if I could fix it for myself from "Tuesday"'s stores .. remarkably, after some head scratching, SUCCESS! .. (I feel a bit guilty about wearing a smug smile afterwards, but it's really quite pleasing!)

   Horta is nice .. peaceful, island mentality .. most shop-owners etc speak English very well, and so far everyone is helpful and patient .. very easy-going friendly crews on the boats, truly international .. Doug, one of the Americans, pointed out to me that every one of these crews has SAILED here, over an open ocean, so none of them are likely to be the typical English-marina-type of yottie at all .. quite right .. hadn't thought of it like that ..

   The sad thing is that most boats don't stay here long, just using the wall-rafts as a stepping stone to Europe and the Med .. so unless I stay rafted up on the wall, with all its comings and goings, and tidal range etc, it's possible I may miss out on the people I would most like to meet .. nevertheless, when this afternoon the staff here offered me the opportunity of a berth on a finger-pontoon I jumped at it .. simply for security and peace of mind if I'm going to leave the ship to go on an Exploring-Expedition when Tot arrives tomorrow..

   Much to my surprise, the tight manoeuvring to move the ship in this crowded harbour went particularly well, though I suspect a brand-new British boat's crew had a few heartstopping moments while Tuesday rotated slowly and elegantly on the spot, in LESS than her own length, swinging her overhanging bow anchor above their heads in their cockpit .. no wind, no current at the time .. Doug was on board with me to help moor up, and he said afterwards that he particularly enjoyed that moment! .. (I have to confess, so did I!) .. the victims laughed about it, but didn't really relax until the sky appeared overhead again .. But it was all good-natured, as all the time they fully understood what was going on down in the other end of Tuesday ..

   Hey Ho, time to sleep again ..

   Thanks for all your moral support, which has been much appreciated
      Love from
         Tuesday'n'me.

(RECEIVED) Tue 29/06/2004 15:01

Well, it seems you have not stopped writing either....

We are so happy to know that you are safe and well and have stopped drinking the greeny water and eating the M&Ms!

We will write a longer message soon, right now we just wanted to say WELL DONE TUESDAY AND DAVID!!!

Ciao

Philippe and Paola

SY 'Why Not?'

(RECEIVED) Wed 30/06/2004 15:14

hi Doc

Well done!!! some trip and a great daily average your obviously a real sailor.

I'm still in Brazil but will be leaving in the next few days for Tobago. Have been offered some work their for about 6-8 months if I can get their before end of July.

Enjoy the Azores the're great islands, hire a car if you get to Pta delgada, the island is spectacular and well worth it.

regards

bill, buddy and shusha

Thu 01/07/2004 22:36

Dear Everybodies,

Tot arrived! ... full of smiles and chuckles and fun ... it's really nice to see her again, and we've been beginning to explore a little ... and she brought warmer weather and sunshine ...

Swimming in the middle of a volcano, in a mixture of warm water and very cold ... Soren came with us (he's the Swedish skipper of a retired English racing boat, whose crew stole his money and cashcards as they fled the country last week), but he was eaten by a jellyfish while we were swimming .. recovering now ..

Climbing up the big tunnel that the dead whales used to be dragged up, before they were cut up into little bits in the whale-processing-factory (now long-since defunct) ... there was a strange sense of quiet reverence in the place, like being in a garden-of-remembrance ...

Collecting more samples of volcanic effluent ... each bit seems different from all the other examples from other island volcanoes I've seen during this trip ....

Spent 80 minutes in full scuba gear under the ship today, (once again Chris'n'Tashi, I thank you!), seriously "beasting" the rudder-bearings ...found the source of the clunking noise to be a small VERTICAL movement of the rudder itself and not a LATERAL bearing-wear ... it is not a significant risk at present, so I don't need to haul the boat out, thank heavens ... the noise only occurred when pitching heavily, which fits with my findings ... I will review the underwater photos I took when the film is developed in a day or two ...

Five days ago the underside of the hull was coated with big fat goose-barnacles everywhere, one every inch or so ... today I was amazed to find NONE at all ... not even a straggler ... SOMETHING must have upset them to make them leave suddenly ... makes me worry about what they know that I don't! ... maybe it was due to the temperature change? ... whatever it was it's certainly very effective ..

Sadly, Doug and his son Eric, left today for Spain/Portugal on their bright yellow, home-built, 40' catamaran called "Jo Do Beer", (from JOanne, DOug, BErt and ERic) ... one of the few catamarans I've been very impressed by, with its simplicity and strength and functionality ...

There are so many stories about this remarkable duo ... but as an example, they have an additional crew of ten aggressive looking, heavily armed, pirates ... each is about 3" high, and Doug was given them, to look after him, when he retired ... they move around the deck a bit when it's rough, and occasionally one of them falls over, or hides ... Doug then lines them all up for a rollcall, and gives them stiff dressing down for falling down on the job, before putting them back to work as lookouts or guardians...

Doug lives in the port hull, while Eric lives in the starboard one, each pretty well totally independent from the other, with no intervening superstructure on the brigedeck ... but the two of them get on really well together, and were a great pleasure to meet ...

Hired a car today, to look further afield ... chauffeur-driven most expertly by Tot ... (I've always wanted to be a back-seat-driver!) ... it's been a great day, while she drove Soren and I round the island ... exploring all sorts of volcanic places ...

The last big eruption here was in 1957 ... it partially buried a lighthouse (which we inspected carefully, especially as I have photos of the actual event) ... and it had buried a village (where we noted the ash/soil is still hot underfoot, and even more so if you dig away the top few inches) ... a stunningly stark landscape where a whole new kilometre of high headland was built onto the island in a matter of a few months ... very difficult to grasp the mindboggling forces at work to produce these effects ... and for me certainly an unexpected, eye-opening addition to my journey that I could never forget ...

Naturally growing flowers lining the roads everywhere, in all shades of blue (Hydrangeas) ... very pretty indeed ...

Beautiful views of the blue sea and the steep green/brown cliffs ...every shade of green in the foliage, some almost fluorescent ... birdsong everywhere in the hot sunshine ...

 Then meeting a charming Dutchman and his wife here who carve intricate pictures onto the teeth of long-dead Sperm whales ("scrimshaw") ... very interesting, the history of this form of art, we found ... Tuesday now has her own Sperm whale baby-tooth on board, but an UNcarved one ...

Yes, Horta is certainly a nice, mellow place, with several surprises to show you ... well worth a visit if you possibly can ...

Time to stop ... so much more to tell you about ... but another time, I'm afraid ....
>   With Love from
>   **Tuesday'n'me.**

(RECEIVED) Thu 01/07/2004 01:15
>   *Dear Tuesday, David and Tot,*

>   *Wow... all that way! It's hard to believe it. Anyway, first of all a most hearty welcome to Tot; I hope you are feeding her well... or is it the other way round? It was so delightful to see her when she came round a few days ago. We are as proud of her as you are!*

>   *All that's happened here is that the other day it occurred to me that the car might be nearly due for a service. So I rang up Potters and a nice lady there told me that not only was it two months overdue but that I had also been driving around all that time without an MOT! So today it went in; and I asked them also to look at a squeak (more of a grunt actually) in the rear suspension when I go over a large bump. Well they've cured it.... but there are now three new rattles which were not there before. Think I'll just drive around for a bit and see if they go away by themselves.*

>   *It is such a relief to know, at the moment anyway, that you are not on the high seas, but are safely tied up alongside. I am sure that you will not venture out again until you are 101% sure your rudder is absolutely OK. Yes, I think I'm sure! Your "everybodies" are so wonderful and we look forward to the next ones. Chris also gets selected ones of them.*

>   *We all send our love, to you and to Tot. We miss you.* **Daddy.**

Fri 02/07/2004 02:22
> **Dear Daddy,**
> Loved your Email thank you!
> MOTs and cars:-
> Tell 'em your son's been struck by lightning, and that's why you forgot...um....er....whatever it was ....
(at least you've GOT a car ... I've still got to find one somewhere when I get back) ...
> Rattles in cars :-
> Long ago you taught me that rattles do one of three things :-
either they get better (so no action needed), or they get worse (so now you can find them and fix'em), or they stay the same, (in which case you'll be no worse off than you are at present) ... That philosophy has applied to so many things in the last 10 years or so, particularly during this trip ...so Thank you for this collection of Wise-Thoughts ...
> I'm sorry you've got the dreaded Rattles ... and I hope it's resolved soon!
> I'll see you soon, so stay well both of you ...
> **T,T'n'me.**

(RECEIVED)Mon 05/07/2004 07:12
> *Just a quickie - did you get my text message about looking at the paintings on the harbour wall?*
> *There is one by the daughter of one of my customers who visits there and is supposed to be very good.*
> *Hope you are doing the same - or that Tots has done one for you!!*
> *L.O.L.*
> *Jonesey*

Mon 12/07/2004 04:15
> **Subject: "Eleanor Mary"**
> Dear Unudderedbwudderbuddy,
> Bit of a problem about the painted sign for "Eleanor Mary" ... there's bleedin' MILLIONS of painted motifs, but we're still looking hard ... if there's any chance of a clue about roughly WHERE to look, that would be nice ... better not tell your customer that we might threaten to paint ours over the top of it tho'!...
> I really miss the radio skeds, but the QRN in here is "suffn kronik" as they say at home ... S8-9 noise, all bands, 24hours per day, so although I try for the Nets most days, it's almost always sweet f.a. ......
> Keep de peace!
> Toodle-pip!
> **Me.**

(RECEIVED)Mon 12/07/2004 06:55
> *Ta eva so for that - the painting is roughly half way along the wall as I understand it.*
> *Yes I too miss the skeds but hopefully we can resume when you get going again - whenever that might be.*
> *t.t.f.n.*
> *J.*

Tue 20/07/2004 02:54
> **Subject: "Eleanor Mary"**
> Fin found it! ... and it's still in good condition ... obviously good paint! ...
> **D.**

207

(RECEIVED) *Mon 05/07/2004 15:24*
Dear David,

We are happy to know that you are enjoying a bit of rest and recuperation in the company of Tot.

But where was our medical advisor when we most needed him?.... Playing with the green slime in his drinking water more than half way across the Atlantic. Not really very professional! No, this time a bite on the neck, just under the chin by some form of vicious insect, which injected its poison without Philippe's knowledge or, indeed, any awareness at all.

However, the result was a neck blown up so that Philippe rather resembled his image of Mr Pumblechook (the corpulent lawyer in Great Expectations), which necessitated a flying visit to the Albert Einstein Hospital in Sao Paulo. This hospital, is the leading (Jewish) hospital in South America. They did various blood tests and a CAT scan and thankfully confirmed that the swelling was only external and not internal, which might have proved very problematic. Various pills were prescribed and within a couple of days Philippe's swan-like neck reappeared.

Pantaenius, which covers us also for medical emergencies, have been really very good and helpful.

Some Brazilian friends with an ENORMOUS gin palace were kind enough to drive us to Sao Paulo and accommodate us in their substantial residence, guarded by two enormous dogs (with fangs) and an assortment of Brazilian guards with guns. It was very kind of them and it just goes to show that not all Brazilians are like those in the Policia and Receita Federal, whose sole purpose in life seems to be centred on making the life of a retired Suffolk GP a misery.

We are still immigrants in Paraty, in the Ilha Grande/Angra dos Reis region and do not plan on moving until at least mid August. It is a very beautiful part of Brazil and we are very sorry that you did not manage to see it. Next time???

Anyway, we hope you have a fantastic time in the Azores and a safe trip back home, when the time comes.

Do not forget that if you feel like a bit of South American sailing you can always come and play with us. From all the info and charts we are acquiring Argentina and Uruguay look really very interesting, besides being even cheaper than Brazil!

Keep drinking mango juice.

    Ciao!

      Paola and Philippe
        SY 'Why Not?'

Mon 12/07/2004 04:15
    Subject: Mango juice
    Dear P'n'P,

Lovely surprise to get your Email tonight! ... but I'm sorry about the exploding neck problem ... wonder what the poison/infection was ... I doubt whether I could have helped much anyway, I'm sorry to say ... but it sounds like you did all the right things, so well done! ... it must have been a nasty and very worrying time for you both though ... I sympathise ...

Thanks for the kind offer about sailing more on that coast ... much appreciated, but don't worry, you're quite safe for the moment! ... I regret very much not seeing more of Brazil, but on the other hand I wouldn't have had all that fun on Itiparica with Yvan'n'Christina's new house ...

Present plan is to return to England for the winter, and then contemplate on what I've learnt before deciding what I want to do ... Fin (my Ladywife) is here with me in the Azores for two weeks, and we've had tremendous fun realising yet again why we married each other 31 years ago (it's been 9 months since we last saw each other) ...

Maybe you've seen the Azores already, but I'm impressed by Faial and Pico Islands ... and we hope to see Flores Island together before she flies back home (to return to work, because otherwise she can't afford me ... at least, that's MY story!) ...

And the mango-juices? ... the stuff here is CRAP compared to the Brazilian ones, so far, but it brings back a hint of memory of the taste in that nice old guy's tiny bar in Salvador ...

Oh, and by the way, they say they're still looking for my electronicals in Sao Paulo, the thieving b*st*rds, (you know who I mean!) ...

Stay well, you lucky B's ...

Keep in touch!

Tuesday and the doc.

Sun 04/07/2004 03:15

Dear Everybodies,

I know I said this Island is a place of surprises, but even so it's always got at least one more trick up it's sleeve ... I don't want to spoil it for when you come here yourselves, so I won't tell you about ALL of the things we've seen in the few days while Tot has been here ...

However, you MUST take a picnic lunch with you when you visit the top of the mountain ... to give yourself time to sit and gradually accept what you see ... to savour the unexpected moment ...

By chance, found a photo album in a shop today, on discreet display ... contemporary photos showing all the stages of the 1957 eruption ... it began quietly with bubbles in the sea ... then increased to an overwhelming display of Mother Nature's sheer, raw, undiluted POWER ... it's very humbling to compare those pictures with what remains there today ... difficult to take in the extent of what's happened there ... and it's still very hot in that area even now, nearly 50 years later ...

Alongside that album is another one, equally mind-stopping ... I had thought that some of the buildings on the Island seemed a bit weak, cracked and split with age and poor quality mortar ... WRONG again! ... in 1998 there was a big earthquake here, and the before-and-after photos take a bit of swallowing ... the wall cracks I'd seen in the buildings today were all due to that one very short-lived event 6 years ago, all across the island ... in Suffolk, England, we consider the stuff we walk around on to be fairly solid and immovable, but clearly that's not the case here ... makes me look at the ground somewhat more circumspectly now ...

We took the ferry to Pico Island this afternoon ...Pico seemed to be "shut" (Saturday afternoon) ... but we came across a large area of empty ash-covered land, with lots of people sitting round it on walls and rooftops ... wondered why they were there ... perhaps a religious occasion? ...or was a parachutist expected? ... or maybe they were waiting to watch the grass begin to grow? ...or for a new volcano to start blowing? ... very strange! ... so we sat on the seawall to see what happened ...

Abruptly, two loud explosions high in the air ... obviously fireworks ... immediately followed by the unexpected appearance, from a large box, of an angry BULL on a very long rope loosely controlled by eight men on the end of it ... the very healthy but bad tempered animal then ran at anything that moved, and knocked over and trampled a young man foolish enough to try to taunt it (he got up and walked away, presumably accepting tomorrow's aches and bruises) ...

At one stage the bull overshot an umbrella waved by an extravert-in-line-for-a-Darwin-Award, and ran smack into a lamppost ... heck of a bang ... lamppost wrecked ... bull not in the least bit put off by it at all ...(though Tot was very concerned that he might cut his feet in all the broken glass) ... we realised that this is the Portuguese version of bullfighting that we'd stumbled into, but we were impressed that the bull seemed healthy and uninjured, although angry at first ...

After about 10 minutes the beast got fed up with the game, and was gradually reeled back in again towards his box, but was a bit reluctant to enter it ... another single explosion high overhead changed his mind though, and he shot back in like a startled rabbit ...

There were three other bulls there, presumably similarly encouraged to let off steam ... all unhurt ...

Mixed feelings about all this ... but overall it did seem that the real victims were the young men who wanted to show off their mettle by trying to out-manoeuvre the animal ... somehow, activities which are more dangerous to the humans than to the animals seem slightly less unacceptable ... but as Tot commented, "what's the point of this weird human behaviour? ... It doesn't prove anything really, in this day and age" .... Hmm ...

My old backpack/haversack has finally fallen to bits ... salt air and sun ... nice new one today, lighter and stronger ... much more comfortable ...

And I'll have to retrim my beard a bit, soon ... gets caught in my zip ... (er, no ... the one the top of my overalls) ...

Stay Well!,

With love from

Tuesday, Tot, and me.

(RECEIVED) Sun 04/07/2004 15:54

Subject: Nasty Noises

Darling David,

Hope you get this. It is just because I think Charlotte leaves you to-day and you will feel very bereft without her until Fin joins you in about forty eight hours time.

I don't know what you and Daddy are talking about, but how to deal with strange noises is quite easy. You do as I did driving alone; you simply turn on the radio, preferaby to Jimmy Young, turn up the volume and the strange noise immediately vanishes.By the time you have got to Edinbro, or Builth Wells, you have forgotten all about it, providing off course that the car has got there. So in future, remember, nasty noise, Jimmy Young, turn up volume, utter peace, worries all gone.

Heaps of love, **Mother**

Mon 12/07/2004 04:15

Dear Mother,

Loved your Emails! ... just received them ... and I THINK this is the correct address? ... it's a bit confusing with all these alias's you have! ...

The nasty "clunk" noise I mentioned got beyond sound-masking techniques I'm afraid, because I could FEEL it through the ship ...no amount of Jimmy Young would have hid it, so it was constantly reminding me that I was a long way from home ... but now I know what caused it I can sail in a way to minimise it ...

It's LOVELY having Fin here, even though she's got a cold at present, poor thing ... suddenly I can relax and take things at a slower pace ... not living "on the edge" for a while ... she's quite some girl, isn't she! .... (except for the right-hand driving, perhaps)...

And it's always a great pleasure, and FUN, to speak to you on the phone ... thanks for putting up with my rambling on, and on, and on, and on, ...

Ship maintenance and repairs all going well ... already reloaded with diesel, oils, greases, water, non-perishable foods etc etc, together with some small improvements here and there which the last 7,000 miles have taught me ... (total mileage since Orford so far is 13,223 ... so expecting 15,000 or so by the time we get home) ...

It's late ... must stop ...

See you soon!

LoadzaLove, D.

Mon 12/07/2004 00:32
   Dear Everybodies,
        A total delight to greet Fin (complete with her passport this time) at the nearby airport! ... WONDERFUL, after 9 months apart! ...
   Mind you, being driven by her in a hire-car, round the island, has got to be one of the three most terrifying events of this whole trip ... however, we (and the poor car) survived OK ...
   And we found more unexpected surprises ...
   A second uninhabitable lighthouse, this time cracked and shattered by the 1998 earthquake (which lasted all of 6 seconds, but 6 very l-o-n-g seconds as a taxidriver told me when he was recounting what he was doing at the time) .... It's interesting to note that this mighty and imposing building, now split apart, displaced and leaning, has been replaced by a simple steel pole held up by four wires ... on the top of it is a modern lamp, powered by a solar panel ... it does the same job as that original huge lighthouse, possibly even better ... and it's almost earthquake-proof too ...
   A red Martian landscape, less than 50 years old, where the volcanic ash is part buried by larva and pumice "bombs" ... you clamber up the unstable (and still hot) side of a volcano ... you reach the edge ...and suddenly feel most unwell when you realise that the rest of the mountain has been eroded by the sea to leave a vertical cliff ... 300 metres straight down into the ocean ... I can assure you that it was two quick (and rather shaky) photos and we were out of there, sharpish! ... I get the impression that this island could bite, if it decided to do so ...
   Gentler things this weekend ... ship maintenance, engine servicing, and Fin very kindly volunteered to sandpaper and revarnish the hatchways and cockpit woodwork ... she did it better than I would have done too, (in spite of out-of-date and sludgy varnish, because the chandlers shop is shut today) ...
   Nice people all around here, with common interests and a variety of useful skills ... but I've met only a few who have that fiercely self-reliant independence which I noted amongst the yachtsmen who had reached Brazil (in particular the singlehanders) ... Horta, here in the Azores, is effectively a "pit-stop" along the classical milk-run from the West Indies to Europe and the Med ... a different type of mentality, perhaps a little like the "ARC" boats I met in the Canaries? ... (A gross over-generalisation, but that's the impression I receive) ...
   Many boats change their crews here ... (unfortunately, signs on some vessels of considerable disharmony amongst them) ... where drop-dead GORGEOUS superyachts lie alongside 23ft. ex MiniTransat racers ... lots of bendy Benneteaus ... all nationalities, but more British yachts than I've seen in the whole of the last year .... a most interesting place, particularly if you just sit and listen for a while! ...
   Some harbours have fish populations which live on weeds and barnacles ... but the fish here in Horta are most industrious at cleaning all the accumulations off the bottoms of the boats ... it happens in many ports, but these little chaps put all the others to shame ... I don't think they removed the goose-barnacles from "Tuesday", which I suspect left voluntarily due to the temperature change (or something), but you should see a shoal of these "cleaner" fish at work on a visiting boat with a waterline "beard" ... very impressive! ...
   Seems to me that you have to keep continuously on the move here ... if you stay still, you'll either be nibbled by the cleaner-fish, or some enthusiastic yacht's crew will paint the name and logo of their boat on you ... no flat surface is safe, and it seems it is unlucky NOT to have left your mark somewhere on the harbour wall/ pavement/ embankment/ wheelie-bin etc ... even on the back of a No-Parking sign ... the quality of some designs is truly superb ...some are very humorous ... you have to compete for a space, but Fin and I think we may have found a site for our own effort, though the design of the picture isn't finalised yet ... "watch this space!" ...
   More Inconsequential Ramblings from "Tuesday" soon ...

Stay Well!
        with love from,
            Fin'n'T'n'me.
PS. Why was it the SECOND uninhabitable lighthouse? ... well, the first one we saw, at the other end of the island, was scorched and blackened by the 1957 eruption, then buried to the level of the first floor by hot ash and cinders... not only that, even if its light could still work, it would be invisible to ships because of the new mountain created to seaward of it ... I don't mean to discourage anybody, but personally speaking, I would NOT apply for a job as lighthouse-keeper on Faial Island, Azores ...

(RECEIVED)

David, I wish you knew how much enjoyment your letters give us. We cant wait for the next instalment even though your laval walk gave me, personally, the horrors. You see, unlike Daddy much of my childhood was spent exploring locally with my younger brother Dan. South Yorkshire was full of coal mines and that means slag heaps. Great fun to play on since the rain creates lots of deepish valleys. One of them was near our home and we would ride our ponies up them. The stuff was very soft and we and the ponies would sink in a bit and if you put your hand on it even in the depth of winter it would feel pleasantly warm. Admittedly, an occasional passing old man would yell at us to come down but we ignored them. A few years later we dscovered that at night the whole slag heap would be glowing a dark red which worried the powers that be because of air raid precautions. By that time I was wise enough to realise that my brother and I had been what my father (your grandfather) would have called "Damn Fools"-- and almost felt sick at the thought of how our ponies could have been killed. So,thank goodness your lava was firm enough!

Heaps and heaps of love to you and Tuesday,
            Mother.

(RECEIVED) Mon 12/07/2004 19:26
    Subject: Did you know your wife is on holiday ?
        Hello Fin !
At long last I know where I can find you !!

Just to wish you a VERY happy holiday with your husband - forgot you had one . Bit like me, I used to have a brother but he went off his rocker and disappeared somewhere down south.....

Rumour has it that you sandpaper boats, but love to hear your version of that later .... Next time David p*sses off and Jean-marc has a business meeting somewhere foreign, come with me to Britanny and have a real holiday . Just got back. Bit lonely at times but fell in love with the place, so determined to go back there as a real tourist.

David thinks he sees it all from a boat's point of view but from a land lubbers point of view there are very different sensations, but lots of pleasure...................

Have a lovely holiday !
        Lots of love
            Mary
P:S By the way if you see David , if you are not too busy sandpapering, do send him my fondest xxxxxxxxx !!

(RECEIVED) Sat 03/07/2004 12:41
    Dear David,
        I do hope you get this as I wanted to say how much Chris and I are enjoying the installments winging their way to us via your father. We are on our annual sailing pilgrimage to Holland until 1 August but I have

had to fly back for a few days to relieve the house sitter.

I've just spent a happy time retrieving all the e-mails backlogged on the computer while we've been away and, as I said to your pa, feel like I've had to put down a most exciting book mid chapter. They are now printed off to take back to Chris and we shall look forward to more instalments in August.

So pleased that you'n'Tuesday seem to be having a good, if eventful time, and not only enjoying your enforced aloneness, but meeting such interesting people along the way.

On behalf of the Royal Harwich Yacht Club (I am taking this on myself even though I am only one half of a member), I hope you would consider giving us all a 'Winter Talk' before you get too busy on the lecture circuit!!

But long before that Chris and I will look forward to having you and Fin over for dinner and videos.

Have a safe rest of the trip and love from two English-marina-type yotties - (always the exceptions that prove the rule)

Gill xx

Mon 12/07/2004 00:32
> **Subject: thanks for your kind comments**
> > **Dear Chris'n'Gill,**

What a lovely surprise to open your Email, which I thoroughly appreciated with all its news ... Thanks for all your kind comments, which are a great help giving me more confidence before attacking the last leg back to England ... very much appreciated! ...

It's strange for me to admit, but yes, I DO want to tell people about what I've learnt on this trip ... not normally my scene at all, and there is so much one could mull over .... but I would love to be asked to relive, with strangers, some of the times I've had ... but maybe not until I've had a chance to put into some sort of order my thoughts and my films and photos ...

Very envious of you in Holland ... many times on this adventure I've longed to be doing precisely what you're doing, instead of spending days scaring myself half to death ... I wished often that I had the sense to stay in my own pond, and relax'n'enjoy ... enjoy yourselves, you lucky devils! ...

Take good care of you both ... I'll see you soon ... (you won't be able to shut me up, I'm afraid ... there's so much to tell you!) ...

> Much Love,
> > **Tuesday'n'me.**

(RECEIVED) Sat 03/07/2004 16:25
> *Hello David*

> *We (Joyce and me) have followed your travels with great interest, when you have arrived at a destination, we have been prompted to look up the details of that place, (mainly on the internet, but with maps and atlas too) all because you have given fine descriptions of either the area or the people.*

I particularly recall you mentioning a group of men paddling out to your boat - after the lightning strike - say they had been aggressive! but they were not, thankfully. So now its the Azores...did'nt know that there were so many Islands making up the group, just getting into this subject.

Weather, must mention the weather- 68deg here now, blowing a 6, had thunder storms and heavy rain during this last week.

Reflecting on all your previous emails, the one thing which comes over most strongly is the 'niceness' of the majority of the people you have met and contacted via radio, long may it continue.

*Best regards **Joe and Joyce***

Sat 17/07/2004 01:04
Dear Everybodies,

Great time here ... a most interesting group of singlehanders gradually finding each other and swapping all sorts of useful (and humorous) information ... remarkable how many friends and acquaintances we have in common ... many nationalities ...

Only had two scuba-dives so far, but both were onto undisturbed seamount-peaks, out in the Atlantic between the islands ... difficult to find the correct spot each time at first, even with GPS, but the very clear water (and my knowledge of wave patterns helped a little bit too) enabled us to place the 90HP rubber boat's anchor in the right position ...

Four divers, and one man left in the boat ... and 25 metres down the anchor-rope is an amazingly colourful and fascinating world, where I couldn't stop smiling ... there's just so much to take in ... many Moray/Conger eels, Scorpion fish, Jacks, Barracuda, etc amongst the myriads of other smaller, brightly coloured beasts ... excellent   visibility ...

Never deeper than 30 (and a bit) metres, and always constantly aware of all the training that had been drummed into me, this was the first time I'd dived in a group with anyone less experienced than me ... acutely aware that for the first time no-one was carefully keeping an eye on me ... so it was with a sense of slight pride that I was able to take my time and do it all carefully and properly ... and you see so much more by staying close to your "buddy-diver", pointing things out to each other ... very relaxing and THOROUGHLY enjoyable ... (Tashi and Chris, I can never thank you enough for opening up this world to me ... very grateful indeed to you both ... the "Doc" fishes are bigger here, but slightly less aggressive) ...

Quite a bit of current on the second dive ... but just like when sailing a small dinghy in a tide, you could use the eddies and backflows to help you get where you wanted, round a pinnacle, down a crevice, behind a rock, over a cliff edge ... exploring everywhere with minimum effort ... Yes, quite an experience for me, in the open sea ...

With Fin's artistic talent, (and my abilities with papertowels and paint REMOVER when I'd messed it up), we managed to leave our graffiti on the harbour wall, as is the custom in Horta ... it is said to be unlucky if you do NOT paint your ship's motif here ... our picture (which took two days to do, as we had to watch the first background layer of paint drying) is based on the Panic Button Club flag, which (defaced) is "Tuesday"'s Battle Flag ... but there's also a little picture of Orford castle in the corner, loosely copied from the ODSC flag ... we're hoping the outer skin of the paint has dried enough before persistent rain set in this evening ... we'll see what wreckage remains tomorrow! ...

Unusual meal out, the other evening ... beautifully prepared raw meat is brought to you (beef, pork, chicken and several varieties of fish/squid etc) ... you cook it yourself at the table, on very hot volcanic rocks which the staff keep renewing as they slowly cool down ... DELICIOUS! ... and you're sitting in the window overlooking the harbour, too ... lovely ambience ... Tot had tried it when she was here, but was sworn to secrecy so that Fin wouldn't know what she was in for ... a very pleasant gentle evening ... nice! ...

Nothing "boaty" in this one, I'm afraid, but it's a great place here for rest and recuperation ... it's not going to be easy to get back into "seagoing-mode", I suspect ...

With love from,
Fin, Tuesday'n'me.

(RECEIVED)Sun 04/07/2004 17:07

David,

You have no idea how much we love your Dear Everybodies. They must take ages to write but Gosh! They aren't 'alf appreciated, bless you! Sending you heaps of love, and hope you and Fin have a wonderful holiday.

P.S.Isn't it nice that Gill says having read the letters from you waiting at Wickham when she came back, she feels that when she returns to Holland she is having to interrupt reading an exciting book. This is exactly how much your Dear Everybodies delight every one.

Again, heaps of love, Mother.

Tue 20/07/2004 02:54

Subject: Horta(vii)

Dear Everybodies,

Imagine the nightmare scene, if you will ...

Pitch dark night, no wind, a dead engine, breakers nearby, and it's too deep to anchor ... painfully slowly the yacht, with her powerless sails slatting noisily, drifts ever closer to the blackness of razor sharp larva rocks under a cliff, showing dimly in between the white crashing waves ... no hope of rescue ... there's very little you can do except stand by to try and fend off with the spinnaker-pole when the time comes ... every wave brings you a little closer, and as you sink down in each trough in the swells your stomach tightens, anticipating the shock of impact ...

Eventually you do hit ... shocking, cracking, rending, ghastly blows to the ship which has been your only home for several years ... each crash bruises you and knocks you over as you are thrown off your feet, first one way then the other, again and again and again ... and with each wave the boat wriggles her way even further in amongst the black teeth, hammering forwards and upwards into the knife-edges on each wave-crest, then grinding heavily as she slides back down again in the troughs ...

Horrible, but it actually happened here two nights ago to Peter, an American singlehander I had met several times some days earlier ... one of the nicest people you could meet, quiet, unassuming, always friendly ... his boat was a pretty, well-cared-for, GRP, 34' American design, with a centreboard in a ballast keel, and a separate full-depth-skeg rudder ...

Amazingly, after he'd survived forty minutes of grinding and crashing, with debris floating around the boat, a light offshore breeze appeared ... with the added help of Peter pushing the rocks with the pole (now quite bent by the strain), the yacht began to bounce her way into deep water again ...

He expected her to sink, but somehow she didn't ...

Neither he nor I really understand quite how he did it, but this remarkable gentleman, (not a young man, and not in the best of health) managed to use the light airs to SAIL his ruined boat, in the dark, several miles back to Horta, where he anchored her safely at dawn ...

It's even more extraordinary, when we know now that only the upper halves of the rudder and skeg remain ... his centreboard is chewed off at the base of the keel, ... 3' of the heel of the keel is broken open, one side of it (3' x 18") missing completely ... the hull itself is seriously chewed up, but, unbelievably, still intact because of a false floor above the ballast ... the bobstay has broken, and the plank-bowsprit is smashed (a quarter of it missing).....and there is a great deal of serious structural damage inside as well ...

I've spent a long time listening to Peter, as naturally he is still in some considerable state of shock ... he cannot believe he's still alive, let alone that his ship carried him to safety ...

If you wrote a novel with this story in it, it would never be believable ... but this is what happened, here in Horta, two nights ago ...

Also, it's worth noting that "Tuesday" herself would not have survived such terrible injuries to her keel, as her own false floor doesn't run all the way to the very back end of the fin ...

It's been a very sobering experience talking to Peter ... but what a remarkable chap he is ...

My apologies that this is a somewhat sombre Email this time, but (as Jo has already said about Brazilian Whizzbangs) "when you take on Mother Nature, sometimes she bites back" ...

Stay Safe yourselves!

Love from,

Fin,T'n'me.

(RECEIVED)Wed 21/07/2004 03:04

Subject: Near disaster.....

David, dear boy,

Don't DO that to us!   We were absolutely horrified while reading the first half of Horta (VII), but at the same time, of course, very relieved to realise that you must have survived it because you were sending us an e-mail.

Poor Peter.... I suppose he'll now have to spend ages, and a lot of money, repairing his ship. Remarkable chap, as indeed are all you lot who will persist in messing about in boats in all the corners of the Earth.

Did we tell you about the parcel which they couldn't deliver because we were out shopping when they called? When we got back I rang them up and was told it would be delivered next day.   Great excitement... would it, at last, be the box of O-rings which Keith said he'd send me.... OR WAIT, surely it couldn't by any chance be your missing one from Sao Paulo.... could it?   Well, all it was was a packet of bags for the vacuum cleaner. Ah well....

Yes, thank you, we are both well... and so is Ben, who came to see us again yesterday, with Meg, before going off next morning to meet Fin at Gatwick. We feel so sorry when we think how lonely it must be for you now that Tot and Fin have both gone home.

Keep well, and keep safe.   We can't wait for the day when we hear that you are back in Orford.

Much love, and respect, etc.

Your **Daddy..**

(RECEIVED) Tue 20/07/2004 19:52

Subject: Sympathy & Horror.

David,

Turning on my flat top intending to write to you since it must be awfully lonely without Fin, especially as Charlotte was with you before Fin so you have had part of your family with you for some time, I decided to look for an EM before writing, though never expected one from you, and there was your No.VII..

My heart has nearly recovered since it seemed that YOU had had an awful BangWhizz, (and of course, it is TUESDAY!) but thank God you are safe, and also, praise be, Peter. Will you tell him we can't imagine what a nightmare he went through, nor how on earth he managed to sail back to Horta with such a damaged boat. The boat being not only his ship but his home. Like you, he is a blo--- marvel. As you say, if you wrote a novel folk would say it is too far fetched to be true.I imagine that not only Peter but you too will have ghastly dreams about it------makes me terrified to think about it. It has shaken me even more since I have been re-reading in the last day or two your telephone messages when you got the WhizzBang.

We told you that Joe has had a very bad back but Mick told me that your Dear Everybodies has had a very good effect on her since she loves to read them and was obviously extremely touched when she got your message of condolence which you asked us to give her when you rang up.She asked me to be sure to thank you and she is improving fairly rapidly. Heaps and heaps of love, **Mother.**

216

Wed 21/07/2004 00:24
   Dear Mother and Daddy,
      Ben has explained to me about the cheque you very kindly gave him, although he's very embarrassed about it and wishes he'd kept his mouth shut, poor chap! ... nevertheless we're SO grateful to you, not only for this but also for effectively supplying all the phone links when I was in a such a mess in Brazil ... it's so nice to be have that moral support from within the family, and this trip has really brought it home for me ...

   I had a WONDERFUL time while Fin was here, and once again the ship was a cold, empty and hollow box when I got back from the airport this afternoon (Fin's safely back in Sax now) .. support and cheer from other singlehanders here who understand how it feels ... But preparations are well in hand to set off towards Plymouth sometime in the next 2-3 days, hopefully ... looks like a reasonable weather window for the first few days, so I might as well use it ...

   I trust you are behaving yourselves as parents should? ...
      Deepest thanks again ... Baxoon!
         Much Love,
         Tuesday'n'me.

(RECEIVED) Wed 21/07/2004 21:01
   Dear David,
      Good to hear you and Fin are having such a fantastic time. By the way, have we missed some episode of the story? What do you mean when you say about Fin "complete with passport this time"? Had she left it behind some other time?

   We have never been to the Azores and it is lovely to imagine them through your descriptions. Philippe has no experience of volcanoes or earthquakes, but Paola has been on top of Vesuvio and Etna, which is still very active and is so high that there is a ski resort on one of the peaks. As the lava flows in rivers it eventually "cools down" and hardens on the surface whilst it still is running underneath. As the lower, more mobile, lava runs away, long tunnels are formed under the surface that can be explored by the adventurous ones. Paola has also experienced an earthquake when one struck the north-east of Italy in 1976. Despite the fact that the epicentre of the quake was a few hundred miles away from Milan some of the furniture of her 3rd floor flat moved around! People on higher floors got an even spookier experience.

   We are having the occasional Pangalactic not to loose the habit. By the way, the Pangalactics seem to be the remedy of choice for Paola's very sore shoulder/elbow. Things were actually getting better, with the help of the occasional Diclofenac Sodium (2 years out of date – courtesy of a certain Suffolk ex-Doc) when stupidly she carried a full gas bottle across town. Anyway, we are at the end of the first week of treatment and though the arm's mobility has greatly increased the pain is still very much there.
      A big kiss to Fin, Tuesday'n'you
         Love
            P & P
P.S. Philippe says it is not actually quite true that he has no experience of volcanoes and earthquakes: "I was at school with a boy called Ridgway, who suffered acute flatulence .... I need say no more".

(RECEIVED)Wed 21/07/2004 09:25
   Subject: Horta (vii)-gave me a nasty turn!
      Hello David...& Fiona too if you are still there.
   Sad story (well told) my thoughts go out to Peter, lets hope he is fit enough to continue his sailing in some way. As you may know, we have been having 'old fashioned' summer weather the type you don't remember from

your school days, but it appeared during last week end that Monday would be a fine flying day, so one of our hangar members - a Jodel owner suggested we have a day flying, we would use the Jodel with him as PIC and me side/k and visit strips not landed on before in (mainly) Norfolk ...... after a pleasant day, lets go home, the wind had got up to a gusty 12 mph at right-angles to the strip at Parham, didn't bother us, got this flying stuff cracked. The touch down was a bit fast as was the diversion to the right hand side of the runway, the removal of the right tyre and damage to the undercarriage happened quickly also, but the nose going down and tail coming up happened much slower, all this whilst surrounded by growing wheat, fortunately the cross wind then became helpful and returned the tail to the ground before we became inverted! So, no injuries, no witnesses, limp side of aircraft lifted onto a dolly and retrieved to the hangar, 3" thick concrete man hole cover replaced (if it had jumped out of the way there would have been no damage).

There you have it - complacency – 'I can do it'.. & Mother Nature - 'gotcha'!!!

Stay Careful   best regards

Joe

Wed 21/07/2004 22:57
  Subject: Gulp!
    Dear J'n'J,

Bloody hell, that was nearly a nasty one! ... YOU are the one living close to the edge, not me! ... Well done, salvaging both occupants and aircraft ... I bet it wouldn't have happened in a Streak/Shadow though, what d'yer think? ... food for thought ...

This place is fast emptying of boats ... what do they know that they haven't told me? ... whilst in Brazil I was advised to get out of the Azores by August 1st, or I'd regret it, so planning to leave in the next few days ... no more long trips of settled weather and sunshine though ... this could be a WET journey ... hope not! ...

Stay Well, shiny side up & dirty side down, preferably with the full complement of legs and undercart ...

Baxoon!

  T'n'me.

Wed 21/07/2004 22:57
  Subject: ?Leaving Horta soon?
    Dear Everybodies,

Sadly, Fin had to fly home yesterday to return to work (otherwise she can't afford me) ... once again the ship felt empty and cold for the first 24 hours, but now I'm busy preparing to set sail again it's not quite so bad ...

I've had a wonderful time here, and I'd like to return sometime to explore some more of this group of nine islands ... one thing I've enjoyed on this trip so far has been comparing and contrasting all the islands ... Culatra(Portugal), Porto Santo, Madeira, Graciosa, Lanzarote, Sao Vincenti(Cap Verdes), Itaparica, St.Helena, and now Faial(Azores) ... each is very different from the others ...

Although on paper it may seem a simple journey back to England from here, I have the usual pre-voyage concerns and worries, but they're much more in perspective these days ... I still think the optimum time to spend in any one place is about one week, then you never get out of seagoing-mode ...

I'll not sail tonight, but I am considering possibly doing so tomorrow ... the ship is all set, checks/repairs/improvements done, fresh fruit'n'veg stowed, fresh-water tanks full (with CLEAN water this time!) etc etc ... favourable winds today, but I hadn't finished getting ready (actually it's started raining heavily anyway, with lousy visibility, cold dark and grey, so I'm not in the right mood to be adventurous at the moment anyway) ...

Anticipating 1300-1400 miles to Plymouth, depending on the wind direction and strength, so expecting about 2-3 weeks, hopefully less ...we will see ...

Stay Well!

With love from,

Tuesday'n'me.

(RECEIVED) Thu 22/07/2004 01:00

Hi Daddy,

Glad you had a nice time with Mummy. Hope the boat isn't tooo lonely without her (or me of course!) around. Mind you, not long til you're back here in the UK anyway. Hope the passage goes well. Thinking of you, as always. Stay safe. And hope to see you in the next few weeks. When you get to Angleterre let me know cos if free will come down to see you on the south coast.

Hope the fishing floats are kind to you & Tuesday.

Loads of Love

Tot xx.....

Wed 21/07/2004 00:24

Dear Yvan, Christina, Thais and Jeremie,

Greetings again!

Had a wonderful time here in Horta, first with Tot (my elder daughter, you remember?) and then two weeks with Fin (The "Boss") ... Fin and I had a really gentle "mellow" two weeks, just like a second honeymoon, so the 9 month separation has done no harm, so far! ... it remains to be seen how we re-adapt to my returning home to England, but I'll let you know (Yvan, your advice is still ringing clearly in my ears!) ...

Planning to sail from Horta in the next 2 or 3 days, 1400 miles towards Plymouth, and then eastwards through The Straits of Dover and up to my home-port on the east coast ... Probably will take an old and trustworthy friend as crew through the actual Straits, as there are so many ships, fishing-boats and yachts there, going in all sorts of directions ...

I do hope all continues well for you, and I often think back with pleasure on the good times you gave me on Itiparica ... I haven't forgotten the pictures of your house and I will send them when I get home ...

Stay Well!, (and best wishes to Tinho when you see him),

Fondest wishes,

"Tuesday" and DocDavid.

(RECEIVED) Mon 26/07/2004 20:35

Hi, doc, we are all going on, the house is almost ready, I am sure you can't imagine how nice she is... School is alwrite and every body is quite happy.

Best wishes for your trip home and congradulations for the succesfull final of your adventure, hopping that it will go on...

Your friends

Yvan, Cristina, Jeremie and Thais

Fri 23/07/2004 23:27

Subject: Still here in Horta

Dear Everybodies,

Good news! ... Peter's boat is to be repaired, and NOT written off ... work on her has started already ...and Peter himself is looking and sounding much more confident now ...

It's not just me who wimped out of leaving here yesterday (Thursday 22nd)... all the other boats which had also planned to sail from Horta around the same time have stayed in harbour, as we've had strong, cold winds from the north, with heavy rain and poor visibility ... I think things may improve in the next 48/72 hours, so we're all monitoring the situation, but I do hope it's not going to be an uphill beat all the way to England ...

It's most interesting to find we're each using different weather information sources, and to compare the variations between them ... the points where the predictions overlap each other would appear to be the most reliable forecasts ...

HF radio conditions here in the harbour have been appalling all month, with gross electrical interference across the whole spectrum wiping out the signals on virtually every day... it will be nice to be able to hear everyone on the Nets once more... I'm looking forward to it...

I've made several new friends here, and I've learnt a lot of clever mechanical wheezes and bodges ... (for example, I didn't know that a useful method of freeing machinery where stainless-steel and aluminium-alloy have corroded together is to soak them in BLEACH ... the clever bit is that you chuck a piece of aluminium foil (cooking foil?) into the mix to make the chemistry work) ...

It's now late on Friday, 23rd. ... Tuesday'n'me are already cleared with Customs, Harbour Authorities, Police, etc to leave early in the morning, Saturday ... hopefully around dawn it will be calmer, and make manoeuvring out of this berth a bit easier ...

The wind is still adverse, and the local weather is still pretty changeable, but we're now ready to go for another little sail again ... it may well be that this trip will be a harder and wetter one, as conditions will be much more unsettled, and colder, as we move northwards, but we shall see ...

Please don't forget that NO NEWS is GOOD NEWS ... but I will do my very best to stay in touch when I can ...

Stay Safe and Well yourselves too ...

Love from,
Tuesday'n'me

(RECEIVED)Wed 21/07/2004 18:41

David,

Fair winds and a good view of the Lizard!
Amazing.
Looking forward to catching up in person over the winter.
Richard.

(RECEIVED) Thu 22/07/2004 22:15

Hello sailor

Bumped into Fin in usual place Somerfields, so got all the updates including the info on the pony tail. thought real sailors had pigtails !!!

We have had a nice couple of days here but prior to that masses of heavy rain and storms...had a quick shower this evening but didnt amount to much.

They are selling off the Suffolk navy (HMS Grafton I think its called) so if you need somthing bigger for next time?.

Ok take care see you soon
John

(RECEIVED) 20/7/04 19:20

A Rival for Alliz Motte?

I hope things are going well for you and that you have enjoyed the Azores. I was reading the other day that conditions can be a little unpredictable despite the 'high'. Europe has been experiencing a very unsettled weather pattern this summer though I have been fortunate with my own sailing excursions.

I decided not to pursue Matador (she sold last week) and my aspirations are now set on another Rival 41. A centre cockpit this time. She seems to be in much better condition, (weekend sailing in Chesaspeake Bay for the last 17 years and the loving attention of a besotted owner), she had an epoxy job last year and has a 65HP Yanmar with 'only' 2000nm on the clock. She has an Aries and at current rates the asking price is very reasonable.

We are now off family sailing on Aliz Motte in South Brittany followed for me by a delivery trip home returning in mid-August. By then I hope to have an inbox full of digital pictures. It looks very promising. The only hitch is the VAT, but even so! I still have moments of hesitation about the sail area to displacement ratio but all boats are a compromise (I've spoken to two friends who have chartered both 38's and 41's and each reckoned the 38 sailed better). I'd be happy if she were a 38 but the a 38 owner I said this to said he would trade for the extra storage (he was living aboard in Ipswich wet dock in winter at the time!).

The long and the short of it is that you need to get back for mid-August so that you can help me through this. (If you don't mind!).

> *Have a great trip back.*
>> *Love to Tuesday and you.*
>>> **Eric**

Chapter 11

Leaving the Azores

Sat 24/07/2004 20:40
    Subject: Horta delay...
       Dear Everybodies,

Delayed here for yet another 24 hours ...

There's a moderate but small "Low" messing things up, drifting around rather aimlessly just to the east of Horta (although the forecasters insist it's to the north) ...I felt like a complete wimp, but this morning visibility was less than 1 mile in persistent heavy rain, with a cold and strong North-East wind (dead on the nose again!) ... it would have been frankly stupid to sail out amongst these islands, solo, in such conditions, when it wasn't essential to do so, and I have been considerably cheered by friends here saying the same thing ...

The Harbour Authorities say they don't want to know about the extra day ... nor do Customs ... how refreshingly simple and practical! ...

So we'll have another look, at around dawn tomorrow (Sunday) ... maybe head south-about round Pico Island, taking the opportunity to pass through THE classical whale-sighting area of the Azores ...

    Take Care!

       Tuesday'n'me.

(RECEIVED) Sat 24/07/2004 12:25
    Subject: Godspeed
       Hi there,

So good to hear that your brain waves are somewhat back in sync enough to realize that you should wait for fair weather to start your last leg.

What will you do when you get back to land? We do hope to see you somewhere on the big blue one day.

Good luck and safe sailing to home. It will be a bittersweet moment and we will be with you in the wind and the waves, singing with the rigging and smiling in the sun.

    Godspeed our friend.

      *Love, **Capt. Ron & Bonnie***

(RECEIVED) Thu 29/07/2004 02:49
    Dear Ron'n'Bonnie,

It's no use your sending fond farewell messages ... you don't get rid of me so easily! ... you've got to suffer a bit longer yet, I'm afraid! ...

Yeah, all is well here, thank you ... keen to get home again now, planning to do a lot more FLAT-water sailing before the season ends in late November ... maybe in little boats too, I hope ...

During the winter refit I shall be trying to sort my thoughts, sifting memories, finding out what I want to do in the future ... Next year Tuesday'n'me are almost certainly heading off up into the Baltic for a few months (before it sets solid again for the following winter) ... After that, who knows? ... I'd love to go back to Brazil again, but as I left that country illegally it might be a bit awkward ...

And sometime I'd like to sail right round Britain and Ireland, s-l-o-w-l-y ...

This coming November Fin and I will be flying to Lanzarote to do some more diving there ... Chris'n'Tashi

222

have set up their own diving school in the building at the entrance to the boat park in Rubicon where Sam'n'Lee were working on their "dropped" boat, (you remember?} ...they've asked us both back there, and I'm keen to get more skills towards being a Rescue Diver ... Tashi won't be diving as (great news) she's "heavily married" and "in the pudding club", baby girl due in December ...

Meantime, listen to the Windsong, and wonder at the Stars ... or you might even hear me still struggling to master the harmonica, (on those occasions when the slider on it hasn't grabbed hold of my moustache again in mid symphony ... makes the eyes water as it clings on your face like a vicious rodent!) ...

I'm still determined to find a set of Caribbean dominoes when I get home ... I want to introduce it to the locals ... (that'll fox them! ... too many dots, you see ...)

Lovely to hear from you! ... stay in touch ... and Stay Well!
        Tuesday and the Doc.

(RECEIVED) Sat 24/07/2004 22:19
        Subject: Common Sense.
        David,
        It would be madness to set sail when the weather is so unsettled and changeable. Even the weather forecast we had here said there was a large black cloud in mid Atlantic heading our way so I imagine it is near you. Not nice! Fin and Ellen came round this evening and Ellen said she had had your text message this morning; and later, I was talking to Rosalie who told me Gerald had also received it to say you were not going yet.

        From the map I imagine it is more than a bit tricky to get out of all the islands even in good weather, so tell Tuesday to refuse to budge until conditions are perfect. It must be frustrating for you but at least you are safe tonight (though not, alas! in Abraham's Bosom near Orford. Daddy and I, and umpteen other folk, are full of admiration for your guts, good humour, and incredible manual dexterity in mending and making things.

        I do so wish my father were alive, he would be full of praise for all you have achieved. I'm just off to bed and looked for a last time at my flat top and there was your EM only just sent. Hope you, and I, have a peaceful sleep, and don't be in too much hurry to set sail.

        Heaps and heaps of love,
                *from **Mother**. Bon Voyage!!!*

(RECEIVED) Sun 25/07/2004 01:17
        So glad that you are still where ever you are.
        Be careful , Dany is crossing the channel next week to go to Dover, spending the night in a youth hostel in Dover and then going on to Holyhead to arrive in Dublin beginning of August for the European Junior 420 Championship. Please don't run over him ....

        How on earth can you adapt to cold winds and water and how are you going back to England without your smelly wellies ....? Knew that you had gone off your rocker leaving in the first place but never even imagined that you would be mad enough to come back ....

        Have a nice trip, give a little wave to Britanny as you go past .... fell in love with the place ....must go back some time ....

                Enjoy your trip!
                        Heh ho! It's back to sea you go !!!!
                                Mary

(RECEIVED) Wed 28/07/2004 13:34
Dear David,

We have no doubt your decision to leave Horta will be taken by you with the greatest of care, you are approaching the closing stages of your incredible journey and we know you will not drop your guard.

Once again take the greatest of care and God bless.

Love **Bob & Brenda.**

Thu 29/07/2004 02:46
Dear Everybodies,

Fin had brought with her (courtesy of the Great and Good Dr.PMWM) powerful magical poisons to fix the damaged elbow ... wonderful result after several days, so that I can now pull a rope with BOTH hands ... no longer (at times) sailing literally singlehanded ... thank you both for making a significant improvement to the day to day running of "Tuesday" ...

Before setting sail again, I noted that one of the seamounts I'd been diving to was labelled as "reported 1980", with no name attached, on the large scale Admiralty chart of the area ... having actually FELT how hard and solid (and pointed) it was, and measured the depth quite accurately with my wrist depth gauge, I will now look on vague "reported" shoals with a great deal more respect!

"Tuesday" left Horta very quietly, just as the sun came up out of the sea, on Sunday 25th July ... it took an uncomfortable 12 hours to find my sealegs again, but this was pleasantly less time than expected ...

Then three days of much better progress than anticipated, in good (if a bit lumpy) conditions, pretty well exactly on the Great Circle route towards England ... goosewinged with a small genoa, staysail and single-reefed mainsail, surging down the seas like the fruit-carrying schooners used to many years ago ...

A few more sperm-whale-spouts seen, (but not the actual animals themselves unfortunately) ... they're a lot easier to spot now that I know what I'm looking for, but even then I thought the first one was a ship on the horizon until it de-materialised in the wind ...

Got a bit overtired at one point ... too many ships around, together with showers and squalls requiring extra deckwork ... wasn't helped by two French yachts on a parallel course to ours coming within 2 miles, and I was somewhat disappointed that neither of them showed on radar ... it meant I couldn't rest till they'd cleared off out of our "patch", as I could only monitor them visually ...

Today has been "busy", with a fast moving and aggressive cold front going through, but now we're in more settled airs the sea has flattened out nicely ... tonight we're closehauled on the port tack, just about able to lay the course, sliding quietly and peacefully along under the moon ... the nasty wet wind'n'rain clouds are scurrying off towards the leeward horizon, while the remnant of yesterday's 3 metre swell from the west still lifts the transom to help us on our way ... not bad, not bad at all now ...

But my goodness how COLD it feels! ... I try to disbelieve the cabin thermometer which insists it's summertime still ... acCLIMATisation seems a very appropriate word! ...

Nearly half way to Plymouth now ... Home Soon, I hope...

Love from,
Tuesday'n'me.

(RECEIVED) Sun 01/08/2004 15:17
Subject: Better Weather!
David,

Turned on flat-top just in case there was a ShipTrak up-date (there wasn/t, too early) but to our great joy there was an email from you only sent a very short time ago. I read out your news about better weather than when you spoke to us last night, and long may it continue if it is 100% what is needed to get you back quickly!

Daddy tells me to give you his love and come home soon. It is wonderful that you can now measure distances in hundreds instead of thousands and we have your position and Plymouth on the same map.

Heaps and heaps of love,

Mother.

Sun 01/08/2004 11:06

Subject: Alien life-forms ... (marine)

Dear Everybodies,

Grey, gloomy, drizzly, dull and dismal ... overcast and cold ... often heavy rain ... three days of it ... everything aboard is slightly damp due to the temperature change, though the triple skinned cabin walls and ceiling remain dry ... Why on earth would anyone want to live in such a climate? ... in my own case, it's because the pull towards my family is greater than the pull to the Tropics, but as Jack said yesterday, "Welcome to the Northern climate!" ... (Hmm, YOU'RE welcome to it!) ...

For those three days the wind was dead on the nose ... the first was in light airs with a bit of motor-sailing (not my usual style, so I must have been pretty fed up!) ... then two separate 8 hour sessions of 30 knot winds for a day, the tops of the crests being torn off ... crashing to windward, when like a lemon I reckon I must have sat under a small local cold-front moving at the same speed as me ... should have stopped and let it pass, I think ...

Then yesterday it was back to a light frustrating breeze again, still from exactly the wrong direction ... (I must have done something wicked as a child, I think!) ...

But last night, only two hours earlier than Gerard's forecast predicted (remarkably accurate ... many thanks!), came a welcome southeast wind ... the clearer skies revealed low cloud whipping across the face of the moon, so that now we're scampering along at 7 knots, heading north of the direct track to anticipate northerly winds later ... still reefed down a bit for comfort and peace of mind, with about 550 miles to go to Plymouth ... we'll use this wind while it lasts ...

The radio maritime/mobile nets are a great comfort when things are "low" on board ... good forecasts, good company, always reassuring and fun ... nice to talk to my brother-in-law most days, to hear the family news etc ...

It means being able to keep in contact with other boats too ... like "Topas" whom I'd met in Portugal over a year ago, "Kite" whom I spent much time talking to in Horta, "Puddleduck" who was my neighbour in Horta where we were helping fit her new selfsteering gear, etc ...("Puddleduck" is 1-2 days ahead of me at present, on her way to the Isle of Man) ... I don't feel alone out here at all! ...

Why "alien life-forms"? ... well, for the last 24 hours the sea has revealed lots of a strange beast/plant which looks like an egg (or a pale apple) with 3-5 limbs like soft barnacles arranged round the edge ... it's probably as common as muck, but I've never noticed them before ... I haven't captured one yet in case it doesn't like humans ... maybe I'll summon up the courage later ...

For all Star-Trek fans, "It's Life, Jim, but not as we know it..." ...

Meantime, please don't use up all the good weather in the UK ... wait until I get back ...

Stay Well!

with love from,

Tuesday'n'me.

Sat 07/08/2004 11:32
> **Subject: Nearly there ...**
>> **Dear Everybodies,**

After the adverse winds for three days it was a relief to be heading in the right direction with "downwind sails" pulling well, even though it was still raining, wet, and cold ... still rolling around a bit in the swells, but a softer, mile-eating pace ...

Two close encounters with ships, one of them in a potentially very nasty set of circumstances ... (early morning, heavy rain partially blinding the radar and reducing visibility to considerably less than 2 miles ... my course and heading meaning that the radar reflector was partially screened by the mast ... just after dawn when the light was still poor, etc) ... the problem was that obviously he hadn't seen me, but I couldn't alter course until I was sure that it wouldn't conflict with any collision avoidance action he might take at the last minute ... remember that because of the Whizzbang I still have no main VHF transmit ability, so I used a handheld 5 watt radio to inform him when I made a 90 degree course change, to pass down his starboard side, with his agreement? ...

Poor chap (the ship's watchkeeper), he was as shaken as I was ... but we had a pleasant mutually reassuring chat for a couple of minutes as he hared by, about 500 yards away ... clearly a professional seaman, from the conversation we had ... he commented that I hadn't appeared on his radar screen until I did the violent course change, thus showing him the reflector clear from the mast ... we shared views on the fallibility of radar reflectors on yachts ...

But the other ship which I spoke to with the handheld radio said Tuesday'n'me were radar-visible at 7 miles, so there's a lot more to this radar reflector business than at first sight ...

There is a very clear demarcation line between the deep waters of the Atlantic and the shallower seas of the Continental Shelf ... there are up-currents swirls in the water, causing a change in the wave patterns, with an occasional, irregular, and considerably larger, lump of sea ... the result is there's more "mixing" of the water, and more nutrients available for fish ...

So the continental edge is marked by packs of dolphins (who take delight in racing over to the boat and then showing off to her ... MAGIC!), and many fishing boats charging about hither and dither... and also a warship/fishery-protection-vessel which insisted on altering course to come a little too close for comfort, and then proceeded to shadow me at about 5 miles range ... all this meant that I couldn't get much rest for a couple of days, hoping for a patch of clear water ...

Disappointed not to see any more whales though ...

One unexpected hazard I hadn't previously considered was due to the seas which had been regularly dousing the ship's upperworks ... they carried with them some of these MILLIONS of baby Portuguese-Men-of-War, so that it was potentially dangerous to move around the deck with exposed skin ... when they die they leave a vivid but elegant deep blue stain ... one of them clearly got flung up into the mainsail, up by the second reef level, before it died ... the mark it has left in the sail is another of Tuesday's honourable battle-scars, admittedly a somewhat unusual one! ...

Managed to capture and inspect one of those "aliens" yesterday ... it's a colony of big fat healthy goose-barnacles (each about 3" long) with their roots deeply embedded in a central float looking like a type of sponge ... but touch any one of the 5 or more barnacles, however lightly, and all the others instantly respond ... there must be a direct neural connection between them all ... intriguing to see what experiments Mother Nature has tried ...

Must be getting closer to England now ... I can now j-u-s-t hear the BBC on longwave ... useful for forecasts ... More soon!
> **Tuesday'n'me.**

(RECEIVED) Sat 07/08/2004 16:14

Dear Bill,

Thank you for forwarding the account of David's latest adventure. He now sems to be making splendid progress and judging by today's map position it looks as if he is now only days - two perhaps ? - from reaching Plymouth. I don't know how long it will then take him to sail round to Orford but what a happy and triumphant homecoming that will be. You and Alex must be feeling very proud and, I guess, more than a little relieved ! I wish one could still send greetings telegrams so that I could send one c/o the Harbourmaster at Plymouth. At an appropriate moment, do give him a welcome back and wrmest congratulations from Paul and me. And so many thanks for sending on reports of his voyage.

Teresa

Sat 07/08/2004 11:33

Subject: Plymouth again.

Dear Everybodies,

Exactly one year, one month, and one day after leaving here, we're back again ... 14,600 miles have passed the keel between-times ... but it's a well known fact that The Almighty does not count those days actually spent at sea, so I myself am only about 5 months older ...

The last night (5-6/8/04) at sea (as expected) was murder, with ships, fishing boats, invisible yachts, and vaguely determined tidal currents leaving no room for sleep ... none at all ...and then it started to drizzle in the cold wind, with rotten visibility for a few hours as a small front went through ... thank heavens for cups of tea and bars of chocolate ... (a LOT of chocolate!) ...

England showed up where I last left it ... Lands End and The Lizard lighthouse ... a strangely moving and emotional moment ... I wondered how I would react, and now I know ...

Dawdled for a few hours with a backed staysail to slow her down a bit, to make an easy approach to Plymouth in the clearer air behind the drizzly weatherfront ...

1415 miles from Horta in 12 days ...

Nice cheery welcome on the fuel pontoon (my first stop, as it's an easier berth to come alongside when I'm a bit out of practice at this close-in stuff) ... equally pleasant Dockmaster, not in the least bit phased by my mentioning that for the same cost as one day here I had a WEEK in Horta and more than a MONTH in Brazil, with the same facilities ... chuckles all round! ...

The Customs said to the Dockmaster over the radio " Does he LOOK British?" ... "OK then, just see his Passport is reasonable, and that'll do.." ... the Dockmaster says that's the very first time he's ever been asked to be a deputy Customs and Immigration Officer ... he enjoyed it! ...

Lovely warm welcome from Mike and Julie from Pantaenius ... when I said how worried I had been when we last met a year ago, Mike said, " Huh! Not half as worried as I had been when I realised that we'd agreed to insure you!" ...

Lounging on deck chatting in the evening sunshine ... WONDERFUL tasting fish'n'chips in the dark, sitting on the seawall by the Mayflower Steps, just where I'd eaten The Last Supper a year last July ...

And everyone speaks ENGLISH! ...

Mind you, they all drive on the wrong side of the road, which is very confusing ...

I've spoken face-to-face with Peter and Andy of the chandlery, Plymouth (who kindly organised the Vanishing Brazilian Package), and then we went together to shake the Shipping Agent warmly by the throat ... We've come up with a dirty tricks plan to try to outsmart the company's complacency, mainly by uniting the primary shipping agent, the chandler, and Tuesday against them, thus preventing their "divide-and-confuse" policy ... we will see what happens now, since very little has been happening so far ...

227

Note that I can deliver a letter from St.Helena, under SAIL, quicker than the "professional" Express Delivery service to Brazil...

A little rest and recuperation ... some fresh bread ... clothes washing ... looking forward to a visit from Ju and John today ... waiting for some pooey weather to go through ... then who knows, maybe a 14,500 mile lap-of-honour? ...

Still another 500 miles or so to do before we're home, but absolutely no rush now ...

Stay Well, ... and prepare yourselves for the most boring home-video you could imagine ... ("that's a wave ... ooh look, there's another one" ...) ... 18+ HOURS of it ... I recommend you go into hiding, or leave the country, now ...

> Much Love
> **Tuesday'n'me.**

Tue 10/08/2004 19:11

> **Dear Nick,**

Arrived safely in Plymouth 6th Aug 04 ... 1415 miles from Horta in 12 days (three of those days were headwinds up to 30+ knots) ...

Now sitting out bad weather for a few days, before heading east and up to home, 20 miles north of Harwich on the East Coast ...

> Keep in touch ...
> Stay safe!
> **Tuesday'n'the Doc.**

(RECEIVED)10/8/04 1911

Stop complaining.. If it was easy everybody would be doing it.."PARABENS"...Brazilian for "Congratulations" if you have forgotten..Nice one my old mucker..God Bless..See UUUUU soon..Send me a tele no..God Bless..

> **NICK...**
> *See you soon!*

(RECEIVED) Wed 04/08/2004 21:49

> *Dear David*
> *I may be a few hours to early but*
> ## WELCOME HOME!

I know it's not Suffolk but at least it's England and you haven't got far to go to be here, but probably more traffic in this bit than most of the other. Have a good rest in Plymouth and tackle the channel with new strength, looking forward to seeing you again, and to hear more of your adventure, some of which I would have loved but most I would have been terrified of. I hope that now you are so near home you will not have any problems, like those for which I have shed some tears for you, and for your friend Peter, whom I hope is OK now, think of all the friends you had before you left and how many you have now, they have treblrubled in number I'm sure, but all those you have meet have benefited for your Knowledge and experience, they will remember you with great affection and pleasure. My spelling leaves a lot to be desired and the spell check doesn't understand so you will have to guess what I mean.

> *Lots of Love*
> *From **Joyce and Himself.***

Sun 08/08/2004 18:06

Dear J'n'J,

Thanks so much for the Email welcoming T'n'me back to the UK ... still can't believe we're really here, as the sleep pattern I adopted at sea meant I dreamed a lot (and I mean a LOT) so at times it was easy to believe it was ALL a dream ... confusing for a young man, it is ...

Nasty gale coming ... staying put for as long as is necessary ...

See you soon ... and remember that the bit of the aeroplane with the wheels on it is the bit 'sposed to stay closest to the ground ...

... unless it's a Zlin or a Pitts or something, of course ...

> Love,
> **T'n'me.**

(RECEIVED) Thu 05/08/2004 20:43

Subject: I shall close my hymne book

Welcome to the land where eveywhere is wet smelly sticky chilly which reminds me , you'd better quickly run and buy some wellys cause otherwise people won't know who you are at Orford . You put them on your FEET remember, that's why there are two of them.

Dany's sailing in Dublin bay , says that they've just broken a record , had a summer that's lasted four days, been fairly nice weather .... he thinks that's terribly funny .....learning bits of Italien apparently cos they've spent two days training with the Italien team and some of them are female. There was me thinking naively that he could at long last practice his English ......

Hope you're getting used to the climate , now you know why I've been living in Switzerland for 30 years , it may be the northern hemisphere but at least it's warmer and drier .

See you some time , I suppose I should come over to England but there is so much going on here........

> *Yours never on your nelly or anywhere else*
> *MARY*

(RECEIVED) Fri 06/08/2004 02:42

Subject: Welcome home!

David, dear boy,

My, my! I didn't much like the business with that ship... where you seem to have "Seen them both!".... (but fortunately did not go between).

So a big WELCOME BACK HOME! I imagine that you have somewhat mixed feelings... the climate is not so nice... the big adventure is over... you will not be sleeping on your beloved ship (Bless her... she's taken our son half way round the world and brought him safely back)... you will come back to all the hassle, traffic problems, appalling government and hooliganism which is England; at least I think it's still called England. BUT, on the other hand, you will be reunited with your family and that is the big plus which will cancel all these things completely out.

Well done. You have achieved much more than you will probably ever admit. We are incredibly proud of you.

See you soon.

> **Daddy and Mother.**

(RECEIVED) Sat 07/08/2004 00:56

Subject: Welcome back to England

We're glad you got back here ok (i.e. in one piece and alive). I saw your parents earlier and I think it's fair to say that Gran was pleased/relieved (i.e. very happy).

I just wanted to let you know that no one will be here tomorrow (except the dog) so if you phone you'll only get the answer phone. It's nothing personal though (we haven't really all upped and left now that you are back!), I'm playing cricket and Fin/Ellen are going on a Surgery day out to Ipswich having a meal onboard a boat on the Orwell (I don't know where and what on, sorry).

Granddaddy mentioned earlier that you might need a chart of the Orford Haven but I haven't been able to find one yet.

It doesn't look like you'll be getting anywhere for a while after Sunday, judging by the weather... Welcome back to England!

Take it easy,

Ben

Mon 09/08/2004 10:13

Subject: Parked in Plymouth

Dear Ben,

Can't thank you enough for all your industry ... WELL DONE! ...

Ju drove down to Plymouth and stayed on the ship for 24 hours ... great fun going round the Aquarium, the shops, the docks, etc ... had a bit of a spending and eating spree, (like I bought two of those clockwork things you hold in your palm when you shake hands with people ... gives them a bit of a buzz ... I'm hoping it will give the lightning story a bit of a pep-up when I tell it!) ... we ate far too much fish'n'chips, but it's delicious here! ... She's gone back to Winthing Basswotsit now, which is a pity ...

Really looking forward to seeing you soon ... meantime I'm absolutely knackered now the adrenalin's wearing off ... quite happy to sit here in the rain and wind for a few days and read a book, even if it's costing a fortune in marina fees ...

Take care of yourself,

Much Love,

Dad.

(RECEIVED) Sat 07/08/2004 14:41

Hallo dear David,

Thank you so much for the last two E-mails, and thank you for all of the others, that now reside in the mailbox under the name of "David + Tuesday".

This is mainly to tell you that poor Gerard is now busy repairing damage from lightning that has destroyed a lot of his electronics, as well as in the neighbourhood! And he said his first thought was of David!

I hope you still know how to sleep in a bed that does not move.......

88 – Trudi

(RECEIVED) Sat 07/08/2004 16:36

Subject: Hi Plymouth.

Glad to you are back -thus far- safe and well (the flights not over until the aircraft is in the hangar) David Cook sends his best wishes.

O/K now come clean, you've 'bugged' everyones house haven't you, would we not look foreward to 18 and

230

a bit hours of your video? One horrid person suggested we all get together and hire a hall so that the video could be shown once, but a far nicer person remarked that this would not be fair to you, as you would have maximum enjoyment showing the pictures several times----Joyce and me are looking foreward to seeing the films, so there!

We were afraid that your arrivall in the UK could have been a bit of an anticlimax, however, your latest email seems to suggest the whole thing is still a big adventure....have you used all your emotions yet, or, I bet you have used more of them since retiring than you did in your last year at work. This makes me wonder, how many emotions are there?

We have taken our lugger to Orford on two trips, on each occasion stopping at the first large buoy - Aldeburgh end - is this 'Tuesday's' mooring? do hope we haven't dragged it!

'Thank you' for the entertaining emails, still more to come we hope.

Best regards *J&J*

(RECEIVED) Sat 07/08/2004 19:59

David,

Just got both your EMs and read them to Daddy who is sitting with me at the table. They are WONDERFUL! Not just for the news and vivid accounts they contain but also knowing you are at least in England and we could almost come to you by train--plus a bit of swimming. This time next week you may even be in this room (the light thing in the kitchen has gone wonky). Heaps and heaps of love from Daddy and me to our incredibly brave and courageous son..

(RECEIVED) Sat 07/08/2004 23:22

Wow David, what a trip you've had. I hope you get Tuesday and it's equipment back in order with little difficulty. Gerard, you and David seem to be a favorite target for lightning. **Jack.**

Sunday 8/9/2004 0613:

Dear Trudi,

As a result of your Email, and the graciousness of the gods of propagation, I had a nice clear chat with Gerard last night, on 14.2975 MHz, to commiserate about the lightning ... poor chap, it's all very sad ... but at least it can honestly by labelled "an act of God", so one's conscience is clear ...

Still here in Plymouth awaiting good weather and a colleague to help through the Dover Straits ... horrified by how many people remember me here, by name, from last year, but delighted by how pleasant they are ...

Fin's gorgeous sister came to stay on board for 24 hours so we could explore shops, museums, the Aquarium etc in the strong wind and heavy rain ... nice! ...

Meantime starting to replace the missing electronics (at additional expense though) ...

Trudi, any news of Mark and Paula, and the two young children, on "Kite", GM0LNT/mm ? ... they may have left Horta in time to run smack into force 8,9 in Romeo or Sole ... they're totally competent, but I still worry a bit for them ...

I will continue to monitor the Nets as much as local QRN allows ....Thanks again for all you do ... I'll be in touch (hopefully by radio) soon ...

David and Tuesday.

RECEIVED) Mon 09/08/2004 19:34
   Subject: R & R in Plymouth
      Hallo David,
   Sorry - I did not realize you had not actually reached home, I thought Plymouth was the end of your line. But I am glad you will have help for the Channel trip.
   There was no Transatlantic Net from this end today, we had a tropical wave and a thunder storm, also the power went off and it bucketed, so I left everything disconnected!
   But yesterday and the day before we called Mark and heard nothing, so I don't know whether they are underway yet.
   I have just been talking to Jack and Gerard on the Italian Net, which also was a non-event!
            Take care, best wishes from **Trudi.**

Tue 10/08/2004 23:38
   For info only, no action required ..
   Just to confirm that the yacht "Kite" with GM0LNT/mm (Mark, Paula and the two children) is today (Tuesday 10th Aug) still sitting safely in Horta awaiting better weather before heading out to Scotland ... I spoke to Mark by radio today (with a relay) ...
   Sorry I was fussing unnecessarily ...
   And it's a pity these marinas breed so much QRN ... I can hear very little at all on the Nets while here in Plymouth ...
      Warmest Wishes!
      David.

(RECEIVED) Tue 10/08/2004 01:56
   Hi David,
   CONGRATULATIONS ON YOUR SAIING ACHIEVMENT .... DOWN AND UP THE ATLANTIC!
   Nice to hear all is fine and your arrival was safe....great!
   I did check in for you on 21.400khz Fri pm but Trudi said you had already arrived early that morning so.... Anyway, hope you have a nice break and will mail you soon.
      Regards from
         Barrie, Val & Shane *who also send their best wishes.*

(RECEIVED)Tue 10/08/2004 15:56
   Subject: Free Spirit
      Hi Doc,
   Wonderful to hear from you and know your back across the pond. You have earned you right to passage. What a trip and you did it your way. Will you be able to go back and forget long passages or do you want to? Will you be able to put around in your area and be content? These are some of the thoughts I have about going back. One reason I did not go back this year.
   Marsha and I are doing great here in the DM. Everything is inexpensive here and there is no tourism in this part of the DM. The people are honest hard working people. Did not find this in the other islands in the Caribbean. We plan to see more if this country while we are here. The transportation system is very inexpensive here if you don't mind riding with someone on your lap or hanging on the side of the door way while it is open. You would love it here.
   When you arrive back home and if you get a wild hair up your A__ please come over for a visit and bring

Fin. We could find a good place for you to stay. Because when we get back to the States and settle in, we want to come to England for a visit and guess where we want to come???

  Take care Doc and give your family our regards.

   Allen and Marsha

Wed 11/08/2004 12:43

  Subject: Future Plans? ... hmm ...

   Dear Allen'n'Marsha,

Lovely to hear from you again, and all your news ... sounds like a good place you've landed in ... Well Done! ... I'm already envious ...

I still have another 500 miles to do, through one of the busiest waterways in the world, so I'm certainly not home yet ... but I'm resting here in Plymouth for a few days first ...

"Tuesday'n'me"s future? ... Well, I will have a lot of thinking to do this winter to decide what I want to do ... long ago I'd already planned to sail up into the Baltic next summer ... Finland etc ... Then I'd like to do Round Britain and Ireland s-l-o-w-l-y sometime ... One thing I'm sure of, I do NOT want to do a circumnavigation ... I never had that ambition at all ... Cape Horn yes, but not the Pacific, thank you! ... Who knows? ... but I'll let you know what's cooking anyway ...

Keep in touch, please ... if you're ever in England, it is a part of this country's immigration regulations that you HAVE to give us a telephone call, however brief ..

   Stay Well yourselves!

   Tuesday'n'the doc.

(RECEIVED) Thu 05/08/2004 18:51

  Dear David,

Hopefully you are in the UK by now, relatively cold and wet but able to buy all the Marmite and Branston pickle – not to mention ginger biscuits – you may wish to, whilst we are still here in the winter sun (26ºC today) with the mango juice and the pangalactics.

We know what you mean by acclimatisation: we have been sleeping under a heavy duty British duvet since the night temperature has on occasion reached something like 19ºC.

We shall be leaving Paraty in a couple of weeks and we are slaving around the boat to make sure she will be OK once we get out there again. We have spent the last 24 hours cleaning the bilges and playing with the bilge pumps and have to say that we can see lots of advantages in having some paid crew, whom you can order to take care of tiring unpleasant tasks of this kind.

A few comments about some of your last messages:

We would like to know – so that we can learn – how Peter got into the terrifying situation you described a few weeks ago. Why was he so close to land? Also, why did his engine fail? Did he call for help? If he did, did anyone respond?

Glad to hear that this time you are sailing with clean water. We were afraid you had developed a taste for the greeny stuff…

Lastly, thanks for the reassuring professional comments about Paola's arm problems. As she still is rather uncomfortable we have now booked an appointment with a consultant in Rio where we were planning to go anyway on other business.

 We hope you will not stop writing once you are back home. Give our love to the fleshpots of Plymouth.

  Love

   Paola, Philippe and the fiftyquidders

Sun 08/08/2004 18:06
Subject: Marmite? ... not for me, thanks ... I hate the stuff ...
    Dear P'n'P,

        Thanks for all the news ... and (in answer to your questions) Peter's attempt to take the overland route with his boat was due to several things :-

    - He had absolutely no wind at all, from more than two miles off the rocks ...

    - His engine wouldn't start because it was the original PETROL engine ... everything was ok except the contact- breaker was too worn away. He didn't find out till the post-mortem ...

    - He tried to call for help on channel 16, but there was no reply ... probably by that time he was already too close to the cliffs ...

    - He realises now that in the Azores current he should never have put himself in that position ...

    - He may have overslept (reading between the lines ... I've slept through the kitchen timer alarms myself, on more than one occasion ... terrible guilt afterwards) ...

    - It could have been any of us, I suspect ...

    - (etc)

        Anyway, I really miss the FiftyQuid birds and the Gargle Blaster Pan Galactix ... and watching the "wet-leg-dancing" (an expression in the vertical for the desire for the horizontal)...

        Get well soon, and yes, please keep in touch ...

        Lots of Love,
            Tuesday'n'the Doc.

(RECEIVED) Tue 03/08/2004 17:33
    Subject: Homeward Bound!
      Dear Doc,

So glad to hear that all is well with you as you near the end of your great adventure. As you will see from the following, our great adventure has also ended & we struggle to move on with the next stage of our lives. Of course, the past 12 years will always remain a very significant part of us.

We have so much news, & must apologize for being so slow to write. We have just been so overwhelmed with things to do, not the least of which is learning to cope with 21st Century life in America.

We sold Pendragon in Mexico to a very nice couple from Minnesota who have taken her to Lake Superior. They plan to go cruising in a few years.

David & I flew from Puerto Vallarta to San Diego on 15 May where we rented a truck to transport our belongings which had been brought from Mexico by two fellows who brought them over the border for us.

We drove to Redding in Northern California where we visited our son Steve, his wife & our grandson. We witnessed son Matt's graduation with a Masters Degree in Social Work in Sacramento, bought a car in Redding, & continued our trek north to Port Ludlow.

On 9 June we spent the first night in our house at Port Ludlow.

Since then we have been very busy accumulating furniture & other necessities to living in a house. This task has been made a bit easier by frineds who have donated pieces they don't need. Our property has suffered from several years of neglect & presents a rather daunting task to bring it back to a civilized state. So far this had produced almost five truck loads of yard debris kindly carried away by very helpful neighbors.

The area in which we live is very beautiful with wonderful evergreen forests, the water with many bays & islands & views of the Olympic Mountains. We have difficulty realizing that we actually live here & aren't just visiting. Our magnificent adventures with Pendragon seem far away sometimes, almost like something we read about once... We did wonderful things and risked so much and now it is over and perhaps we feel a little lost and out of kilter. It will be a while before we are really comfortable in our new life.

Meanwhile we enjoy the many comforts of living in a house, having a car, and best of all being closer to our family. We miss our cruising life & our many friends on land & sea.

As ever,

David & Sally

Sun 08/08/2004 18:04

Subject: LOVELY to hear from you!

Dear Sally'n'Dave,

Thanks for all the news ... I can only begin to try to imagine what the upheaval of your change of life-style must be like ... don't envy you at all, but how sensible of you both to quit while you're ahead ... too often you see people who don't know when to stop, until they're forced to... so WELL DONE, the pair of you! ...

Stay Well! and keep in touch, please ... if you're ever in England, it is a part of this country's immigration regulations that you HAVE to give us a telephone call, however brief ...

We're on the East Coast of the UK, about 20 miles north of Harwich ...

Hope your return to land-mode isn't too upsetting for you ...

Byee, fer now! .

Tuesday'n'Doc.

(RECEIVED)Fri 20/08/2004 19:24

Subject: LIFE

Hi David,

Thank you for your e-mail. Nice to hear that you were safely almost at home already. I am in Trinidad, 3 months already. I found serious rust inside my 40 yrs old steel boat and have to take 1/4 of the interior off and repair. It will take one month more. I am not in a hurry. My rig is now O.K. and transmission is better. I chanced bearings again. Like to sail later to Margarita and December to Panama, maybe?

*Regards **Matti Lappalainen**, The Lone Sailor*

Wed 11/08/2004 12:44

Subject: Sorry radio propagation is so rubbishy at present

Dear Jack,

Had an Email from Staale the other day ... he's left "Rozinante" in South Africa for the moment while he does a delivery job of a new boat from France to Norway ... then he's going back to work for 2 months before returning to his ship ... who knows from there onwards! ...

Warmest greetings, Jack ... Stay Well!

DocDavid on "Tuesday", (still stuck in Plymouth, UK).

Wed 11/08/2004 12:43

Dear Everybodies,

The only thing wrong with this place is that it is so HIDEOUSLY expensive ... otherwise it's really friendly and fun ... lots to see, in spite of heavy rain, as Julia (Fin's sister) and I found out when she came down to stay on the boat for 24 hours ... the Aquarium is quite something! ... the fish'n'chips is excellent here too ...

Then tonight, Tuesday 10th, has been the first of two nights of the Finals of the British National Fireworks Championship, held here each year ... six teams, three tonight and three tomorrow, put on a fantastic display from the Mountbatten Breakwater, just across the harbour, trying to set the sky on fire ... don't ask me the rules, but I think they each have the same tons of explosives, and the test is what they do with it ...

STUNNING! ... (and all to celebrate "Tuesday's" return to England ... ah, isn't that nice of them!) ...

More gentle repairs and improvements to the ship, although very little actually needed to be done ... (I must have been getting to grips with the wear and chafe problems better, I think) ... and a new VHF antenna and wind-direction-thingy fitted at the mast head (lovely view over all of Plymouth Sound from up there!), but I need help to push/pull the cable down through the mast, top to bottom, so I still don't have a working main VHF set-up on board, annoyingly ...

I'm still very tired after the last leg from the Azores ... maybe it will wear off soon ...

More diplomacy about the Brazilian Electronics, while we up the "anti" for the Shipping Agent ...

It's more than likely I'm going to have to sail on from here solo, at least some of the way home ... everyone I would choose has all sorts of other commitments unfortunately (or are they all not telling me something?), and I think I could be stuck here for ever waiting for things to sort out, so I might just as well go ahead and get on with it ... I am surprised to find I can't wait to get back to the sea, or to a quiet anchorage somewhere ... marinas, though very convenient, are simply not my style ...

(Wednesday 11th. Aug) .... RAMMED by a big speedboat here in the marina this morning ... not once but twice ... first time he bounced off the pulpit and the anchor ... a few moments later he smashed my bow navigation light ... offered me a bottle of wine in recompense, but I explained that it wouldn't really help me get through the Straits of Dover, now would it ...

So I've had to buy a new one, which of course has different mountings from the original one ... I've had to make an adapter plate out of bits, and I've suggested that he come back this afternoon and stand on my deck to help me feed the VHF antenna cable down the mast ... (I thought that calling it "community service" was pushing my luck a bit, so I haven't mentioned that ... yet ...)

We will see what sort of Man he is by seeing if he turns up this afternoon ... I think he will ...

The weather's bad (rain, poor visiility, and still some East in the wind)...

And on top of all that, I think I m-i-g-h-t be going a little bit bald ... ah well, as my sister Mary keeps saying, "worse things happen at sea!" ...

More news soon!

Tuesday'n'me.

Thu 12/08/2004 23:20
Dear Everybodies,

The powerboat man DID come back, and was very helpful and apologetic ... I nipped up the mast yet again to sort out the top end, while he very gently tried to tease the VHF coax out from the bottom ... it didn't work, dammit ... the old, lightning burnt coax broke, so the new cable now runs down inside the mast correctly but I can't get hold of the bottom end to feed it out and into the deck ... more thought required, but I think I may have worked out how to do it ...

A very pleasant evening watching the second night of the Fireworks Final, in pouring rain, but in the shelter of the balcony of the Pantaenius offices ... food-nibbles and a little champagne in good company, to celebrate "Tuesday"'s return to the UK ... very enjoyable ...

Today I've met some most interesting people too ... the owner of an AFT cockpit version of "Tuesday" ... a couple sailing a Contessa 32 all over the place ... and a Dutchman with a lovely aluminium boat which looks like it's been through a mincing machine ...

It turns out that the Dutchman bought the boat as a wreck at Porto Calera (spelling?) on Lanzarote ... she'd been washed up on the rocks there in a gale, the hull cut and battered with at least 7 punctures through the metal (nasty sharp lava rocks there) ... the mast and fittings had been sold off ... virtually a stripped bare hull ... Yet this remarkable elderly man, and his son, patched the hull with plates, built a small jury rig from parts from another write-off (the boom is 3 pieces of wood bolted and lashed together), and sailed the thing from the Canaries, via Madeira, to Plymouth, on the way back to Holland to rebuild her ... quite extraordinary persistence and vision, I reckon! ... I'm proud to have met him ...

Tomorrow is Friday 13th ... but the weather conditions look good for heading eastwards, so I'm going to give it a try ... hopefully, aiming to reach Sovereign Yacht Harbour (near Eastbourne) in the next two days or so ... staying well out to sea on the way, to keep all the options open ... we'll see how it develops, anyway ...

Lots more snippets of interest soon, but that's enough for now ...

Lots of love,
Tuesday'n'me.

(RECEIVED) Wed 11/08/2004 20:30
Hallo David,

Sorry you can't find anybody to help you sail to Dover Straits, but you had better wait for something that has no EAST in it first, anyway. As long as the next westerly is not chased by what we send over, remnants of all these tropical storms and hurricanes!

Thank you for telling me the "Kite" has not left yet. And propagation is terrible - today I heard nobody on 15m, it's not only the QRM and QRN in the marinas!

88 – Trudi

(RECEIVED)Thu 12/08/2004 09:48

If I had the time, the guts, the ability and the audacity to be part of a threesome (you and Tuesday that is) I would love to help you sail back. (I have none of these things) Should you wish it and if it were at a reasonable time, I would be pleased to video Tuesdays return into the Ore - I promise to hand over to you the original images! -just a thought.

Time 10:44, now going back to bed to build up my stamina for a possible 18 hour film show!

*Regards **Joe***

(RECEIVED) Fri 13/08/2004 17:20
David,

Totally BRILLIANT. What a trip. You must put all the e mails together to go with the video!

I would have loved to join you on the trip back east if only this work stuff didn't get in the way and we hadn't just got back from a week on L'acushla (damp but still good - managed to stay away from civilisation for 5 days en famille and everyone in the spirit of it). Anyway, perhaps it's going to be hard to share your little vessel with anyone else after what you've been through together.

Richard

Chapter 12

Eastwards from Plymouth

Sun 15/08/2004 18:25
> **Subject: From Plymouth, eastwards ...**
> **Dear Everybodies,**

On leaving the over-expensive marina in Plymouth, on Friday 13th, I found 25-30 knot winds outside ... from the right direction, but there was quite a heavy sea running outside the harbour ... so Tuesday'n'me ducked into Cawsand Bay under a wooded cliff, completely protected from the westerly wind ... nice quiet anchorage ... very pleasant in the sunshine while wisps of cloud raced by overhead ...

Quietly lifted the anchor before dawn next day, under the stars ... not much wind, but worked the strong tides round each headland quite nicely ... covered 8.4 miles in one hour at one point ...

In the afternoon, one particular idiot port-tack-and-engine yacht, veering all over the place , made it difficult to finally have to keep out of HIS way (since it's obvious that he doesn't know the international rules to avoid collisions at sea) ... I reckon he had no idea at all that he forced me to take fairly violent avoiding action ... sporting a blue ensign too ...?should I feel guilty for failing to acknowledge his cheery wave of greeting? ... (I can live with it, I think) ...

But at night there was very heavy traffic (ships, fishing boats, and many yachts which only show on the radar when quite close) ... some of the bigger ships move quite fast too ...

I managed to clamber into bed on many occasions, but every time some new potential crisis arose ... eventually it seemed quite amusingly predictable ... but I got very tired by dawn, once more having had no sleep at all ...

Heavy rain by Beachy Head, but as it cleared, I noticed Eastbourne had put on a public airshow, along the seafront ... and a very good show it was too, as "Tuesday", with sails lowered, drifted lazily on the swells while I watched ..... maybe they didn't know it was just for me, but I accepted it as such, (as with the Plymouth fireworks) ...

Nice welcome here in Sovereign Harbour, and 2/3 the price of Plymouth, with the same or better facilities ... I had remembered Nick's (the Aussie in Brazil) advice about having a Pepsi or a strong coffee/tea 30 minutes before entering a new marina ... just about starting to wake you up a bit when you arrive ... it works!!

Tomorrow, all being well, James should be joining the ship for the trip through the Dover Straits (VERY busy!) towards Harwich ... I'm looking forward to sharing the workload for a change ... (besides, when he left "Tuesday" in the Isle of Wight 14 months ago, he marked the fluid level in the whisky bottle to make sure nobody stole his favourite tipple ... I hope it passes inspection, after all those miles!) ...

More later, but for now I'm going to get my head down, to try to catch up a bit ...

> Love from,
> Tuesday'n'me.

(RECEIVED) Tue 24/08/2004 09:11
> *Subject: 'Tuesday'*
> *Dear David,*

It was a real pleasure to meet you again in Plymouth. The next time I am in your part of the world the beer will be on me-Adnam's(?) I will miss your newsletters .. little gems buried amid all the routine traffic. Always good to hear of some poor soul battling the elements and the bureaucrat in far off places.

Every day we have to make decisions about who to cover and how/where to cover. Often the decision is one of gut instinct based upon relatively little information. In your own case I never had a moments doubt. I think I became totally convinced when you said that you were apprehensive before each passage. This, in my view, is an appropriate emotion and one that leads to proper preparation and a successful outcome.

Best wishes
Mike

Sun 15/08/2004 19:35
    Subject: Rival hunting
        Dear Eric,
"Aeolia" looks much loved and cared for, looking at your picture ...I note the single backstay, so probably the original rig, but I believe there may be more variants of the USA Tall Rig than I thought... I spoke to the owner of "Rival Star", and he is convinced that he has a Tall Rig, after measuring up for new sails with Rob Kemp of Kemp Sails ... (Rob knows a fair bit about Rivals, but I didn't know that until after I'd decided to ask him to build MY sails) ...

The point is that I compared the mast heights of Tuesday and Rival Star with a fair amount of exactitude (I was working at the top of Tuesday's mast at the time), and if he's right, then my OLD mast was a tall one too ... but my present one is nearly 5' higher again ... I give up, I'm afraid!

"Rival Star" was the one advertised very cheaply after "cattle-market" chartering (up to 10 paying punters at a time) in Poole 2-3 years ago ... she was not fitted out in a Rival pattern nor manner, and I'm not surprised she was cheap (good value though) ... she has NOT just returned from a circumnavigation, as I had been told by the marina-staff ...

Coming back to "Aeolia" ... it is probable that she was completed by Southern Boatbuilders, in which case she will be far superior inside than Tuesday (who was completed OUTSIDE Southern Boatbuilders, but probably from kits of their design) ... this would make her a very attractive buy indeed, since the quality of the INSIDE of these boats seems to be the main factor governing the price in the UK ...

In other words, yes you have to take a good look, at the very least, and if you DO decide to go ahead, I personally don't think you will regret it ... you'd never lose much money if you decided to sell her, but I very much doubt you'd want to anyway ...

Personally? .... I think she looks mouthwateringly STUNNING, as I'm still in love with the look of the 41 ...

GO for it, Eric! ... if you were to die in the next few years you would be kicking yourself for missing an opportunity ... if there are many obstructions to the purchase along the way then maybe it's not meant to be .... with "Tuesday" I had the same terrors or worse, but it all rolled along smoothly almost as though I wasn't in charge of the process ...

However I will fervently deny all this if I get grilled by your family ... why not ask THEM what you should do, because they will be involved in using the vessel too ....

I'm not much help to you I'm afraid ... but I've missed two big opportunities in my life by being "sensible", and I was NOT going to let "Tuesday" slip out of my fingers ...

(By the way, "Tuesday" isn't home yet ... arrived here in Sovereign Yacht Harbour, Eastbourne this afternoon (Sunday), after a totally sleep-free night dodging ships, fishing boats and yachts all the way from Plymouth to here ... so I'm completely cream-crackered at present, though planning to move to Harwich, with a friend's help, in the next two days ...)

    Keep in touch!
        Tuesday'n'the Doc.

239

(RECEIVED)Sun 15/08/2004 21:53

Great to hear your latest news that you are almost on your final leg of this cruise. You say you will be coming with James towards Harwich - does that mean Orford? I know that we and others would love to meet you down river on your return to the Ore and hope you will let us know when you are coming!

Look forward to hearing all about it.

Cheers,

Ben (J)

Fri 20/08/2004 09:02
   Subject: Harwich Harbour.
      Dear Everybodies,

Yes, the spirit level in the whiskey bottle passed James's inspection ... unchanged since 18th June last year ... but I'll bet it's gone down a bit by now though (he took it home with him when he jumped ship again in Levington ...)

Very pleasant meal overlooking the water in Sovereign Yacht Harbour, discussing with the Portuguese waiter the excellence of the Brazilian/Portuguese singers.

Then nice sunny weather after a leisurely start from Eastbourne, but a slowly dying wind ... the Straits of Dover were as busy as ever, and so was the crossing of the Thames Estuary ... I would not have liked to do it solo, as two pairs of experienced eyes made it dramatically easier and safer ...

During the night we threaded our way through the narrow short-cut in the banks and shallows 25 miles off the coast, whilst thunderstorms and heavy rain slowly caught us up ... the short pauses between lightning flashes didn't really leave time to recover our night vision ... impressive forked lightning hitting the sea only 200 yards behind us concentrated the mind a bit ... sailing at maximum speed in strong winds and a down-pour, and minimal visibility, was testing but exhilarating too ...

After 18 hours, finally entered a predawn Harwich, to rest alongside the fuel-pontoon in Levington ... topped up the diesel and water tanks, while working out a Cunning Plan to enable the ship to pull herself sideways off the berth, against a strong wind which was pinning her there ...

It involved a very long piece of rope and the willing help of the fuel-pump attendant, who stood on the tail end of the rope where it went several times round a bollard ... it all went remarkably well, with a distinct absence of fright, much to the helper's amused surprise ("well well! We learn something new every day!" he shouted) ...

At the appointed moment, and a signal from me, he lifted his foot, and the rope swished out into the water, to be hauled aboard before it could get near the propeller ... I enjoyed that whole manoeuvre, (which I myself have never seen before ... I'll use it again someday!) ...

Three days of lazy recuperation ... trying to eat up all the perishable stores on board ... relearning how to sleep at night and stay awake by day ... winds up to 40 knots, but we're safely tucked up at anchor and can enjoy it ... making plans for the difficult entrance to the Orford River in a few days time, (it's not an easy task, as the entrance changes its shallow shingle banks all the time) ...

So we're not quite home yet ... about 18 miles to do still ... but it looks like a useful weather window is coming along ...

I had forgotten just how pleasant this area of England is, even in the rain and wind ... it's GREAT to be back in home waters again! ...

More news in a few days ...
      with love from,
         Tuesday'n'me.

(RECEIVED) Fri 20/08/2004 09:02

Yes this is a lovely part of the world isn't it!

Glad you had a good trip. At what point did you feel you were in home waters? Rounding South Foreland?

Or perhaps you have felt you were in home waters since Plymouth. I guess it's relative. You have been a long way.

We shall be aboard Aliz Motte this weekend but with no fixed plans. If you are still in the Orwell on Saturday evening we could bring Aliz Motte round and have you over for a meal. Of course we don't want to intrude but we would like to welcome you home (if you don't mind being welcomed!). Your trip has been an inspiration to me.

The purchase of R41 Aeolia is rolling along with its own momentum. I have commissioned a survey and all being well will fly out to conclude the deal in mid-September. I have some anxiety that I am buying a bigger boat than I really need but fate seems to have taken a hand. I am a bit worried about its effect on our sailing economy as at present we only pay around £50 per year for our mooring and our fairway committee will find it difficult to accommodate a 41'at with 6' draft!

Good sailing - enjoy your last few days and don't forget to make all those technical notes for your next trip BEFORE you get ashore.

> *Eric*

(RECEIVED) Sun 15/08/2004 23:42

My goodness, David, we are going to miss G0CBE on the net in future!

Although the miserable propagation has sort of eased us in that direction in the last few weeks.

I want to say thank you for being a wonderful and faithful check-in, fair winds for the rest of the trip, and have a good rest, and if you are writing a book, I would, please, like to buy an autographed copy!

For the meantime I shall keep your E-mails in their mailbox, if I may?

> *88 – Trudi*

8/19/2004 20:50

Dear Trudi,

But of course, those "Tuesday'n'me" Emails are your personal property to do with entirely as you wish ... I have no plans for a book at this stage, but maybe one or two short Yachting magazine articles, if they're interested ...

I have been asked if I would give several public talks about the trip, and I'd like to try that too ... and I hope to be able to pass on some of the vast range of information, which others have given me, to sailing students going through the local sailing school (I sometimes help out on the Practical courses as I've had a commercial ticket for many years).

I'll send an Email to you, Jack and Gerard when I get home ... but I'm not quite there yet, and I have one more difficult and dangerous hazard to negotiate, namely my own home river entrance, with its constantly shifting shingle banks and its 6 knot tide in the rivermouth ...

Apparently, at Orford, they are planning a big Welcome Home small-boat flotilla to meet me on Sunday morning, local newspaper there etc etc ... a year ago I would have run like hell to avoid it, but now I think it might be fun, and each one of them will have shared a little piece of the adventure for themselves ... we will see what happens when we get there, and I will try to be brave! ...

Meantime, Warmest Greetings to you and yours!

> (more to follow in a few days)
> **DocDavid.**

Tue 24/08/2004 08:35
    Subject: Finally home at Orford.
      Dear Everybodies,

Three days of gentle unwinding, at anchor in the River Orwell, in thundery showers and gusts up to 40 knots ... but we were in sheltered waters now, and felt safe and secure enough to enjoy it... still had to move anchorages twice to stay in the lee of the land more effectively, though ...

Lovely warm sunny Force 4, to sail round along the coast, up to the (potentially) dangerous River Ore entrance, in close company with Chris and Gill on "Lady of Deben" ... I had forgotten what an exceptionally beautiful coastline this area is ... wide range of birdlife etc ... all this part of the world needs to be PERFECT, is clean transparent seawater instead of the 'soup' we float our boats in here, plus the climate of Itaparica ... (oh, and the price structure of Bahia, Brazil too please)....

A very special moment when I dropped anchor in Abraham's Bosom, behind Havergate Island ... 14 months and 14,960 miles since leaving the same spot last year ... it's so peaceful here ... flat water, high cloud, birdsong, and distant views of Orford castle and the lighthouse on Orfordness ... a quiet night and a good sleep ...

Finally, the last 3 miles up to Orford itself ...

... to be waylaid by a veritable armada of other local yachts, all dressed overall with flags, sounding their hooters and sirens as they fell into formation astern to welcome dear old "Tuesday" home ... the rows of happy faces on the quay, waving flags and shouting greetings to us ... Anglia Television was there too ... I confess it brought a tear to my eyes for a moment, as it was all so overwhelming ...

Interview with the TV people ... speech and presentation at the Clubhouse, when I gave the tattered remnants of "Tuesday's" old burgee to the club (who want to frame it!), and in return was given a brand new one to replace it ... message from Suffolk Radio ("?OK to come to the studio in Ipswich for live interview on Tuesday?") ...

... and I'm feeling a fraud, because I met several other remarkable people on my adventure who would think nothing of the trip I've just completed, and would be surprised to find such a fuss being made of yet another safe voyage ... but it wasn't my idea to have such a welcome, and it makes me feel proud and tall to accept it from my friends ....

I was truly alone on this trip for only a very few days ... in particular after the Whizzbang .. after radio failure near St.Helena .. after I discovered the bad water supply .. and when the rudder problem cast definite doubt on the ship's ability to stay afloat (I was wrong, and worrying unnecessarily, but I didn't know it at the time) ... through all the other adversities and successes, tears and smiles, fears and elations, were Trudi, Gerard, and Jack of the TransAtlantic MaritimeMobile Nets, and my brother Jonesy ... my constant companions (by radio), day after day after day ... I would have found it very much harder without their constant support, encouragement and humour ... lovely people ...

And the main thing I've learnt from Tuesday's Atlantic Wanderings? .... quite simply, the immense value of ones own family (which includes those very special friends I count as being part of my family) ... the support and reassurance from them felt like a physical prop, carrying me through some nasty times, helping me make the right decisions at the right times ... it was a sensation that I had not expected, but I was so very glad of it when I needed it ...

What next? ... probably the Baltic Sea next summer, but after that, who knows? ... I have much to think on this winter! ...

Thanks for all your help, each one of you, in different ways, over the past few years ... but now, sadly, this series of "Dear Everybodies" must come to a .   (full stop)

    Please keep in touch!,
      Grateful Thanks, and lots of Love, from,
        Tuesday'n'me.

(RECEIVED)Fri 27/08/2004 17:36

(copy)

"Dear Paul and Teresa,

Just to tell you that David finally tied up at Orford on Sunday 22nd August at 11.00am. he was escorted up the river by a flotilla of 23 boats, all displaying masses of flags, etc. and to the accompaniment of foghorns, clapping, a crowd of wellwishers on the quay, and general happiness and congratulation. Anglia Television were there, for pictures and interview. At a reception in the clubhouse the Commodore accepted David's gift of a very tattered ODSC pennant ... only about 20% of it remained. It will be put on display in the clubhouse. In return, the Commodore presented him with a brand new flag ... "for your next voyage!". David reminded the assembled company that there is an ODSC burgee now firmly fixed on the wall of the well known cafe in St Helena.

He is fit and well but does not feel he has quite come down to earth yet. He sends his regards to you, and his thanks for all your help and support.

> *Bill"*

(RECEIVED) Wed 25/08/2004 14:09

Subject: CONGRATS!

> ***CONGRATULATIONS ON THE COMPLETION OF YOUR FIGURE OF EIGHT!!!!!!***
ALBEIT, WITH A SLIGHT DEVIATION TO THE SOUTH FOR BOTH
TUESDAY AND YOUR FRIED BRAIN!!

We are glad you are home safely and are proud to have you in our circle of family/friends that we have met on these tiny beautiful oceans of life.

Enjoy the first "real" shower, flush the head forever and fresh milk for all!

Let us know how you assimilate to your new (old) surroundings.

> *Love,* **Capt. Ron & Bonnie**

(RECEIVED)Thu 26/08/2004 10:31

Missing you already!!!!

> **Cathy and Dave,** *NZ*

(RECEIVED) Mon 30/08/2004 18:36

Subject: Greetings from Sweden

> *Dear David*

Long time no see. I´m sorry that we couldn´t say goodbye before we left Horta. We went by your boat but you and your wife were out. Fredrik was very sorry that he couldnt say goodbye. He looked up to you very much....well we all do!!! He has started his career to be a doctor. You gave him some good advice he told me.

We had a nice sailing up to Falmouth onboard Symphonie. Just 2 days of hard weather with gale. I met my family there and we had a wonderful sailing in 10 days along the coast up to Portsmouth. There 2 men from Sweden came down to sail our boat to Sweden. Leona and my 2 son´s went by returning car up to Sweden.

Soren had a hard time from Horta to Falmouth. We tried to stay close him and did soo for 4 days. Then we lost contact outside Portugal in a gale. We came to Falmouth after 12 days. No Soren there. When I had waited for 4 days I started a SAR with the help of English coastguard and MRCC in Sweden. He was found by Bishop Rock with a rope in his propeller. He had no electricity or power onboard and was very tired. Now he is in Falmouth trying to sell his boat. If he doesnt succeed he will try to sail it home and sell it in Sweden.

We have used our boat several times here at home. We are very pleased with the boat. I'm longing (to go) out again and will fit the boat for my family's needs and then in some years try to get down to Azores and Spain. I'm back in the navy now and the days goes by. My colleges can see me look out at sea in a different way now. They say "look at him, he is out there again". They can't understand how much I miss the trip over the Atlantic. But next time I want to have my boys with me.

How is everything with you and your family. Would be nice to hear from you if you have the time to email. Say hello to your family. I guess they also can see the need for sailing in your eyes too.

Hope to meet you in the future.

Best regards

Jörgen Bergman

S/Y Symphonie.

Mon 06/09/2004 23:23

Subject: ...and Greetings from Orford (East of England) to you too ...

Hi Jorgen!,

Thanks for all the news and information ... if you come across Soren again soon, please do give him Best Wishes from my daughter and me ("Tot" and "Doc") ...

I'm glad to know that "Symphonie" arrived in Sweden safely ... well done, Sir!

Here I'm having a few minor problems settling into a more normal lifestyle again, as you can imagine ...

It's been 15,000 miles in 14 months, so I'm not surprised ... so I spent another 10 days cruising alone along the coast of the Thames Estuary .. it's a particularly interesting area for me, even though I was born and brought up in this part of the world ... it was a real pleasure to rediscover the little creeks and backwaters, seeing them through wiser eyes now! ...

Take good care of yourself too ...

Fair Winds and Safe Landfalls!

DocDavid on Tuesday.

(RECEIVED)Wed 01/09/2004 20:43

WELL DONE!!

always new you were a great yachtsman, just wish I had the same dedication to reach my goals. I'm still drifting along, heading for Tobago at the moment with a vague idea of Cuba for xmas. Great to have met you and perhaps our paths will cross on your next trip!!

regards

Bill

WJPogson on s/v British Tiger

Mon 06/09/2004 23:23

Subject: Keep in touch!

Dear Bill, Buddy and Shusha,

Great to hear from you again! ... and no, you're not just drifting along, you're looking in various doorways as you travel the corridor of time, looking for the one which will interest you most ... (do you remember our conversation?) ...

I hadn't got the guts to do that, so I've simply dabbled my feet in various Atlantic waters for 14 months, scared meself on many occasions, and have now returned home to review what I've seen and learnt ... I confess that at the moment I don't care how hard the wind blows as long as the water stays FLAT, so I've been sailing around the rivers and creeks of the Thames Estuary for the last 10 days ... We'll see how I feel after the winter ...

In England we're all taking a close interest in the paths of the hurricanes this year, so you may feel the moral support from the UK should one of them head you're way ...

Meantime take special care of yourself, and be sure to give us a call by phone each and every time you're back in the UK ... it's compulsory ...

Stay Well, Stay Safe!

"Tuesday" and the Doc.

Fri 27/08/2004 17:36

   Subject: Home safe again

   Dear Y,C,T and J,

On 22nd August 2004, "Tuesday"'n'me arrived safely at Orford (our home port) on the East Coast of England, after 14,963 miles in 14 months ... word had obviously got around, and there was a most unexpected flotilla of 20+ yachts, all dressed overall with flags, blowing whistles, sirens and hooters, clapping and shouting "Welcome Home!" ... they popped out from the back of an island as I came past ... a very emotional (if noisy!) moment ... unforgettable ... made my eyes water a bit, I confess ...

And then the quay at Orford was full of people, waving, shouting, cheering ... when I finally got ashore an hour later, there were interviews to be given to both the TV and the Radio ...

But I feel embarrassed by it all because you guys have been doing a lot more than me, for a heck of a lot longer too ... however, these friends of mine here in this area clearly wanted a party and I was the excuse for one I think ...

Anyway, the point of this Email is to tell you it's been an honour to have met you during my trip, and to thank you for all the information and friendship I've gained from you ... keep sending details of what you're up to, please ... I look forward to hearing about all your adventures! ...

Your Autohelm 4000, which I modified to work with a Navico motor and used some Plastimo bits in it, has behaved very well, though it's for calm weather only ... many thanks again! ...

By the way, my Dad was delighted with his samples of Iron Wood from your new house, (?"Chateau Voitchovsky"?), and took great delight in showing my Mum how they sink in water ... good fun! ... However I've kept the blue sand-in-a-jar art painting for Fin and me (it's too nice to give away to anyone) ... And so far, relationships at home have been better than ever, although I appreciate it's still early days ...

Please don't lose contact ... and Stay Well! ...(CD of your piccies to follow soon, if the address is correct?)

   Grateful thanks,

      "Tuesday" and the Doc.

(RECEIVED)Sun 12/09/2004 04:33

   Dear Doc,

Congratulations on the successful completion of your voyage! What a marvelous welcome... so glad you shared it with us. Sounds like you rank right up there with Chichester and such.

Again we thank you so much for helping Sally to know the proper dosage of Stugeron... which made our last passages completely free of seasickness... too bad we didn't meet you 11 years earlier!

All goes well here as we settle into life ashore. We are blessed with good friends here & new neighbors and are enjoying the amenities not available on a boat. Of course we miss our cruising life sometimes, but it was time to move on & it is wonderful to be able to pick up the phone to call our family whenever we wish.

One of our very fond memories will always be the time we spent with you & the group in Rubicon... the dominoes games, & the preparations for our Atlantic crossing... really heady stuff!

Enjoy your family & friends & the ease of life ashore.

   As always, ***Dave & Sally***

Mon 06/09/2004 23:23
>
> **Subject: ...Best Wishes from East Anglia! ...**
>
> **Dear Trudi, Jack and Gerard,**

I am really beginning to appreciate what you three (and my brother) did for me during my trip, now that I have been going through some of the 22 hours of video I recorded ... the film has reminded me just how wearing was the constant movement, the noise and the worry for all those months, and the Nets were a valuable part of each day for me ...

I've found it a bit difficult to re-adjust to life ashore, so I ran away back to sea again, in the Thames Estuary creeks and rivers, for about 10 days, to unwind slowly ... we will see how long it takes to come down to earth again ... haven't finished unloading the ship yet ...

> Meantime, very best wishes to all four of you,
>
> > More news later,
> >
> > > Tuesday'n'me

Tue 14/09/2004 00:26
>
> **Subject: Reviewing piccies.**
>
> **Dear P'n'P,**

Glad to hear you're sensibly waiting for the better part of the season ... Take care! ...

Here, taking a little while to re-adapt back to "civilisation", but in between more short trips around the creeks and islands of this area, I'm slowly being tamed! ... I've enjoyed starting to look through the piccies and the videos ... nice movies of you both in Alvor while you were saving the topless beauty and her sugardaddy from being washed into town ... (I was starting to get my dinghy out of the bilge to inflate it when you beat me to it!) ...

Many nice memories with you two ... Stay safe and happy! ... (and don't you DARE lose contact) ...

> > **Tuesday and the Doc.**

(RECEIVED)Wed 22/09/2004 19:18
>
> *Subject: Reviewing piccies ...*
>
> *Dear David,*

Have they re-educated you yet? Are you eating proper food and drinking non-rain water? And what about clothes?

Spooky to think of you in the UK looking at images of us back in Portugal!

Here in lovely Paraty everything is fine, though we really can't wait to leave for Uruguay. We are definitively done with Brazil for the rest of our lives. Just another six weeks before we start moving again.

We are thinking of making a list of Brazil's top 5 best and worst things.

Any suggestions?

Changing subject, we have just found out that a friend of ours – name Alan – has just launched his new home-built Hunter on the river Orwell. The yacht's name is "Another Planet", rather like the place you get to after a caipirinha too many, so keep your eyes open for it. We have told Alan about you so you can say hi if you see them.

Be worried because we surely do not intend to lose contact.

> *Love,* **Philippe and Paola.**

PS We are still making fun of M..... "Mo....., Mo...., I am locked up in he lavatory!!

Fri 24/09/2004 00:56
Subject: Brazilian List
Dear P'n'P,

Lovely to hear all your news, and thanks for the medical details which I find fascinating. I'm glad Paola's bits are all successfully overhauled, or nearly so ... well done!

And yes, I've nearly stopped drinking rainwater from the water butt now ... still can't stop eating too much though, since I don't have to cook it!

You asked about my personal BRAZILIAN HIGHS and LOWS :-
HITS:-
   - CiapirinhaPanGalacticGargleBlasshhtersshhhhh....(hic!)
   - Drinks and ices made from fresh mango's.
   - The Bossa Nova, and certain Brazilian singers, especially Galcosta .... (oh, and one particular song by Adriana Calcanhotto).
   - Watching Saturday evening "wet-leg dancing" in the marketplace on Itiparica (expressing in the vertical the desire for the horizontal) ...... mmm, nice!
    - The sheer engineering-poetry of almost every Brazilian girl I saw ....(yeah, OK, maybe I'd been away from home too long...)

MISSES:-
   - The Shipping Agent (Brazil).
   - Police Federale.
   - Anything to do with Costumes & Intimidation(Customs & Immigration), and the Marmite(Maritime) Police.
   - Salvador City thieves, robbers, and Hobbits.
   - The French in general.

From this you will gather that I'm a dry-mouthed, overheated dipsomaniac and a dirty old man, with strong tribal prejudices and a total disregard for those in authority, ... so you can understand how I got a job in the NHS ...

Meantime, look after you carefully please ...
    (and continue to keep in touch!)
      Much Love,
        Tuesday and the doc.

SOME PERSONAL COMMENTS after a SINGLEHANDED 14 MONTHS, and 15000 MILES, voyage in the NORTH and SOUTH ATLANTIC in 2003/2004.
By David Foreman.

1. WHY?

Ever since I was a schoolboy I've always wanted to see, hear, (and maybe even to smell) the different weather systems and the ocean wildlife in the various climate belts of this planet. Reading as many books as possible about the old sailing ships' explorations and about the Horse Latitudes, the Doldrums, the Tradewinds, and the Westerlies, kept reinforcing this wish. Seeing views of it on television wasn't enough .. I wanted to experience it for myself. I longed to be able to actually LIVE in the open ocean for a while, to feel what it was like to become a tiny part of that world, and to see some of the wonders as sailors of 500 years ago saw them. Although I have enjoyed racing in the past I had no ambition during this particular trip to get my sailing over and done with as fast possible, as I wanted to savour every moment of it. I didn't want to dawdle either, but to travel at a safe speed which was as comfortable as possible for both the ship and me. It would be nice to visit all sorts of islands and foreign places, but for me this would be merely a bonus, and not the main reason for my travels.

2. THE ROUTE?

Because of the circulation of the winds and currents (clockwise in the north Atlantic, anti-clockwise in the south), and in order to be able to cut ACROSS the weather systems, a giant figure-of-eight route seemed best. Starting in the UK this meant sailing south to the Algarve, then out to the islands of the Madeira archipelago. Thence to the Canaries, and on southwards to the Cap Verde Islands, before crossing through the Doldrums, staying well east and upwind for the southeast trades to Salvador in Brazil. From there southwards down to Argentina, before turning eastwards towards the Falklands and Tristan de Cunha Island, which would be the halfway point, approximately.

The return trip would involve sailing north to St.Helena
Island, past Ascension, over the Equator once more (maybe managing to stay far enough east to see the Cap Verdes again if I were lucky with the winds), before slicing across and upwind against the Northeast Trades, and eventually into calms of the Horse Latitudes. I should be able to work the ship slowly through the calms northwards to the Azores group, and thus homewards to the UK again.

Unfortunately, both the ship and I myself were severely damaged by a direct hit by lightning in Brazil (which caused four separate fires on board), and due to a combination of events the ship was unable to continue southwards along the South American coast. So, after three months of hard work achieving only basic repairs, the journey continued southeastwards towards Tristan de Cunha. However, the early winter weather down there turned particularly aggressive, so to protect the damaged ship, the course was changed direct to St.Helena as soon as I could pick up some easterly winds off the African coast.

Overall distance sailed was 14,963 miles in 14 months, the longest stretch being 7,500 miles from Salvador to the Azores with a 7 day pause at anchor at St.Helena. The longest continuous passage at sea was 4200 miles in 40 days. Fastest weekly run was 1024 miles in 7 days, and the best daily run was exactly 160 miles, (all these are Nautical miles). Average daily run for all the days actually spent at sea was just under 110 miles/day, which includes all the calms etc.

3. WHEN?

The intention was to have a northern hemisphere summer, then a southern summer below the Equator, followed by summer again in the north. The plan was to avoid bad weather if at all possible, and it involved leaving England in June/July to avoid gales in Biscay, but delaying the crossing to Brazil until November/December to avoid the hurricane season. The last bit of the return voyage would require leaving the Azores (towards the UK) by the 1stAugust the following year.

4. OVERALL POLICY.

I consider ocean sailing to be like tiptoeing past a vast dragon in its cave. Try to choose a time when it is asleep, be prepared to run back if it stirs, but make sure both you and the ship are strong enough to survive if by chance it rolls over on top of you. There is nothing personal in its behaviour, it's so big it doesn't even know you're there, but it's just as lethal if you get it wrong. The ship and the crew become one single entity, each unable to survive without the other, so, just as the ship is there to protect me, it is up to me to look after her carefully to enable her to do her job.

5. WHY ALONE?

Most certainly I was not out to prove anything, nor was I running away from anything.

On ocean voyages it is often simpler to sail alone, as long as the ship is suitably arranged for one person (which will require considerable forethought). It all hinges on one's attitude, and the ability to work out a way to sidestep a problem, rather than simply to bludgeon a way head-on through it. The singlehander is able to alter the voyage plan with ease if necessary, and is much more able to adapt to circumstances than if he had other people to consider as well. The responsibilities are less, and as far as emotions are concerned, the Lows may be deeper but the Highs are very much greater. Many natural events you will witness will be a source of absolute wonder and delight. I longed to be able to share these emotions, but the presence of someone nearby would have diluted them perhaps.

I found reprovisioning and general restocking of ship's supplies to be very much simpler and quicker for a solo sailor when he touches land. It seems to be the rule that everything which comes on board will have to be physically carried there by the crew, and usually rowed out to the anchorage in an inflatable, but one person needs only a small amount of stores.

The downside is that the singlehander must be prepared for the total absence of reassurance and advice when things go wrong, and at times will have to remain a detached "observer" of this little human, who may often be considered as merely another part of the boat's equipment (and a very fragile one). This ability to detach oneself from the drama of the event will enable you to prevent "panic", by reducing it to "fear", then to "worry" and finally down to "concern", (which Tristan Jones described as a proper and seamanlike emotion in times of trouble). Personally, I get frightened very easily, and I get seasick easily too, but a balanced outlook carried me through, so that I could continue to think ahead and work out what to do.

6. THE SHIP.

I needed the right tool for the job.

I found "Tuesday" (named after a derelict Thames barge, some of whose timbers are incorporated into her rebuild) in Majorca in 1997 after a long search. Built in 1975, she is a centre-cockpit Rival 41 (Hull No.7), modified by a small but massive bowsprit bringing her to 43' overall. When fully loaded with stores etc. she displaces 14 tons, and draws 2.1 metres. I knew she had severe osmosis, which meant the removal of quite a thickness of glass before we reached something we could work with, but the outer three layers are now glass-reinforced-epoxy, much stronger than the original. It was a 15-month job, but it gave me the time and opportunity to make many other improvements.

Chain plates were a potential weakness, so a long area of reinforcement was built under each sidedeck. Together with the new 12mm standing-intermediate-shrouds ("fixed runners") which pick up into the main bulkhead, they make the rig much safer. The mast step had already been strengthened.

I had very clear ideas of what I needed from her sailpower and so I asked Selden if they would agree to build her new mast and rig to my specifications, and Rob Kemp kindly added to my ideas for the new sails. So now she has a taller, boomed-staysail cutter rig giving her 38% more sail than the standard plan, which has transformed her power and performance, while remaining within the capabilities of one person. This cutter rig has proved to be an excellent choice for what I had in mind. The most comfortable rig for downwind sailing was NOT twin genoas, but a single reefed main with firm preventers, and a poled-out genoa, with the staysail pinned in flat fore-and-aft to kill any vortices from the other two sails. This dramatically damped down the rolling. A longer than usual genny pole means that the sail can be carried well onto a beam reach, maintaining full power with a lighter helm. As the wind rises sail area is reduced progressively until we end up running under a pinned-in staysail only (slab-reefed on its own boom if necessary). The storm sails were always ready to hoist, but never actually needed during this trip.

A replacement 5 cylinder Nanni engine has turned out to be nearly twice as powerful as the original Perkins 4.108, while giving 50% more range from the same amount of fuel (an example of 25 years of diesel evolution). In fact I used the engine hardly at all, and certainly not simply for charging the batteries, as there are solar cells, a towed generator and a wind-generator for the electricity supply, with full spares for each. The simplest, cheapest radar I could find was very reliable and ran virtually continuously, until the lightning Whizzbang. Its spare control-head has been used successfully since then.

The general rule I followed was to keep everything as simple and repairable as possible, without needing specialist tools. I had to be able to do all the maintenance and repairs myself at sea, and designed things accordingly. If something was essential could I fix it? If I couldn't, and it really was essential, then reluctantly I'd have to carry a spare, or two. This policy paid off very well indeed when the ship's electrics were destroyed by the Whizzbang in Brazil, as the repairs I carried out had to be done by using the ship's stores only. This was because almost none of the replacement parts sent out from England managed to reach me, which caused considerable anguish, and over a year later was still a matter of legal discussion. Unfortunately most of the spare electronics on board had been ruined as well, even those stowed below in their boxes, but lateral thinking found temporary and primitive solutions to circumvent the problems, enough to enable me to sail for home.

After the primary refit, the whole ship was tested in 2001 in a horribly rough North Sea crossing, then more thoroughly the next year with a ten week cruise up the western coast of Norway. Throughout her recent travels, whether during the shakedown cruise north of the Arctic circle in 2002 or south of Capricorn in 2004, the ship did her job admirably, and time and time again I was thankful for the design genius of Peter Brett. To watch the sea-kindly way she dealt with awkward conditions, sitting in the water comfortably with a soft motion, making it all look so easy, was a joy. Her passage times were always respectable, although I admit her light airs windward-pointing ability is nothing special. However, as soon as it gets rough she quickly shows why she is the shape she is. Truly she is a very civilised and safe means of transport, (and in my opinion, elegant and graceful too).

In combination with her Aries self-steering gear (which, with some modifications I made, was a revelation in itself) she looked after me very well.

7. NAVIGATION

I enjoy exercising the ability to navigate by traditional methods (such as daylight Venus transits etc), and this was a great help during the return journey when the lightning damaged electronic gear was unreliable. It was very reassuring to be able to check the one method with the other.

Observing the tropical night sky, I was surprised to discover a comet all of our own, which I called the

Tuesday Comet partly because I confirmed its direction and rate of travel in the early hours of a Tuesday. (I know now that it had been discovered several months before, and given the name "Comet C/2001 Q4 (NEAT)", but nevertheless I was able to experience a glimmer of the pride those ancient sailors must have felt when they named a new natural phenomenon).

As a general rule I aimed to make landfalls at sunset, heave-to 30-40 miles off, and then make harbour late the following morning. I consider most night arrivals require more than one pair of eyes to be safe.

8. HEALTH.

ILLNESS or INJURY would incapacitate a singlehanded vessel. I was very aware not to put myself at risk of either. I spent quite a bit of time and effort before each leg of the voyage trying to get physically very fit, in an attempt to minimize the chances of injuries due to falling etc. Early on in the journey I would be literally covered with bruises by the time I sighted land again, but I learnt rapidly, and one or two remarkably simple modifications around the deck and cabin helped enormously. However, a damaged elbow caused several weeks of trouble, and I had to find a way round the difficulties it caused.

 SLEEP. The biggest problem was making sure I could get enough sleep and yet maintain a good lookout/weather eye etc. I found it best to try to sleep for 15 minutes out of every hour, day and night regardless, as I did when coming back from western Norway in 2002. When shipping was about, the rest periods would be shorter and more frequent, often in the cockpit. Initially I couldn't get any sleep, but at least getting some rest helps, so I made a point of getting onto my bunk if only to read a book (preferably a boring and longwinded "classic"). I was often convinced I hadn't slept, but stopped worrying about it once I realised I must have done so because I had dreamed. Kitchen-timers, a minimum of two of them at a time, under the pillow ensure regular awakening. Mind you, I hadn't got a clue what time of day or night it was, or even WHICH day it was, unless I checked my watch first.

In the beginning I was upset and cross if something broke into my short sleeps (such as a weather change, or a ship appearing for example, when I would have to stay up until the situation was fully resolved), but then I realised I could start again, reset the timers and be able to get back to bed with another full 15 minutes ahead of me. Later in the open ocean I was happy to extend the sleep times to 30 minutes, depending on conditions. It required great discipline to keep making myself rest when I didn't want to miss anything on deck, but tiredness causes mistakes, injuries, and (as is well recorded, and I know from past personal experience) eventually delusions. Think of sleep as behaving like a lead acid battery .. easy to manage if you keep it topped up all the time, but it takes absolutely ages to recharge it once it's partly empty, (unless you can get two consecutive full nights' rest, which was impossible on this trip). However you can store only just so much sleep, so there's no point in trying to OVERcharge "the battery". Incidentally, the most tiring bits of the whole voyage were when doing 36 hour passages in the English Channel, amongst all the other ships and radar-invisible yachts, when I wasn't able to get any rest at all.

The price I paid for all this was that it took more than four weeks before I could sleep normally again on returning home.

CLOTHING. With all the number of times I was taking my waterproofs and life-harness off and on, I found it useful to wear thin nylon overalls, so that the outer layers of clothing slipped over them easily and quickly. Near the equator clothes were unnecessary (another advantage of sailing singlehanded), but protection was still needed from the overhead sun and from the sea when it was rough. A lifejacket was of absolutely no use to me at all in the open ocean, but a comfortable harness most definitely was.

TEETH. I had spent a long time getting dental treatment before this trip, to make sure I was as safe as possible, but even so I was unlucky to crack an upper tooth just as I was leaving Brazil. So I super-glued the carefully cleaned remains together, which involved kneeling, forehead on the floor, balancing a mirror and torch against the ship's movement, while dripping the glue in place. Not easy, but the wreckage held together (with further repairs) until back home in the UK. Sadly it then became apparent that the tooth did not survive the event.

9. PROVISIONS.

I found this a particularly difficult problem to sort out before setting off, with the absence of refrigeration (due to lack of electricity power), particularly as I am the world's most unwilling cook. So I evolved a simple system .. Divide stores into three categories .. the first 7-10 days I would live on fresh stuff, ie. bought just before departure. The last category was about 6 weeks of emergency rations (tins of high protein meats etc) in case I was dismasted and stuck out in the middle somewhere. The middle portion was 3 months supply of tinned meats, soups, beans, vegetables, fruits, and pastas of various types. I preserved 6 dozen eggs before each of the longest legs of the trip by flash-boiling them in very weak vinegar for 10 seconds, on a rotation system in a large saucepan .. very successful indeed. (Note also that with only one person on board there was no difficulty deciding who would have the last egg). I learnt how to make bread, but I had to be careful with adequate vitamins etc. if at sea for more than 6 weeks at a time.

The diet was supplemented by plentiful fresh fish, mainly Flying-Fish and Dorado. I was careful not to eat anything I wasn't absolutely sure of, but in the event I ate everything I caught except for two (poisonous) Puffer Fish hooked by accident. The line was deliberately a weak one to make sure I didn't catch anything too big to deal with.

I collected rainwater as often as it was easy to do so, which came in handy when the ship's main water supply went bad in mid-ocean. I had previously evolved a simple way of making up an emergency supply of water .. keep all your empty 2 litre fizzy-drink bottles .. fill them with rainwater, or water from ashore, then leave them in the sun for a week .. if there's nothing growing in them by then, store the bottles and contents low down in the bilge .. I found I had accumulated 170 litres of separate emergency fluid this way by the time I returned to England, so perhaps I overdid it! In the event, I made a filtering/precipitating system for the bad water supply, and lived on that for 8 weeks.

Incidentally, the rubbish which is not biodegradable can be very firmly packed with a screwdriver into the used (and now empty) fizzy-drink bottles, which are then placed back where they came from, thus not wasting any stowage space.

10. THE ISLANDS.

I was able to land on ten separate islands, six of them still actively volcanic. The variation of the landscapes, geology, and types of animals and plants fascinated me. There was an almost universal "Island Mentality" of the people and animals who lived on each of them .. slower, peaceful, and very tolerant and friendly. But each island was completely different from the next.

There were some fascinating contrasts too. For example, I note there are some soft volcanic rock samples I collected on Faial Island (in the Azores) which FLOAT when put in water; but some samples of WOOD collected from Itaparica Island (in Brazil) actually SINK in water.

11. WILDLIFE.

I found the ocean is teeming with life in some places, and apparently deserted in others. But just to mention a few of the beasts, some of which even now I still don't understand:-

Mullet in the Azores will clean the weed off your boat in no time at all. No scrubbing is necessary.

Dolphins (many types seen, all of them very curious about the boat) were an absolute delight to watch .. the novelty never wore off. On one occasion at night they used the boat's keel to help them round up a large shoal of sprats .. thousands of eyes reflecting the torchlight.

Whales, a surprising number of them, mainly Sperm Whales. They often passed close, but ignored the ship altogether .. however, when they "breech", leaping clear of the water after a long dive, I was acutely aware that this was their territory and not mine! There were VAST Fin Whales in Biscay (they are SERIOUSLY big from the deck of a yacht, virtually twice the length of "Tuesday", which was a bit daunting), and there was a solo Humpback Whale which became a bit amorous towards the ship's bottom in the South Atlantic one night (I didn't know whether to sit down, stand up, or jump overboard).

Albatrosses, the large southern variety, are very big animals, with a bodysize comparable to a swan's, but with literally twice the wingspan. They are capable of unbroken, gliding, soaring flight as long as the wavetops are moving through the air .. very beautiful indeed to watch, with not a trace of a flap of a wing .. now I understand the awe that sailors of old felt for them.

Angry poisonous footballs, with spikes, called Puffer Fish. I felt bad for accidentally catching two of them, as they were reluctant to deflate again when I put them back. The chances are that they would get sunburnt floating on the surface before they recovered.

Millions of tiny white snails, every one of them dead, stuck to a type of grass on Porto Santo, giving the impression of a huge field of cotton bolls .. I have absolutely no idea what the story is.

Portuguese-Men-of-War, every 2-3 feet, covering the sea continuously for three days' of sailing, millions upon millions of them. The smaller and younger they are, the closer they are together. Why haven't they taken over the world? And what on earth can control such a vast stinging machine? Certainly you'd be dead if you fell overboard there.

Buoy Barnacles, of a type I've only just been able to identify, were very common on one particular day. A colony of big fat 3" barnacles, each stuck into a float they've made in the middle. I was able to demonstrate that they communicate with each other through the "float". How?

A group of Gannets were seen happily fishing 234 miles from the nearest rocks/land. This worried me, as it meant my navigation could be wrong, since I believed they went only 70 miles offshore. A hasty sextant check confirmed the position, and I have since found they have been seen "up to 200 miles" off the land. Interesting that even the experts may not yet know all the answers yet.

There is a yellow-breasted bird in Brazil with a characteristic cry of "Fifty Quid! Fifty Quid!" (at least, that's how we interpreted it), promptly answered by another one "What? Fifty Quid! W-o-w!" They have long conversations about this exorbitant fee, becoming more and more agitated about it. The Brazilians call it the "Bem-ti-vi" (meaning I saw you well, ie. "I CAUGHT you!"), but the French called it the Kiscadee (from Qu'est ce que dit, ie. "?What was said?", clearly believing the bird was deaf) all named from the bird's cry. Personally I think "Fifty Quid" is the best though!

How about the Walking Batfish of Brazil, a remarkably ugly fish I came across on the harbour seabed while scuba diving in Salvador? It looks so ugly that it might have been designed by a committee. The extraordinary thing about this fish is that it CAN'T EVEN SWIM! Pick it off the bottom and it flails around vigorously getting nowhere while it sinks rapidly. Once it lands onto the bottom it sets off at a respectable speed by walking, hopping and jumping on its heavily modified pelvic fins. Its front fins have evolved into two tiny front paws underneath, so it behaves just like a rabbit. Weird but wonderful!

12. PEOPLE.

I was privileged to meet some truly remarkable sailing people, whom I would never have been able to get to know if I hadn't been sailing singlehanded ("let's go and be nice to him before he dies"). It is impossible to mention them all, but they are amongst the most resourceful, adaptable, and resilient humans I've come across, yet they were utterly charming, and supportive, although a little shy. I'm still in contact with them now, and they made me feel proud to be human, when there is much in the media these days to cause doubt. They are modest unsung heroes and heroines, and they will remain deep sincere friends for the rest of my life.

Officials on the islands were almost invariably helpful, (though one in the Azores was an outright liar, and two separate officials on mainland Brazil were verging on the certifiably insane).

Almost everyone else was courteous, helpful and friendly, more so than I suspect the British would be in similar circumstances.

13. EMOTIONS

I was surprised how emotional an Suffolk Anglo-Saxon could be in the special circumstances in which I was living. There were episodes of tears of elation, or rarely of despair, and other tears of simple happiness while listening to gentle music reminding me of friends and home .. most unBritish!   Bad temper, however, was easily recognised as a sign that I was not coping very well with the relevant situation, so take control of it, try to get one step ahead of it, and very quickly rational calm descends again. Recognising the early signs of a "Mr.Cockup" day, when everything seems to be going wrong, saved me no end of problems, enabling me to break a chain of events which would have led to injury or damage.

Even though I've been sailing all my life, I had to learn how to live with my own fears and lack of confidence, but both of these feelings may actually be helpful for survival. But I had not anticipated the mountain of support and encouragement I felt from my family, and those few true friends I consider as family. I was surprised to find that Emails enabled them to do the journey with me (in spirit), and it was an absolute joy to meet up with those who came to join me briefly on some of the islands. The downside was the empty coldness of the ship for a day or two when they left to go home again.

I was surprised at my reaction when a Brazilian in a motorboat rammed poor old "Tuesday" while she was moored up in a marina, and then blamed me for being in his way. It got rather physical I'm afraid when I frogmarched him up to the authorities; not my scene at all normally, but I felt exceptionally protective towards the ship which had become my home for over a year.

At sea I would try to save 20 minutes most evenings for a concert, either on the cassette-player or while I learned to play the Chromatic Harmonica, as a way of having some "time off" for a short while. It was a precious time. Other joys were when making pairs of earrings out of Mid-South-Atlantic barnacles, for my daughters (very rare jewellery indeed), and making artistic pictures from flying fishes wings.

Ham Radio allowed me to speak to my brother in Yorkshire a few times a week, and to chat virtually every day to special members of the Maritime Mobile Networks in a variety of countries. They were always interested and concerned how things were going, as well as passing weather information both to and from the ship. They have become trusted friends even now, and I still miss the daily check-ins with other Radio Hams at sea around the world. It felt like a "mobile village", where everyone knew everyone. I needed only 8 watts output for world-wide communication, and only the simplest of equipment.

I felt truly alone very rarely, such as when leaving Plymouth, and when I left Portugal for Madeira and promptly ran into unforecasted 45 knot winds. Salvador was a lonely city at first, when I dearly missed the friends I'd made in the Canaries. Another time was in Brazil when the lightning strike suddenly left both myself and the ship physically disabled, 6000 miles from home .. and then again when a rudder problem cast definite doubt on the ship's ability to stay afloat (I was wrong, and worrying unnecessarily, but I didn't know it at the time). A further episode occurred 1600 miles from the nearest mainland when I discovered the freshwater supply was going bad. And yet another time was when the replacement ham radio blew an RF transistor near St.Helena, leaving me with minimal communication until I could repair it.

I tried to record as much of the voyage as I could, in the ship's diary, on stills cameras, and on video. I'm so glad I did, because today I cannot truly see myself "in the picture" any more .. it seems as though it must have happened to someone I knew very well, someone very much braver than me. While filming I took some comfort from talking to the camera I think.

I had worried that this 15 month, solo odyssey might form a barrier between my family and myself. To my delight, I found that because of the emails, text messages and hamradio conversations, my family felt they had shared fully in the emotions and the experience, and on my return home I found relationships with family and friends were even closer than before. I wonder if this would have happened without modern communications.

14. WOULD I DO IT AGAIN?

Yes, if I didn't wish to stay in the UK with my family. The rules out there are completely honest and fair, but totally binding. I'm still just as timorous as I was when I started out, but I'm a bit wiser now about how to cope with it.

15. SOME RELEVANT SAYINGS, which seemed to help at times:

"Never doubt your motives if they lead you to something you really want to do, something which is yours and yours alone. You may question the results, you may not succeed, you may even give it up, but at least try as hard as you can to try to make it work first. You'll regret it for the rest of your days otherwise."

"In the future you will be more disappointed by the things that you didn't do, than by the ones you did do."

"But if there's something you really want to do, and you don't yet know how to achieve it, then maybe you don't really want it hard enough yet."

"Decide what you want to do .. then decide what you are willing to risk or lose in order to achieve it .. then (hardest of all) actually get up and go and do it".

"A mountain is only as steep as it appears to the person who is climbing it".

"Indecision causes Worry .. Remember that a problem will do one of three things .. (i)Get better (in which case problem solved) (ii) get worse (in which case the remedy becomes more obvious) (iii) stay the same (in which case you are no worse off than you were before). Only in one of these do you need to take IMMEDIATE action, so there is usually time to calmly organise a cunning plan to deal with the problem."

"Courage isn't about not being afraid. It's about understanding that something else is more important than being afraid."

"The greatest fear is due to Fear itself, not due to the actual reality of the situation."

(And finally, written on a washroom wall in the Canaries, from an ancient comment, possibly with the singlehander in mind?)

"Happy is the Man, and happy he alone
  He who can call this day his own.
 He, who secure within, can say
  'Tomorrow do thy worst,
    For I have LIVED today!'".

Index

Equipment:

Dinghy	16,57,104,172,173,
Hull	60,67,85,87,191,193,215,236,249
Provisions	15,136,252
Pulley	182,193
Radar	16,40,52,54,86,143,166,167,200,224,226, 238,250,251
Radio	76,86,100,109,143,162,165,174,177
Rig	37,188,236,250
Rudder	33,71,193,199,200,205,215,242
Sails	126,167,188,250
Selfsteering(Aries)	8,15,38,143,250
Selfsteering(other)	54,60,71,134,143,151,179,180,187,245
Sextant	15,65,66,119,143,161
Water supply	160,242,252,254

Countries:

Brazil	25,59,65,69,75,80,99,100,105,110,148,150
Cap Verdes	55,56,58,59,69,71,190,248
Portugal	14,27,48,254
Spain (Canaries)	8,39,45,46,55,57

Islands:

Ascension	168,182,186,192
Culatra	23
Faial	199,212,252
Graciosa	39,40,42
Havergate	242
Itaparica	127,135,136,141,145,150,157,188,242,252
Lanzarote	39,40,41,42,50,124,236
Madeira	28,30,32,36,48,80,110
Pico	200,209
Porto Santo	24,28,29
Sao Vincenti	55
St.Helena	176,177,178,183,188,192,243,248
Tristan de Cunha	76,127,160,180,189,248

Communications:

Fax	108,138,165,173
Ham radio	18,26,27,37,53,76,108,143,162,168,202,254
Internet	60,162,213
Mobile phone	58,83,85,86,174
Morse	18,78,202
Satellite phone	13,14,58,158,163,174
Shiptrak	81,105,155,156

Incidents:

Broach	54
Calms	14,15,57,138,162,190
Collision	16,53,115,190,226,236,238
Diving	42,48,109,117,146,172,214,224
Diving (ran out of air)	44
Doldrums	61,63,190
Fishing float/pot	15,21,167
Lightning	83,134
Pulley	182,193
Stranding	69,215
Watersupply	160,252
Waves/Swell	15,48,54,59,136,167,169,215

'Ologies:

Comet	161,162
Earthquake	209,211,217
Lava	40,212,217
Squalls	54,67,160,166,184,189,190
Volcano	31,39,59,176,204,211

Wildlife:

Barnacles	8,77,167,194,205,211,224,226,254
Birds	8,17,103,17,162,171,173,253
Gannets	8,66,253
Portuguese Men of War	8,193,197,226,253
Whales	14,38,54,166,190,205,206,253
Fish	15,17,42,43,44,48,55,60,62,64,107,109,146,161, 185,190,211,214,253

List of the main Characters

The Family:

My wife	Fin
My Mother	Mother
My Father	Daddy, D, BA,(Bill and Alex)
My elder daughter	Charlotte or Tot
My younger daughter	Ellie
My son	Ben
My elder sister	Ros or Woddy
My younger sister	Mary or Mayweed
My brother(-in-law)	Gerald or Jonesy or J
My sister (in-law)	Ju-Ju
My neice	Liz, Elizabeth, or EDAM
My nephew	Michael, MOL or MOWL

Long standing family friends

(Strictly in alphabetical order only):

Angie and John	
Ben (J)	(yacht Shelanda)
Bob and Brenda	
Cathy	(in New Zealand)
Eric	(yacht (at the time) Aliz Motte)
Gill and Chris	(yacht Lady of Deben)
Ginny and Graham	
James and Liz	(yacht Petronella)
Jan	In Portugal
Joe and Joyce	J&J
John	(a fellow radio ham)
Richard	(yacht (at the time) Lacushla)
Ruth and Chris	
Teresa	(whose brother Paul gave me his sextant)

Dear and sincere friends gathered during the trip
(strictly in alphabetical order only):

Allen and Marsha	(yacht Free Spirit)
Barrie, Val and Shane	(on St.Helena)
Bill	(singlehanded yacht British Tiger)
Chris and Tashi	(Rubicon Diving Centre, Lanzarote)
Dave and Sally	(yacht Pendragon)
Gerard	(of the Transatlantic Maritime Mobile Nets)
Jack	(of the Transatlantic Maritime Mobile Nets)
Jorgen	(yacht Symphonie)
Manuel	(yacht Stardust)
Matti	(singlehanded yacht Snoopy)
Mike and Julie	(of Pantaenius Yacht Insurance)
Nick	(singlehanded yacht Lala Salama)
Nick and Denise	(ex of Ancasta yachtbrokers)
Philippe and Paola	(yacht Why Not?)
Ron and Bonnie	(yacht Forever)
Staale	(singlehanded yacht Rosinante)
Tinho	(on Itaparica Island)
Trudi	(of the Transatlantic Maritime Mobile Nets)
Yvan and Cristina	(yacht Sailmaker)

Printed in the United Kingdom
by Lightning Source UK Ltd.
117878UK00001B/1-56